ERRATUM

The Motel in America
John A. Jakle, Keith A. Sculle, and Jefferson S. Rogers

The map printed below replaces figure 5.18 on page 144.

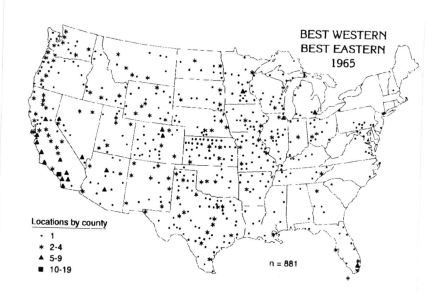

BEST WESTERN
BEST EASTERN
1965

Locations by county
·   1
✳   2-4
▲   5-9
■   10-19

n = 881

THE MOTEL IN AMERICA

THE ROAD AND AMERICAN CULTURE

Drake Hokanson, *Series Editor*
George F. Thompson, *Series Director*

Published in cooperation with the Center for American Places, Harrisonburg, Virginia

THE MOTEL

IN AMERICA

JOHN A. JAKLE

KEITH A. SCULLE

JEFFERSON S. ROGERS

THE JOHNS HOPKINS UNIVERSITY PRESS
BALTIMORE AND LONDON

© 1996 The Johns Hopkins University Press
All rights reserved. Published 1996
Printed in the United States of America on acid-free recycled paper

05 04 03 02 01 00 99 98 97 96 5 4 3 2 1

The Johns Hopkins University Press
2715 North Charles Street
Baltimore, Maryland 21218-4319
The Johns Hopkins Press Ltd., London

Library of Congress Cataloging-in Publication Data
will be found at the end of this book.

A catalog record for this book is available from the British Library.

ISBN 0-8018-5383-4

FRONTISPIECE The 66 Motel, on old Route 66, outside Tulsa, Oklahoma; probably circa 1930. Photo by John A. Jakle, 1993.

FOR ALL WHO HAVE EXPERIENCED

lost reservations and bad directions,

lumpy mattresses and broken ice machines,

burned-out light bulbs and those tiny bars of soap,

grimy towels, empty pools, paper-thin walls,

and forgotten wake-up calls.

Contents

CONTENTS

———

x

Preface and Acknowledgments

WHEN THEY VENTURE AWAY FROM HOME, NEARLY ALL AMERICANS REGU-
larly depend upon motels. The motel is a vital part of the service infra-
structure that insures the geographical mobility so vital to modern American life. Travelers on commercial rounds, movers shifting residences,
tourists on vacation, conferees attending meetings—all require convenient, functional, and secure lodging, and a hospitality industry has
evolved to provide it. Our modern nation would be difficult to imagine
without motels, a fact forcefully reflected in their nearly ubiquitous presence in the American landscape. Motels break down parochialism by
connecting isolated places to one another and to worlds beyond. They
promote homogenization. They facilitate the movement of people and,
through people, the flow of ideas and material goods. For all these reasons,
the motel in America deserves scholarly focus.

We offer an exploration of the commonplace motel—its origins, its
evolution as a form, its changing geographical distribution, and its changing social meaning. How did the motel evolve as a commercial idea? How
did it take form as an architectural expression? How did it spread along
America's highways? What regional patterns did it create? How has it
changed as cultural icon? These are the sorts of questions explored herein.
Because of the multifaceted character of the American motel itself, our
work is at once architectural and social history, historical geography, marketing history, and cultural criticism.

In chapter 1, by way of introduction, we consider our own discovery of
motels in childhoods variously structured by automobile travel. We see
ourselves as typical Americans, dependent upon motels in work and
leisure. What do our experiences say about motels as social reality? Chapter 2 provides an overview of an evolving motel architecture since the

1920s. With roots in the auto camp, the motel evolved from cabin court, cottage court, and other forms into the modern highway hotel. We offer a contrast with the traditional railroad-oriented downtown hotel, the mo-tel's earliest competition. How was the hotel's decline related to the motel's rise? The family-run "mom-and-pop" motel is the focus of chapter 3. Small entrepreneurs experimented by America's roadsides to evolve a new business form. Who were these people, and how did they go about their work? Chapter 4 explores Alamo Plaza Courts, the first motel chain of any size, established in the 1930s. What promises did early chain expansion bring? Chapters 5, 6, and 7 concern place-product-packaging in the motel industry, the chain idea expanded and elaborated from the 1930s onward. How and why were motel chains formed? How did modern business-format franchising evolve? How did today's large motel companies come to dominate the hospitality market? The evolution of the standard motel room as a service package is the focus of chapter 8. What did Americans expect and demand in motel accommodations? What were the fads and fashions of room packaging? Chapter 9 looks at Holiday Inn, the chain that revolutionized the industry in the 1950s. How did Holiday Inn de-velop its well-engineered place-product-packaging system? Chapter 10 offers a case study of the motel industry in Albuquerque, New Mexico, elaborating the changing geography of motel location. Remade by the automobile with the coming of Route 66 and other highways in the 1930s and by interstate freeways more recently, Albuquerque typifies urban America in many ways. How and why did motel location strategies change in the city over time? What were the distinctive landscape responses? How have motel chains competed in Albuquerque for market penetration? Fi-nally, in chapter 11 we offer a synthesis in drawing together our diverse themes. Just what do motels contribute to life in modern America?

Even the casual observer is aware of the vast changes that have occurred in the American motel industry over the years. The remains of old tourist courts can be seen along American roadsides. Rising near suburban office parks, peripheral airports, and downtown convention centers are new highway hotels—in scale and function recalling the old downtown hotels. Our task is to tell the story of the motel industry's fascinating maturation. It is a story of entrepreneurship playing out primarily along the nation's highways, driven by a rapidly evolving automobility. It is a story of the American roadside come of age in function, form, and meaning. It is the story of a changing cultural icon suggestive of much that is America's own invention. In the motel, Americans can see themselves clearly reflected. The motel is quintessentially American.

Until the 1960s, motels catered largely to white middle-class Americans. Most motel owners and operators were of the same class; excluded were black Americans and, in certain parts of the United States, members of other minority groups as well. Gaining access to motel services and entree to the economic opportunities of ownership and management came with the civil-rights movement. Indeed, it could be said that the cause of civil rights was advanced substantially from motels as leaders traveled across the country coordinating activities. It was in the Lorraine Motel in Memphis that Martin Luther King Jr. was assassinated, and the building now stands as a memorial to his accomplishments. Today a substantial proportion of the nation's motels are owned and operated by Asian Americans, who have focused on the hospitality industry as a window to economic opportunity. The motel in America, therefore, reflects variously who we have been, who we are, and who we are becoming as a nation. Its stories are central to the American experience.

We owe much to cooperating individuals and organizations who aided us in our endeavor:

Jane Domier, cartographer at the University of Illinois at Urbana-Champaign, drafted the maps for chapters 5, 6, and 7. Barbara Bonnell at the University of Illinois and Jacqueline Hughes provided invaluable clerical assistance.

Marilyn Irvin Holt read chapter 3 of the manuscript for us, and Larry Ford read the entire manuscript for the Johns Hopkins University Press. Many of their very insightful recommendations were gladly considered and incorporated in the final text. Michael Wiant graciously took the time to identify anthropological works on the "deconstructionist" controversy that helped clarify our thinking.

We thank the following individuals for sharing their recollections or opening their files to us, or both: Mrs. Myra Alprin, Mrs. D. W. Bartlett, Holst C. Beall Jr., Madeline Bluestein, William W. Bond Sr., Mrs. Edward Bruce, Basil E. Butler, Gilbert C. Chandler Jr., Agnes Chastain, Anna Conner, E. O. Cypent, Mrs. Harry F. Dole, Chris Dykes and the Tulsa City-County Library, William L. Edmundson III, Ted Farner, Mrs. W. H. Farner, George P. Gardner Jr., Gwendolyn Gosnell, Clare A. Gunn, F. Randolph Helms and F. Randolph Helms Associates, Opal Henson, Helon Torrance Hiatt, Jacqueline Hughes, C. Humbert, Lawrence P. Ingram, Michael Jackson, Annie Mae Johnson, James J. Jolly, Hugh Jones, W. Dwayne Jones of the Texas Historical Commission, Mrs. W. H. Legge, Robert H. Lightfoot, Thomas Lightfoot, W. G. McGrady, E. L. McLallen III, Harold Metzger, John Noel III, Rufus Nims, Mrs. Carl B. Olsen, Vernon W. Phillips, Mrs. W. P. Robinson, Sherman Pryor, Mrs. S. E. Ulmer Jr., Marian M. Warren, Harold Whittington, and Kemmons Wilson.

For assistance in identifying and locating local materials we are especially indebted to the following: Ray L. Bellande, Vicki Betts and the library of the University of Texas at Tyler, Virginia Buchanan and the Smith County Historical Society at Tyler, Texas, Mary Catron and the Metropolitan Library System at Oklahoma City, the Central Arkansas Library System at Little Rock, John Cloninger and the Dallas Public Library, Anne Douglas and the Houston Public Library, Eric Erickson and the Chatham-Effingham-Liberty Regional Library at Savannah, Georgia, Pete Gillies, Mary Glenn Hearne and the Public Library of Nashville, Tennessee, Dan Hyslett and the Waco-McLennan County Library at Waco, Texas, Mary Irving and the Railroad and Pioneer Museum at Temple, Texas, Ned Irwin and the Chattanooga-Hamilton County Bicentennial Library at Chattanooga, Tennessee, Rosemary J. Lands and the Public Library of Charlotte and Mecklenburg County, North Carolina, Patricia M. LaPointe and the Memphis Shelby County Public Library at Memphis, Carol Marcks and the East Baton Rouge Parish Library at Baton Rouge, David Montgomery and the Tyrrell Historical Library at Beaumont, Texas, William A. Montgomery and the Atlanta-Fulton Public Library at Atlanta, Frank Murphy and the Harrison County Library at Gulfport, Mississippi, the New Orleans Public Library, Mr. and Mrs. Henry Ward Owen, Mo Palmer, the Albuquerque Museum at Albuquerque, New Mexico, Marella Powell and the Biloxi Public Library at Biloxi, Mississippi, Anne V. Swallow, Laura Street and the library archives of the Louisiana State University in Shreveport, the Eudora Welty Library at Jackson, Mississippi, James Lewis Wilkins and the Smith County Historical Society at Tyler, Texas, Brenda Williams and the Shreve Memorial Library at Shreveport, Louisiana, and Martha E. Wright and the Indiana State Library at Indianapolis.

Invaluable library aid was provided by Kathryn Harris, Janet Noecker, and William Tubbs of the Illinois Historical Library at Springfield, Illinois, and by Katherine Laurence and the staff of the Cornell Hotel School Library at Ithaca, New York. We express our appreciation to George F. Thompson for his personal attention to this project and his leadership role in establishing the Center for American Places, dedicated to the study of the American landscape. Thanks also to Joanne Allen for her thoughtful editing of this book.

Last, but not least, we wish to acknowledge the help and encouragement of Cynthia Jakle and Tracey Sculle, wives who have shared with their husbands a fascination with America's roadside landscape.

THE MOTEL IN AMERICA

1

Introduction

REFLECTION TINGED BY DEGREES OF NOSTALGIA INFORMS WHAT FOLLOWS, a history and geography of the motel in America. Each of the authors developed an infatuation with motels largely before our distinctive scholarly orientations had matured. Our passion for the subject matter is rooted in the past, when we were mere consumers of motel services. Two authors are geographers. Their interests in motels date from trips taken as children with their parents. Travel was clearly part of their preparation for becoming geographers. Middle-class families traveled for pleasure and relaxation but also to broaden their experience, especially the experience of their children. Touring by automobile was a matter of connecting attractions deemed important. But much of a child's education in travel derived from close observation of the roadside, including the places of the roadside that served tourists directly.

One author is a historian. His interest in motels is of later origin, as his parents took few automobile trips. His primary fascination was with the motor car and all that it represented. As an adult he traveled by car with his own family in search of roadside relics, to make up, perhaps, for earlier travel missed. Such retrospection ultimately became central to his being a historian. Like his co-authors, he became committed to understanding the fundamentals of American popular culture. Nothing has been more popular in America than the travel by automobile, which motels have helped to sustain.

Collectively, we are of two different generations. The historian and one of the geographers were born at the start of World War II. Their coming of age was rooted in postwar landscapes of the late 1940s and early 1950s. The other geographer was born toward the beginning of the Vietnam War, and his coming of age was rooted in landscapes of the late 1960s and early 1970s. His remembering of motels starts with the Holiday Inns and the Motel 6s of a rapidly maturing franchise era. His co-authors' remembering, on the other hand, necessarily embraces more the mom-and-pop tourist courts of the prefranchise era, when "referral chains" were just getting started. But the younger of us did something that his older colleagues did not: he parlayed his interest in motels into employment, landing a job as a front-desk clerk to earn money for college. Thus his reflection involves two kinds of role playing: that of the "guest" and that of the employee.

Autobiographical accounts of our involvement with motels serve several methodological purposes. Each is important in its own right, and cumulatively they amount to a credo. First, our recollections release some of the emotional charge that built up in the excitement of conceptualizing and researching this book. We can therefore be less nostalgic as we seek more complete objectivity in the chapters to come. Second, we afford thoughtful readers the opportunity to see our personal and cultural moorings, our biases, in other words. In an era when scholarship's self-critical reflection has been taken to extremes, questioning the very existence of an objective reality, for example, the value of historical and geographical analysis has been discounted by some as no more than personal view.[1] We acknowledge the contemporary scholarly dictum that all efforts at objectivity are ultimately dogged by an author's predispositions. We attempt no contribution here to the raging epistemological debate besetting academia, yet we believe that it is responsible writing to tell the reader where we come from before inviting company for further exploration.[2] Third and last, recollection also serves to place the motel firmly into a cultural context. Thus we begin by assessing why motels struck us as deserving of special attention. Later we look at the imperatives that have driven scholars, ourselves included, to embrace the motel as serious subject matter indeed.

The motel is more than a place where people stay in transit. The motel is an important icon, a social symbol. Just what it symbolizes is a function of how Americans have traditionally experienced the motel—the satisfactions they have sought to enjoy and the dissatisfactions they have sought to avoid. The motel is a commercial manifestation developed over three or four generations of entrepreneurial experimentation. It is an idea that did not take form all at once but evolved incrementally as increasingly larger market niches were discovered and developed in an emergent hospitality industry. Americans did not rush to embrace the motel "overnight": they needed the coaxing of product refinement and maturation.

PERSONAL DISCOVERY

John Jakle Discovers Motels

The Jakles lived in a suburb of Detroit. Family travel during and immediately after World War II had been primarily by railroad. The stringent gas rationing of the period and the lack of a new automobile made a road trip out of the question. But in 1948 we bought a new Buick and set out on a three-week trip to the "East," vaguely defined as including New York City and New England. We reserved rooms in advance in several large cities, but between these destinations our nightly lodging was a matter of chance. We stayed not only in large commercial hotels but also in small-town hotels, resort inns, tourist homes, and, of course, tourist courts and motels. During our later travels through the 1950s and into the 1960s we would come to patronize motels more and the other kinds of accommodation less.

A drive of more than 450 miles in a single day was an accomplishment in 1948. Up before dawn, we drove until after dark, crossing northern Ohio and then dropping south to Pittsburgh and the new Pennsylvania Turnpike. In the early days of the automobile, auto touring was championed as a way of traveling leisurely through landscapes beyond the control of railroad timetables and the corporate powers that those timetables represented. Motoring was promoted as a means of getting to know the country through slow, firsthand encounter. As highways improved, however, touring became increasingly a matter of "making time" between big attractions more distantly spaced. How quickly Americans came to trade landscapes glimpsed rapidly through train windows for landscapes glimpsed rapidly through windshields. Our family was no exception.

The new turnpike road in Pennsylvania, with its separated traffic lanes and limited-access cloverleafs, offered uninterrupted high-speed driving. As the modern overpasses flashed by, Bedford, nearly halfway across Pennsylvania, was our first day's goal. Arriving late, we were greeted by the "no vacancy" signs at the town's newer motels located close to the turnpike interchange. Bedford had been a spa town, and numerous nineteenth-century resort hotels enjoyed partial revival in the automobile era. Nonetheless, we selected an older cabin court west of town, on the old Lincoln Highway, a motel that had been "marooned" by the new turnpike. This was my first cabin court. It dated from the early 1930s, and although our cabin had been modernized with indoor plumbing, it had a run-down aspect. Lying on my cot, I could look through the cracks in the wainscotting and see that the insulation was provided primarily by Depression-era newspapers. Bare light bulbs hung from the ceiling. It rained that night,

FIGURE 1.1 The Benjamin Franklin Hotel, Philadelphia, circa 1940. The post-card reads: "Philadelphia's foremost hotel as well as the largest and most modern and ideally located close to shops, theatres, and historic shrines." Such luxury hotels dominated the big-city travel market through the 1950s.

and through the ceiling came a steady drip of water. My mother was not pleased.

The next six nights were spent in the luxury of big, first-class city hotels—the Benjamin Franklin in Philadelphia and then the Park Sheraton in New York City. Here were palatial lobbies, extensive corridors with stores, barbershops, and newsstands, formal dining rooms, and less formal coffee shops (see Fig. 1.1). At the Bedford cabin court we had seen only the proprietor, the other guests being known to us only by their automobiles, parked at cabin doors. In the hotels, on the other hand, the public spaces were crowded with people, especially cigarette- and cigar-smoking businessmen in business suits. Giving the car to a valet for parking, being escorted by the doorman to the front desk, the ritual of registering, and the elevator ride to our room escorted by a bellhop, though not totally novel to me, were nonetheless intimidating. My most vivid memory of the Park Sheraton is of a television set being wheeled down the hall to my room. It was a tall box on wheels with a screen not more than six inches across. Two or three channels broadcast for a few hours each evening. This was "my" first TV. It added substantially to my sense of being in a place of sophistication.

We spent two nights in Boston, where we did not have hotel reservations. Because of a convention in the city, we could not stay at the Statler, which had been our plan. Instead we stayed at a lesser hostelry overlooking a railroad yard with a large sign advertising Gillette safety razors visible immediately below the window. The rooms were small, poorly ventilated, and ill furnished in a pre–World War I style. Thus we left Boston a day early. The several nights at the Hawthorne Hotel in nearby Salem, on the other hand, were a pure delight. Built in the 1920s, the hotel had originally been oriented to travelers coming from the nearby Boston and Maine Railroad depot. But it also had a motor entrance and a parking lot. It was a small-town drummer's hotel that also catered to vacationers who came to see the house made famous by Hawthorne's *House of Seven Gables* and the other attractions of the locality. I remember dinner in the dining room, which looked out on the public square. A drum and fife corps in Revolutionary War uniforms paraded up and down the green that night.

After Salem came a night at a summer resort in the White Mountains. It was selected by my mother, as were most of the other lodgings on the trip, from the listings in an American Automobile Association *Tourguide*. Like the hotels of Bedford, it dated from the nineteenth century. It would be years before I understood the difference between the "American plan" (in which meals were included in the room price) and the "European plan" (in which they were not). Here was a clientele made up almost exclusively of families on vacation, especially mothers and children. Most of the guests had made reservations for the week or the month and seemed to know one another.

We decided to return home by way of Quebec. Having lost our way north from Sherbrooke, we discovered the new defense highway completed during the war (today's TransCanada), which ran in nearly a straight line from Montreal to Quebec City. It was only a single lane of concrete with a gravel shoulder on either side. Almost all of the vehicles were horse-drawn. Even though travel brochures advertised Quebec as the next thing to seventeenth-century Normandy, the backwardness of the country was a surprise. Here was sharp contrast with the modernity of the turnpike in Pennsylvania of the bucolic Merritt Parkway, which we had driven in Connecticut. We entered Quebec City late in the evening. Since the tourist season was at its height, we found the downtown hotels filled, so we settled for an ancient resort hotel on the edge of the city. I remember a wooden veranda with rocking chairs filled with elderly guests all speaking French. As the hotel was reserved for a wedding the next night, we went to a tourist home very much of the bathroom-down-the-hall variety. The proprietor, in undershirt and suspenders, showed us to our rooms, the smell of cooking permeating everywhere. The house was new, and the family was taking in tourists, the owner said, to help pay the mortgage.

Although we had made a reservation at Montreal's new Laurentien Hotel on Dominion Square, no rooms had been set aside for us. In compensation, we were given a suite on the top floor for the price of a regular room (a source of considerable pride for my father). The suite had a living room, a dining room and kitchenette, and two bedrooms. It looked down on the Basilica of Mary, Queen of the World, across the roof of which marched, during the daytime hours, a stream of priests saying their devotions. Here was true luxury. A basket of fruit on the table, bottles of wine in the refrigerator, and for the wide-eyed youngster a magnificent view of the city. I remember joking with the bellboys, who spoke little English, collecting every piece of give-away literature from the hotel travel bureau, and otherwise making a nuisance of myself. I was the "rich" kid in the penthouse.

We returned to Detroit by way of Old Forge in New York's Adirondacks and Niagara Falls. In Old Forge at the Flamingo Court (the sign out front featured a pink flamingo in neon) a pipe burst in the wall of our cabin late at night. With water gushing out of the wall, I joked that we no longer had to visit Niagara. The motel owner appeared with a coat thrown over his pajamas, ripped a section of wall away with a crowbar, tightened a joint in a pipe with a wrench, and left with apologies. Luckily, the motel at Niagara Falls was as modern as it was new, veneered in brick and equipped with a radio in every room. Units elbowed one another in a straight line connected under a single roof, integrated further by a long porch, or veranda. Across the parking lot was a lawn with a shuffleboard court. What more could a nine-year-old boy desire?

We had seen much on our trip, although our experience of places had been rushed and very superficial. We had lived off the land (it was on this trip that I discovered chocolate milkshakes at Howard Johnson's) and quartered in a wide range of accommodations. This was a period of transition in American vacation travel. Touring, at least in the East, was not yet out of the railroad age. Even those who traveled by car depended substantially on railroad-era hotels, especially in the cities but also in the small towns and country resorts. The cabin courts and the more up-to-date motels provided alternatives along the highways connecting major tourist destinations. Only in an emergency did we rely on a tourist home. I am glad my family took that trip. Not only did I see Independence Hall, the Rockettes at Radio City Music Hall, Bunker Hill, the villages of French Canada, and, of course, the Niagara Gorge but I experienced the American roadside firsthand. Indeed, measured in time, my attention was mostly focused there. Places of accommodation were especially interesting to me and remain vivid in my memory. Save to visit relatives, I had never before been away from home for a long period of time. That such a diverse world of packaged hospitality awaited me came as a revelation.

During the 1950s, travel with my parents included trips to Northern

Michigan (several visits to Mackinac Island's Grand Hotel), the West (including cabins in Yellowstone and a dude ranch in Colorado), and return visits to New York City and Quebec (the Savoy Plaza and the Chateau Frontenac). But always a wide diversity of motels figured in our travels to and from major destinations. In the 1960s, camping came to the fore. Now with my own family to support on a graduate student's and then a lowly assistant professor's income, state and national park campgrounds became an important means of stretching the travel dollar. Although our accommodations tended to be the older and cheaper mom-and-pop courts, occasionally we worked the Holiday Inns into our touring, for there children stayed "free" and the swimming pools delighted our two young daughters.

Memorable motel stays included the night in New Jersey when passionate moans and groans from the other side of paper thin walls interrupted the silence at roughly half-hour intervals and the night in Maine when two male members of a well-lubricated wedding party engaged in a 3:00 A.M. fistfight in the next room over who would escort a certain young female "home." Except in such instances, motels had become thoroughly ordinary to me, merely offering the convenience of a "home away from home" when I was traveling. Only when I decided to focus my scholarly endeavors on travel, and especially travel by automobile in the early twentieth century, did the motel suddenly loom as significant. My entry into motel scholarship came primarily through the analysis of industry trade journals, particularly in a search for evolving motel prototypes.

Keith Sculle Discovers Motels

I remember only fragments of two family vacations. The first was to Niagara Falls in the late 1940s. We drove across southern Michigan and southern Ontario. Niagara Falls was the kind of vacation destination that a less affluent middle-class family of Eastern and Southern European immigrant origins might select for their first long automobile trip in America. The trip was broken with relatives near Detroit. Staying with friends or relatives to renew acquaintances as well as reduce travel costs was a feature of most Americans' travel then (and may be even today). Niagara and the Great Smoky Mountains, the other vacation destination of the mid-1950s, evoke no special memories of specific motels. My memories instead are of selecting the routes in Tennessee as I took my first turn behind the wheel of the family's Nash. Simply put, hotels and motels were taken for granted.

In 1968 my wife, our young daughter, and I took our first long vacation trip. Our destinations were Washington, D.C., and nearby colonial Williamsburg in Virginia. We sought a last bit of leisured learning before formal immersion in graduate school at the University of Illinois. Off we dashed across Indiana and Ohio, paying little attention to the locales through which we passed. We had made reservations in advance, presuming that the corporate reservation system would somehow guarantee satisfaction. The first night found us in a motel at Washington, Pennsylvania, following a 425-mile day, a short driving distance by the standards of interstate travel but considerable for our one-year-old. Prompt delivery of a crib to our room, as stipulated in the reservation, considerably reassured us that we had chosen the right motel.

We spent the following three nights in the national capital at a hotel of moderate pretensions within walking and stroller distance from the tourist attractions clustered around the White House. Legendary hotel protocol, so discouraging to many early automobile vacationers seeking total relaxation, was not a problem for me despite my general lack of experience in hotels. Already hotels had forgone much of their formality in responding to the competition of motels. Washington's sites delighted us. Quite contented at having seen much of what we had anticipated from the travel brochures, we departed for Williamsburg, which proved an easy day's drive even with a stop at Mt. Vernon.

A spacious motel room with a crib awaited us. A sliding glass door that opened onto a central courtyard gave us the feeling of being in a kind of resort. We spent several relaxed days sightseeing in the morning, returning to the motel for rest and our daughter's nap, and then making late afternoon and evening forays back into the historic village. Everything was quite casual, just as motels liked to advertise. In Williamsburg we were surrounded by other families on tour dressed casually in the bermuda shorts and blue jeans that were the new fashion.

Our return home included another stay in a motel before we reached Bloomington, Indiana. There we stayed with friends, repeating my parents' earlier travel habit. Visiting friends always loomed as something special. Motel stays, in contrast, were merely for convenience—a kind of minimal experience when set in the context of visiting special people and, of course, of experiencing advertised tourist destinations. As a traveler I had been easily programmed into the motel scene, giving little thought or special consideration to motels. Most of the travail of overnight accommodation had been taken out of highway travel. With their standardized format, especially within a given motel chain, there was little to excite the imagination.

Motels grew more memorable as travel became more an intellectual experience for me. With a new Ph.D. in history, I did historic-site survey work between 1972 and 1975 under contract to the Illinois Department of Conservation. Many were the days I spent driving the twenty-seven counties of east-central Illinois, and many were the nights passed at mostly small-town motels. Small mom-and-pop motels were ideal in terms of cleanliness, price, and pure human interest. My choice of a motel, always made from behind the windshield of my car, was determined by the "look" of a place and, of course, by the appearance of a "vacancy" sign. I carefully avoided small-town hotels, most of which were the disheveled remains of the railroad era. The older motels residual along Illinois highways had a sense of nostalgia for me, but I found the hotels merely old and obsolete.

I clearly remember the Pinnell Motel on the northern edge of Paris, Illinois. There I stayed but one night in March of 1973, alternately writing sections of my day's report and watching TV to break the stony silence. Toward town, on the Route 1 commercial strip, stood the usual farm-implement yards, liquid-fertilizer stores, gasoline stations, and drive-in restaurants. Breakfast downtown at a stool-and-counter diner near the courthouse square satisfied my taste for "road food" and nourished my need for social interchange, if only in the random chatter of the cook and his customers. I have since realized that my nights and early mornings were similar to those of the traditional small-town drummers, the traveling salesmen who helped stock the retail stores in towns along regular routes. The Pinnell Motel symbolizes for me that whole travel experience as documenter of historical architecture in a program calculated to sell landscape appreciation to an Illinois citizenry.

Today at the Pinnell, gloss-varnished woods of light hue (pine doors, maple baseboards) still trim the textured-plaster walls in each room. Ceramic tiles in contrasting colors (pink with blue or turquoise or gray, or dark blue with aqua) make bathroom interiors gleam. The blond brick façade punctuated by white-painted aluminum storm doors still sparkles. In its scale and its room furnishings the Pinnell reads as middlebrow, quintessentially 1950s American. Obviously worn but spotlessly maintained, it is an elegant survivor from the once common postwar world of mom-and-pop ownership and management, giving a historian cause for vivid recollection and periodic revisits.

The requirement of physical integrity and the fifty-year restriction on sites for the *National Register of Historic Places* kept me from designating any "historic motels" in state survey reports. The closest I came was to check the box marked "miscellaneous significance" for four deteriorated 1930s tourist cabins that seemed to exemplify the persistence of nineteenth-century log building technology in the twentieth century. The Five-Star Motel, built in the late 1940s on U.S. 40 (the old National Road) east of Greenup, Illinois, should have been recorded and nominated. Built by a returning veteran immediately after World War II (five-star generals are the highest-ranking officers), it had an extended L-shaped configuration of beige block and was located in a grove of mature trees. Even today the motel is wonderfully preserved, looking as if time had stood still.

Scholarly study in the United States focusing on roadside architecture began in the 1970s, making motels an intriguing topic for those of us enamored with ordinary things in ordinary places. Professional networking structured my serious interest in motels in the early 1980s. My discovery of the fanciful architecture of the Wigwam Village near Mammoth Cave, Kentucky, on a trip to a professional conference led to an oral-history project involving interviews with an early motel entrepreneur, her employees, and several of her customers. It was not long before I co-authored the *National Register* nomination for the Wigwam Village. I had been totally smitten by the motel as an intellectual pursuit.

Jefferson Rogers Discovers Motels

From the mid-1960s to the mid-1970s my family regularly took summer vacation trips. While our destinations varied from year to year, we always spent our nights at the same place: Holiday Inn. My parents' loyalty made sense. The rooms were large enough to accommodate all six of us, and my two sisters, my brother, and I stayed "for free." These motels were usually conveniently located at the edge of towns, they had family-oriented restaurants on the premises, and the quality of the rooms and the services offered remained the same wherever we went. Often the best part of these trips, as far as I was concerned, was not the tourist destinations or the visits with relatives or friends but the stays at "the Nation's Innkeeper." Each night, when we reached our destination my father would challenge us by asking, "OK, who can spot the Holiday Inn sign first?" (I usually won.) The motel's swimming pool was the ultimate entertainment venue; there we children would have splashing wars and diving contests, try underwater handstands and somersaults, and engage in other forms of horseplay (see Fig. 1.2).

These annual summer road trips ended in the mid-1970s, when my father, a university professor, began to reserve summers for teaching, research, and writing. For the rest of us, summer camp and other activities filled our vacation time. The few trips we took were sporadic, and usually one or more of us were missing. Moreover, during this period Holiday Inn lost my family's business after my mother discovered Motel 6 on a trip to Phoenix as a swim-team chaperone. Like many other cost-conscious travelers during the recession-plagued 1970s, my parents were willing, if not eager, to exchange the restaurants, free TVs, and in-room telephones for Motel 6's substantially lower rates. At the same time, Holiday Inns were becoming more expensive as they added amenities and facilities my par-

FIGURE 1.2 Advertising postcard for Holiday Inns of America, circa 1970. The swimming pool figured prominently in the development of Holiday Inn's family-oriented image. Luxury motels had captured more than half of the traditional hotel market by the 1970s.

ents had no interest in subsidizing. In effect, the Rogers family and the Holiday Inns went their separate ways.

In the mid-1980s, however, a new relationship emerged. My brother and I both went to work for the company. In May 1984, at the end of my junior year at the University of Kansas, I needed a summer job. My brother, who had quickly worked his way up from the kitchen to the front desk at the Holiday Inn in our hometown of Las Cruces, New Mexico, informed me that they needed another desk clerk and would hire me if I applied.

The Holiday Inn de Las Cruces was my hometown's premiere lodging facility. It was far more elaborate than the typical glass-walled "roadsides" that had dominated the chain since the early 1960s. Located adjacent to the I-10 interchange at the southern entrance to town, it had been built by a local entrepreneur in 1976. Like many "Holidomes," externally it was a plain, two-story structure, but it had a richly decorated, if not festive, interior. The Holidome featured Mexican-style tile walkways, a double-tiered pool, an "open-air" cantina and cafe in which guests were serenaded by a strolling mariachi band, two restored stagecoaches that had traveled along the Camino Real during New Mexico's territorial era, various pieces of Mexican art, and lush vegetation. About one-third of the facility's some one hundred rooms opened into the Holidome. Also located in the inn were two plush suites completely furnished with territorial-era antiques, the Billy the Kid Saloon, various meeting and convention rooms, and several small giftshops. The Las Cruces property won Holiday Inn's international design award in 1976 and regularly earned Mobil's four-star and AAA's four-diamond rating.

The nexus of the Holiday Inn de Las Cruces was the front desk. Built into an adobe structure resembling a small, two-story New Mexican house, the front desk played a part in every operation of the facility. During the first week of work, as my brother and other clerks trained me, my preconception of what desk clerks did was totally shattered. Instead of just taking people's money and handing them a room key, I was also expected to handle five-figure audits, produce occupancy counts, deal with reservations, print out hundreds of pages of computer reports for every department, inform housekeeping of every room's status, make coffee for the continental breakfast, program the wake-up calls into the private branch exchange, or PBX, take incoming calls when the switchboard operator was out, and provide guests with detailed directions to restaurants and attractions across southern New Mexico. The eight-hour shifts, whether morning, evening, or graveyard, were rarely dull.

I quickly realized that the motel in which I was working manifested important changes taking place in Holiday Inns nationwide. When I began working as a desk clerk, I assumed that the motel's clientele would mostly replicate my family—folks traveling across the country to visit relatives or visit the Grand Canyon or Disneyland. Instead, our guests included internationally famous entertainers (with one-hundred-member entourages), U.S. senators, wealthy corporate executives, rocket scientists, military officers, and construction workers. The typical vacationing family—parents with their 2.3 children and a dog in a station wagon—were, in fact, quite rare.

The Holiday Inn de Las Cruces was less interested in who its clients were than in whom they were affiliated with. The sales and reservations personnel worked hard to develop long-term relationships with organizations that could consistently deliver large numbers of guests. Holiday Inn had strong ties with the people who booked rock concerts at New Mexico State University's basketball arena, with corporations such as SpaceCom and Lockheed (both of which always had engineers and executives traveling to and from the White Sands Missile Range), and with major tourist companies that brought affluent retirees through the area by the busload. Not only did these people get substantially lower rates but they were also given the better rooms. Front-desk clerks were also explicitly instructed to give high discounts to travel agents, military personnel on travel orders, and state officials from Santa Fe. Personal friends of the owner and Republican Party political candidates usually had their rooms and meals "comped" by the management. Only the walk-ins—folks such as the Rogers family—paid the full price for whatever rooms remained.

The transition from emphasizing walk-ins to emphasizing corporate-affiliated travelers became apparent in other ways. Every few evenings, usually around midnight, a message would come in on the "Holidex II" reservation system tersely stating that a property somewhere in the country was no longer a Holiday Inn—"effective immediately." Often it was one of the older roadside properties whose owners chose not to upgrade to a more costly Holidome design upon renewal of their franchise agreement. I recall the employee meeting during which the owner announced the upcoming replacement of the Holiday Inn "Great Sign" with the more subdued script and starburst on a green marquee. He explained that although the old sign was indeed a powerful symbol for the chain, "times had changed." It was costly to build, light, and maintain. As Holiday Inn's business came increasingly through organized networks and less from off-the-road highway travelers, the Great Sign was no longer cost-effective. Moreover, it promoted an outdated image. The new sign would better portray Holiday Inn's role as a sophisticated, progressive leader in the international hospitality market.

I worked at Holiday Inn de Las Cruces for three consecutive summers and one Christmas vacation. It was a good job, and it gave me an opportunity to spend time at home. Several years later my former employer declared bankruptcy, and the motel was taken over by his creditors. Almost in poetic parallel, the columns that supported the roof of the Holidome nearly collapsed, and ugly reinforcement beams were temporarily installed to prevent the place from literally caving in. Two large competing motels—a Quality Inn and a Hilton Inn—have also had severe financial problems. Las Cruces, like most cities in the United States, developed a substantially overbuilt lodging environment during the boom period of the 1980s.

Today when my oldest sister travels, primarily by air on business, her accommodations are designated by her employer. My brother prefers to camp in wilderness areas when he leaves his home, and my other sister has too many local obligations to allow many excursions. My parents still choose Motel 6. Perhaps in latent reaction to my parent's persistent brand loyalty, as well as because of my evolving scholarly interest in lodging-market segmentation, I usually try to find a chain that I can afford and have not yet experienced. On occasion during a summer month, however, I will stay at an old roadside Holiday Inn (often converted to a Days Inn or a Comfort Inn or run as an independent) and enjoy the big pool in the center courtyard.

MOTEL SCHOLARSHIP

We are not the first to write about motels, nor are we the first to explore the commonplace in the American landscape. Scholarly focus on that elusive thing called "landscape" is rooted in many disciplines, from art history to architectural history to geography and beyond. We consider motels an element of the landscape, an orientation that derives from cultural geography, especially the brand of cultural geography advocated by Carl Sauer, a professor at the University of California from the 1920s through the 1960s.[3] Sauer saw landscapes as containers for human life, and their structuring and organization as reflecting essential cultural or social values. Landscapes and the elements they comprised (such as motels) were to be read for their social meaning.[4]

The word *landscape* originally was used for scenic depictions, painted representations of what one could see when one looked out over a geographical area.[5] During the Renaissance, painters revolutionized the art of realistic landscape depiction, especially by replicating graphically the linear perspective of distance. Artists such as Claude Lorraine and Nicholas Poussin established important compositional devices, the former using multiple horizons and enframements (which led the viewer's eye into a painting toward a focal point) and the latter adding strong diagonal elements (which strengthened further the sense of vista). European aristocrats in the sixteenth and seventeenth centuries, especially in England, turned to creating "picturesque" rural estates configured to look like landscape paintings. Thus the word *landscape* came to connote actual places. Ultimately, the meaning of the term changed to embrace the material realities of what could be visualized in a given place, for example, the material realities of the roadside.

Sauer's contribution was to focus attention on how landscapes, as built environments, evolved over time. He emphasized how underlying cultural values drove decision making, although he rarely fully explained how individual human actors actually behaved within specific social contexts in their articulation of landscape. Rather, culture was conceptualized more as a kind of superorganic agency restricting options and encouraging actions according to basic value systems. This stance was expanded upon and widely popularized by another key figure in landscape study, John Brinkerhoff Jackson, a colleague of Sauer's at Berkeley for a short period.[6] In 1951 Jackson founded *Landscape,* a magazine devoted to the study and appreciation of common landscapes. The magazine embraced the vernacular of ordinary places, such as the American roadside and its motels.[7] Even architectural historians, who remain largely preoccupied with the polite architecture of society's elites, have come to recognize the significance of the vernacular realm, where the vast majority of a society's buildings exist.[8] Cultural geographers have encouraged architectural historians and other scholars to consider the geographical contexts within which buildings, both sophisticated and ordinary, evolve. They have focused attention on building groupings as settlement patterns.[9]

Much attention has been paid to the architectural elements of landscape, especially to understanding the origin and diffusion of various building types. Common houses have received the most attention, especially those built in earlier historical periods, which are relics in contemporary landscapes.[10] Their rapid disappearance has contributed a sense of urgency to recording their distribution and understanding their historical meaning. Builder houses, those constructed not by owner-occupiers but by professional builders for specific clients or constructed on speculation, have also received attention. The building industry, sustained nationally by professional organizations, quickly spread the fads and fashions of new architectural ideas through the media of trade journals, order catalogs, and the like. Only relatively recently, however, has attention turned to the commercial architecture of the American roadside.[11] For example, John Jakle's article "Motel by the Roadside: America's Room for the Night" focused on successive motel prototypes in the United States.[12]

The historian of the American motel, however, is Warren Belasco. His *Americans on the Road: From Autocamp to Motel, 1910–1945* not only examines the evolving motel form but also seeks to locate the American motel in changing cultural and social contexts.[13] It is our intention in this book to expand upon Belasco's work by retracing some of his steps and, more importantly, extending his path into more recent time. Clearly, the better part of the motel story takes place in the post–World War II era. Belasco examined the motel's roots in the auto camp. Large numbers of automobilists traveling on the nation's highways in the early twentieth century carried tents and cooking pots for camping along the nation's highways. Localities organized free municipal auto camps to control such activity. Private entrepreneurs saw an opportunity to profit by upgrading facilities, often through the provisioning of rental cabins, and so the cabin court was born. Belasco saw auto camping as "an inexpensive, individualistic sport with antimodernist implications." "As antimodernists gypsies," he wrote, "these tourists wanted simplicity, self-sufficiency, and comradeship; as modern consumers, however, they valued comfort, service, and security. Ultimately, the gypsy gave way to the consumer, not because the urge to stray off the beaten path was insincere or unimportant but because the bourgeois route was safer and easier."[14] The motel quickly came of age.

It is surprising that social and economic historians have given little attention to the hospitality industry and, more specifically, to motels. What literature exists is dominated by biography, with many works overly solicitous of the men celebrated: E. M. Statler, Conrad Hilton, Kemmons Wilson, J. Willard Marriott.[15] Robert Woods, decrying the lack of serious scholarship, sees these biographies as following the same pattern. The works emphasize individual accomplishment and provide little insight into the development of the hospitality industry. Likewise, company histories, most of which were commissioned by the corporations treated, do little more than give names, dates, and events. Rarely do they elaborate on failures. As Woods notes, they leave readers largely on their own to figure out causes and consequences.[16]

The motel story, so far as it has been told, has been buried in the pages of obscure industry trade journals and popular magazines and newspapers. The literature reviewed and synthesized in the chapters that follow is diverse and highly fragmented. Some of it is well worth reading. For example, "The Great American Roadside," ghostwritten by James Agee and published in *Fortune* in September 1934, captures much of the spirit of early roadside America.[17] Agee wrote exuberantly of the cabin court's underlying rationale: "Casually yet eagerly this American people has spun away the summer length of day, in cars, along the great road; the lifted dark brings them down like sea birds, wherever night finds them, to rest along their line of flight. The shaky truck is quiet now, and the slick sedan garnished with emblems of speed." Agee asserted that the "great" American roadside made for rich anthropological study. There old folkways were playing out in new forms. But as Agee emphasized, the roadside was also "a mighty market place, 900,000 miles in length, $3,000,000,000 in girth, and founded upon a single word: restlessness."[18]

Other writers besides Agee have woven the motel into their writings. And, indeed, anthropologists and other social scientists also have focused on motels, if only modestly. Vladimir Nabokov, comfortable in widely diverse languages and cultures, recognized early, as most Americans perhaps could not, the motel's significance in American life. Motels amplified individual prerogatives, providing privacy in relative anonymity—a complement to the restlessness of car travel. Vladimir Nabokov begins his novel *Lolita* with the words: "It was then that began our extensive travels all over the States. To any other type of tourist accommodation I soon grew to prefer the Functional Motel—clean, neat, safe nooks, ideal places for sleep, argument, reconciliation, insatiable illicit love."[19] Indeed, motel guests enjoyed a degree of freedom previously unknown in other kinds of accommodation. In his 1940 article "Camps of Crime," published in *The American Magazine*, FBI director J. Edgar Hoover warned of an implicit immorality and tendency to criminality fostered by the motel.[20] The lead-in to the article read: "Behind many alluring roadside signs are dens of vice and corruption, says America's head G-Man. . . . He points out the menace to the public from hundreds of unsupervised tourist camps, 1940-style hideaways for public enemies." Certainly, there was something about motels that seemed to encourage "deviant" behavior. Or was it simply social change playing out in these places of relative freedom?

Even as early as the 1930s a few social scientists were intrigued by the rapidly evolving roadside and its motels. Sociologist Norman Hayner drove the highways of the Pacific Northwest to inventory and assess the accelerating phenomenon of highway travel and, more specifically, the role tourist courts played. His "Auto Camps in the Evergreen Playground," published in *Social Forces* in 1930, has a profound sense of discovery.[21] Here was something potentially important in the American experience. But what? Hayner anticipated much of what Warren Belasco would later write about.[22] Sociologist Elbert Hooker, on the other hand, focused directly on the motel's deviant implications. In a 1935 study of motels in the greater Dallas area, Hooker established that a large proportion of big-city tourist courts catered to, and thus promoted, an illicit sex trade, the "hot pillow joints," in the vernacular of the time.[23] Hollywood used the motel to advantage. The 1934 Frank Capra film *It Happened One Night,* with Clark Gable and Claudette Colbert, explored the implications of an unmarried couple innocently spending a night together in a motel. The heroine, in what then passed as something of a racy scene, undressed behind a blanket draped over a clothesline to separate two halves of a cabin. The motel served as a democratizing venue for the heroine of leisure wealth and the hero of average means, forced to share limited accommodations. Motel proprietors who worked hard at improving their industry's public image were necessarily concerned with the tendency of moviemakers and of Americans generally to link geographical mobility, motels, and illicit behavior. Clearly, there was anonymity in motel use. Most motels were located beyond the city limits—beyond the force of municipal law. Perhaps a loosening of mores should have been expected in the peripheral highway zone beyond legislated virtue. The motel could even be seen as a thing of evil, the most sinister motel of all being the Bates Motel in Alfred Hitchcock's *Psycho.*

Through the 1960s, architects and architectural critics gave little thought to motels, and architectural historians were totally oblivious. Indeed, few scholars considered motels or other elements of America's evolving roadsides to be architecture. Not until Geoffrey Baker and Bruno Funaro's book *Motels,* published in 1955, was there a serious attempt to explore the design implications of the motel function.[24] A few architects were at work designing motels, for example, Wayne McAllister, who adopted a convoluted rustic-ranch or Spanish-bungalow style for his design of the

El Rancho Vegas Motel in Las Vegas. Alan Hess reminds us in his *Viva Las Vegas: After Hours Architecture* that the motel was the progenitor of the Las Vegas casino and that the casino, in turn, was the progenitor of the Las Vegas strip, a very new kind of urban landscape. "Whereas San Francisco was based on the row house set on a twenty-five foot lot, the Las Vegas Strip was based on the motel set on a thousand-foot frontage," says Hess. "El Rancho set the pattern of the large highway resort hotel. With its opening the builders of Las Vegas varied the motel archetype a bit: the sign was expanded, the lobby was enlarged to include a casino, and the room wings were surrounded by recreational facilities and lush plantings. A bigger budget, a slightly different program, but a motel nonetheless." [25]

Thus scholars have come not only to value motels as an element of the modern American landscape in America but also to see them as fundamentally reflecting and indeed contributing to a changing America. The restless freedom implicit in transient mobility quite literally has resided in motels. Changing social mores, not just sexual mores, seem to have been encouraged by the anonymity and the convenience offered by motels. Today the motel business, part of what is termed the "hospitality industry," is a far bigger industry than even James Agee possibly could have imagined. And the motel helped to set the template for the highway commercial strip, so fundamental to the new automobile city, the city of exaggerated consumption in the "postindustrial" age.

Our knowledge of motels may be based on personal experience from trips taken or jobs held, but we must look beyond this personal discovery to assess the motel as an important cultural and social icon. Herein lies the rationale for this book. As we begin, however, we need to agree on a definition of the motel. The motel in America has never been a set piece defined once and for all. It has been ever changing, its form and function reflecting and contributing to societal change.

THE MOTEL DEFINED

What exactly is a motel? The first use of the term was apparently in the name of Arthur Heineman's Milestone Mo-tel, opened in San Luis Obispo, California, in 1926.[26] The word was a contraction of *motor* and *hotel*, with *motor hotel* the implied full form.[27] Thereafter, the word *motel* became a generic descriptor labeling a wide variety of highway-oriented accommodations. Many other labels were also applied, but none had the staying power to describe the whole class of business enterprise. Table 1.1 provides a summary of the designations used by motels listed in a 1950 accommodations guide. *Motel, motor court, court(s), tourist court, auto court, cottages, motel court, hotel court,* and *cottage court* led the field in the directory, which was focused primarily on the eastern portion of the United States.

Just where the first motel was established remains a matter of conjecture, hinging, again, on the definition one uses. The first motel may have been the Askins' Cottage Camp, established in 1901 at the edge of Douglas, Arizona, a copper mining town. William Askins's creation, a rooming house made up of nine cottages arrayed in rows facing a public street, was a remarkable approximation of the future motel. Indeed, after 1910, when automobile tourists began to replace transient miners and their families, a new name was chosen: Askins Tourist Court. Each small house contained a kitchenette, a bedroom, and "front room." Bedding and kitchen utensils were furnished. The charge initially was fifty cents a night, with an additional charge of twenty-five cents per bucket of coal. Water was available from a communal pump driven by a windmill.[28] Later, six one-room cabins connected by garages were built in a row across the back of the property, and yet another name adopted: Askin's Auto Court.

In the 1920s and 1930s it was easier to define a motel in terms of what it was not. It was not a traditional hotel located either downtown in a city (or a town) or in a rural resort. It was not a large, multistory structure with formal spaces such as lobbies, dining rooms, and ballrooms. Instead, the motel was a single-story affair often comprising several small buildings. It lacked formal spaces in which dress and other codes of social conduct were strictly regulated by a surveillant management. Such distinctions quickly blurred in the 1940s as motels grew in size and began to incorporate large public areas as well. In Las Vegas these spaces were gambling floors. As we demonstrate, the large highway hotels blended the features of the traditional hotel and motel. As late as the 1960s, however, some

TABLE 1.1 Designations Used in Motel Names, *Federal Hi-way Guide*, 1950

Descriptor	No.	Descriptor	No.	Descriptor	No.
1. Motel	104	11. Motor court	3	21. City	1
2. Motor court	87	12. Tourist cabins	3	22. Homes	1
3. Court(s)	78	13. Tour-o-tel	3	23. Hotel cottages	1
4. Tourist court	64	14. Motor hotel	2	24. Motor inn	1
5. Cabins	29	15. Tourist cottages	2	25. Tourist camp	1
6. Auto court	18	16. Travelodge	2	26. Tourist town	1
7. Cottages	12	17. Village	2	27. Trav-o-tel	1
8. Motel court	9	18. Auto hotel	1	28. Plaza court	1
9. Hotel court	6	19. Bungalow court	1		
10. Cottage court	3	20. Cabin court	1		

Source: Federal Hi-Way Guide, *Federal Hi-way Guide to America's Better Motor Courts/Tourist Homes* (St. Paul, Minn., 1950).

commentators still struggled to differentiate hotels from motels. "The line of demarcation is at the point where the guest is obligated to pay something more than the actual price of his room," argued Scott King, the president of the TraveLodge chain.[29] If a guest had to pay for a garage or tip a bellboy for a bucket of ice, then he or she was not in a motel.

By whatever name, motels rapidly increased in number through the 1930s and then again in the two decades after World War II (see Table 1.2). Of course, the lack of a clear definition for the motel makes these figures only crude approximations. The peak seems to have been reached in the early 1960s, when approximately 61,000 motels operated in the United States. As the industry matured and many of the older, smaller tourist courts dropped out in favor of newer, larger establishments, total numbers declined. The Bureau of the Census reported some 52,000 motel operations in 1972 and some 40,000 in 1987.[30] Both hotels and motels were included in later census tabulations, reflecting their virtual merger as a single lodging industry. Although the number of motels decreased, the total number of motel and hotel rooms did not. In 1972 there were some 2.5 million rooms available, and in 1994, roughly 3.1 million.[31]

The rise of the motel (and the reorientation of the traditional hotel to accommodate motorists) followed from the automobile's adoption as America's preferred mode of transportation. The increase in the number

TABLE 1.2 Estimated Number of Motels in the United States, 1928–1987

Year	Number	Year	Number
1928	c. 3,000	1957	56,248
1935	9,848	1959	60,500
1939	13,521	1961	60,951
1946	c. 20,000	1972	51,860[a]
1948	25,874	1987	40,424[a]
1954	29,426		

Sources: For 1928, Frank E. Brimmer, "Fundamentals of Motor Camping," *Official AAA Camp Directory* (Washington, D.C.: American Automobile Association, 1928), 16; for 1935, E. L. Barringer, "Uncle Sam Takes Census of Tourist Camps," *National Petroleum News* 29 (December 15, 1937): 44; for 1939, "Complete Court Census Released," *Tourist Court Journal* 5 (February, 1942): 23; for 1946, C. Vernon Kane, *Motor Courts: From Planning to Profits* (New York: Ahrens, 1954): 1; for 1948, "Bureau of Census Report of Courts," *Tourist Court Journal* 13 (September, 1950): 12; for 1954, "Motel Census Completed," ibid. 19 (September, 1956): 68; for 1957, "Latest Motel Census," *American Motel Magazine* 14 (January, 1957): 37; for 1959, Carl Rieser, "Sheraton vs. Hilton: Playing Checkers with 60,000 Rooms," *Fortune* 62 (January, 1961): 162; for 1961, "How Big Is Your Motel Industry?" *Tourist Court Journal* 25 (July, 1962): 24; for 1972, "How Big Is the Motel Industry?" *Motel/Motor Inn Journal* 37 (July, 1974): 9; and for 1987, U.S. Bureau of the Census, *Census of Service Industries, 1987* (Washington, D.C.: U.S. Government Printing Office, 1989), US-9.

[a]Includes both hotels and motels.

of motels followed closely the increase in automobile registrations. In 1956, 24 million passenger cars were registered in the United States; in 1958, 57 million; and in 1991, 143 million.[32] By 1958, Americans were traveling some 281,253,000 miles by auto on rural roads each year, the average household accumulating some 6,000 miles per year.[33] Much of this mileage represented vacation travel requiring overnight accommodation. The average traveler spent 14.6 nights per year away from home in 1967.[34] Of course, through the 1970s and 1980s motels came to rely more on the business traveler, as Jefferson Rogers discovered at Las Cruces. But business people also traveled by automobile, including rental cars obtained at airports and other locations. Increased automobile use was encouraged by the building of the nation's highway system, which was paid for by gasoline-tax revenue—a kind of "pay as you go" system. As more highways were constructed, more automobiles could be accommodated; and as more automobiles were used, more tax was generated. As this system of automobile orientation energized, the motel came fully into its own.

Traveling with parents, most of us discovered early the motel as a way station to somewhere else. A few of the accoutrements of home, along with much of its sense of privacy, familiarity, and security, could be had in a motel. If automobiles were private containers for movement, motels were places for pause where travelers reenergized in order to move on. The motel followed from the automobile as night followed day. What was there to marvel at? The idea of the motel was so logical. Only unusual variations on the theme caught and held attention, and then only momentarily—the motel painted pink and advertised as "The Flamingo" or the motel with the landscaped courtyard and pool configured as a "resort." Successful entrepreneurs sought clear visibility for themselves, usually by titillating travelers' fantasies. They learned to speak in simile and metaphor, to associate themselves and their motels with cultural and historical themes central to the American experience. They learned to promote the exotic associations that suggested escape from mundane routines. They sought to amplify the overnight motel in a way that home could rarely or never be amplified.

As students of landscape, however, we cannot let the motel merely be an architectural item. Because motels have come to be taken for granted, they demand careful interpretation. They illustrate much that is central to the American experience. In this book we adopt a simple strategy for interpreting motels as an element of landscape. We seek to define what has been average or normative about motels over time. We also seek to understand significant deviations from those norms. Motels represent a kind of place, albeit one defined on the scale of the retail business establishment. People choose these places based on the kinds of satisfaction desired. What kinds of satisfaction do they expect? And how have entrepreneurs worked to create and sustain these dispositions? Motels, as places, are commodified. They are packaged as a commercial product. How has the packaging of motel services evolved in the United States? Who has been responsible? How have they gone about their business?

Motels have not only a history (both as individual establishments and as part of an industry) but also a geography. They take architectural form as they fill specific sites. They occupy specific locations and specific kinds of locations vis-à-vis other things or other land uses. As standardized packages formulated by large corporations, they relate to one another today in networks of shared brand identity. Their geographical configuration in America is substantially informed by place-product-packaging, the systematic formulation of standardized motel chains in which each motel employs the same logo, has the same exterior architecture and interior room decor, provides the same level of service, and charges roughly the same price. Through chains of look-alike motels, large corporations battle territorially, seeking to optimize market penetration. Many of today's giant franchisers have segmented the motel market in the United States with different but complementary chains targeted at different kinds of travelers. The motel provides an important window through which to view and comprehend change in America today.

2

The Motel as Architecture

THE NEED FOR INEXPENSIVE OVERNIGHT ACCOMMODATIONS CONVENIENT to highways led to the establishment of auto camps, especially in the American West.[1] In the East, tourist homes came to serve a similar function. The highway traveler's rejection of hotels, located in congested downtown areas and lacking adequate parking, prompted the rapid rise of cabin courts, cottage courts, motor courts, motor inns, and eventually highway hotels on the periphery of urban places. In this chapter we describe the emergence of each of these distinctive motel types. Standardizing influences were reinforced through trade associations, referral chains, and then franchise corporations. Thus, motel morphology tended to follow set prototypes introduced and popularized over decades. Eventually the large motel came to be very much like the traditional hotel, with stress placed on various public facilities in addition to the rental of private rooms. Hotels, on the other hand, came to emphasize much of the convenience and informality that motels represented.

HOTELS

We begin our story with the hotel. Both in cities and in small towns downtown hotels dominated the lodging industry in the early 1900s. Few were convenient for automobiles. The Park Hotel in Lake Orion, Michigan, was typical of the nation's small-town hotels (see Fig. 2.1). Such establishments catered to salesmen and other travelers arriving on foot or by livery van from nearby railroad depots. When guests arrived by automobile in the years before World War I, their vehicles were shunted off to distant livery stables or storage garages. Motorists supervised the unloading of their luggage, turned their cars over to doormen, and entered the

FIGURE 2.1 The Park Hotel, Lake Orion, Michigan, circa 1910. The hotel was the dated centerpiece of the town. The town remained in the gaslight era, although the photographer's car and a superimposed picture of an airplane suggested that Lake Orion was indeed modern.

FIGURE 2.2 The Kavanaugh Hotel, Harrisonburg, Virginia, circa 1920. New hotels appeared in more prosperous small towns oriented to the automobile traveler. The Kavanaugh had a garage and a main entrance that was decidedly convenient for automobiles.

FIGURE 2.3 The Park Hotel, Chattanooga, circa 1920. Like most World War I–vintage hotels in small cities, the Park was not designed for the automobile traveler. The hotel's advertising instead emphasized the building's fireproofing and the fact that every room contained a bath and a ceiling fan.

ceremonial hotel lobby to face the ritual of registering (see Fig. 2.2). The Park Hotel in Chattanooga, Tennessee, was representative of hotels in small cities. Oriented to streetcar lines and accessible by taxicab, the hotel, built about 1910, made no special provision for automobiles (see Fig. 2.3). Yet, as the American Automobile Association (AAA) insignia on the postcard in Figure 2.3 indicates, automobile travelers had become very important.

During the 1920s, large towns and small cities subsidized the building of hotels, often through the agency of the local chamber of commerce. Investor groups acted not only out of self-interest but also to bolster civic pride, for no town or city could prosper without a modern hotel to accommodate visitors, especially automobile travelers. The full range of hotel facilities such as dining rooms and coffee shops were important adjuncts to private business dealing and public entertainment. Hotels were intended to stand as landmarks symbolic of economic and social vigor. The amenities they provided signified decorum and civility. The building of hotels like the one at Medford, Massachusetts, produced a nationwide building boom and an oversupply of hotel rooms in the nation's larger cities at the time of the stock market crash in 1929 (see Fig. 2.4).[2]

FIGURE 2.4 The Hotel Medford, Medford, Massachusetts, circa 1940. Cars lined the street, and a gasoline station occupied the corner opposite. The hotel sported a "motor entrance" and an adjacent parking lot. Medford had entered the automobile age.

Although these new hotels served the automobile traveler reasonably well, especially hotels that featured automobile entrances and garages, they were still located in or at the edge of congested business districts. Accordingly, they were difficult to reach, especially during the evening rush hour, when highway travelers, tired from a days's drive, were least able to cope with traffic frustration. Constructed on expensive land in urban centers, hotels necessarily charged high prices for rooms kept deliberately small in order to reduce construction and operating costs. Profits came primarily from a hotel's public spaces, and, accordingly, guest rooms functioned primarily to guarantee business in dining rooms, coffee shops, and rented meeting spaces.

Of course, relatively few of the nation's smallest towns could sustain the building of a modern hotels after World War I. The hostelries constructed during the railroad era necessarily continued to serve these towns. Sinclair Lewis explored this situation in his novel *Free Air,* in which the heroine, Clair Boltwood, motored alone across the upper Middle West. "The state of mind of the touring motorist entering a strange place at night, is as peculiar and definite as that of a prospector," Lewis mused. "It is compounded of gratitude at having got safely in; of perception of a new town, yet with all eagerness about new things dulled by weariness; of hope that there is going to be a good hotel, but small expectation—and absolutely

FIGURE 2.5 The Book-Cadillac Hotel, Detroit, circa 1930. Ostentatious ornamentation characterized the public spaces of Detroit's most prestigious downtown hotel. Here the aspiring middle classes could experience a taste of the aristocratic.

FIGURE 2.6 The Sheraton-Cadillac Hotel, Detroit, circa 1950. Originally named the Book-Cadillac, this grand hotel, refurbished as the Radisson-Cadillac in the 1980s, today stands derelict in Detroit's largely abandoned downtown, the Motor City's economic energies having shifted substantially to its suburbs.

FIGURE 2.7 Capitola, California, circa 1920. Ocean, beach, boardwalk, and hotel were the focus of this railroad-era resort reinforced after World War I by automobile tourists. Here an interurban electric car departs for nearby Santa Clara.

FIGURE 2.8 The Lewis Bay Lodge, Hyannis, Massachusetts, 1924. The lodge has been signposted for the automobile trade. Its advertisement in the 1923 *Automobile Blue Book* reads: "A Homelike Hotel Near the Water; Comfortable Rooms—Excellent Food; We Cater to the Motorists."

no probability—that there will really be one." Lewis described the hotel in the fictional town of Gopher Prairie as follows: "In the hotel Claire was conscious of the ugliness of the poison-green walls and brass cuspidors and insurance calendars and bare floor of the office; conscious of the interesting scientific fact that all air had been replaced by the essence of cigar smoke and cooking cabbage; of the stares of the traveling men lounging in bored lines; and of the lack of welcome on the part of the night clerk, an oldish bleached man with whiskers instead of a collar."[3] Lacking funds, few provincial hotels bothered to keep up with the current fashions.

By contrast, in the largest cities the leading hotels were brought to the highest level of perfection. The Benjamin Franklin Hotel in Philadelphia long symbolized the pinnacle of that city's social sophistication (see Fig. 1.1). Detroit's Book-Cadillac Hotel (later the Sheraton-Cadillac) was an opulent "palace" with lavish ornamentation throughout (see Figs. 2.5 and 2.6). A mammoth block, the hotel anchored one end of downtown Detroit's fashionable Washington Boulevard, while the equally elegant Statler Hotel anchored the other. A grand ballroom swept across the entire front of the second floor of the Book-Cadillac. On the ground floor there was a grand arcade lined with exclusive shops selling expensive men's clothing and other luxury items. The dining room simulated the great hall of a European palace. With its 1,000 guest rooms and several floors of meeting rooms, the hotel attracted large conventions. Penthouse suites catered to the affluent and the influential, drawn to the booming motor city on business or pleasure.

Downtown commercial hotels catered primarily to male tastes. Food served in hotel dining rooms tended to red meat, starch, and spices. What hotels earned on food sales they redoubled on liquor sales. Unescorted women were discouraged from using commercial hotels, and married women accompanying their husbands were expected to remain for the most part in the background. Warren Belasco observed that "the public lobby, with its coterie of traveling salesmen, was off limits to respectable unaccompanied women; many hotels provided separate ladies' entrances and waiting rooms. Women traveling with husbands remained at a discrete distance from the main desk, out of public view, while husbands registered."[4]

The resort hotel was another form of accommodation available to early automobile tourists. Located in the mountains or at the seaside, most of these facilities were originally also aimed at railroad passengers, such as at Capitola, California, where interurban electric cars connected to nearby Santa Clara (see Fig. 2.7). Parking lots were provided, and hotels listed themselves in AAA guides not only as resort destinations but as overnight accommodations between destinations (see Fig. 2.8). Even hotels and taverns that had once catered to stagecoach travelers sprang to life once again along highways once forgotten but now swarming with automobiles (see Fig. 2.9).

Traditionally, vacation hotels catered mostly to women. In well-to-do families men worked year round in the city so that their wives and children could enjoy the finer things of life, such as summer leisure in the country.[5] But many resorts, such as Capitola-by-the-Sea, catered also to the middle and lower classes, who came on short excursions in family groups that included both sexes. It was this vacation crowd that automobile travel tended to reinforce. Only a very few resorts remained strictly elite preserves. Theodore Dreiser approached Indiana's French Lick Hotel with some trepidation. He wrote in *A Hoosier Holiday,* "Various black porters pounced on our bags like vultures. We were escorted through a marble lobby such as Arabian romances once dreamed of as rare, and to an altar like desk, where a high priest of American profit deigned to permit us to register." Dreiser and his companions were "ushered down two miles of hall on the fifth or sixth floor" to "very plain, very white, but tastefully furnished rooms, where we were permitted to pay various slaves who had attended us."[6]

The hotel industry suffered during the Depression. By 1932, 80 percent of all hotel mortgages were in default, and 32 percent of the nation's hotels could not even cover property taxes from revenues. Fifteen percent could not meet payrolls.[7] Although excess room capacity and mismanagement

FIGURE 2.9 The Table Rock Inn on U.S. 50, Backbone Mountain, Maryland, circa 1925. The inn confronts the motorist with gas pumps, restaurant, hotel rooms, and cabins. Here was opportunity to cool the engine and partake of a mountaintop view.

FIGURE 2.10 Postcard parody, 1942. Older hotels were stereotyped as antiquated and obsolete in the new "motel age."

accounted for much of the difficulty, motels were also cutting substantially into the hotel customer base. Hotel owners began to take serious notice of what some called the "motel menace." Hotel prices were cut to meet the new motel competition. Generally, motels operated with lower fixed and variable costs and could charge less. Price cutting undermined the ability of hotel owners to repair or upgrade their establishments. Thus motel competition helped force marginal hotels into a downward spiral of delayed maintenance and obsolescence. Postcard art poked fun at the hotel predicament (see Fig. 2.10). The AAA had reported in 1929 that some 75 percent of its members stayed in hotels when traveling, but in 1936 the percentage fell to only 60 percent.[8]

AUTO CAMPS

Auto camps first evolved in the western United States as an alternative to hotels. They appealed both to seasonal tourists and to migratory transients in search of work. Automobile tourists had swarmed onto western highways just before World War I in search of the adventure and the change of pace that getting closer to nature promised. They were called "tin can" tourists, a reference to both the debris they left along the roadsides and the "tin lizzies" many drove. They dominated a short "squatter" period in travel, during which campers set up campsites wherever they chose, often squatting on private property, usually without permission.[9] Once equip-

FIGURE 2.11 Georgia roadside, circa 1920. "Tin can" tourists, traveling in "tin lizzies" and eating from tin cans, squatted by the roadside in the years before auto camps became widespread.

UNDER THE COTTONWOODS IN ROCKY MOUNTAIN LAKE PARK, DENVER, COLO.

FIGURE 2.12 Rocky Mountain Lake Park, Denver, circa 1920. Commissaries at the larger public auto camps sold groceries and provided toilets, showers, and often laundry facilities. They diverted campers from the roadside itself.

ment had been purchased, camping was an inexpensive way to travel (see Fig. 2.11). Those who pitched tents by the roadside and cooked their own meals avoided room costs, meal costs, parking fees, tips, and all the other charges that accumulated in hotels. Money that might have been spent on accommodations could be spent on gasoline and longer trips.

Partly out of civic pride and partly in order to protect themselves against uncivil campers, towns along principal migratory routes took to roping off areas for campers. Thus camping was confined to specific locations that were easily policed by local authorities. Municipal campgrounds were developed in large cities also, for example, in Denver, where a fairgrounds was converted seasonally into a mammoth tent city (see Fig. 2.12). The better equipped of these facilities featured public toilets and showers and provided water and firewood. The Denver campground had a commissary that sold groceries and other camping supplies, a gasoline station and a garage, a lunchroom, a laundry, and a large playground for children. Local businessmen, especially retailers, could profit from the touring families attracted to their town's campground. But hotel owners harbored great resentment. Initially, campers paid no fee in most places. Since campgrounds were paid for in part by property taxes levied on hotels, the hotel owners viewed campgrounds as unfair competition.

While merchants might want to attract tourists, they generally did not want to attract unemployed transients. Like the Joad family in John Steinbeck's *Grapes of Wrath,* transients in search of work moved slowly

FIGURE 2.13 The Woodland Beach Tourist Park, Lake Mills, Wisconsin, circa 1940. House trailers became increasingly common in auto camps after 1930. Some private auto camps survived World War II as trailer courts.

PURE WATER FROM CITY   ELECTRIC LIGHTS AND MODERN CONVENIENCES

SITUATED JUST OUTSIDE OF KINGSTREE ON THE NORTH SIDE

S. D. GUYTON,
PROP. & OWNER

DIXIE TOURIST CAMP

HEATED CABINS AND TENT GROUNDS

COMFORTABLE CABINS IN A BEAUTIFUL GROVE OF HICKORY AND OAKS

HOT SHOWER BATH, HOT LUNCH AND GARAGE, STORE AND SERVICE STATION

40 MILES SOUTH OF FLORENCE :: 70 MILES NORTH OF CHARLESTON, S. C.

ON COASTAL HIGHWAY NO. 17   KINGSTREE, S. C.

FIGURE 2.14 Advertisement for the Dixie Tourist Camp, Kingstree, South Carolina, circa 1930.

from campground to campground, often lingering for weeks or months.[10] Poverty-stricken, their household goods crammed into ancient, asthmatic cars and trucks, transients tended to discourage tourism wherever they lingered. Although automobile camping was romanticized as essentially "democratic" in that people of various backgrounds and origins could mix in the camaraderie of the camp, a profound social stratification tended to operate along class lines where tourists and transients were thrown together. By 1925 most municipal auto camps had begun to impose entrance fees, to charge for firewood, and to enforce strict limitations on lengths of stay—all to discourage migrants. Once such fees were widely assessed, then private operators were attracted to the auto-camp business (see Fig. 2.13).[11]

Commercial auto camps quickly replaced the municipal campgrounds in most places. Fireplaces, picnic tables, coin-operated stoves in community kitchens, electrical outlets, electrical lighting, tent floors, and even tents were provided. The next logical step was to rent primitive cabins in lieu of tents. Campers still carried their own bedding and cooking utensils and tended for themselves in an essentially outdoor situation. Permanent cabins at a campground signaled an important change: the development of the cabin camp. As cabins were weatherproofed and provided with stoves, they began to define a kind of overnight experience removed from the rustic outdoors. In the late 1920s the Dixie Tourist Camp, at Kingstree, South Carolina, could advertise heated cabins in addition to its tent grounds (see Fig. 2.14). The cabins were complemented by a central lavatory building, a gasoline station and garage, and a store with a lunch counter.

TOURIST HOMES

In the eastern United States the tourist home came to function in much the same way as the western auto camp.[12] The typical tourist home was a private house, usually located near the downtown area on a major thoroughfare carrying a through highway, where one or more bedrooms were "let for the night" (see Fig. 2.15). A sign reading "Tourists Accommodated" or some such adorned the front lawn. The Coastal Tourist Home, in Savannah, Georgia, offered meals and, according to its advertising card, provided garage space for a fee (see Fig. 2.16). Operators of tourist homes were stereotyped in the 1930s as either widows struggling to make ends meet or bankrupt former businessmen struggling to regain their business composure. Taking in guests was a way of profiting from equity invested

FIGURE 2.15 The Lawnsette Tourist Home, Lewisburg, Ohio, circa 1940. Rooms, bath, and home cooking were the enticements offered by this tourist home located beside U.S. 40 on the Old National Road.

FIGURE 2.16 Advertisement for the Coastal Tourist Home, Savannah, Georgia, circa 1930.

FIGURE 2.17 Irvine's Tourist Court, Bardstown, Kentucky, circa 1950. This tourist home was expanded into a cabin camp, a motel aborning.

in private homes otherwise jeopardized by the Depression. A tourist-home craze swept through eastern cities. For example, the *Hotel Monthly* reported in 1935 that there were about a thousand tourist homes licensed in Richmond, Virginia, alone.[13] Throughout the country, tourist-home operators built cabins in side and back yards as an easy way to expand successful businesses, creating cabin camps in the process (see Fig. 2.17).

CABIN CAMPS

In 1933 John McCarthy and Robert Littell wrote in *Harper's Magazine* that "the tourist cottages are anything but standardized. The travelers who use them may roll up in the same cars, all exactly alike; . . . they may listen to Amos an' Andy at seven fifteen and brush their teeth by national advertising, but the places where they sleep by the side of the road are the products of individual taste and effort."[14] Diversity seemed to rule as the cabin camp was reinvented over and over again. Actually, a relatively narrow range of prototypes quickly came to characterize these new motels; in truth, they were anything but the product of independent invention.

Understanding evolving motel morphology requires focusing on (1) building types and (2) building arrangement. Evolving building types are illustrated in Figure 2.18. Cabin camps, the first motels, emerged from the auto camp and the tourist home. But three varieties of cabin camp evolved: (1) the auto camp with cabins added; (2) the cabin camp built

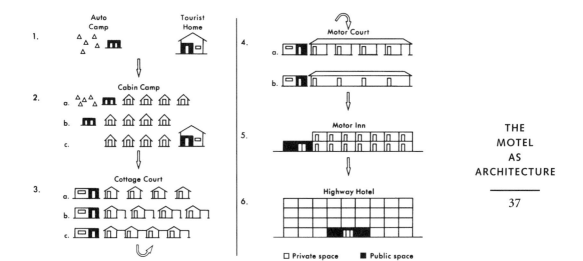

FIGURE 2.18 The evolution of the American motel as a building type.

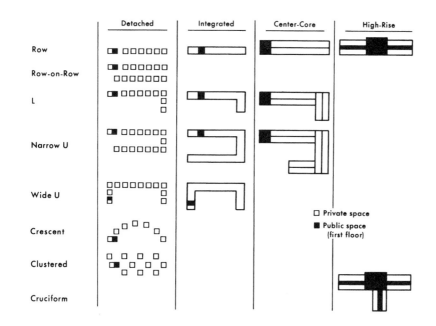

FIGURE 2.19 Dominant variations in the spatial organization of the motel.

FIGURE 2.20 Lakeside Cabins, Detroit Lakes, Minnesota, circa 1935. A row of cabins and intervening carports was placed perpendicular to both highway and lake.

from scratch, without tent camping or a tourist-home facility; and (3) the tourist home with cabins added. The prevailing patterns of building arrangement are illustrated in Figure 2.19. Shown are the row, row-on-row, L, narrow U, wide U, crescent, clustered, and cruciform arrangements, which applied variously to detached, integrated, center-core, and high-rise buildings. Cabin camps, as a motel type, tended to be arranged in row, row-on-row, L, crescent, and clustered patterns.

Standardization followed from the logic of the small cabin (a simple geometric box built on a rectangular or square floor plan and capped with a simple gable roof), usually only large enough to enclose a bed, table, and chair. Standardization also resulted from the size and maneuverability of the automobile. Motel owners were limited in the arrangement of their cabins by the need to provide each guest with a parking place in front of or adjacent to his or her room. Where carports or garages were provided, a simple row configuration was a logical solution (see Fig. 2.20). Standardization also followed from the provision of sanitary facilities, usually located in a central building to which guests walked from their cabins. Only later did motel operators build "bathrooms" within cabins, one of the distinguishing features of the more solidly built cottage courts.

In the early years, most motel owners literally built their own motels. To assist them, companies such as the Economy Housing Company, of Onawa, Iowa, sold kits of prefabricated lumber to cabin camp owners. Kits could be purchased at local lumberyards or from traveling salesmen. Popular magazines, farm journals, and other trade publications regularly carried plans showing how to erect simple cabins.[15] Owners of cabin courts traveled to observe what other owners were accomplishing. They formed state and regional trade associations in order to share information and to set specific standards for operations. These standards had definite building implications. A rather restricted design vocabulary developed. Motels had not only to function as motels were expected to function but to look like motels were expected to look in order to attract customers, who were increasingly demanding. Often several design prototypes appeared in a single motel built incrementally over a number of years.

In 1933, *Architectural Record* declared cabin-camp construction to be one of the few "booming" building sectors of the Depression. At least 400,000 "shacks" had been constructed in the previous four years.[16] Of course, architects played hardly any role in this activity, which had already produced some 30,000 cabin camps in the United States.[17] Of the 714 camps the sociologist Norman Hayner studied in the Pacific Northwest in 1930, 77 percent already had cabins.[18] The secret to success lay in the jack-of-all-trades, do-it-yourself nature of the business. John McCarthy and Robert Littell speculated that a farmer located beside a highway could add gas pumps to his produce stand and that from the profits he could build a cafe and a few cabins. "The money trickles steadily in and rolls in during the summer. Your overhead is low. Your wife does the cooking, your daughter makes the beds, your son tends the gas pumps. The food, for yourself and your guests, all comes from the farm."[19]

Their convenience was what made the cabin camps popular. In 1936 *Hotel Magazine* featured a short article entitled "I'll Answer Your Questions on Tourist Camps." In answer to the question, What induced travelers to stop at cabin camps? it emphasized "sixteen separate and distinct" conveniences: "car at cottage door; economy; housekeeping facilities; more privacy; no street car or other city traffic noises; no tipping required; speed in checking out; speed in emergency exits; home-like atmosphere; limited removal of baggage from car; individual control of heating system; direct contacts with owner; elimination of driving in down-town traffic; no garage storage, or pick-up and delivery service; car servicing on premises; personal appearance after driving all day not embarrassing as there are not lobbies to pass through."[20]

At the U-Smile Cabin Camp, in Kansas City, Missouri, arriving guests signed the registry and then paid their money. A cabin without a mattress rented for one dollar; a mattress for two people cost an extra twenty-five cents, and blankets, sheets, and pillows another fifty cents. The manager rode the running boards to show guests to their cabins. Each guest was given a bucket of water from an outside hydrant, along with a scuttle of

FIGURE 2.21 Postcard parody, 1954. Older cabin camps, like older hotels, came to be stereotyped as old-fashioned and out of date.

firewood in the winter. Such cabin camps required little investment. Initially the motel business attracted people with little capital who were willing to work long hours. *Fortune* magazine commented: "There was a time when the sailor home from the sea went to chicken farming. Nowadays he buys a motel by the side of the road."[21]

Many cabin camps were combined with gasoline stations, cafes, and other businesses. In 1935 the *Census of Business* counted 9,848 "tourist camps," of which 20 percent sold gasoline.[22] The petroleum industry encouraged jobbers and agents to invest in cabin camps. A *National Petroleum News* editorial advised: "The lower the cost of touring the farther down the economic scale touring is made possible, and as sleeping and eating costs less the tourist can cover more territory consuming [more] gasoline and oil."[23] Thus, a camp might sell groceries and offer roadside entertainment, as at the Red Hat Tourist Camp, in Baxley, Georgia. The camp's menagerie featured a black bear, a monkey, an alligator, and some peacocks. "The bear imbibes about 40 cold drinks a day . . . and the proprietor of the place frequently sells as much as fifteen cases of drinks on Sunday."[24]

Cabin camps were flimsily constructed, and few were winterized. In the North, many cabin camps were seasonal businesses. Where indoor plumbing had been added, it was usually makeshift, and very small cabins were made smaller still by the enclosure of minuscule bathrooms. Cabins deteriorated quickly and could become quite disheveled after only a few operating seasons. With the arrival of newer, more solidly constructed motels, the early cabin camps, like the older hotels before them, became the focus of humorous postcard art (see Fig. 2.21).

COTTAGE COURTS

As cabin camps became more substantial, the word *cottage* increasingly was used in their names (see Fig. 2.22). Cottages were not only more durable but also larger and winterized for year-round business. Permanence was not really a construction objective, for as the *Tourist Court Plan Book* warned, the motel business changed constantly and if a motel were built "too permanently," the materials would outlast the style. "It is wise to build out of materials that will last say 15 or 20 years," the *Plan Book* recommended, "for by that time the court will likely be outmoded."[25] Each cottage contained a private bathroom and a closet. Initially, kitchens or kitchenettes were widespread, but by World War II they had largely disappeared from newer motels because of low demand and because they were costly to build. Cottage units were added to preexisting cabin arrays in the older motels, as at the Colonial Cottages Tourist Court, in Gulfport, Mississippi (see Fig. 2.23). Eventually, older cabins might be torn down and replaced by modern units, bringing a motel entirely up-to-date.

After 1930 motel names increasingly included the word *court*. Cottages were increasingly arranged geometrically around a central open space, or court. The width of U-shaped courts was dependent on the depth of the lot and the extent of highway frontage (see Fig. 2.24). Cottages were usually arrayed as individual units with open spaces between the units.

FIGURE 2.22 The sign at the Locust Grove Cottages, Palmyra, Indiana, 1978. Cottage courts were winterized and provided with fully appointed private bathrooms, representing a substantial step up from primitive cabins.

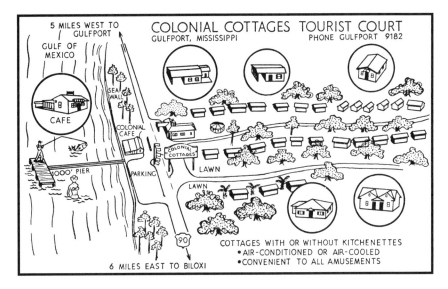

FIGURE 2.23 Postcard advertisement for the Colonial Cottages Tourist Court, Gulfport, Mississippi, circa 1940. The cottages, some with air conditioning and kitchenettes, are located back from the Coastal Highway, U.S. 90.

FIGURE 2.24 The Oaks Tourist Court, Atlanta, circa 1950. The Oaks promoted its fireproof cottages, steam heat, private baths, and innerspring mattresses.

FIGURE 2.25 The Koronado Hotel Kourts, Joplin, Missouri, circa 1930. Part of a small chain, this motel claimed on its postcards to be "the finest and most up-to-date tourist courts in the entire Southwest on U.S. 66 Highway."

Attached garages were popular after 1930, and it was not uncommon to find cottage-garage combinations linked wall to wall to form continuous façades, the integrity of each building preserved in individual roof lines, since the units were usually freestanding.

The typical cottage court contained an office building that usually included private apartment space for the motel manager and his family. Another building might contain a coffee shop (see Fig. 2.25). As in the case of the cabin camps, public space was primarily outdoors. Space not given to parking was often landscaped to give motels a more gentrified aspect. Architecturally, cottages were made to look like little suburban houses in order to enhance their appeal for the middle-class tourist and the traveling businessman. Cottages were furnished like suburban houses, with rugs, dressing tables and bureaus, radios, and the like. Sometimes they were provided with steam heat from central heating plants.

MOTOR COURTS

Motor courts were structured like cottage courts except that room units were totally integrated under single rooflines usually as a single building (see Fig. 2.26). Long porches enhanced the sense of visual integration and sheltered open windows in inclement weather. Motor courts were single-story structures. Many contained coffee shops or restaurants as part of an integrated complex, for example, Harlan Sanders's establishment in

FIGURE 2.26 The Park Plaza Hotel Court, New Orleans, circa 1950. A motor court organized around a narrow U-shaped court, the Park Plaza offered fully carpeted, air-conditioned, and centrally heated rooms. The motel promoted its memberships in the American Motor Hotel Association (AMHA), the Louisiana Motel Court Association (LMCA), and the New Orleans Motor Court Association (NOMCA).

FIGURE 2.27 The Sanders Court and Cafe, Corbin, Kentucky, circa 1950. The cafe and motel where Kentucky Fried Chicken began is now preserved as a museum. The caption on this early postcard reads: "Offer complete accommodations with tile baths (abundance of hot water), carpeted floors, 'Perfect Sleeper' bed, air conditioning, steam heat, radio in every room, open all year, serving excellent food."

Corbin, Kentucky (see Fig. 2.27). In 1960 the average motel had only about twenty units.[26] Approximately 18 percent contained coffee shops or restaurants, and 25 percent operated gasoline stations as at Sanders Court and Cafe.[27] Although motor courts were built in a range of architectural styles, from Tudor Revival to Colonial Revival, "western" themes were the most popular. Motor courts with façades integrated around interior courtyards were reminiscent of Spanish haciendas, especially when they were constructed of stucco to stimulate adobe. Motels with names such as El Rancho and Casa Grande appeared from coast to coast.

After World War II the word *motel* quickly came to describe the new motor courts, although other words, such as *autel*, continued to thrive (see Fig. 2.28). Many motels were organized around large courtyards rendered as informal outdoor "lobbies." Here the increasingly popular swimming pool was located in a landscaped ground suggestive of a resort (see Fig. 2.29). In these motels parking was restricted to the outside of the U-shaped courts, and rooms were provided with doors both front and back. On the pool side, sliding doors accessed small "patios."

Motel construction boomed in the late 1950s and 1960s, and by 1964 there were at least 61,000 motels in the country.[28] Many factors fostered the rapid growth. Motels benefited from the general decentralization of cities and towns that came with increased automobile ownership. The federal interstate highway program, begun in 1956, was an important part of this decentralization process. More important, however, were factors internal to the motel industry. The motel business was characterized by a higher cash flow than most other types of real estate investment; thus, interest and principal on loans could be easily amortized. New motel properties in growth areas appreciated rapidly, producing substantial capital gains when they were sold, which invited speculation. Banks and insurance companies looked favorably on motel investments and required small cash down payments. Such leverage produced higher rates of cash return on initial investments, enabling investors to gain more appreciated value when motels were sold.[29]

The 1954 tax code not only stimulated new construction but also tended to limit the life expectancy of motel buildings, thus precipitating short-term ownership and cyclical renovation and modernization. The tax code remained a built-in mechanism for change until the late 1980s. Equity was sheltered through accelerated depreciation in the early life of a purchase, but in eight to ten years, when amortization payments become greater than depreciation allowances, it was time for the purchaser to sell and take his or her long-term capital gain. The investor was then ready to reinvest in another motel and repeat the process.[30] Owners took part of their profits by disinvesting their buildings, which meant providing only

FIGURE 2.28 The American Autel, Salt Lake City, circa 1950. The bold neon sign out front prompted the logo "Look for the Indian Head."

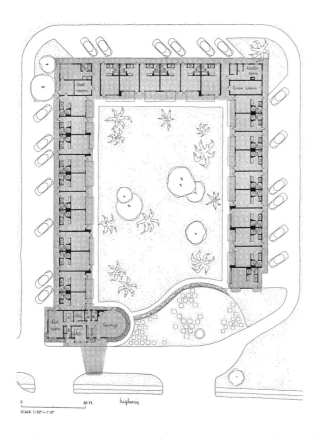

FIGURE 2.29 Motor court plan, 1955. (*Source:* Baker and Funaro, *Motels,* 38.)

FIGURE 2.30 The Bo-Peep Motel, South Fulton, Kentucky, circa 1955. Described by its owner as a "ranch style" motel, the Bo-Peep exemplifies a simple row configuration.

minimal maintenance and repair. Buildings deteriorated until a change in ownership brought renovation, often embracing the latest fads and fashions in construction and styling. Architectural integrity in motel buildings was short-lived. The tax code encouraged a brisk trade in second-, third-, and even fourthhand motels, many of which would otherwise have been abandoned.[31] It also encouraged builders to put up junky, flimsy buildings and to otherwise foster impermanence on the roadside. In 1960 the average life span of a motel building was calculated to be only nine years.[32]

Not all motor courts had courtyard configurations. The motor-court idea played out in simpler row and L-shaped room arrangements (see Fig. 2.30). But space was usually reserved for complete court configurations should the motel prove sufficiently profitable. Motor courts began to sport giant signs that dominated the motel grounds visually, as at the American Motel, in Newport, Arkansas (see Fig. 2.31). The sign, with its elaborate neon display, was intended to provide a vertical dimension to an otherwise low-to-the-ground building configuration. Located at the driveway entrance, the sign carried iconography symbolic of the motel's quality and range of services. Motor-court rooms became increasing standardized around furnishings supplied by supply houses specializing in hotel and motel outfitting (see Fig. 2.32). To the chairs and bureaus of the cottage camps were added writing desks. Air conditioning became a necessity, especially in the Southwest and the Southeast. Brand names became increasingly important in advertising. Crosley air conditioners, Simmons mat-

FIGURE 2.31 The American Motel, Newport, Arkansas, circa 1960. The caption on the postcard reads: "All rooms on ground floor with free parking in front of door. TV, room phone, music, air conditioned. Private swimming pool and sun deck. Spacious well equipped play ground. Restaurant, banquet and meeting facility."

FIGURE 2.32 The Pines Motel, Orange, Texas, circa 1960. Except for the television set and clothes rack, all of the furnishings of the typical motor court room are shown here. Knotty pine was a common feature of the decor through the 1960s.

tresses, Ivory soap, and RCA televisions were among the items regularly promoted on motel signs as guarantees of quality.

MOTOR INNS

Motor inns appeared in the 1950s and were located largely in metropolitan areas, either downtown in urban-renewal zones, near airports, or at the new interchanges of peripheral freeways. Substantially larger and more luxurious than motor courts, they were most often complexes made up of two- or three-story buildings organized around a courtyard (see Figs. 2.33 and 2.34). Besides an elaborate outdoor area focused on the swimming pool, the typical motor inns featured expanded public space indoors. The coffee shop became a full-fledged dining room with an adjacent cocktail lounge as well as banquet and meeting rooms. The registration desk expanded into a small lobby with a magazine counter and gift shop. Guest rooms were large: the typical room contained two double beds, a night table with telephone, a baggage rack, several lounge chairs, a chest of drawers, and a desk or table, and there was a dressing and bath area with vanity separated from the shower and toilet. Rooms were air-conditioned, and of course there was a television set. In many motor inns rooms were built back to back, the utilities placed down a center core (see Fig. 2.19). The center-core buildings were noisier, but construction costs were lower, and they were cheaper to heat and cool.[33] Inns with 150 to 300 rooms could be accommodated on sites where only 50 to 60 rooms had been possible before.

The motor inn was promoted as a motel type by several competing motel chains. The small businessman dominated the motel industry until the 1950s, when motor-inn construction began to require vast capital outlays. Although investment money was readily available, lenders wanted assurances that new motels would profit, and affiliation with one or another motel chain seemed to provide that assurance through national brand-name recognition. Motel chains were not new in the 1950s. The idea had been applied in the 1920s, albeit prematurely, to both primitive cabin camps and luxurious highway hotels, early predecessors of today's motel-like hotel complexes. In 1929, for example, the Pierce Petroleum Corporation opened five forty-room hotels along U.S. 66 in Missouri and Oklahoma.[34] The facilities included an emergency hospital with a nurse on duty and a restaurant equipped with an "electrola radiola."

Brand identity through standardized signage and buildings had long characterized industries dominated by relatively few corporations, for example, the petroleum industry, in its development and use of gasoline station chains.[35] But motels, which were locally controlled, were late in

FIGURE 2.33 The Centre Denver Motor Lodge, Denver, circa 1960. "Big enough to serve you! Small enough to know you!" was this motor inn's motto. It featured 140 rooms in three multistory units, a dining room, a coffee shop, a cocktail lounge, and five banquet rooms in a separate structure. A gasoline station stood adjacent.

FIGURE 2.34 The Shore Drive Motel, Chicago, circa 1970. This motor inn brought suburban lodging amenities to the center of Chicago.

seeking the benefits of brand recognition. Motel chains, such as Holiday Inn or Best Western, brought substantial regimentation to motel architecture. Not only did motels have to look like motels were expected to look but, ideally, motels within a given chain should look alike. The Howard Johnson's motor inns of the 1960s shared the following features. Guests arrived at a gatehouse, where the registration desk was located. Once registered, guests drove to their assigned room. On entering their room, they faced a partition comprising a built-in rack and coat closet where bags could be conveniently dropped; the partition allowed only a partial view of the room, its furnishings, and the sliding patio door beyond. A dressing area with a large mirror, counter, and lavatory came next. Thus a specific traffic flow was planned to heighten first impressions: from car to luggage rack to bathroom to bed and sitting area to a view out over the patio and landscaped grounds. A company restaurant was immediately adjacent at many facilities.[36]

Modular construction became increasingly common during the motor-inn era. Room "kits" in which all electrical and plumbing fixtures were already installed were hauled to construction sites from factory floors and arrayed and stacked in the appropriate configurations. Factory assembly reduced labor costs, the largest single expense in motel construction. Not only were assembly-line procedures economical but factory labor tended to be nonunion, with wage rates considerably lower than those of skilled carpenters, plumbers, and electricians. However, modular construction placed certain limitations on motel planning. For example, an outside width of twelve feet was the maximum allowed on most highways along which modular units were transported, so that modular motel rooms tended to be very small.

HIGHWAY HOTELS

The highway hotel, an unsuccessful experiment in the 1920s and 1930s, reappeared in the 1960s as an assemblage of rooms partially if not wholly contained in a highrise structure (see Fig. 2.35). Traditional motel design, which favored row, L, and court building arrangements, gave way to the multistory box or other simple geometrical forms, including cruciform, round, and curvilinear structures (see Fig. 2.19).[37] The typical 1970s highway hotel included a high-rise unit in which the bulk of the public space was on the first floor and most of the private rooms were above, as well as one or more low-rise wings that also contained rental rooms. Rooms in the tower were entered from central hallways as in traditional hotels, but rooms in the wings could be approached directly from adjacent parking lots. In the 1980s the low-rise wings were eliminated from most new construction. Restaurants, cocktail lounges, and meeting rooms in high-way hotels were larger than those in motor inns. Nonetheless, at least in the more luxurious establishments, motel design still focused on large guest rooms. Most highway hotels were located in large urban areas along suburban roadways, near airports, and in downtown redevelopment areas.

An important variation on the highway hotel was the new resort hotel, which perhaps should be considered a design category in its own right. In places like Las Vegas and Miami Beach the highway motel was raised to a higher power. Rooms might number more than a thousand. Public spaces were massive, many opulently furnished as pseudo fantasylands. The Sands Hotel, on the Las Vegas Strip, displayed all of the elements of the highway hotel (see Fig. 2.36). The large sign out front beckoned to motorists, as did the giant porte-cochere marking the main entrance. The front parking lot reassured potential guests that here was a place easily accessed by automobile. The low-rise "wings" offered additional persuasion by suggesting traditional motel convenience. There some guests could still park adjacent to or near their rooms. The largest proportion of the new resort hotels, however, was dedicated to the casinos, the nightclubs, and the restaurants that made the Sands a self-contained vacation destination.

The 1980s brought an important highway-hotel innovation: the all-suite motel.[38] Oriented to the business traveler, all-suite motels involved a reduction in front-door services and a scaling-down or even elimination of restaurant and/or meeting-room facilities. Guest rooms, on the other hand, were made larger, often by combining several rooms *en suite.* Equipped with large desks, suites accommodated the evening work routines of traveling business people. Kitchenettes facilitated extended-stay housekeeping. Designed as small efficiency apartments, suites were organized with separate complementary spaces, if not in separate rooms then in a single room organized by room dividers. Eating, working, sleeping, and bathroom spaces were carefully segregated and related. Embassy Suites, the leader in the field, built many of its hotels around large, multi-story atriums.

FINANCING MOTEL CONSTRUCTION

The rise of the motel was rapid, driven by America's enthusiasm for automobile travel. However, investment in the motel industry was amplified by tax-code revision and other federal legislation. The motel boom, and particularly the rise of the highway hotel, by no means resulted merely from a laissez-faire market. Through the 1970s most motels were constructed through local initiative, the profit incentive focused on the construction activity itself and not on long-term motel operation. For ex-

FIGURE 2.35 The Hill Wheat-
ley Downtowner, Hot Springs,
Arkansas, circa 1975. Part of
a national chain, the Downtowner emphasized central-city
locations.

FIGURE 2.36 The Sands Hotel, Las Vegas, circa 1980. The postcard caption
reads: "Now a gleaming new tower symbolizes the Sands reputation as the world's
most exciting luxury resort and convention hotel."

ample, a local builder might construct a motel. Generally, he would build with as small a cash investment as possible, perhaps by pyramiding a series of second, chattel, and other mortgages on top of an initial mortgage. As journalist Seymour Freedgood noted in *Fortune* in 1963, "He then sells his thin equity to an investor syndicate and takes back an operating lease, which, in turn, he sells to a motel operator, thus ending his own involvement entirely. This operation ordinarily leaves the builder with a fair profit, but the new owners and the operator may have a time bomb on their hands. The dynamite lies in the high debt charges that the owners and the operator are obliged to pay on such properties."[39]

Joseph Molinaro, president of the Motel Brokers Association of America, outlined the reasons why investors might buy into a motel. Leverage, the ability to borrow in excess of the cost of funds borrowed, topped his list. Cash flow tended to be greater for motels than for other businesses similar in size, making leverage easier. Leverage enhanced capital appreciation and tax-sheltered income. Thus, a relatively small cash down payment produced a relatively high rate of cash return on the initial investment.[40] However, it was the provisions for accelerated depreciation write-off and the capital-gains advantages permitted by the 1954 tax code that truly led to increased investment in motels. Under the 1954 tax code, 67 percent of the cost of constructing a motel could be written off in five years by the so-called double declining-balance method.[41]

In the 1960s, motel investment, like commercial real estate generally, was seen as a hedge against inflation. A primary vehicle for investment was the real estate investment trust, a kind of mutual fund for real estate loans that provided small investors easy access to potentially lucrative real estate deals.[42] Banks, in turn, extended credit, allowing the investment trusts to leverage themselves with commercial paper. The result was a substantial overbuilding of motels. The building craze continued in the 1970s, with new and even more flexible methods of real estate finance: limited partnership syndications, joint ventures, and land lease with lease-back arrangements, for example. Insurance companies, savings-and-loan associations, and corporate pension funds, as well as banks, joined in the investment binge.

The Economic Recovery Act of 1981 encouraged developers by allowing them to receive tax benefits on accelerated depreciation and interest even sooner. This legislation encouraged formation of real estate syndications designed primarily for professionals in high tax brackets. However, the Tax Reform Act of 1986 substantially decreased the attractiveness of motel investment by eliminating investment tax credit, lengthening the depreciation period from 19 to 31.5 years, restricting deductible passive losses, lowering individual tax rates, and raising taxes on capital gains.[43] Thus, motel construction in the 1990s slowed considerably, and fiscal restructuring in the motel industry was widespread. In 1991, 60 percent of all motels and hotels in the United States lost money.[44] Hotel and motel values were 35 percent lower than their mid-1980s levels, a situation highly reminiscent of the hotel industry in the 1930s.

The development of the American motel has come full circle in approximately fifty years. Initially conceived in contrast to, if not in direct competition with, hotel interests, the motel has become hotel-like. Not only has the motel penetrated the heart of the city but it has expanded its services and now seeks increased profits from enlarged public spaces just as traditional hotels do. In the large highway hotels parking is not necessarily adjacent to or even near most private rooms. In most high-rise motels corridors and elevators lead to a central lobby and a registration desk, so that guests no longer escape public scrutiny. Public space has become formal, with informality surviving primarily at poolside. Hotels have become motel-like, with parking garages, large atriums (simulating the informality of the out-of-doors), and swimming and other recreational facilities. Hotels differ from motels primarily in their larger size and their orientation toward convention and packaged-tour clientele. Thus, they continue to derive a larger proportion of their profits from restaurants, banquet rooms, and other public facilities.

The large corporation did not exert a standardizing influence on motel architecture until the motel chains matured in the late 1950s. Nonetheless, a tyranny of taste and fashion brought a surprising degree of uniformity to motels from one part of the country to another decade by decade. Uniformity manifested itself in the size and furnishing of rooms as well as in the arrangement of rooms in overall motel configurations. The primitive cabin camp gave way to the more substantial cottage court. From the cottage court came the motor court, the motor inn, and finally the luxurious highway hotel. Motel owners watched and copied from one another, a process encouraged by the adoption of operating standards through chains of cooperating motels.

Changing motel morphology was characterized by evolution rather than revolution. The growth of automobile travel and the demand for new automobile-convenient lodging facilities along American highways prompted the trend toward larger and more luxurious facilities in order to capture more and more of the traditional hotel trade. Older, obsolete motels continued to serve less affluent travelers or lent themselves to ready recycling as low-cost weekly or monthly apartment rental, especially for low-income migrants.

The revised 1954 tax code and the Highway Act of 1956 combined to energize the motel industry as it had never been before. Accelerated depreciation as a tax option greatly stimulated new construction, older motels receiving new life with each investment cycle. Compared with other features of the American roadside, such as gasoline stations and quick-service restaurants, motels tended to hold to their original function, although not necessarily their design integrity, longer. Until 1986 the tax code invited cyclical disinvestment, resale, and remodeling, usually at eight- to ten-year intervals. The motel was at once a stabilizing influence, given the fluid use of land along the nation's highways, and a symbol of change, through the superficialities of facelifting and remodeling.

The motel not only remains an important fixture along America's highways but has invaded airport and downtown locations as well because it offers travelers a vital service. The motel is an interface with the private automobile, further cocooning and protecting the traveler away from home. It provides privacy. The motel has tended to lessen formality in favor of providing a homelike atmosphere. The motel has become, and remains, America's home away from home—a significant travel refinement in a society of hyper geographical mobility.

3

Mom-and-Pop Enterprise

IN THIS CHAPTER WE EXPLORE THE MOTEL'S ORIGINS IN SPECIFIC HISTORI-
cal circumstances and trace its development through the advent of the
large chains. Our path begins in the 1930s and extends into the 1960s. The
colloquial term *mom-and-pop* was made legitimate in the professional
literature as small, independent, owner-managed motels dominated the
roadside-lodging industry in these years. An examination of how mom-
and-pop motels were run helps us to appreciate the complexity of the motel trade even at its most elementary level before the era of multimillion-
dollar financing and units of occupancy numbering in the hundreds or the
thousands. *Mom-and-pop*, of course, is broadly interpreted as a comparative term comprehending all manner of smaller relationships, including
closed corporations, multimember partnerships, as well as husbands and
wives, which, in fact, represented the largest group of motel entrepreneurs
from the 1930s to the 1960s. Individual entrepreneurs' tastes, cultural values, and financial calculations coincided to determine the life of a specific
mom-and-pop motel, from its creation through its demise or successive
redefinitions.

THE 1920s AND 1930s

The 1920s and 1930s brought a set of circumstances with special rele-
vance to the evolving roadside-lodging trade.[1] Many Americans became
acutely aware of an essential transformation of values and institutions in
the 1920s. That decade constituted a watershed in the way people experienced life and imputed meaning to ordinary things. Problems that had
been brewing for a long time erupted in this tense time.[2] Although it is
not easily summarized and or named, much less easily explained, recent

scholars have made a convincing case for the advent of a consumer culture. Those who advocated the values and goals of this consumer culture spoke of a "modern" way of life, while those who opposed them came to be called traditionalists. The former found inspiration in the future; the latter looked to the past for guidance. Much of the early twentieth century's anxieties and the efforts to reconcile them can be understood as resulting from a conflict between the moderns' and the traditionalists' world-views. The traditionalists essentially ranked production above consumption, hard work above indulgence, self-control above self-expression, and character above acclaim. For example, future-minded people characteristically envisioned a machine age measuring success in terms of efficiency and material progress.[3] Thus, arbiters of elite architectural taste heralded the functionalism of modern design as superior to the long-popular eclecticism that popular taste coveted all the more for its references to the past.[4]

In the political arena, the 1920s can be interpreted as a decade of growing discontent pitting rural, Protestant Americans against urban dwellers of various faiths, including secularism, with its own set of values and aims. Accordingly, a crescendo was reached in the 1928 presidential election campaign, when the Republican candidate, Herbert Hoover, distinguished himself as a traditionalist in comparison with the Democrat, Al Smith. Whereas Hoover spoke in favor of largely Protestant-inspired Prohibition and identified strongly with his rural Iowa roots, Smith's very speech and linkage to New York City's Tammany Hall pointed up his big-city orientation, and his Catholicism underscored it further. In a time when the most recent census, that of 1920, had shown that the urban population outnumbered the rural for the first time, Smith seemed a harbinger of an uncertain future, while Hoover seemed to embody a reassuring past.[5]

Changing sexual mores characterized the 1920s and the 1930s, and motels were viewed by some as potential sites for immorality. What role motels would play was an important issue in an age given to great moral controversies. The link between sex and the automobile involved many questions of right and wrong. The automobile was treated as a facilitator to courtship, providing couples a means of escaping parental surveillance, and, worse, a place for illicit sexual relations.[6] The evolving roadside not only presented welcome opportunities for consumers and entrepreneurs alike but also was the scene of shifting societal mores. It was not organized crime and vice so much as the "hot pillow," or "couple," trade that caused concern.[7]

This concern can be understood if one thinks of the automobile roadside as a frontier, an unsettled land. The Del Haven Hotel Cabins and its surroundings exemplify the growth of a roadside complex built around a

FIGURE 3.1 Felix Irwin, a store owner from rural North Carolina, attracted by
Washington, D.C.'s economic growth after World War I, bought a farm along
Route 1 in Bel Air, Maryland, where he and his wife opened the Del Haven Cottages in 1923. By the late 1930s the family, including five daughters, was operating
what had grown into a private park, here pictured on a matchbook cover, that included twenty-three cabins, a hotel, a restaurant, an outdoor dollhouse, pony
rides, a miniature golf course, and a zoo. Such complexes soon "civilized" the
roadside.

motel (see Fig. 3.1). Questions about what kind of civilization would grow
from these first roadside businesses on the new land came at a critical time
in American culture. A moral revolution seemed under way as part of the
overall shift in cultural consciousness in the early years of the twentieth
century. Secularization was on the rise. Family authority seemed to have
eroded. Women sought independence. Divorce was more common. Sex
was more openly discussed. In short, a new range of choices was available.
To traditionalists, society appeared to teeter on the brink of chaos because
moral choices too often hinged on individual preference rather than on
established code.[8] The automobile frontier threatened to become a veri-
table Sodom and Gomorrah. Anyone starting a business that was subject
to public vigilance had to consider the prevailing norms. Landscapes
created in the wake of highway travel suggested a vacuum that could be
filled by antisocial behavior. Many motel owners organized themselves in
associations in order to promote a "clean" reputation for their trade; they
knew the impression that less careful competitors, concerned only with
hourly profits, had made on the public. Ceaseless informal discussions
occurred among alarmed motel owners.[9] Owners began to make their
standards known by posting rules and regulations in plain view at their
motels (Fig. 3.2 shows the list posted at the Lighthouse Lodge, in Longview, Texas). But it was hotel competitors who dragged the discussion into
the open for serious scrutiny. The American Hotel Association prepared
to launch a formal advertising campaign based on moral charges against

RULES AND REGULATIONS
of the
LIGHTHOUSE LODGE
Longview, Texas

Member of United Motor Courts • Member International Motor Court Association

THE RATE ON THIS ROOM IS $......................PER DAY IN ADVANCE. SAME PRICE TO EVERY-
ONE. There is no extra charge for the second guest in this room. Every Guest Must Register.

LODGE DAY BEGINS AT 7 A. M. CHECKING OUT TIME IS 5 P. M.

When no baggage is left in room it is notification that the room has been vacated, unless you notify
the office. PLEASE LEAVE KEY ON DRESSER WHEN CHECKING OUT, and lock the door.

Absolutely no one except those originally registering for the room will be allowed to occupy same.

No boisterous or profane language or undue noise will be tolerated, and we reserve the right to demand
possession immediately upon violation of this rule, and no refunds will be made.

Money, jewelry and other valuables should be left at the office where receipt will be given for same, as
we are not responsible for valuables left in rooms or cars.

We take the number of all cars and retain same until the room is checked and found to be in order after
the guest leaves.

Kindly assist us in our effort to provide a clean, comfortable place for you and others to sleep at a
minimum of expense. Kindly report any complaints and suggestions to the office as they will be
cheerfully received.

COURTESY, CONVENIENCE, CLEANLINESS AND COMFORT for every guest is our goal. This is
the original TRAVELING MEN'S HEADQUARTERS in Longview.

Please Turn Off Fan and Lights On Leaving Room

* Cottages patented; patent No. 1985789; see framed patent in office . . . Ground layout copyrighted
"Lighthouse" trademark registered.

FIGURE 3.2 In addition to the bare essentials of rate and check-out time, the owner of the Lighthouse Lodge, in Longview, Texas, made it known by this sign displayed in each room that the lodger was not to permit others in the room, be boisterous or profane, or fail to secure valuables at the desk. The intent was to provide "COURTESY, CONVENIENCE, CLEANLINESS AND COMFORT for every guest."

the motels but apparently backed off when a consultant's report warned of the danger of casting the first stone. Nonetheless, some hotel owners could not resist the temptation to circulate J. Edgar Hoover's "Camps of Crime." [10]

The concern about lodger morality was consistent with the moral tone of the times. And insofar as some motels facilitated the "couple" trade, they reinforced changing attitudes toward sexual relations. Motels as a new landscape form became both cause and consequence in a new cultural consciousness. [11]

A belief that a portentous cultural shift was in progress and the consequent call to cling to certain values influenced the young motel trade. Belonging, community, and dedication became cherished traits in the predominantly conservative American culture. [12] Overnight lodging on the roadside frontier had to be carefully named, and this theoretically offered an opportunity for new nomenclature. The names given were suggestive of a security-seeking age. [13] Chapter 2 explains names in terms of place. Here we offer a reinforcing historical explanation.

Nowhere in the trade literature were the basic names used on the roadside—*cabins, camp, cottages, village*—clearly defined. And yet these names, with their innumerable modifiers, were ubiquitous; names such as Kirk's Cabins, The Y Tourist Camp, Gould's Cottages, and Nite's Rest Village abounded. Did they reflect cultural constants and, perhaps, time-bound associations? We can only speculate because contemporaries did not fully explore alternative meanings and thereby offer tidy explanations.[14] The words *cabin, cottage, camp,* and *village* all connote security amidst flux, dependability despite adventure, a home on the road. *Cabin* and *cottage* likely derive from woodsy sanctuaries to which people repaired for psychic renewal in the time before the automobile. A sense of isolation resonates. The sportsman's getaway comes to mind. *Cabin* may even hearken back to earlier homesteading. *Camp* and *village* also impart a sense of the pre-automobile past, but a past rooted in community, not one of individuals separated. For automobile travelers who were whirling down the highway and amazed at how effortlessly they could do so, might it not have been reassuring to chance upon a place defined for people of their own kind? A place where they might find a small group of people living in a kind of mutual dependence, more or less in harmony, for a time more intimately related to one another than to the world beyond? Although the word *camp* implies impermanency, a short-lived or seasonal residence for a people on the move, and *village* connotes a more permanent arrangement, neither was a chance aggregation. Here instead was promised a functioning social entity for the traveler loosed from his domestic moorings. Might this not have been especially cherished in the 1920s and 1930s, when basic social assumptions seemed to be so fundamentally challenged?

The names that were fashioned reflected a business strategy. As the years passed, *cabins* and *camp* were used less often, and *cottages* and *village*, more. Perhaps the latter were considered more sophisticated than the former. Col. Arthur T. Nelson's entrepreneurship in Lebanon, Missouri, is illustrative (see Figs. 3.3, 3.4, and 3.5). Inexorable progress toward better living standards was an American cultural imperative. *Court* and *inn* would later prevail for the same reasons. *Motel* would carry a higher charge of modernism in its direct reference to the motor car as machine.

The culturally conservative origins of the motel trade in the 1930s are nowhere more strongly reflected than in its financial structure. Discovery of the new industry along the roadside during the Great Depression drew amazement from the newspaper and magazine reporters who were the motels' first students. They concluded that the capitalistic system was fundamentally sound after all, at least in its capacity to provide investment opportunities for the small entrepreneur. An entirely new industry had

FIGURE 3.3 Accommodations at the Top O' the Ozarks Camp were tents *(right)* the Nelson family rented beside Route 66 in Lebanon, Missouri. Patriarch of an elite regional family, Colonel Arthur T. Nelson began his family's roadside business with a gasoline station *(left)* after persuading authorities to build Route 66 through Lebanon.

FIGURE 3.4 Nelson's campground was renamed the Top O' the Ozarks Inn when frame cabins *(center)* and a hamburger stand *(left)* were added in the late 1920s.

FIGURE 3.5 Dream Village, twelve stone cottages built around a landscaped courtyard, replaced the frame cabins in 1934. A line of garages behind the courtyard *(top)* completed the site's progression from temporary shelters to residential community.

risen, and it had risen not from capitalism's ashes but because of capitalism's inspiration.[15] "Two years ago I was busted. Next season I plan to build twenty cottages more," one small owner was quoted as saying before government ended its urgently improvised remedies in the Hundred Days.[16]

Mom and Pop approached business expenses in the same way that they did their personal budget: they bought only what they could afford with cash on hand. No wonder big suppliers looked covetously on the untapped yet solvent motel market as a place to sell their products—furniture, mattresses, linens, soaps, foods, and drinks.[17] Ironically, these mom-and-pop exemplars of resurgent small capitalism were invaded by the troubled big corporations, whose trademarked products began place-product-packaging in the motel industry literally from within. Owners of the burgeoning tourist camps, meanwhile, were portrayed as refreshingly direct, and their almost taciturn transactions with lodgers were said to reflect a healthy pragmatism.[18] The Spartan lodgings—a bed, chairs, mirror, sink, and toilet all housed in a single small room—seemed of a piece with the owners' manner.

Popular Mechanics advised do-it-yourselfers: "If you live near a well-traveled highway, or can lease space near one, a few low-cost tourists' cabins . . . will afford you a substantial income during the summer months." Regarding amenities, the article advised: "If the cabins are erected in a well-kept grove where there is an adequate supply of pure, fresh water, so much the better."[19] H. O. "Doc" Woodward, a stock raiser, demonstrated how to take advantage of a crossroads amidst a maple grove that offered refreshing shade from the parched plains and hot pavement when he built and named Shady Bend Motel, at the eastern edge of Grand Island, Nebraska, in 1930 (see Fig. 3.6). The prescient James Agee best characterized the sturdy and stolid mom-and-pop entrepreneurs in his 1934 article for *Fortune*, a popular periodical dedicated to capitalism, where he described a lodger's approach to a motel:

> If you are a novice the routine is so simple as to take your breath away. The farmer or the filling-station proprietor or either's daughter appears, puts a casual foot upon the running board, and opens the negotiation with a silent nod. "How much are your cabins?" He or she says "Dollar a head. Drive in by No. 7." He or she accompanies you, riding with the ease of habit on the side of your car. You make your inspection. . . . you nod "O.K." and give the proprietor two dollars. He may, but probably won't, give you a card or a register in which to sign a name. He doesn't care what name you write because in case you seriously misbehave he has your car license number, noted as part of his professional routine. So he pockets the two dollars and walks away. That's all.[20]

The general feeling was that the old values of ingenuity, hard work, and a good product would be rewarded with profit. One could start small, build by increments, innovate to satisfy consumer requests, and succeed. Here was a great palliative for a nation in the profoundest economic turmoil since its inception, a nation in which many people had not only suffered bankruptcy but also lost self-esteem. People were advised to be their own boss, get rich, and depend on their own resources; the petit-bourgeois ideology of the Jeffersonian vision for America seemed to be confirmed. And, it seemed to be further confirmed by the rural and small-town places in which the mom-and-pop tourist cabins sprang up. The mythic yeoman farmer and the small shopkeeper once again proved America's strength. By the end of the thirties the search for an "American way of life" had become a crusade; the mom-and-pop entrepreneurs by the roadside showed that it was alive and well in the hinterlands.[21] (Stationery used at the George-Anna Cottages in Jackson, Tennessee, illustrates Mom and Pop's traditional moorings [see Fig. 3.7].) The mom-and-pop entrepreneurs were capitalism's cultural heroes. Most of these popularly depicted founders of the new industry were not upwardly mobile or newly wealthy; they were property owners who were converting or diversifying their investments in response to temporary market constraints.

FIGURE 3.6 Located on a curve in Route 6, Woodward's Shady Bend seems poised to scoop travelers into its lush confines.

FIGURE 3.7 Inner leaf of folded stationery for the George-Anna Cottages, Jackson, Tennessee, early 1930s. Roadside domesticity is advertised here in round-the-clock service for every traveler's needs. The family-centered focus of many early motel entrepreneurs is manifest in the portraits of the children for whom George P. Gardner named his business.

In many ways they embodied the rugged individualism so loved of small business people. Self-made men freewheeling through successive deals to open their business in a booming market, the new motel owners contentedly worked alone until the fear of profit lost or a scheme for profit increase stimulated them to combine their efforts. When the hotel owners threatened to formulate a National Recovery Administration (NRA) lodging code that motel owners considered disadvantageous to their business, some of them hurriedly coalesced to represent their interests because the NRA would not recognize a trade unless it had an organization. Cooperation with government was expedient. Hence, the National Tourist Lodge–Motor Court Trade Association (NTL-MCTA) was formed in 1933. After the NRA rejected the code finally recommended by the NTL-MCTA because it seemed unrepresentative of the whole industry, the NTL-MCTA virtually disappeared in 1934. A decade would pass before motel owners again welcomed governmental help. Meanwhile, a group of southeastern owners banned together to form the Tourist Court Owners Association (TCOA) in 1932, and a group of California owners followed by forming United Motor Courts (UMC) in 1933, to exert pressure for improved architectural standards and against the "hot pillow" trade throughout the industry. They made progress toward their goals as they increased membership throughout the decade before World War II. The motel owner who had headed the NTL-MCTA in 1933–34 also headed the TCOA.[22] The TCOA merged with the UMC in 1937 and became the UMC, Eastern Division.[23] Organization and standardization thus went hand in hand.[24] Yet, individual owners staunchly maintained independent ownership.

In 1937 the reinvigorated NTL-MCTA was renamed the International Motor Court Association (IMCA) and contracted with the Gresham family of Temple, Texas, to publish the first important motel trade magazine, the *Tourist Court Journal*.[25] None of the Greshams owned a motel; they were printers and stationers. But "Bob" Gresham, as he was commonly known, became committed to counseling the motel trade. The first issue of his new journal appeared in October 1937. Filled with brief articles on various managerial questions in hopes of making the mom-and-pop owners even more successful, the *Tourist Court Journal* rapidly became the trade's standard reference. Growing numbers of subscribers read it for advice as well as advertisements, and the popular press regularly cited the periodical in its own reports about the motel trade. Professionalization was afoot in the rising young industry.[26]

Too much can be attributed to the small entrepreneur's pluck, common sense, and accruing professionalism in explaining the motel's origins during the Great Depression. Certainly the small entrepreneurs' risk taking and native intelligence were factors. But the economic constellation of the times rendered considerable advantages to these "first movers" of the fledgling motel industry. Most of all, there was a considerable popular demand; and although it was greatest in the West, the market was truly national. Enough has been written about Americans' passion for mobility and their incredible comparative wealth—they have been described as the only people who went to the Depression in a Ford.[27] Several other factors should also be emphasized in order to render a balanced historical account.

The relationship between supply and demand was more complicated than a willingness to answer a nationally felt need. The vacationing nuclear family has usually been identified as the new industry's main consumer. In fact, the traveling businessman, termed the "commercial traveler" in the trade literature, accounted for a substantial percentage of the motel trade from its inception. Motels were significantly cheaper than hotels, where the commercial traveler had stayed through the 1920s. Budget-conscious businesses decreased their travel allowances during the Depression, thereby providing a strong incentive for patronizing the new motel market. Partly as a result, hotels suffered greatly because of the Depression. By one account, while 75 percent of all travelers lodged in hotels in 1929, the height of the hotel trade, by 1939 hotels had lost most of their business to motels and accommodated only 32 percent of the lodgers. Hotel owners reacted variously to the new competition. Some emphasized the negative aspects of motels in advertising and other promotions. Others lowered their rates, for example, allowing the wives of regular lodgers to stay free of charge. New York's hotels lowered their rates by 20 percent in the summer of 1940 in hopes of competing successfully with the motels. Many commercial travelers took advantage of lower motel rates, submitting higher hotel bills while staying at motels and pocketing the difference. This practice became so common that the American Hotel Association, together with victimized corporations, took action against such bogus claims.[28]

Motels offered an economic opportunity in the classic sense of frontier property manipulated for financial gain. It was comparatively easy to start a motel. Knowledge was not yet specialized enough to deter the merely willing. Little capital was required. In many cases the land was farm acreage no longer profitable because of depressed agricultural prices or rendered otherwise useless along a recently laid highway. Conversion, not purchase, was required. Construction seemed easy. Builders' magazines beckoned with unsubstantiated claims of low costs while facilitating cabin construction with plans giving specific dimensions and materials.[29] The

American Builder magazine, for example, typically encouraged investment through plans presented for easy construction (see Fig. 3.8). Many utilized such plans, created their own, used prefabricated kits, or adapted existing structures. Construction actually was cheap. One frugal owner built his own cabins for $300 apiece. *Hotel Management* claimed that a comfortable unit with bath could be built and furnished for $750 and that the range was between $50 and $5,000.[30] With regular occupancy, a few cabins could be paid off in a short time and the owner could consider building more. The hidden advantage was sweat equity, for Mom and Pop, sometimes with the help of their family, not only built but also maintained their business. Few calculated their own labor in figuring profit and loss. Profit was good. After paying wages to a hired man and a maid, a tourist camp with eleven cabins might have an income as high as $2,870.25 in 1931. The New Deal's Federal Housing Administration further spurred investment by categorizing small structures built for less than $2,000, including motel cabins, as remodeling, which required no down payment to receive a loan if real property was debt-free.[31] "One of the few oases of the Depression, this business has thrived on hard times and limited purchasing power," one writer observed.[32] Motels indeed were born and flourished because of the Depression, not despite it.

Traditional divisions of labor carried over into this economic frontier. Men managed the overall operation, did the necessary construction and repairs, and, at motels where a gas station had been added to attract the traveler seeking convenience in a single stop meeting all of his or her needs, also serviced automobiles. Women also contributed substantially to motel ownership and management. Female hired help and wives certainly

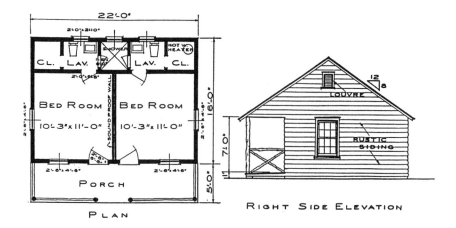

FIGURE 3.8 Floor plan and elevation of cabins built in Bethel, Connecticut, circa 1940. (*Source: American Builder* 62 [July 1940]: 69.)

FIGURE 3.9 Frank Redford *(second from right)* and his wife, Vetra *(to Frank's right),* managed the staff of their Wigwam Village at Cave City, Kentucky. They are accompanied in this photograph by waitresses at the motel's restaurant and attendants at the motel's gas station.

supplied at least an equal share of the physical labor required to run a competitive motel (see Fig. 3.9). Some helped build and repair cabins and changed oil and pumped gasoline at the motel's adjacent station. They commonly washed the mountainous piles of bedding and toweling for the lodgers, made their beds, and cleaned their rooms. Daughters might also work, as did one required by her father in the temporary capacity of housekeeper, but only after she had graduated from high school.

Women also doubled as cooks in the short-order grills appended to some family-run motels. Wives frequently accepted these added tasks as part of an existing marriage. Some cases suggest that male entrepreneurs may have sought wives partly on the basis of the contributions they might make to a family-run enterprise. In several cases, recent brides were active in formulating plans for what remained nevertheless their husband's business. In another case, a recent bride devolved into an additional, albeit specialized, member of the work force tied to a daily routine at the motel, becoming what the trade literature named a "work hermit." Her husband, meanwhile, worked away from the site on promotional campaigns and/or spent leisure time. Regardless of their extensive labor at the motel, it was the young wives become mothers who were expected to feed and raise the family when they returned home from their official chores. Thus, women clearly provided the preponderant amount of labor for these family businesses.[33]

Different women responded differently to these arrangements. Several looked back affectionately on those years, seeing themselves as valued partners in developing a business with their hard-working husbands. One disgruntled woman, however, simply declined politely to talk about the experience now that it was past and her children enjoyed fulfilling lives. Motel ownership was a means to an end for women in such families. This family orientation could short-circuit development of some mom-and-pop motels. Many motels closed or were sold after grown children had left for less laborious careers. On the other hand, in cases where families plowed profits back into their businesses and aggressively expanded, parents and children might be celebrated as pioneers in a dynasty of motel entrepreneurs.[34]

Who were the early motel pioneers? Leona Combs Flanagan, of Macon, Georgia, is a well-documented motel entrepreneur.[35] Flanagan was in her forties when poor health forced her husband to retire from work and she assumed the role of family breadwinner: "I opened a filling station near our home and operated it myself, with only two helpers. That was in 1922. Those were the days of the 'tin can tourists' and I began to let them camp on our property in their tents which they carried along with them." Later in 1922, Flanagan erected two cottages, each having two rooms. By 1936 Flanagan's Camp comprised about thirty-five rooms in twenty-seven cottages. A traditional homemaker's touch contributed to the quality of the rooms. Each room had fans against hot weather, heaters against cold weather, "beautiful furniture, nice rugs, and every floor covered with easy-to-clean, sanitary, linoleum," a journalist visiting Flanagan in 1936 reported. "And such pretty curtains at the window! 'I make them myself,' Mrs. Flanagan admitted when questioned. 'I have an electric sewing machine and it's fun making them.'"[36]

High maintenance standards and a rigorously enforced code of ethics created an aura of wholesomeness that greatly benefited Flanagan's Camp. Ministers, who often led crusades against immorality as they saw it in roadhouses and motels, directed inquiring travelers to Flanagan's as the only appropriate tourist camp in the vicinity. No questionable couples nor radios or liquor were permitted. An ambiance of home pervaded. "It is a pretty spot out there with soft green grass down the center of the court and little green and white cottages reposing on each side. Note that the trailer has displaced the old-fashioned tent-er and is almost displacing the rooming tourist, accommodations have to be made for the family trailer too, and there are plug-ins and parking spots to take care of its needs too" (see Fig. 3.10).[37]

Flanagan's indomitable spirit and commitment to traditional values enabled her to achieve a rather celebrated life. Still caring for her husband

FIGURE 3.10 Flanagan's Camp, circa 1940, with its cottages, is further domesticated by a central line of trees and flowers, which adds relief to the otherwise bare driveway and parking lot.

and having raised a daughter, Leona Combs Flanagan found time to be second vice president of the TCOA beginning in May 1936. Her strict standards at Flanagan's Camp had long made her a welcome member of the association, which was attempting to improve motels' image. Flanagan warned against the common illusion that running a motel was easy work: "Many folks mention that they would like to go into this sort of business, but they do not realize how very much attention and care it requires. I have to have my bookkeeper figure the profits of every room down to a penny. We have to watch every cent. That is the only way one can see a profit in a business and that is not so easy." [38]

Her family did prosper. She felt comfortable withdrawing to a less active role as general overseer at least by 1936 while her daughter Polly ran the motel and her son-in-law Holst ran the service station. They purchased a store across the road and converted it into a hotel in 1939–40. Whereas motels languished in World War II, deprived of their tourist trade, Flanagan's was located closed to Robins Air Base. Built as overnight tourist housing, the cabins became "efficiency apartments," provisioned with iceboxes and two-burner gas grills. The complex survived until the competitive onslaught of chains along a new interstate highway built nearby in the 1950s. [39]

Wigwam Village illustrates the fortunes of a mom-and-pop motel moving toward a larger-scale operation beginning in the 1930s. Opened in

FIGURE 3.11 Redford's highly memorable "teepee" architecture appears in this earliest surviving view of Wigwam Village Number 1. Rickrack on the waitresses' uniforms (see Fig. 3.9) extended the "Indian" motif to a small detail.

1933 by Frank Redford in Horse Cave, Kentucky, Wigwam Village eventually comprised seven motels operating throughout the South and the Southwest by 1950.[40] Redford created a unique place-product-packaging design utilizing an "Indian" motif and principally "teepee" architecture (see Fig. 3.11), and he drew other owners into the referral chain without profiting from any regular participation fee or suing infringers on his patented design. Perhaps no other single image in early motels fired the imagination as did Redford's "teepees," which captured the eye of photographers, cartoonists, and journalists.[41] The basis of a chain was laid. Redford, however, profited modestly by working with friends and equally independent owners to operate his small chain; failing to establish a corporate structure, Wigwam Village faded as a competitor by the 1960s. Three of his motels survive on trade drawn to them as curiosities, a testimony to the strength of their place-making architecture.

Opportunities were not open to all, however. Although too little is known to attempt a definitive treatment of opportunities for racial minorities in early motels, it is highly probable that they were victims of discrimination and a small, segregated market. Among blacks, the best-known minority, few motel entrepreneurs have been identified. Where did the comparatively few blacks who could afford the luxury of owning a car and traveling long distances in it spend the night?[42] It is not imaginable that they were welcomed at most mom-and-pop motels, whose owners not only shared traditional mores but also were hyperattentive to those mores in hopes of winning local approval. The *Green-Book,* an annual directory for blacks first published in 1936, listed not only lodgings but restaurants, gasoline stations, taverns, liquor stores, and barber and beauty shops where they were welcome, and the *Directory of Negro Hotels and*

Guest Houses in the United States, published in 1939 by the U.S. Travel Bureau, a branch of the Department of the Interior, probably did not provide a comprehensive list.[43] The *Green-Book,* the longer of the two, included a disclaimer to that effect.[44] Only a tiny fraction of the entries in both directions were for "motels," the several period names for motels appearing rarely. Hotels, private homes (named "tourist homes"), and Young Men's and Young Women's Christian Associations constitute virtually all the entries. Might older, declining hotels and tourist homes that once had refused blacks lodging now have grasped for their business? Were new motels capable of restricting themselves to the affluent who expected racial segregation and shutting out black lodgers until the time when they welcomed blacks as they tried to make the most of their aging investment?

Given the unstudied market for blacks traveling by automobile, it is appropriate to speculate about alternatives to the directories mentioned above. Informal networks of communication through churches perhaps helped blacks to locate friendly families with rooms for rent and rooming houses. Might blacks and other minorities have had recourse to sleeping in their cars in the absence of lodging for minorities? As in other regards, lodging on the roadside frontier was often both prey and prospect to the values and practices of the culture from which it sprang.[45]

THE 1940s–1960s

Four lengthy guides for those already in or entering the motel trade were published between the end of World War II and the early 1960s: Harry Barclay Love's *Establishing and Operating a Year-Round Motor Court* (1945); the *Tourist Court Journal* staff's *Tourist Court Plan Book* (1950); C. Vernon Kane's *Motor Courts: From Planning to Profits* (1954), and Harold Whittington's *Starting and Managing a Small . . . Motel* (1963).[46] Also available were instructional films, short articles in popular and trade magazines, and college publications, especially from Michigan State University and Cornell. But the four abovementioned guides are representative of the dawn of formal motel-management training. Not only do they reveal several of the persons and organizations that drove the industry's rapid maturation but they allow rare access to the decision-making process from a general perspective of a business heretofore introduced to Americans through case descriptions. Published at nearly even intervals, their comparison demonstrates the increasingly problematic nature of postwar entrepreneurship. It was the boom time of the mom-and-pop motels, a time when more motels were opened than ever before or since. In advising better business practices, these guides reflected as well as spurred the period's fierce competition.

Although the yearnings for professionalism stirred in the late 1930s, these four postwar publications reflect the culture of professionalism that was rapidly and fully coming to describe motel entrepreneurship. Relatively few of the many motel owners could claim expertise in systematized knowledge. Those who authored guides earned their income from full-time advising. They represent the professional's attempt to gain control through "scientific" management procedures. Although they intended to raise everyone's standards, in fact an eventual consequence of their advising would be to eliminate the untutored mom-and-pop operations from industry dominance. Aggressive entrepreneurs adopted ever more expensive and elaborate management procedures in moving to ever larger scales of operation. The corporation in its various forms became increasingly dominant. Intended to help the small operators, the new advice hastened their demise, the seeds of change coming from within the trade.[47]

Who wrote and who published these guides is thus instructive about the era. Not surprisingly, the federal agency charged with assisting small businesses published the first and the last, and the fact that they conveniently bracket the period perhaps suggests something of their publisher's seldom stated but persistent rationale: Cold War military preparedness. Throughout the boom in motel building, coincident with the onset of the Cold War, the federal government was critically aware, because of the experience of World War II, that a considerable amount of dependable housing was necessary especially for defense workers but also for non-war-related workers in a highly mobile nation. Motels were the answer, and small owners dominated the industry, so Mom and Pop were offered federal help. Thus, the motel came of age as a government-acknowledged fact of life. Like the Department of Agriculture, which championed the family farm while promoting corporate agribusiness, the Small Business Administration (SBA) championed the mom-and-pop motel while advocating management procedures that effectively pointed away from small operators. After World War II the agency targeted returning veterans, and the Veterans Administration funded its 1945 publication.[48]

As the foremost trade publication for the small motel owner, the *Tourist Court Journal* eventually came to chronicle the small entrepreneur's declining competitiveness amidst increasing investments and specializing professionals. Bob Gresham's editorial staff at the time of the 1963 guide comprised a former staff member of the American Automobile Association and two former newspaper men, the *Temple (Tex.) Daily Telegram*'s ex-managing editor and an ex-photographer and journalist. Himself exemplifying the small entrepreneur's generalist tendencies, Gresham contentedly ran the *Journal* from the upstairs offices of his stationer's and job printery. His business was reputed locally as a printing shop, and not as the source of a nationally known trade publication. He held on to the passé descriptor *tourist court* in the title of his journal not only because it had name recognition but also because he was slow to change.[49] He adopted the more current title *Motel/Motor Inn Journal* in 1970, only four years before he died.

William L. Edmundson Jr., a rapidly rising figure in the maturing post-war motel industry, was acknowledged for his contributions to the 1945 self-help guide. Edmundson, president of United Motor Courts at the time and owner of Oleander Court, in Houston, Texas, won wider recognition as the most outspoken advocate for the motel industry in its opposition to the Office of Price Administration's anti-inflation policies, which restrained motel profits during the 1940s boom. The aggressive Edmundson also had led UMC insurgents dissatisfied with owners of older facilities who were unwilling to modernize in leaving the UMC and had helped found the more prominent motel trade association, the American Motor Hotel Association (AMHA). Under Edmundson's leadership in the late 1940s the association aimed at organizing the entire industry, which then numbered approximately 18,000 motels. Fast professional friends, Edmundson and Gresham together helped further professionalize the trade by invoking college training through many short courses in hotel and motel management at the University of Houston.[50]

C. Vernon Kane represented a new phase in motel professionalization when he authored the third self-help publication. Although he had never owned or operated a motel, Kane had had six years of indirect experience in Florida, where he was a certified public accountant specializing in motels and had been a partner since 1949 in Horwath and Horwath, a well-known hotel-auditing firm. Also a professor at the University of Miami, Kane espoused the Jeffersonian credo about the wellsprings of American genius in no uncertain terms: "The backbone of America's economic structure has always been 'small business.' Motor courts belong in this category and are probably one of the best examples. Next to the farmer, the motor court owner is one of the most self-sufficient individuals. . . . In this country, whoever wants to be his own employer can find ample opportunity."[51] Like the other authors, Kane espoused the notion that success lay in carefully assessing past experience. All four guides disclaimed a guarantee of success, although each was progressively more certain about the advice given.

Each of the guides agreed that location was by far the most important factor. The very first guide, despite its comparatively elementary approach on other aspects, attempted to impress the reader with the multifaceted nature of site selection. Climate was imperative to any year-round operation, the emphasis having shifted from the seasonal auto camps common as adjunct incomes before World War II. Highway access was also important. A host of other factors were added: the attractiveness of the immediate natural surroundings, sufficient space for parking, landscaping and expansion, building codes, the nature and quality of the immediate neighborhood, the traffic count of adjacent highways, land costs, the availability of public utilities, competition, proximity to towns, proximity to tourist destinations, the origin and destination of adjacent highways, and highway regulations. Clearly, the prospective entrepreneur had to consider a potentially baffling array of overlapping real-estate, governmental, social, and natural authorities.[52]

Even the buoyantly folksy *Tourist Court Plan Book* warned against the impulsive site selection all too common among the earlier mom-and-pop entrepreneurs. It advised motel owners to be "hard-boiled and businesslike."[53] Volatility of location potentially undermined every site selected, however cautiously, for the expanding investment opportunities were predicated primarily on the rapidly expanding postwar highway system. What some roads provided, newer ones could take away. The 1945 guide admonished owners to keep up with their state highway department's plans and legislation regarding all roadside business. The 1963 recommendations were even more ambiguous: "Keep Your Plans Flexible." The 1963 guide warned that the architecture of a mere decade earlier likely discouraged trade with travelers who demanded the newest. The first guide thus seemed comparatively naive in holding that a new motel would be good for at least twenty years.[54] The postwar motel was a microcosm for a culture chasing ever evolving novelty reciprocally pushed by consumer and producer alike.

Architecture, by which people judged the desirability and status even of temporary housing, was a critical, if secondary, concern in all four guides. The SBA's initial publication declared about layout: "When individual rooms are spaced about an open landscaped court, they present a 'show window' of overnight accommodations to the passing motorist."[55] A domestic illusion was contrived: "The open court should be landscaped and made into an outdoor living room."[56] The Colonial Motor Court, in Cincinnati, Ohio, for example, made its domestic setting central to its postcard advertising (see Fig. 3.12). Comfort and cleanliness also had instantly to be signaled, the architect Tom E. Lightfoot wrote in the 1950 guide.[57]

The entrepreneur sought to achieve the greatest consumer attraction at the lowest possible construction cost. Saying that the proper ambiance could be conveyed by either a modern or a revival style, Lightfoot preferred the modern because it was cheaper. Kane dismissed the loss of the "picturesque" in center-core construction (in which there were rooms on

FIGURE 3.12 Frame houses with window boxes opening onto a communal lawn exude a feeling of community at the Colonial Motor Court in the late 1940s.

both sides of a common plumbing line), saying that it was outweighed by its cheaper cost. Mom and Pop could decide between economy and ambience, but their choice was not easy. Whatever their decision, an illusion was to be maintained for the consumer. The fourth guide stated most urgently the need for a motel's "image" or "personality" to bring the lodger and the owner-operator together. Behind the scenes, endless labor readied the motel for guests' reception (see Fig. 3.13); however, one's stay should fulfill every expectation for blithe living, from the homey or resort look of the place to the breezy and chatty manner of its personnel. Contrived "atmosphere" is another aspect of modern culture that sets it apart from traditional merchandising, which de-emphasized display.[58]

Mom and Pop's contribution to the important modernizing effects of "atmosphere" deserves emphasis. Although the mom-and-pop business arrangement was an elementary one, it was the entrepreneurial means of many and thereby fostered the radical implications of mass marketing. As mom-and-pop motel owners consciously contrived "atmosphere" for consumer delight, they helped break down the unquestioned belief in a single system, which numerous scholars have found to be at the root of modernity.[59] Making a rational choice between alternative ways of doing things became the norm. Threatened was the security of derived and immutable knowledge. Axes of power, not right and wrong, determined what prevailed. Hardly philosophers, Mom and Pop nonetheless brokered consumers' choices regarding their roadside lodging. Thus, given the pro-

MOTEL/MOTOR INN JOURNAL

"Come, Miss Becker . . . what went wrong on the job today? Plumbing?
Rude guests? Too many units? Overwork?"

FIGURE 3.13 The crush of meeting the public could find humorous release, as in
this cartoon. (*Source: Motel/Motor Inn Journal* 34 [September 1971]: 28.)

found influence of landscape in the structuring of culture, mom-and-pop
motels, with their creature comforts, were harbingers of bigger agents with
more sweeping schemes dividing consciousness between reality and pretense, fact and façade.[60]

Other business aspects—financing, services, bookkeeping, housekeeping, allied services (restaurants and service stations), and planning—received their due in the postwar guides. Financial advice varied greatly from
guide to guide. Whereas possible sources of funds went unmentioned in
the first guide, they gained but slight mention in the second. Assurance
was given that money could easily be borrowed as long as the lender was
satisfied that the applicant had rigorously analyzed a prospective site. The
next guide sketched a very complex picture of lending, which it described
as dependent on the availability of mortgage money at any particular time,
the intended motel's geographic region, and the lender type. More initial
money was needed in 1954 than in the previous postwar years; on average
initial investments had tripled as the motel industry had matured. Nine
years later soaring competition and construction costs would make it necessary for the would-be owner to form a partnership or corporation or to
participate in an investor syndicate.

Services too proliferated in the time between publication of the first and fourth guides. Telephones in each room were optional in 1945 but essential for motels catering to commercial travelers in 1963. The motel picture postcard (ironically one of the most ephemeral items when printed but often surviving as the only vestige of a long vanished motel) was required, along with a host of other advertising items, in 1945. In 1963, however, the postcard was not mentioned, but more expensive promotional strategies were outlined. High housekeeping standards were a preoccupation of all the guides. Chapters in both the first and the fourth guide of the series illustrate the drive toward standardization. A uniform classification of business transactions advocated by the AMHA was outlined, and a widely accepted bookkeeping system devised by one of the new experts, Kemper W. Merriam, of the University of Arizona, was promoted. Owner-operated service stations and restaurants adjacent to and part of motels received less treatment with each guide and were barely mentioned in the last guide.[61] Service stations and restaurants only multiplied the complexity of the motel owner's challenge in an age of increasing specialization.

Prospective owners had been warned from the first that running a motel was hard work entailing long hours seven days a week. But by 1963 the industry had become so overbuilt that the tone of that year's guide was discouraging to those who had little more than sweat equity to invest. Mom and Pop of the sixties were well advised to hire an attorney, an architect, and an accountant, just as in the forties; but unlike their predecessors, they were advised further to consider employing a motel consultant, interior decorator (with contract furnisher), building contractor, and specialized staff.[62] Entrepreneurial leadership was no longer feasible for a jack-of-all-trades (see Fig. 3.14).

Mom and Pop were engulfed in the rising tide of big investors by the 1960s. They were not driven from the roadside. Many mom-and-pop motels, such as the El Rancho Rankin, in Cincinnati, Ohio, tried to compete in size and amenities (see Fig. 3.15). By 1972 mom-and-pop motels still made up 59 percent of motels, whereas they had represented 98.2 percent in 1948. But they came to provide the least number of units as well as the least desired form of lodging after 1945.[63] Mom and Pop found themselves victims of the very consumer culture in which their hopes and industry had taken root.

Perhaps no other society experienced more profound changes than the U.S. society did in the fifteen years after 1945. Demands pent up during the Depression and World War II broke loose in every facet of life during an unprecedented era of peace and prosperity. By the mid-1950s Americans, who constituted but 6 percent of the world's population, consumed more than one-third of the earth's goods and services. In 1956 the average

A. H. Patterson

FIGURE 3.14 Small entrepreneurship meant direct involvement with every aspect of the motel. The owner, building, and highway sign of the Fleetwood Motel, in Burlington, North Carolina, are three parts of a single image on this advertising postcard.

American income was 50 percent higher than in 1929, the year of the previous high. The decade after the war was that of the legendary "baby boom," when the number of newborns grew by 50 percent each year. Suburbs mushroomed as refuges of the newly affluent.[64]

The federal government energized the economy in many ways. Housing laws in 1949 and 1954 aimed at providing desirable housing for every American family and granted funds to raze and rebuild inner-city neighborhoods. Veterans had their own boon: whereas prewar mortgages had demanded 50 percent down payments and repayment in ten years, full mortgages repayable over thirty years enabled 3.75 million veterans to buy homes. Banks also liberalized their terms to borrowers who were not federally insured, with the result that by 1960, one-quarter of all American housing was new, built in the previous decade. The accelerated-depreciation provision of the 1954 tax code and the construction commenced by the 1956 interstate highway act had their own effects on roadside investment, as noted in chapter 2. These were the agents for a profoundly reshaped American landscape.[65]

Leisure became an industry. Whereas in the 1920s the average industrial worker had labored fifty-two weeks a year without vacation, by the 1960s the average industrial worker labored fewer than forty hours per week and earned eight paid vacation days. By 1950 Americans were spending twice as much on entertainment as they did on rent.[66] Many of the mom-and-

FIGURE 3.15 El Rancho Rankin, Cincinnati, Ohio, one of the last members of the small owner-oriented United Motor Courts, showed its huge investment and size as well as illustrated its amenities on this postcard in the late 1950s.

pop purveyors of roadside lodging were themselves looking for an easy way to earn a small living after retirement, made possible by their own and others' affluence.

The culture responded to and encouraged consumption. Sociologist Daniel Bell's *End of Ideology* (1960) held that America was on the verge of solving all of its fundamental problems and that it could do so if government called on experts to implement their ideas. Although Bell himself denied conservative moorings, others could invoke Bell to absolve the prosperous from guilt regarding the large minority who did not yet share the bounty. A consumer culture was believed to have shaped the entire twentieth century, an idea seemingly validated by the unprecedented postwar prosperity. Another sociologist, David Riesman, argued in the *The Lonely Crowd* (1950) that personality was "other-directed" in an age of abundance, focused to please others rather than regimented according to traditional codes. The student of landscape J. B. Jackson deduced that motels were part of the age's "other-directed" roadside architecture, aimed at pleasing the pleasure seekers.[67]

Concurrently the tide against racial discrimination attacked motels, since they were the prime providers of public accommodations. Despite English common law's longstanding principle of equal access and service at wayside inns, it took the civil-rights movement's relentless pressure beginning in the 1950s and the Civil Rights Act of 1964 to bring about the practice in motels. As highly prominent places of social interaction, motels became the sites of "historic" events associated in national memory with both the pluses and minuses of democracy's fortunes, such as the *Heart of Atlanta Motel, Inc. v. United States* (1964), upholding the Civil Rights Act of 1964's constitutionality, and the Algiers Motel incident in Detroit (1967), witnessing to racism's persistence. The fact that the Lorraine Motel in Memphis, where Martin Luther King was assassinated in 1968, later became part of a civil-rights museum dramatically confirms the ambiguity of roadside lodging in the national experience. Ultimately one of the strongest forces diminishing racial discrimination in motels, both for lodgers and for employees, was the growth of chains. Not only did many indirectly prod racially biased local business communities when they refused to invest in cities beset with sit-ins and riots but they more readily hired blacks. Expanding profits and a refined image were goals of corporate investment, which coincidentally had democratizing benefits. Moms and Pops' provincially structured industry was being revolutionized in many ways.[68]

The trajectory of new motel construction was meteoric. Between 1946 and 1953 the numbers doubled, to approximately 45,000, even before the stimulating accelerated-income-tax-depreciation clause of 1954. This was startling growth, and almost unprecedented in American history for any industry. California and Florida especially overbuilt motels. Mom and Pop immigrated to resort destinations, thinking they could live in a sunlit retirement off profits made while owning and managing a motel, only to find too many others with the same false hope. Motel turnover was rapid. In 1953 the widely circulated *Saturday Evening Post* detailed the sobering realities of year-round work without relief, of waiting to make a profit after enduring many years of earning just enough to pay off the mortgage, furniture payments, and payroll while also watching the rising tide of competition. The *Post* article "Troubles of a Motel Keeper" summarized the new popular perception of the mom-and-pop motel trade, one in stark contrast with the romantic allure of the popular prewar treatments.[69]

A glimpse of Mom and Pop's work routine gives some idea of their challenges. Many lived at their motel, in small quarters hardly larger than the rooms rented. While this meant that they were able to instantly address any need, Mom and Pop also lived in a "fishbowl," subject to continual scrutiny by passersby as well as customers. Furthermore, warned the *Post*, "the confinement is killing. You never get away. Lots of couples say it's like being in jail" (see Fig. 3.16).[70] The daily frenzy could begin at six o'clock in the morning with a lodger leaving his key in the office rather than in the room. Within an hour all hope of rest ended: the driveway roared with revving engines, slamming doors, and crying children as lodgers readied to leave. Hasty exits often meant tangled blinds and walls and portals nicked by suitcases. Normal occupancy often revealed cigarette-burned furnishings and ashtrays as well as stolen towels. Lodgers' behavior was not always easy to anticipate based on their appearance. One trusting owner, for example, was surprised to find that the sheriff had arrested a mother and daughter, the latter embarrassed to admit she was a schoolteacher, for stealing towels. While some repairs were made to keep rooms in daily use, the office hummed with calls for the next reservations, inspections following the maids' work, and forgotten items being added to the "lost and found." By late afternoon Mom and Pop had to wash and redress to meet their new guests, wait through frequent room inspections as guests decided whether to lodge at the motel, and furnish various items (e.g., extra blankets and aspirin) to meet guests' special needs. Mom and Pop squeezed dinner in, seldom together, between intermittent calls to the desk and before sunset brought its own rounds—checking lights, sprinklers, and customer comfort (because repeat business was coveted). Bookkeeping was usually reserved for evenings, when interruptions decreased. For one team, weekends could be the hardest times because that was when Pop completed repairs forestalled during the week while Mom turned the mattresses and cleaned bedspreads and pillows.[71] Seasonal cycles of repair and maintenance varied, of course, according to location. Snow removal, for example, was a necessity in northern climes that was absent in southern climes, where more time had to be given year-round to shrubs and lawns.[72]

DON'T BE A SLAVE

TO YOUR MOTEL

HEDY McDOWELL, Town House Motel, Sunnyside, Wash., above, combines business with hobby by painting a huge mural in oils for the motel lobby. A part of the painting is shown here. At left are Harry and Dorothy Christy, Red Apple Motel, Yakima, Wash., who find that a vital interest in people—their guests—keeps their minds fresh and their own motel problems in perspective.

by **LEONE TEETERS**

Confining pressures of the motel business can ruin your health unless you can learn how to relax and enjoy life. Here's how other motel operators face the same problem that you face.

MOST MOTEL OPERATORS will admit that the motel business is confining. Some become so frustrated that their attitudes with their clientele are strained. Others adjust to the situation in various ways in order to remain relaxed and happy as motel managers.

"Pressure problems which are going to face a motel operator should be considered right in the beginning if it is at all possible," said Leonard Johnson, AAA field supervisor in Seattle, Wash. "And if I can, I try to help."

Occasionally, a retired couple approaches Johnson.

"We've sold our wheat farm," one couple told him, "and we would like to buy a motel and run it."

Johnson says he is quite blunt in cases like this. He asks them three specific questions.

"Do you really like people?"

If their answer is 'yes,' his next questions are even more blunt.

"Are you willing to work harder than you have ever worked before?" And finally, "Will you mind being confined day after day after day?"

When Johnson is satisfied that the answers are sincerely affirmative, he tells them to go ahead and buy their motel. But—he suggests that they talk to persons who have been in the business for several years to find out from them how they have coped with some of the problems which arise.

Facing managerial problems ahead with the new managers was accomplished successfully by the Henry Lack-

FIGURE 3.16 Overcoming the boredom of job confinement was a chronic challenge for which the *Tourist Court Journal* offered therapeutic advice in a February 1963 article. Hedy McDowell, of the Town House Motel in Sunnyside, Washington *(top right)*, painted the mural beside her, and Harry and Dorothy Christy *(left)*, of the Red Apple Motel in Yakima, Washington, took renewed pleasure in personal service to their guests in order to maintain a positive attitude about their work. (*Source: Tourist Court Journal* 25 [February 1963]: 46.)

One should never discount the industrious small owners who insisted on their relative rewards: a proportionately high income compared with that from investment in other businesses, for example, or an acknowledged life of hard work, but one that was still easier than they might have had. The letters to the editor in the next month's issue of the *Post* article tapped into "motel fever," as the magazine labeled small owners' ardent feeling for their their trade. Yet, despite denials, Mom and Pop were buffeted. By 1956 it was estimated that about one-half of all motels earned no more than a modest income from their twenty or fewer rooms. Hotel rivals exacerbated competition. From their quarter-century of doldrums, hotel investors rebounded in the late 1950s as aggressive builders. Federally funded urban renewal opened important center-city tracts for new hotel investment. Hotel investors also had clearly heard the automobilists' call for auto convenience. Elitist roadside critic Bernard DeVoto even readily conceded the motel's advantages for ease of access and lack of tipping, since it achieved a reputation for cleanliness and decency (see Fig. 3.17). Hotels thus moved to the roadsides at the edge of town, where motels had earlier incubated (see Fig. 3.18).[73]

Large, plush motels began to flood the market in the 1950s. Memphis, Tennessee, at the convergence of five national highways, beside a major continental river and an important North-South portal, spawned one of the first elaborately documented "motor hotels," the Town Park Motor Hotel. Of more enduring importance, however, was the Town Park's competitor, Kemmons Wilson's Holiday Inn, also founded in Memphis. *Business Week* described Wilson's entrepreneurial genius with stunning simplicity: "The idea, Wilson says, is to develop motel rooms along the line of a branded product: the name is your guarantee." Within a decade—by 1964—motels were being built at six times the rate of 1945.[74]

Mom and Pop no longer dominated. H. H. "Joe" Mobley, head of the AMHA, pointed out: "It used to be that Ma and Pa sort of retired into the motel business, but not any more. Nowadays it takes ambition, money and know-how to survive. The mortality rate in this business has become terrific."[75] Mom and Pop were also lost in the stampede of popular attention afforded the big chains, on which the popular press henceforth focused increasingly. Money and imagination both swept past the small entrepreneur.

Mom and Pop still owned 54 percent of all the motels, according to the 1987 federal census.[76] Often their motels were located in small towns (see Figs. 3.19 and 3.20). Advantages obviously remained for them. It cost relatively little to maintain a good-looking motel, and visual appeal persisted as an important, initial consumer attraction.[77] Established mom-and-pop

FIGURE 3.17 In this postcard (circa 1960) the owners of the Driftwood Motel, in St. Petersburg, Florida, tried to impress the potential lodger with the motel's easy access and informality.

FIGURE 3.18 The U.S. Grant Hotel and the Motel U.S. Grant, Mattoon, Illinois, are pictured on a single postcard. Their corporate directors acceded to roadside lodging by building the motel in 1952; the uptown hotel had been built in 1928.

FIGURE 3.19 The Trees Motel, shown here in 1989, was the last occupant of a long prosperous motel site beside Route 30 in Denison, Iowa.

FIGURE 3.20 Fred Ravy, shown here in 1989, owned and operated The Trees Motel until his recent death, when it underwent a conversion to short-term rental units, as older motels often do.

owners also maintained their hard-won reputation for decency. Profit-hungry new owners or absentee owners usually permitted the "hot pillow" trade.[78] Surviving independents also had recourse to advertising the "comforts of home," on which Mom and Pop had long capitalized. Even in 1992 a latter-day referral chain (with some large properties) could advertise: "The Independent Motels of America are a group of motels that believe very strongly that you, the traveling public, should not be forced to stay in large expensive motels. We feel just as strongly that you should not sacrifice full services such as free advance reservations, knowing what each motel has to offer, and certainly most important to all of us, what it will cost."[79] Reliability seems to be verified in the simple and forthright language. Small, accessible, inexpensive, and sufficient: Mom and Pop today echo the appeals of their Depression-era forerunners. Do bed and breakfasts recast the mom-and-pop enterprise of the past in contemporary terms, at once offering the earlier virtues of intimate scale and personal service yet purchased at high rates, including for food, avoided earlier?

Mom and Pop, with their motels, were the first settlers on the roadside frontier. Not only did they live by the road, as did many early operators of the other major roadside businesses—gas stations and restaurants—but they provided overnight lodging for those who were passing through. Having been the first to profit by meeting the needs of the automobile traveler, the more aggressive small entrepreneurs moved quickly in the 1930s to overcome the typical frontier-trade reputation for dumpiness and indecency. All the while the economy begged investment. First, the Depression displaced hotels and beckoned motels; then World War II drove housing demands to record heights. Postwar development raced. Mom-and-pop referral organizations finished sanitizing the motel's image, but they could not finance all the lodging and plush accouterments demanded. The frontier terms of easy admission and hard work for success gave way to others. Big investors sought big profits and wanted to locate their homes far off the roadside. Professionals advised them. Brisk competition closed many small motels and caused others to go through a rapid succession of naive owners. Harsh realities were confessed in the popular press, if not cursed privately by Mom and Pop.

How typically this frontier had ended—quickly, with big capital and regret. Within thirty years of having founded the industry, mom-and-pop entrepreneurs were driven to its margins. They survived, but they no longer flourished on a frontier of their own. In the process, mom-and-pop motels had contributed significantly to America's consciousness. Mom and Pop were exemplars of the American dream. In the Depression, their stiff defiance was a reassurance that "the system" still worked. Their lodgings furnished the extended domesticity a highly mobile nation sought on the road. While their frequent racial discrimination satisfied a generally biased nation, their acquiescence to the civil rights of prospective employees and lodgers eventually contributed to growing equality in public lodging. Although the big chains eventually provided luxurious convention and resort facilities, Mom and Pop had helped make it reasonable for Americans to expect such options in a new culture of highly personalized pleasures.

4

Remember the Alamo Plazas

IN THIS CHAPTER WE MOVE BEYOND THE MOM-AND-POP MOTELS BUT NOT yet to the contemporary corporate giants. What follows is a case study of Alamo Plaza Hotel Courts. Begun in 1929, Alamo Plaza became the largest early motel chain. Here we seek further to gain insight into entrepreneurial decision making and at the same time to document a significant intermediate step in motel-chain development. In the 1950s Holiday Inn, for example, enjoyed an accelerated growth and left Alamo Plaza far behind, the latter chain languishing as a residual curiosity in comparison.

Alamo Plaza Hotel Courts was a referral chain of several independently owned branches. Each was begun and operated by a family member or friend of the founder, Lee Torrance, who emerged as the network's acknowledged patriarch. Torrance's talent lay in sensing the need for inexpensive yet prestigious lodging throughout a large area and providing it by a formula quickly improvised. No conceptual model guided his work; his was the successful businessman's gift of effective action, not intellectual rumination. He perceived an opportunity and took advantage of it to accrue a considerable fortune. His motives can be inferred from his genuine accomplishments and from interviews with his business associates; he left no written record, and but a few spoken words have survived. Lee Torrance was a risk-taking investor and an aggressive owner, an entrepreneur by definition. Yet the term suggests a refinement that does not fully capture the source of his strength: a commonsensical, unambiguous, and, when needed, rough-and-ready character. People who knew Lee Torrance remember him as "one heck of a horse trader," not as an aloof executive directing subalterns.[1] He was a highly motivated originator and an industrious operator before the age of managerial capitalism divided ownership and operation. Like Kemmons Wilson later, Torrance was out and about in his empire, overseeing it personally, attending to the smallest detail when he was convinced of its capacity for profit. He reveled in making his business work.

Torrance's undeniable individuality left its mark on his creation. Even Bill Farner, the most aggressive of Alamo Plaza's branch owners, derived his procedure largely from Torrance. Torrance provides an instructive example of a transitional entrepreneur. If market domination within an area is the measure of success, Torrance's Alamo Plaza Hotel Courts must be taken as a significant but unsuccessful step. Torrance proceeded gradually to build a chain that was big by the standards of its day, but he did not have the indomitable vision of industrywide reform that Tedlow has attributed to the great entrepreneurs of mass marketing.[2] It would be a mistake to see Alamo Plaza Hotel Courts as a link in some inexorable progress toward an ideal or ultimate motel modus operandi. Alamo Plaza Hotel Courts was an ad hoc creation whose periodic pulsations reflected routine business.

ROOTS

E. Lee Torrance was born in 1894 in rural McLennan County, Texas. He moved to Waco, the county seat, as a child, and it was there that he lived and headquartered his business enterprise throughout his life.[3] The center of a prosperous cattle- and cotton-producing hinterland in the last third of the nineteenth century, the city was served by a dense rail net (there were eight railroads and 206 miles of rail countywide by 1904). Called "the Hub of Texas," Waco had a vibrant economy. Amicable Life Insurance Company's twenty-two-story headquarters, built in 1910 and publicized nationally as Texas's first skyscraper, symbolized the young town's vitality. In 1910 Waco's merchants launched the Cotton Palace Festival, which was an annual event through 1930. It opened with a parade to the fairgrounds pursued by hundreds of people in streetcars. A midway with various rides and vendors dazzled and entertained, while the exposition hall's dome and towers, outlined with nighttime lighting, increased the aura of fantasy.[4]

A business culture developed rapidly. Toby's Business College, for example, went from giving private accounting lessons three nights a week in a private house to offering a full curriculum that included shorthand, typing, and auditing in its own downtown building eight years later. However, it was Baylor University, organized from several antecedent schools, that augmented Waco's bid for central Texas prominence and the claim to being "the Athens of Texas."[5] Torrance, although orphaned when he was thirteen, flourished in this environment. After attending Waco's public schools, he studied at Toby's Business College. In 1918, when Waco had an economy pumped high by two local military bases built during the war,

Torrance left his job as a bookkeeper with a hardware company and started his own used-car dealership.[6]

Public lodging had long been profitable in Waco. Besides commercial travelers, tourists had been drawn to the presumed curative waters of several local springs. A new hotel and numerous boardinghouses had sprung up early in the century to satisfy the demand for temporary housing. The mayoral campaign of 1912 turned partly on one candidate's promise to build "the most modern hotel in Texas," but his bankruptcy after the election soon resulted in his enterprise, the Raleigh Hotel, becoming part of the Albert Pick hotel chain. In 1929 local investors built a hotel for Conrad Hilton, who operated it as part of his competing chain.[7]

In 1928 McLennan County passed a bond issue to match state and federal funds for laying eight concrete automobile pavements radiating from Waco. Torrance seems to have seen little investment opportunity in this development, although he did contemplate building a "bachelor's apartment" as he and his friend Judge Drummond W. Bartlett motored about town one Sunday afternoon. Such a place would make a logical residence, bachelor Bartlett thought, and earn additional profit, businessman Torrance hoped.[8]

How could an apartment venture combine respectability appropriate to a district judge and profit too? Where would it be built? What would it look like? After some consideration, the two friends decided to build twenty-four "tourist apartments," as they called them. They were not to be "tourist cabins," a name common at the time. These were to be superior to ordinary motorist lodgings, as the label implied. They chose a site on the east side of Waco, across the street from Grande Courts, a large motel. Perhaps they intended to draw business by developing a locus in the city for temporary lodging. Mimicry of its neighbor, furthermore, probably explains the architectural design adopted for the new undertaking.[9]

But why mimic Grande Courts? Many choices were possible in the evolving repertoire of motel design. A local architect provided Torrance a free interpretation of the Alamo, one of Texas's most famous symbols. Such a retrospective reference implied both respect for tradition and security for the traveler. It was an age of expanding visual communication, and the Alamo was widely recognized not only in Texas but nationally as an icon. Revivalism, which was current in popular design, resulted in once local images being used nationally. The Alamo alluded to the Spanish revival of the Southwest. Roadside architecture had come to appeal to a new consuming market by loudly declaring the old identities. Thus, adobe simulations commonly masked gas stations, restaurants, and tourist cabins in the Southwest.[10]

Torrance was dogmatic about certain issues of architectural design. Most of all, he was proud of his Texas heritage, including the Alamo.[11] During a 1953 interview he disparaged the U-shaped courtyard of many motels as being fit only for a barn. They did not make inviting motels, he said. A skilled horseman, Torrance was familiar with the long, front-facing horse stables on ranches. The richly associative two-story "Alamo" façade, tapered by separate flanking one-story extensions across the front of his "tourist apartments," imparted contrasting elegance. In later additions, another set of "tourist apartments" would be aligned perpendicularly to the highway, their setback visible through driveways piercing the symmetrical main façade. The result was a sense of gracious living not unlike that on a large hacienda (see Fig. 4.1). The restful interior courtyard was screened from the energy of the road, a feature Alan Hess has noted in Las Vegas's later motels.[12] It also embodied the plaza of the motel's name, the open space that commonly defined a community's focal area. Nomenclature reinforced architecture. Would his guests not rest assured by neighboring themselves for a night with other elitists in transit seeking elegant motel services? In short, guests were both told and shown a compound secure physically and socially against outside uncertainties while traveling away from home. Had Torrance or his architect learned intuitively from the fantasy architecture of Waco's Cotton Palace Festival? Did they also learn what they did not want from Texas's mushrooming motels?

During the 1953 interview, Torrance recoiled strongly from the idea of nighttime lighting to outline his buildings: "No sir, no neon. We don't want to look like a beer joint. We have a neon sign in front."[13] In this discrimination, Torrance and his architect may have taken a negative lesson from the Cotton Festival's exhibit hall. He may also have instinctively appreciated that the Alamo façade functioned as a very effective sign, in its breadth and height overwhelming most competing motels, its white color standing out day or night. He may not have fully understood the appeal of a widely popular architectural image when he and Bartlett began, but he certainly did by 1953, when he began to use the expression "Remember the Alamo Plazas."[14]

Torrance's desire for a prestigious image presented one of the most common problems in roadside design: how to offer attractive yet affordable services. By hiring his brother-in-law, W. N. McGrady, a building contractor, to oversee construction and by avoiding the cost of a restaurant, Torrance was able to keep the total start-up bill to $40,000 and room rates to $1 for a single and $2 for a double.[15] Here was hotel-quality accommodation at motel rates, with higher profit margins than were possible at most hotels. Alamo Plaza was not unlike a mansion among

FIGURE 4.1 This postcard view dating from 1948 illustrates Alamo Plaza's fully stated original style.

roadside shacks, which was what contemporary observers often likened the mundane tourist cabins to. Torrance had also contrived a typical boom-town façade—expediently low-cost but good-looking.

Herein lies the brilliance of his business solution as well as a provincial contribution to the twentieth century's growing cultural distinction between reality and illusion, noted in chapter 3. Landscape was both cause and consequence of the period's popular thought and feeling. Masking contemporary retail services in revival architecture was common in the 1920s and 1930s, when people seemed to be torn between the advantages of an apparently secure past and those of an uncertain future characterized by accelerating change. Transition could be eased by historical reference. Masking is the essence of architectural *façadism,* a term coined to describe the use of a building's façade to make a strong public impression. Façadism became an enduring quality of roadside architecture; the speeded communication of travel by machine seemingly required a countervailing show of faith in the past, especially dramatic in Alamo Plaza's case. On April 9, 1929, Torrance and Bartlett opened their motel. It did, indeed, convey the impression of an aristocratic estate, not only then but a half-century later as well. Thus, a recent observer was startled to learn that one motel in the chain had sunk to being a hangout for the oldest profession.[16]

As the nation slumped into the Depression, Torrance prospered. Disappointed by a close relative whom he had selected to manage the Waco motel, Torrance hired an aggressive young manager, a man from nearby McGregor, William "Bill" Farner, who made the operation fully profitable. In a few years, Torrance and Bartlett easily paid off their $37,000 loan.[17] Bartlett's public life precluded his active participation in the partnership, and Torrance found himself virtually alone to pursue the motel trade as he wished. Torrance turned next to Tyler, Texas, approximately 110 miles east of Waco. Blessed with a large number of fresh-water springs, Tyler had grown gradually throughout the nineteenth century. Small industries, fruit growing, and especially King Cotton yielded a good income with good railroad service. Starting in the second decade of the century, Smith County, with Tyler at its center, developed a substantial system of automobile roads. But it was the East Texas oil boom of the 1930s that made Tyler's economy take off. Just when cotton's productivity was declining, in the 1920s, largely as the result of boll-weevil infestations, the richest oil deposits discovered up to that time began to produce in a succession of wells within a thirty-five-mile radius of Tyler.[18]

Oilmen, lawyers, gamblers, and other followers crowded into Tyler and dispersed into the surrounding countryside, all needing temporary housing. Work shanties sprang up, offices were built, and existing facilities were hurriedly adapted to serve the population flooding Smith County. Here was an oil-boom landscape: haphazard, impermanent, and unkempt. Even the regal one-hundred-room Blackstone Hotel, Tyler's largest hostelry, built during the prosperity of the early 1920s and leased to Waco's Raleigh Hotel, had slumped as a result of the demand by 1930, its desk clerk ordered to tell inquiring lodgers to sleep on cots in the lobby or go elsewhere. Autos doubled as beds for many.[19]

On July 5, 1931, Lee Torrance opened his forty-three-unit Alamo Plaza Tourist Apartments on Erwin Street, also known as the Dallas Highway, on Tyler's west side. There four competitors also clustered by 1932, defining the city's first motel strip.[20] A full-page Sunday advertisement in one of Tyler's newspapers clearly proclaimed Torrance's appeal to dignified roadside lodging, amplified since the opening of the first motel two years before. Each of the individual "tourist apartments" was equipped with indoor plumbing (which included "shower baths"), major-brand mattresses, and "hardwood floors." The number of rooms varied—from one to four—to accommodate individual needs. This was no generic tourist facility. These "snow white court apartments," in significant contrast with the grimy industrial landscape of the oil boom, amounted to "America's Finest Tourist Apartments," Torrance bragged.[21] The newspaper carried its own description, and local merchants eagerly promoted the services they had extended. Advertisements were placed by a paint and wallpaper store, an electrical contractor, and the awning shop of an automobile paint and top company. The newspaper concluded that Torrance's facility provided "everything you can find in your own home." By then Torrance had announced his plan to extend the chain.[22]

The fact that Torrance had a plan did not mean that he had a schedule. Torrance never took less than an even chance in the motel trade. In contrast to many motel marketers in the 1930s, for whom the combination of services was as yet undecided and the earnings were insufficient,[23] Torrance had hit on a profitable place-product-packaging scheme. It would be four years, however—1935—before he finally added the third motel to his chain. Intelligent but conservative investment was Torrance's hallmark as a motel entrepreneur. Unlike those who had set the pace in soft drinks, automobiles, and soaps, he never pushed the market.[24] Shreveport, Louisiana, where, on August 1, 1935, he opened the third Alamo Plaza, was nearly as attractive an investment location as Tyler had been.

Shreveport had been linked to East Texas since the early nineteenth century, when the wagon road west out of town was designated the "Texas Trail," and "G. T. T." (Gone to Texas) became a familiar local message left by those seeking opportunity westward. Popularizing its reputation by proclaiming itself the heart of "Ark-La-Tex," a hinterland of an approximately one-hundred-mile radius that included the adjacent corners of Arkansas, Louisiana, and Texas, Shreveport became a river port first and then a rail center for a wealthy and diversified economy, natural gas and oil discoveries further boosting the economy beginning in 1906. Although the agricultural base declined sharply beginning in the 1920s as a result of depressed cotton prices, with serious unemployment resulting, some East Texas oil wealth spilled over to its Louisiana neighbor. Then the big gas field at Rodessa, north of Shreveport, opened in 1930. The nearby Barksdale Air Field, however, became the city's biggest resource. More than nine hundred laborers worked in shifts around the clock in 1931, generating a substantive demand for temporary housing. Barksdale was formally dedicated in 1933.[25]

Torrance located his motel on the west side of Shreveport at the intersection of Greenwood Road, the old trail west, and Mansfield Road, a major route south to the Gulf Coast. That both roads had been among the first paved for automobiles attests to their primacy. His three-member chain now stretched along a busy east-west corridor approximately two hundred miles long. His motels literally towered above the competition. In support of the image of a prestigious place to stay, Torrance's quarter-page newspaper advertisement for his grand opening again highlighted well-furnished "apartments," but he renamed the business Alamo Plaza Courts, *courts* having been popularized in the industry. Torrance aimed at a clientele of businessmen traveling with their wives and married couples in need of household facilities until they could move into permanent housing in Shreveport. Breaking with the average motel's custom of no tipping, Torrance had porters whose income derived largely from tips. Advertisements flanking the notice of his grand opening proclaimed the capacity of the several local contractors who had worked on the motel to deliver high-quality work on short notice. Advertising reciprocally ingrati-

FIGURE 4.2 Torrance advertised Alamo Plaza's opening in Shreveport in order to convince the public that the motel was a community asset as well as a lodgers' oasis. (*Source: Shreveport Times,* August 4, 1935, 13.)

ated the out-of-town chain operator with his new business community. Shreveport and Torrance both intended to gain from their pretension that Alamo Plaza represented the "South's Finest Tourist Courts" (see Fig. 4.2).[26]

Business conditions and sound management proved Torrance's financial instincts right again. Shreveport, for example, suffered no run on its banks during the Depression, and Barksdale continued its remarkable economic patronage as the buildup for World War II began in the late 1930s.[27] Torrance called in a nephew, W. G. McGrady, as manager to ensure close surveillance of his latest enterprise; and he thereby also trained one of the later branch founders. By 1935 Torrance was profiting handsomely from his distinctive marketing strategy at three shrewdly selected sites effectively and loyally managed. He outdistanced all his competitors, the small, often rude cabins mushrooming along the roadside as well as the worn uptown hotels built a decade or more earlier. The chain was firmly rooted.

BRANCHES ON THE FAMILY TREE

Torrance's success depended on a handful of faithful and reliable intimates to whom he could delegate independent management of each motel. Among Torrance's several trusted business companions, however, Bill Farner alone was as ambitious as his mentor. It was not surprising that Farner eventually built a large Alamo Plaza branch that briefly rivaled the larger chains. Farner alone in Torrance's cadre understood the roadside imperative for frequent periodic change in order to stay at the market's forefront. Society frames broad profit-making possibilities, but the entrepreneur with a forceful personality, such as Farner, alone risks taking specific options.

William Henry Farner is remembered as pursuing wealth to overcome his modest origins. He blended sheer grit and determination with common sense and a winning personality to emerge as a noteworthy but unpublicized early motel entrepreneur. Farner had much in common with his mentor Lee Torrance in his early years. Also a native of East Texas and only eight years younger than Torrance, Farner, born in 1902, was likewise raised in a tough and competitive environment fostering faith in material rewards through honesty, persistence, and hard work. His oldest son, Ted, wrote down the family lore of pioneering westward, albeit only some seventy-five miles and in the early twentieth century:

> At some time they loaded up in a covered wagon and moved to McGregor, Tex.
>
> They were poor dirt farmers, 3 girls, 2 boys. All children strong healthy and good looking.
>
> Bill, oldest sister, father, sharecropped, and worked for neighbors to send others to school and feed [and] cloth them.
>
> His father was a little man, had a way with animals, and plants, also people. A good looking man, strong; people did not bother him. Some said even the chickens understood him. Others said he was Apache Indian. Bill and sisters brothers loved him. Clearly so did I. He was up before daylight and made breakfast for everyone while the children took care of the animals, and then went to school. Bill and Mabel had very little schooling.[28]

An epic of loving self-sacrifice for the family's greater good—conservative American ethical bedrock—moored Farner's values. Aspiration and exertion to the uttermost went hand in hand with this ethos. Ted continued: "When Bill became a teenager, his father would take him to the McGregor square on Saturdays and let him fight for money. He never lost; he was beaten sometimes badly, but always won the fight. His sisters said he would come home a bloody mess. Some said he was like Jack Dempsey and would never give up. All money went to my grandfather and he spent it wisely. My grandfather was a kind gentleman, looked after his family."[29]

Bill grew up in McGregor, where he attended school through the fourth grade, married Hazel Kathleen Cawthron, and started in business managing a dairy to support his family, including two sons. Seeking more pay than the ten dollars a month he earned from the dairy, Bill moved his family to Waco, where he worked long hours to earn twenty-two dollars a month as a boilermaker for the Katy Railroad. Despite his reputation as one of the yard's best workers, he was let go in 1930 because of the Depression. From this bitter experience he drew two important conclusions: (1) that big business has no loyalty and (2) that one should be one's own boss. With his small savings he leased a little diner and profited by dint of total family commitment. Although Hazel's arthritis bound her to a wheelchair, she advised him on management. Six days a week Bill opened at dawn and closed at sunset, relying on only his son Ted to clean up. His father's sheer joy in an unimagined income (thirty-one dollars the first month on the sixty-dollar lease) that he did not have to share with another owner created an impression that remained strong in Ted's memory over sixty years later. Proudly depositing the previous day's earnings in the bank each morning became an important ritual validating their success.[30]

Chance presented the next opportunity. Lee Torrance owned the diner and the lot on which it stood, next door to his used-car lot. Eating two meals together each day, the two assiduous young businessmen became fast friends, the older and richer man something of a financial adviser to the younger man. He appreciated the younger man's diligence and honesty. When Torrance and Bartlett saw in Farner a potential remedy for their promising but initially unprofitable Waco motel, Farner was forced to break his pledge against working for others, for the much higher income he would receive as manager of their motel would allow him to pay for his wife's badly needed medical care. Bill negotiated an agreement that included not only a salary plus commission, eighty-seven dollars a month at the beginning, but also free housing for him and his family since he was serving as on-site manager.[31]

Hard work, family commitment, and loyalty to benevolent authority had their rewards. Physically incapable of heavy work, Hazel nonetheless helped her husband significantly in systematizing the motel's management and registering lodgers. A hired woman took care of the children. Bill was "on his way." Bill's basic routine was simple at first: "All he knew was rent the rooms, get the money and take it to Lee Torrance next morning and be sure to get a signed receipt. Mother laid out the program." Torrance greatly valued roadside signs for advertising, and Bill obediently rented sign space from farmers on every major highway out from Waco. In one case, he happened upon a farmer who was chopping cotton, challenged him to a chopping contest just for the sport, and won a free sign spot in return for his vigorous labor. With the help of one of the motel's black porters, Bill dug postholes for the signs and mixed the concrete in which to set them. Bill's standard work days, ranging from ten to eleven hours, would have left most men exhausted. Hazel complemented her husband's raw energy, schooling him in polite manners. She persuaded him to don the air of a respectable merchant by buying a business suit in which to call on local companies that were critical to the motel's success, principally the utilities, the interurban company, and local gas stations. At the latter two he regularly stocked postcards, one of the early industry's more successful advertisements.[32] Alamo Plaza finally started turning the profit Torrance and Bartlett had wanted.

Typically concerned with minimizing labor costs as one way to increase his profit margin, Torrance sought to cap his industrious manager's earnings while at the same time retaining for him a guaranteed good income. Farner was earning $275 a month plus housing when Torrance and Bartlett offered him $50 a month regardless of their earnings. Not only did this tell Farner that his bosses believed he was earning too much but it restored his intention to work for himself. Having learned on the job that sizeable profits could be made in the new motel trade, Farner lacked only capital and legal expertise to set off on his own.[33]

Charles Hill Mooney complemented Farner very well, and they became partners in 1938. Farner would manage and codirect a new enterprise with his exclusively entrepreneurial partner. Six years Farner's junior, born in Waco in 1908, Mooney was another ambitious young man who had come up the hard way. His father had died when he was five years of age, and his mother had supported herself and her son by ironing, washing, and taking in boarders. Mooney was working his way through Baylor University to become a lawyer when he offered one of Farner's sons a job delivering newspapers on an extensive route Mooney had developed. Mooney quickly became good friends with the Farners. After Bill refused Lee Torrance's offer of fifty dollars per month and gave thirty days' notice, he proposed partnership to Mooney.[34]

Business took precedence over feelings. When Torrance learned that the new partners were to become potential competitors, having located a site for their own motel in Beaumont, Texas, Torrance offered to underwrite the new motel and confer the Alamo Plaza name as well. The new partners agreed, advanced a down payment of approximately $3,000 from their own savings, obtained a large loan from a Waco friend, and opened Alamo Plaza's Beaumont branch with sixteen units on April 23, 1938.[35]

Beaumont was only a fair bet for Alamo Plaza's first branch location. Whereas Torrance had staked out booming towns, Farner jumped into one that had had the earmarks of a vital town in the past but was then slumping economically. Cattle and lumber had enriched a few "barons" incredibly during the nineteenth century, but the 1901 discovery of oil at

Spindletop, the legendary oil field southeast of town, had widely diffused great wealth. Decent temporary housing was at a premium, and although the "new" Crosby Hotel had been built in 1903 to replace a predecessor, speculators and swindlers overflowed its rooms, making their fly-by-night offices on its porches. Major oil companies—Texaco, Humble, Mobil, and Gulf—and numerous lesser ones emanated from Spindletop; and even when it had dwindled to a "pumper" by 1904, it spawned more than two hundred new buildings in town and a $3.5 million bond issue for paved streets. Population multiplied fourfold, to 40,000, in the twenty years thereafter, a deep water port finally opened in 1916, and the Spindletop gusher in 1925 transfused more entrepreneurial energy and dispensed more wealth.[36]

The Depression hit Beaumont hard. There was no benevolent equivalent to the East Texas oil boom. Nonetheless, by the late 1930s private housing starts had increased and the remodeled Crosby Hotel typified the Beaumont business community's determination to renew. Merchants and city government cooperated to attract tourists, and Louisiana's own tourist offensive in the nearby "Evangeline country" complemented their effort. Perhaps Farner took his surest sign of hope from the Old Spanish Trail Association, promoters of Highway 90, which skirted the nation's southern border from coast to coast. It was on that busy street, just east of the city's downtown, that the motel was built.[37]

Farner's entrepreneurship reflected his long managerial experience. The attractions named in the opening newspaper advertisement were identical to those Torrance had mentioned: the privacy of separate "rooms and apartments"; three-sided ventilation; the finest building materials and furnishings (tile baths and Beautyrest mattresses); and low rates (two dollars for two people). The overall intent was, similarly, to impress the traveler with this newest link in the nation's chain of "finest economical accommodations" (see Fig. 4.3). Indeed, having a Sunday grand opening, inviting public inspection, and publication on the morning of the event followed the standard Torrance format. Farner departed only in his comparatively smaller advertisement, probably a constraint of his and his partner's smaller budget. Farner's experience at Waco had taught him that sixteen units plus his family's living quarters was the maximum amount that could be cared for with the smallest hired staff, that is, one maid and two porters, one for the day and one for the night (see Figs. 4.4 and 4.5). As they profited, Farner and Mooney gradually added several sixteen-unit sections, which enabled them to create the effect of the interior courtyard integral to Alamo Plaza's architectural signature. Farner was not simply mimicking Torrance. Farner innovated specific routines for all the hired staff; he stocked the minimum amount of supplies necessary for two days'

Announcing the Opening of

ALAMO
PLAZA COURTS

WACO — TYLER - SHREVEPORT - OKLAHOMA CITY — LITTLE ROCK
ON HIGHWAY NO. 90—1900 COLLEGE ST.

W. H. Farner. Owner and Mgr.   Chas. Hill Mooney, Owner

And now we bring to Beaumont the newest unit of the Nationally Famous ALAMO PLAZA COURTS, America's finest economical accommodations. Erected at a cost of more than $50,000.00, they offer you service and comfort without extravagance—at moderate cost. It's years ahead of anything you've ever seen, with tile baths in each apartment. Built of the finest materials and finished throughout like the finest homes . . . Trained attendants will be on hand to show you through.

ENJOY THESE INCOMPARABLE FEATURES

- All Outside Rooms and Apartments
- Perfect Ventilation on Three Sides
- Tile Bath in Every Room or Apartment
- A Beautyrest Mattress on Every Bed
- Complete Privacy for Every Guest
- Thoroughly Modern and Completely Furnished
- Electric Refrigeration

2
PERSONS
$2.00

WE INVITE YOUR INSPECTION TODAY!
11 A. M. to 4 P. M.

FIGURE 4.3 Farner's grand-opening advertisement in Beaumont was similar to Torrance's advertisements for new Alamo Plazas except for its smaller size and the fact that it carried only a single local contractor's claim of excellence. (*Source: Beaumont Enterprise,* May 8, 1938, 8-A.)

operation. Imperative, although not novel, were well-groomed grounds, immaculate rooms, and courtesies especially to commercial lodgers, who made up the majority of Alamo Plaza's customers. Farner cashed their checks, and porters washed their cars, for example. Commercial lodgers could be counted on to pass the word along about Alamo Plaza's special catering. Signs directing prospective lodgers were set out along the incoming highways; and, as with those around Waco, their placement on farmland often led farmers and other locals to recommend Alamo Plaza. Farner sought the respect of city merchants just as he had in Waco.[38] His hard work, honesty, and reputation for a decent motel won him acceptance among those responsible for Beaumont's economic revival.

If Torrance had any hopes of purchasing the Beaumont motel cheaply should Farner's management fail, they were quickly dashed.[39] Farner and Mooney soon paid their loan from an estimated seven hundred dollars' profit earned each month. Baton Rouge, the next major city eastward and nearest the Gulf Coast, became the target for the expanding Farner-Mooney branch. Louisiana's capital held out a good market potential for decent yet inexpensive transient housing by 1940. The Florida Street

FIGURE 4.4 Dependable maids were essential if Alamo Plaza was to fulfill its claim to being a prestigious motel. Blacks, posed here at Beaumont, were often hired as maids. Welcome in work but not in patronage, blacks suffered discrimination throughout the motel trade despite their service to it.

FIGURE 4.5 Porters, often black, were important to Alamo Plaza's claim to rank above the average motel. Shown here calling attention to the street-side sign at the new Beaumont motel, porters performed many errands for lodgers.

FIGURE 4.6 Alamo Plaza's advertising for its grand opening in Baton Rouge oc-cupied a portion of a previous page in addition to this one in the local newspaper. (*Source: Morning Advocate,* March 30, 1941, 7B.)

site the partners purchased was on an artery being considered for widen-ing into a four-lane connector to the new Airline Highway. Thus Alamo Plaza became an east-side sentinel for travelers.[40] On war's eve, local defense industries generated morning-newspaper headlines such as "Ba-ton Rouge Listed by Body As 'Key Defense' City That Is Facing Housing Shortage."[41] Residents were asked to list with the chamber of commerce any available housing for officers and their families. "Act now!" the news-

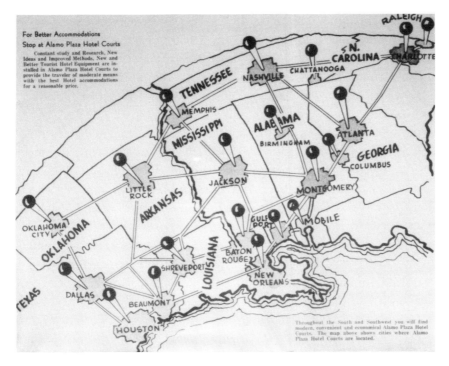

Within the map image:
For Better Accommodations
Stop at Alamo Plaza Hotel Courts

Constant study and Research, New Ideas and Improved Methods, New and Better Tourist Hotel Equipment are installed in Alamo Plaza Hotel Courts to provide the traveler of moderate means with the best Hotel accommodations for a reasonable price.

Throughout the South and Southwest you will find modern, convenient and economical Alamo Plaza Hotel Courts. The map above shows cities where Alamo Plaza Hotel Courts are located.

FIGURE 4.7 Three panels showing Alamo Plaza's southern market made up the largest section of a foldout directory placed in the chain's rooms beginning in the late 1940s.

papers pleaded.[42] Baton Rouge was also the only major city in the central South not served by Alamo Plaza. Farner and Mooney opened their second motel on March 30, 1941. Cooperative merchant advertising echoed Alamo Plaza's earlier grand openings (see Fig. 4.6).[43]

MATURATION

All the elements of Alamo Plaza's evolved formula were in place by the late 1930s: strategy, territory, and management. Their application, however, was not always orderly. Some steps in developing a motel continued more because they were merely convenient than as part of an overarching development scheme. And withal, none of Alamo Plaza's entrepreneurs, investors, or managers aimed consistently at a vast and enduring empire. At its height by the early 1950s, Alamo Plaza's advertisements boasted only twenty-two motels with some two thousand units in the South (see Fig. 4.7).[44] Only viewed in hindsight does the process appear to have been one of smooth progress to maturation. Entrepreneuring the first large motel chain in fact demanded daily fortitude and intelligence, although luck intervened as events unfolded.

The original intention of high-quality lodging rivaling the amenities of home yet rentable at low rates remained central to Torrance's marketing strategy. The challenge was to actually offer this uniformly as the chain grew. Torrance trusted local contractors to reproduce the same motel everywhere, but only under the strict supervision of a loyal team made up of his brother-in-law, a builder, and Jess N. Chastain, a construction site manager. Chastain, originally a flooring contractor, was hired by Torrance in Tyler to rebuild the hardwood floors of the first motel. While Torrance's brother-in-law inspected periodically, Chastain figured the list of building materials, bargained for them with local suppliers, and was daily on the construction site. Torrance also hired nonunion labor, when possible, to keep costs down.[45]

The image of respectability was basic from the start. It was essential for his first partner's own lodging in the first motel, and Torrance demanded it for all his chain additions, and he eventually sought formal endorsements of his motels' respectability from civic leaders in each city added. Exemplary was a Jackson, Mississippi, commissioner's to-whom-it-may-concern letter about the Alamo Plaza there: "It gives me pleasure to recommend this establishment for its honorable type of operation, and especially for the management in selecting with careful screening, not only the personnel of its management, but the type of people they permit to stay in their courts."[46] An endorsement from the general manager of the Shreveport chamber of commerce confirmed: "We have always found the local management of these courts, as well as the ownership, to be courteous and considerate of the traveling public and above average in civic interests and cooperation."[47]

After 1940 each new Alamo Plaza was dubbed a "hotel court." It is uncertain how rigorously Torrance applied the new nomenclature, since Oklahoma City's Alamo Plaza Courts, for example, never was renamed. Torrance's own advertisement in the June 1940 issue of the *Tourist Court Journal* is for Alamo Plaza Courts, although Torrance's preferred mattress supplier, Simmons, carried an endorsement in the same issue with letterhead stationery from Alamo Plaza Hotel Courts.[48]

Torrance briefly investigated alignment with the loosely federated referral organizations that dominated the trade at the end of the 1930s. In a rare public appearance before the motel industry, in May 1938 he addressed a joint meeting of the International Motor Court Association and United Motor Courts on the virtues of radio advertising. He reiterated his appeal in a letter to the editor of the association's *Tourist Court Journal* several months later and added a call for movie advertising in which costs to participating owners would be prorated according to their motel's size. These appeals must not have been persuasive, for neither a letter to the editor nor a *Journal* article appeared in response to Torrance's invitation. This may well have reinforced his independent streak, for although he did advertise in the *Journal* between 1937 and 1940, Torrance developed a reputation for running an independent chain.[49]

He stubbornly refused to list with the American Automobile Association (AAA), claiming that favors required by its inspectors were not worth the advantage of listing since his chain already had an established reputation. Individual managers, however, were at liberty to obtain AAA listing. Farner valued AAA certification and listing as his branch grew, but he too felt secure without the AAA's endorsements. However, there is evidence that some of Farner's managers listed their motels.[50] Neither of Alamo Plaza's primary heads was active in any of the motel trade associations that sprang up after World War II.

Design as well as chance coupled to extend territory. Certain rules of site selection remained unquestioned: location beside a major highway feeding a busy city street, close proximity to the city's central business district, and a sizeable lot to accommodate future expansion. But the possibilities of a regional chain developed slowly as profits mounted.[51] In rapid succession Torrance opened in Oklahoma City (1936), Little Rock (1938), Memphis (1939), and Jackson, Mississippi (1940). A juggernaut eastward might be inferred, but a rare combination of documents surrounding the Memphis opening disclosed the realities of Torrance's very conservative and pragmatic manner.

Torrance claimed to a reporter covering Alamo Plaza's opening in Memphis that he had wanted a location there since 1932. Yet only the year before he had argued in the premier motel trade journal that he had no intention of increasing his chain.[52] However, when an excellent lot came available, he moved rapidly. The forty-eight-unit Alamo Plaza was located at 2862 Summer Avenue, a busy interstate road. After checking with local merchants, including tourist-camp operators, about a desirable site, as he usually did, Torrance personally confirmed the particular location's virtue when he counted fifty cars with out-of-state licenses in thirty-eight minutes during one survey. To the reporter inquiring after the reasons for the new business in town, Torrance served up his usual mix of flattery and logic.

> First, Memphis is a good big town close to Little Rock, where we already have a court, and a logical place for our chain into the Southwest. I noticed lots of traffic across the Mississippi.
>   Then Memphis didn't have a large place fairly close to town. . . .
>   Memphis is a good business town. It is also one of the prettiest towns I ever saw. It has pretty trees and shrubbery. It has the most

careful drivers I ever saw. They sure obey the speed limit, too. Natu-
rally, that helps me. If people are speeding thru town they won't be as
apt to see my tourist courts. . . .

Two major highways (68 and 70) pass this location.[53]

Decisions could be rapid and personally motivated. Torrance's son-in-
law, W. Howard Lee, was taken into the partnership in order to establish
the Memphis motel, and a year later his two brothers were permitted to
start their own short-lived branch in New Orleans. Taste for the Memphis
investment soured before the building was even finished because of a
falling out with the Crump political machine, which controlled Memphis
city government, and organized labor. Not having the establishment's routinely sought approval, Torrance sold the Memphis motel, for a $20,000
profit, after only six months. The purchaser was a Nashville, Tennessee,
lumber merchant, E. L. McLallen.[54]

McLallen and his son further expanded the Alamo Plaza chain and
deleted the word *hotel* from the name after the purchase. McLallens'
"colonial"-style Alamo Plaza Courts opened in Nashville in 1941 (see
Fig. 4.8), and the 1952 addition, of no particular style according to the junior McLallen, opened outside Alamo Plaza's southern territory, in Indianapolis.[55] While the oil companies homogenized the roadside by place-
product-packaging their gas stations to achieve territorial recognition,
Alamo Plaza diversified its image. Clearly, not all roadside entrepreneurs
had learned the lessons of place-product-packaging.[56]

The McLallens' creativity quickly became evident. They were initially
more than salesmen of Torrance's proven product. Attempting to encourage initiative, the *Tourist Court Journal* raved about the end wall of a room
at Nashville's Alamo Plaza Courts cut away to display a sample room.
"Here the prospective guest, inexperienced in travel, therefore inexperienced with the comforts of motor courts, will have all fear of what this
court offers dispelled from his mind immediately."[57] The customer could
see exactly what he was renting. Instant assurance of quality was essential
for an industry still striving for the American public's approval as late as
the early 1950s.[58] Nashville's riveting "show room" was also one more case
of roadside marketing's ever more elaborate play on reality versus illusion,
here underlining a tired lodger's past and promising a wonderful future.
The weary traveler beheld the scene in which he would soon rest. A huge
sign competed for potential lodgers motoring into downtown Nashville.
The *Tourist Court Journal* praised it as an "outstanding idea."[59] Resource-
ful, if not innovative in design, the McLallens also used reflecting highway
signs to overcome wartime's restrictions on the use of electricity. The

FIGURE 4.8 A large supply of shakes available at a low cost from his brother explains McLallen's nonetheless ironic selection of a "colonial" style for the Alamo
Plaza in Nashville.

McLallens belonged not only to the Alamo Plaza referral chain but also to
the UMC. One of their boldest moves was in labor; in 1943 the wartime
manpower shortage encouraged their employment of a black woman to
manage the registration desk, a locally unpopular step.[60]

Farner and Mooney were surely the most creative mavericks. Possibly
without consulting Torrance, Farner helped initiate William P. and Mary
W. Robinson's Plaza Hotel Courts in Columbus, Georgia, opened in 1941.
No fee was collected, but except in its name this branch foreshadowed
the format franchising of a later time. William Robinson was a traveling
hosiery salesman who had become acquainted with Farner while staying in
Beaumont, and his wife was a modestly paid bank employee. They risked
$15,000 of their own money and assumed a $12,000 loan. Nearby Fort
Benning, which was mobilizing for war, was expected to provide much of
the clientele. Farner provided building plans, and familiar Alamo Plaza
features appeared at the new site. They included "very attractive" white
stucco buildings, single and double "apartments," hardwood floors, tiled
baths, and Simmons steel furniture (see Figs. 4.9 and 4.10). The Robinsons
initially built twenty-one units on a five lots measuring 250 feet wide and
100 to 160 feet deep and located five minutes from downtown. As profits
permitted, a lot was added, and four groups of units, a total of forty, were
built in installments through 1950. The Columbus motel also joined the
UMC in order to augment the draw. Torrance willingly accepted the
Columbus motel's link with his business and recognized that his chain had
spread to the East Coast.[61]

FIGURE 4.9 This 1949 view of the Columbus, Georgia, Alamo Plaza, with the sloping street-side façades in the foreground, captures something of Alamo Plaza's pretension. Note the passages between awninged units, which help distinguish Alamo Plaza from the period's generic tourist camps.

FIGURE 4.10 In Columbus, wear necessitated replacement of the original hardwood floors with a synthetic covering and retiled bathrooms by the late 1940s.

Luck played a big hand in the Alamo Plaza chain's maturation. Farner and Mooney's Gulfport motel, for example, may well have been inspired principally by a unique episode reflecting the 1940s wartime housing shortage along Mississippi's Gulf Coast. According to Farner's son Ted, the Keesler Air Base command was distraught over the lack of local temporary housing for airmen and visiting families. Hearing from one of his officers, Col. Ben Farner, Bill's brother, that he might have some influence in acquiring an area motel, the commanding officer asked Farner and Mooney to call on him, whereupon the partners were encouraged to build a motel using land and materials confiscated under war powers.[62] The partners could easily calculate the considerable profit potential around Gulfport during the waning war and afterward. The entire coastal region had been a seasonal resort destination for wealthy southerners since the early years of the nineteenth century, booming as late as the 1920s.[63] Paving the Old Spanish Trail for automobiles along Mississippi's entire Gulf Coast in the 1920s generated further tourism. By 1930 bridges spanned every inlet along the route, as the war pressed the Intercoastal Waterway nearly to completion by 1945.[64] Nightclubs, gambling parlors, restaurants, hotels, and motels honeycombed a coastal playground when Farner and Mooney opened at Gulfport in 1948.[65]

The war made Farner and Mooney overnight millionaires. They had begun in the early 1940s with two debt-free motels that earned two dollars for a single room, and their profits rose when rates inflated during the war.[66] Locations near military installations proved their saving grace.

Mooney and Farner were preparing to launch an elaborate campaign to flood the postwar market with Alamo Plazas when Mooney suffered a debilitating illness. Farner's partnership was sorely tested when Mooney independently constructed a branch in Savannah, Georgia, in 1955. Nonetheless, with Mooney's health failing badly in the early 1950s, Farner assumed sole responsibility for his and his partner's interests. Overwhelming work combined with considerable accumulated wealth to take the edge off Farner's appetite for further expansion. He refused new investors as well. Therefore, Atlanta, Georgia, in 1948 proved to be the last location that Farner developed.[67]

Recounting his career in 1953 for *American Motel Management,* the justifiably proud motel pioneer Torrance detailed his road to success: persistent supervision, room phones especially for commercial lodgers, ample parking, increasingly bigger rooms, coin-operated radios, TVs in the future perhaps, green-painted rooms, married-couple managers, roadside signs, periodic newspaper advertisements, no garages, restaurants only when absent nearby, metal furniture, local contractors only for electricity and plumbing, and strict prohibitions against the "hot pillow" trade. Here

FIGURE 4.11 Architect Art Williams, Jr.'s proposed view of the updated Alamo Plaza for Shreveport in 1965 departed substantially from the image used since the chain's start thirty-six years earlier.

was a list of strategies and tactics all presented in a fashion that implied their seemingly equal importance. Standardization, economy, a market niche, respectability, and consumer satisfaction might be considered a formula, but Torrance's loosely descriptive retrospection honestly reflects the essentially ad hoc manner in which his chain expanded. Analysis would have added the geographic elements of site selection and methods of financing.

Although his convictions about the advantages of Alamo's trademark architecture were firm, he reluctantly accepted a more contemporary adaptation designed by Art Williams Jr., a Waco architect, and first used in 1961 to remodel the nine-year-old motel in Chattanooga, Tennessee. Its two stories, blocky massing, straight lines, minimization of courtyard visible through the office driveway, and abstracted decoration obscured the original image greatly while bringing it clearly into line with 1960s commercial modernism (see Fig. 4.11). The practical demands of keeping the façade clean in Chattanooga's sooty, industrial environment made it reasonable to abandon the traditional white stucco front in favor of a façade of self-cleaning porcelain-steel and aluminum, which contributed to the more contemporary appearance. Notable was the material Lucite, which Du Pont created with the Chattanooga job in mind (see Fig. 4.12). However, in using Beautyrest mattresses, a product Torrance had used consistently since his chain's start, he was acting conservatively, advertising them for the Chattanooga site (see Fig. 4.13).[68]

FIGURE 4.12 "Colorful, durable, glossy sheets that all but clean themselves solved the problems encountered in designing a White archway at the Alamo Plaza Hotel Courts in Chattanooga," Du Pont said of Lucite in its promotional publication, *The Lucite Spectrum* 1 (April 1963): 6. (*Source:* F. Randolph Helms.)

FIGURE 4.13 Torrance did not tinker with features once he was satisfied, as illustrated in this typical early 1950s Alamo Plaza room furnished with his favorite Simmons "152" group furniture in green and gray.

FIGURE 4.14 The renowned St. Francis Hotel, in San Francisco, California, conferred dignity by association on its namesake motel chain in Alabama.

American Motel Magazine's 1953 article respectfully and accurately classified Torrance as a conservative. The reference was to his frugal business practice. Torrance, the article said, stood in "direct contrast to the tendency today of offering the motel guests extra inducements in the form of free newspapers, free coffee, and what have you." Also an inveterate trader who enjoyed the challenge of profitable deals, Torrance, for example, bought and sold the Memphis motel twice between 1953 and 1961.[69] Torrance no longer pushed the market; he responded to it.

Alamo Plaza's congeries of branches no longer set the pace in the motel trade by the 1950s and 1960s. Prominent were loyal managers of long association who made their motels profitable, namely, Torrance's husband-and-wife teams, the Chastains (1936–77), who finished at Charlotte, North Carolina, and the Johnsons (1947–77), who finished at Shreveport, and Farner's son Ted, who was employed throughout his lifetime as a short-term troubleshooter at several motels.[70]

The St. Francis branch illustrates the subtle shift in emphasis from entrepreneurial creativity to managerial competence. Founded by Torrance's nephew W. G. "Mac" McGrady, who had learned motel management at Shreveport and Jackson, and his partners, St. Francis Hotel Courts, later Motor Courts, the St. Francis branch lay claim after World War II to Alabama: Montgomery in 1946, Mobile in 1951, and Birmingham in 1953. Using the original Alamo Plaza architecture, this branch took its name from the prestigious St. Francis Hotel in San Francisco (see Fig. 4.14).

FIGURE 4.15 The original St. Francis motel, in Mobile, copied the original Alamo Plaza look. The American Automobile Association's logo in the upper corners of this postcard denote an affiliation unlike that of the chain's founders.

FIGURE 4.16 The Mobile St. Francis's façade was remodeled in 1968 to give it a more contemporary look.

However, when McGrady and his partners added the Vulcan Motel in Birmingham, "The Waldorf-Astoria of Tourist Courts," as the *Tourist Court Journal* crowned it in 1951, for reasons of economy and existing recognition they did not remodel it in the original Alamo Plaza fashion. When the Mobile motel's façade was remodeled in 1968, this further distinguished it from the remainder of the chain (see Figs. 4.15 and 4.16). McGrady was also the only Alamo Plaza owner to become an officer in a national referral or trade association, thus breaking with the chain's independent tradition by his two terms on the American Motor Hotel Association board beginning in 1959. However, McGrady did follow most of Torrance's management practices, such as insinuating a role in the local business community. Thus, he deserved the sobriquet "Mr. Alabama Travel," which was used to describe him upon his 1977 retirement for promoting the state's post–world war tourism.[71]

The late 1950s witnessed a final burst of entrepreneurial initiative. In 1959, with Mooney's death after a long incapacitation, Farner briefly flirted with expanding Alamo Plaza through franchising. Torrance's declining health, plus his satisfaction with "things as they were," had led him to reject Farner's invitation to participate. Farner offered two franchise plans. One called for motels to change their signs, taking only the Alamo Plaza name, in return for a one-time $25 fee per room (with a $1,000 minimum) and a monthly fee of 5¢ per room per night. The other called for motel owners to use Alamo Plaza's name along with their own in return for a one-time $200 fee and a yearly $250 fee. Farner hired a former regional insurance manager, Vernon W. Phillips, who contacted many motel owners and finally dogged Torrance into listing his own (minus the fee) in a directory that included forty motels. Only a single motel choosing the first franchise plan entered the chain new; the other twenty-two that chose the first plan already belonged to the chain.

Some bulk buying and customer credit cards were under consideration when Farner feared running afoul of different state legal requirements should his empire mushroom. He dropped the franchise scheme within a year. So ephemeral was any benefit to the franchisees that a recent check of Alamo Plaza motels revealed only one that remembered its franchise (see Fig. 4.17).[72] Whereas Kemmons Wilson briefly called his enterprise "hotel courts" at the outset, perhaps borrowing from his Alamo Plaza competitor several blocks down Summer Avenue, it was Bill Farner who copied Wilson's "great sign" in the franchising gambit six years later (see Fig. 4.18).[73] It was the sign, perhaps, as well as Wilson's franchising strategy, that finally excited Farner about his own opportunities in place-product-packaging.

Branches were sold off beginning in the 1970s, first by Mooney's heirs, then by Torrance's, and gradually by Farner's; almost all of Farner's

FIGURE 4.17 One Alamo Plaza franchisee was the preexisting Ambassador Motel in Cave City, Kentucky. Emphasizing its appended miniature golf course and
swimming pool, this L-plan motel with units visible directly from the highway
was linked to Alamo Plaza by a brief business agreement only.

FIGURE 4.18 Bill Farner's franchising scheme included a new
Alamo Plaza sign. Although
Farner claimed to have received
permission for patterning it after
Kemmons Wilson's Great Sign,
the symbol of the rapidly expanding Holiday Inn chain, Wilson denied having granted Farner permission to adapt it.

FIGURE 4.19 The Alamo Plaza in Baton Rouge, Louisiana, is still good commercial real estate, as shown in 1993.

branches had been sold by the time he died. The Baton Rouge and Gulfport Alamo Plazas (see Fig. 4.19) still prosper because of enforced respectability, refurnishing, and the brisk traffic flowing past their front
door. Development took others, the one in Mobile succumbing to a shopping mall and the one in New Orleans to an interstate highway. Still others
fell on hard times. The derelict Chattanooga Plaza, situated in an aging industrial area, was branded a "disgrace to our town" in 1988.[74] Charlotte's
declining inner city led to the closing of Alamo Plaza's successor, a motel
of disrepute, by public order in 1991.[75] An immigrant Asian American
family that owns several Alamo Plazas follows the familiar American pattern of trying to achieve success through sweat equity.[76] Estimates of motels owned by Asian Americans range from 7,000 to 12,000.[77] The experience of Alamo Plazas exemplifies the life cycle of many motels.

Creative entrepreneurs turned energetic overseers, family members
who became effective owners and temporary managers, and friends who
became loyal, long-term managers combined to make Alamo Plaza the
largest motel chain in the precorporate era. The chain aimed for an elite
clientele from the first, all the while charging rates for the average man. A
good location and strenuous management led to profits. Ambition grew as
success mounted, until the vision dawned of a regional chain. By then,
however, the founders had either earned enough to satisfy themselves or
died prematurely. A lifetime's substantial earnings, and not continuous

innovation, had been their motive. Alamo Plaza remained merely the largest nonreferral chain of the closing mom-and-pop era. Its owners' post–world war energies led them to either diverge considerably from the Alamo Plaza association, as in Alabama, or momentarily expand without actually converting the chain permanently into a franchising scheme. At the very time when enormous prosperity and extensive mobility were sparking a new generation of entrepreneurs to build motel chains, Alamo Plaza's elders complacently fell behind simply by maintaining their profitable status quo.

What Alamo Plaza might have been is pointless to investigate. Alamo Plaza did not fail; it was an anomaly. With its twenty-two associated motels, it was a giant in its heyday, but it would not be regarded as a big corporation by today's standards. In the mom-and-pop era it shared all the traits of the dominant business mode except one: size. At the outset of the corporate era it had one characteristic that anticipated the coming giants—size. Even more staunchly independent than many mom-and-pop owners, Alamo Plaza's owners seldom made referral agreements except between their branches and never considered taking many corporate partners. The conditions of competition changed more than the Alamo Plaza owners' motives did. Not only is it unfair to judge their enterprise by standards they never set but it diminishes our capacity for historical appreciation. Alamo Plaza had no mission. It was a means for obtaining a satisfying income. It demonstrates clearly that few remain creative entrepreneurs for long. Equally important is the drama of individuals acting in pursuit of their varied interests within the context of the opportunities as well as the limitations of their time and their place. Alamo Plaza's owners practiced the risk taking and savvy trading as well as the persistence and occasional innovation that produce most good motels.

5

The Rise of Place-Product-Packaging

A FEW SMALL MOTEL CHAINS APPEARED IN THE 1930S, THE ALAMO PLAZA Hotel Courts being one of the most important. Yet the chain phenomenon came late and haltingly to the motel business, in which independent mom-and-pop operations predominated well after World War II. Only in the hotel business were chains well established, but even there the vast majority of hostelries remained outside ownership or referral networks. Unlike the petroleum industry, which early on had embraced what has come to be called "place-product-packaging," the lodging industry did not. The major oil companies established chains of look-alike gasoline stations that competed for a share of the market.[1] Place-product-packaging involved the adoption of readily identifiable logos, color schemes, building designs, and service and product mixes so that each unit in a retail system would reinforce the others, making the whole greater than the sum of its parts. Large corporations financed and largely managed the nation's gasoline stations. Motels, on the other hand, were financed and managed by local entrepreneurs.

How did place-product-packaging eventually win out in the motel industry? How did large corporations come to dominate? In this chapter we outline the motel industry's maturation, starting with the hotel chains, the motel trade associations of the 1930s, and the referral chains of cooperating motels that came to the fore in the late 1940s and early 1950s. In the next chapter we focus on the franchise chains (some of which evolved from referral groups), which have dominated since the 1960s. We organize our discussion principally around today's leading corporations and their highly visible brands. Vignettes describe the evolution of brand names, focusing on geographical distribution over time. How did specific motel brands originate? Why have some brands succeeded and others failed?

Since the Civil War, Americans have become increasingly conscious of brands. Today most consumers prefer branded goods to their generic counterparts. Advertised brands carry implications of high quality and dependability; goods and services without such endorsement are suspected of lacking integrity. At first, everyday consumer goods—soap, crackers, coffee, tea, tobacco—were branded as corporations reached out to penetrate larger and larger trade territories, the distinctive packaging ultimately dominating the shelves of retail stores. As product lines became increasingly standardized through mechanization in manufacturing, industry codes, and governmental regulations, little remained to differentiate products save branding and its associated advertising. Gasoline, for example, was a generic product despite color dyes and other additives intended to make a given company's product appear otherwise. Only through advertising did customers become convinced of brand distinction.

Large consumer items (e.g., pianos or furniture) and implements of work (sewing machines, farm implements) were branded as well. To the national lexicon of Ivory Soap, Uneeda Biscuit, Salada Tea, United Cigars, and Standard Oil were added the likes of Baldwin Pianos and Singer Sewing Machines. Some companies (and the industries that they dominated) went a step beyond mere branding to embrace product franchising. Singer, Standard Oil, and, later, Ford and General Motors, among other automobile makers, marketed their products through licensed retailers, each required to limit selling to the single company's brands.[2] Franchisees agreed to create a business location, stock the company's product, and sell according to the anticipated carrying capacity of a local market. In addition, agents handled the servicing of the product and, in the case of early automobiles, were responsible for aspects of final assembly. Retail stores, although locally owned, carried the corporate logo. Through franchising, regional, national, and even international sales networks could be quickly established by tapping local investment capital. Companies were relieved of financing operations at the local level. Retailers, on the other hand, could enjoy the benefits of national brand visibility and enter business higher up on the "learning curve" by following already proven selling procedures.

Some companies actually owned chains of retail outlets. The Atlantic and Pacific Tea Company became synonymous with grocery retailing early in the twentieth century. Woolworth, Kresge, and Kress became synonymous with the new "five-and-dime" stores. These companies did not pioneer new products so much as they pioneered mass selling, passing on lower prices through economies of scale wrought through more efficient distribution. Central, however, was the creation of brand loyalty through advertising—if not loyalty to a single product, then loyalty to a wide array of associated products marketed as a line of merchandise. It should not be surprising, therefore, that branding, chain development, and franchising ultimately affected even the nation's service industries, including the lodging industry.

HOTEL CHAINS

The hotel chain, established through ownership, lease, or management contract, was already quite common in the early decades of the twentieth century. But such chains only weakly linked individual hotels, each of which usually retained its own clear identity. If there were rationales other than entrepreneurial ego (the "collecting" of hotel properties as business "trophies"), they were the advantages of centralized purchasing and management systems administered from atop a corporate hierarchy. Few guests realized that they were hosted by a corporation or that their hotel was part of a network, for none of the advantages of overall brand identity applied. Each hotel was marketed as a distinctive place.

Among the more prominent hotel chains of the 1920s in the United States were the Boomer-DuPont Properties (the Waldorf-Astoria in New York City, the Bellevue-Stratford in Philadelphia, and the Willard in Washington, D.C.) and the Bowman Hotels (the Biltmore, Ansonia, Belmont, Commodore, and the Murray Hill Hotels in New York City and the Biltmore Hotels of Atlanta, Los Angeles, and Providence). In the latter instance, the name Biltmore did play out in a number of cities, but the name was used by hotels outside the chain in other cities. Frank Dudley's United Hotels Company of America was one of the largest and most vigorous chains. In 1928 the company operated eighteen hotels in the United States, including the Roosevelt in New York City and the Benjamin Franklin in Philadelphia. The elegant St. Francis Hotel in San Francisco was affiliated. Most of the United Hotels were located in the Northeast and Middle West.

Hotel empires were put together by aggressive capitalists expert not only in hosting the traveling public but also in finance. Prime among the early entrepreneurs was Eugene C. Eppley. Starting as a steward in the McKinley Hotel at Canton, Ohio, Eppley worked his way up in hotel management, first in Franklin, Pennsylvania, and then in Minneapolis.[3] By 1923 his own Eppley Hotel Company was operating nine hotels in Nebraska, South Dakota, and Iowa, the Hotel Fontenelle in Omaha being the flagship operation. By 1928 the firm's properties in the Middle West numbered fifteen, and it owned other hotels in Los Angeles and Pittsburgh, including the latter city's prestigious Hotel William Penn. In 1931 Eppley purchased the Seelbach Hotel in Louisville. Eppley was president of both

FIGURE 5.1 Postcard advertisement for the J. B. Pound Hotels, circa 1925. Entre-preneurs collected hotel properties, forming them into loosely structured chains that protected the individuality of individual units.

the Ohio and the Northwestern Hotel Association and was very active on the council of the American Hotel Association.

Most hotel chains were regional in scope, even those like the United and Eppley chains, which had pretenses to national connections. The J. B. Pound Hotels operated in Jacksonville, Savannah, and Chattanooga in the 1920s, and its postcard advertising carried the images of all three hotels (see Fig. 5.1). Theodore DeWitt's Dewitt Operated Hotels were located in Cleveland, Columbus, and Toledo. W. F. Miller's Miller Hotel Company operated in Des Moines and Davenport. Carling Dinkler's Dinkler Hotels Company operated in the 1920s in Atlanta, Birmingham, and Mont-gomery, Jacksonville, and Nashville. T. A. Baker's Baker Hotels were lo-cated primarily in Texas cities, including Austin, Dallas, Fort Worth, and San Antonio. Only one hotel in each of these chains carried the name of the corporate founder (and hence the name of the parent corporation).

The Statler, Albert Pick, Hilton, and Sheraton chains were the first to promote a strong corporate identity, overriding somewhat the personali-ties of its individual hotels. These corporate names would eventually be used in the branding of motel properties as well. It is, therefore, to the ho-tel chains that we necessarily look for the beginnings of and the rationales for place-product-packaging for motels.

Ellsworth M. Statler, a Buffalo restaurateur, entered the hotel business with a temporary hotel of wood and plaster built for the 1901 Pan-American Exposition. Containing more than 2,000 rooms, it was one of the marvels of the fair. Three years later Statler operated a similar facility at the St. Louis Louisiana Purchase Exposition. Profits earned from these temporary ventures were invested in a permanent Statler Hotel in Buffalo, New York, a commercial hotel intended to provide businessmen with luxuries previously reserved for the elite, such as telephones, running ice water, and morning newspapers shoved under guests' doors. "Room with bath for a dollar and a half" was the hotel's motto.[4] Statler Hotels opened in Cleveland and Detroit, booming industrial cities closely connected to Buffalo by steamship and railroad, in 1912 and 1915, respectively. The St. Louis Statler followed in 1917, the large, 2,200-room Hotel Pennsylvania in New York City in 1919, and a new Buffalo Statler in 1923 (see Fig. 5.2).

Ellsworth Statler seemed to have created something new. Henry J. Bohn wrote in *Hotel World* that "any man who has seen the Statler Hotels of Buffalo, Cleveland and Detroit . . . will recognize a Statler Hotel as far as he can see one, and entering it he knows instantly that he is in one of the Statler public places. This means that Statler has created a type. Statler is

FIGURE 5.2 The Hotel Statler, Buffalo, New York, circa 1930. Ellsworth Statler's hotels took on a certain "look" that reinforced name recognition. The chain, rather than its individual units, was the focus of promotions.

the father of hotel standardization in America."[5] The Boston Statler followed in 1927, and after Statler's death in 1928 additional hotels were opened in Pittsburgh, Washington, Los Angeles, Hartford, and Dallas. With the exception of the New York City hotel across from Pennsylvania Station, every hotel in the Statler chain was called "the Statler." Here was instant name recognition. And to the extent that Statler Hotels were similarly appointed, a degree of place-product-packaging was brought to the hotel industry for the first time. In 1954 Conrad Hilton bought the Statler chain, preserving its identity for only a few years.

The Albert Pick Hotels

The Albert Pick Company, named for its founder, was primarily a hotel-supply company. Headquartered in Chicago, the company manufactured furniture and fixtures at plants in New York City and Cincinnati. From the company's catalogs the architect, interior decorator, or hotel manager could order virtually anything related to hotel operation, from china and silverware to carpets and draperies. The company offered design services, specializing in kitchen and other hotel logistical areas.[6] With such expertise at hand, it was perhaps inevitable that the company would create its own chain of hotels, although to move too aggressively in this area was to compete directly with the very hotel entrepreneurs that constituted the firm's principal customer base. Experience running hotels, it was argued, enabled the company to test equipment and architectural programs. By 1937 there were sixteen Albert Pick Hotels in Illinois, Michigan, Indiana, Ohio, Kentucky, Tennessee, Missouri, and Texas. In 1947 there were twenty-three, with new additions located in Kansas, Louisiana, Pennsylvania, and New York. Only the Hotel Pick–Ohio carried the name of the corporation.

In 1955 the company entered the motel field, operating four Holiday Inns under franchise and several additional motor inns under the Albert Pick name. The process of selling off older, central-city hotels had begun. In 1964 the firm began to franchise the Albert Pick name in an attempt to build a nationwide motel chain modeled on the Holiday Inn chain.[7] After purchase by Bass Brothers Enterprises in 1976, the company's motel operations were conducted primarily under the franchised brand names of other chains, including Hilton and Ramada Inn. The purchase of American Airlines's majority interest in Americana Hotels in 1979 resulted in the formation of the Pick Americana Company and a reorientation favoring airport locations. The faltering Albert Pick brand, one of the few names to make the transition from hotels to motels, was retired.

The Hilton Hotels

Conrad Hilton bought his first hotel, the Mobley, in Cisco, Texas, in 1919. Within ten years he had built a Texas chain of seven properties. Hit hard by the Depression, Hilton did not resume his expansion until after World War II, when he purchased the Town House and Rosslyn Hotels in Los Angeles. Hilton perfected management systems (time and motion study, safety innovation, budgetary control, and pricing programs), which enabled him to optimize operating efficiency. For example, a forecasting committee estimated daily, weekly, and monthly demands for each hotel in his chain, and employees were then scheduled according to the volume of business expected. Although management was highly centralized (especially fiscal planning, purchasing, and reservation services), the company worked hard to develop a distinctive personality for each of its hotels. Managers were encouraged to use every square foot of space for revenue production, fitting hotels with restaurants and shops tailored to local markets. Purchase of the Palmer House and the giant Stevens Hotel, then the world's largest hotel, in Chicago and the Waldorf-Astoria Hotel in New York City made Conrad Hilton America's premier hotelier after World War II.[8]

Conrad Hilton leased and bought hotels, in the latter instance through syndicates that he set up as tax havens both for himself and for his investors.[9] In 1946 he consolidated his various properties and leaseholds into the Hilton Hotels Corporation, which as it grew leased more hotels than it owned. Hilton operated forty-one properties comprising 31,313 guest rooms in 1961. A subsidiary, Hilton Hotels International, operated seven properties in Puerto Rico, the Virgin Islands, and Canada. Hilton purchased the Statler chain through a Delaware subsidiary, and the takeover involved a host of banks and insurance companies, including the Equitable Life Assurance Society and the First National Bank of Boston. The Delaware subsidiary represented a base for depreciating fixed assets, both buildings and equipment. Business analyst Donald Lundberg wrote: "By adopting a plan of complete liquidation of the old company and distribution of the assets to the stockholders, a capital gains tax was avoided. By using the new corporation, the benefits of the sale-and-lease-back plan were also exploited."[10]

In 1976 Hilton Hotels operated nineteen owned or leased hotels and managed another twenty-six owned by others. It had sold a 50 percent interest in six of its largest downtown hotels to the Prudential Insurance Company, retaining a management contract.[11] Hilton focused its new construction near downtown convention centers and in the suburbs of growing cities. Typical was the North Shore Hilton in the Skokie suburb

FIGURE 5.3 The North Shore Hilton, Skokie, Illinois, circa 1965. The postcard reads: "Convenient to expressways, golf, horseback riding, year 'round ice skating and major shopping in Old Orchard Shopping Center."

of Chicago, a highway hotel located near the Old Orchard Shopping Center (see Fig. 5.3). The chain derived about 35 percent of its revenues in the 1970s from convention and group business.[12] Like Statler, Hilton targeted the businessman with a standard product. A 1963 article in *Time* summarized the Hilton formula as follows: "Hiltons are assembly-line hostelries with carefully metered luxuries—convenience, automatic, a bit antiseptic. Conrad Hilton's life is rooted in the belief that people are pretty much equal, and that their taste and desires are, too. His hotels have made the world safe for the middle-class travelers. . . . At a Hilton all they need is a reservation and money."[13] All of the company's hotels save the Waldorf-Astoria and the Plaza in New York City and the Palmer House in Chicago carried the name Hilton or Statler. Here was a mature case of place-product-packaging.

A chain of resortlike Hilton Inns was begun in the 1950s, the first in Long Beach, California. At the same time, the company began to franchise a chain of highway hotels, initially under the Statler Hilton name and later under the Hilton Inns logo. The chain enjoyed only modest success: in 1967 there were only 11 franchise operations along with 35 properties owned outright by the company.[14] In 1967 the firm's overseas subsidiary was sold to Trans World Airlines. In subsequent ownership changes, Hilton International was owned by Allegis (the parent of United Airlines), Ladbrook (the British hotel chain), Westin Hotels, Robert Bass, and the

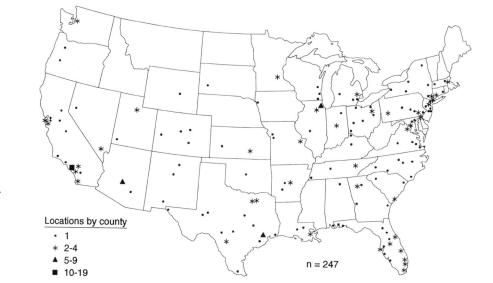

Locations by county
- · 1
- * 2-4
- ▲ 5-9
- ■ 10-19

n = 247

FIGURE 5.4 Hilton Hotels, 1993. The counties with the most properties were Los Angeles in California, with 11; Harris (Houston) in Texas, with 8; and Cook (Chicago) in Illinois and Maricopa (Phoenix) in Arizona, with 7 each. The chain was headquartered in Beverly Hills, California.

Aoki Corporation of Japan. In 1990 there were 45 Hilton Hotels, 210 Hilton Inns, 3 Hilton Suites, and 2 CrestHil Inns (a "clubcourt" motel brand) in the Hilton system renting a total of 92,513 guest rooms.[15] The cities of the original Statler and Hilton hotel chains were still represented, although the chain had come to emphasize smaller cities, especially in California and Florida (see Fig. 5.4). Hilton, a hotel chain that embraced the motel, also remained very much hotel-like in its services and in the configuration of its properties.

The Sheraton Hotels

Sheraton, another successful hotel chain, also turned to the motel format. The Stonehaven, in Springfield, Massachusetts, was the first acquisition of what would become the Sheraton Corporation. Two years later, in 1939, three additional hotels were purchased in the city of Boston, prime among them the Sheraton Hotel. With its large rooftop sign too costly to remove, this hotel gave its name to the entire chain. Ernest Henderson, a Boston investment banker, was the entrepreneurial force behind the firm, named the Sheraton Corporation in 1947. Sheraton was run more like a real estate operation; indeed, Henderson's forte was the use of leverage money. In expanding his chain he expanded his equity ownership, showing only modest profits for tax purposes from year to year. As Donald Lundberg wrote, "There is a time to buy a hotel and a time to sell it, the timing dependent upon the tax base which is left for depreciation in a property, general business conditions, and whether or not the cash might not be put to better use in another property. Henderson put into practice a theory of minimaxing—minimizing costs and maximizing return on one's investment."[16]

Until 1975, when the Philadelphia Sheraton was built, the firm grew through acquisition both of individual hotels and of whole hotel chains. Thus were added the Park Central in New York City (renamed the Park-Sheraton) and the Book-Cadillac in Detroit (renamed the Sheraton-Cadillac) (see Fig. 2.5). In the mid-1950s, Sheraton bought the Eppley Hotel chain, mainly to gain control of the William Penn in Pittsburgh. A competition had begun between Sheraton and Hilton. Indeed, the two big hotel chains were competing in all but three of the fifteen largest U.S. cities by 1960. Henderson's primary interest was the conservation and increase of his capital. His method for building capital was to trade up to better hotels, plowing back earnings in the process. But Henderson was also a savvy hotel host. He provided free parking at all Sheraton Hotels, including those in constricted downtown locations. Indeed, many of the firm's older hotels were promoted as "motor hotels" once they were given motor entrances and adjacent garages (see Fig. 5.5).

Sheraton entered the motel field in 1955 with large highway hotels of one hundred to three hundred rooms. A franchise division was formed in 1962 to promote the new Sheraton Motor Inns. A process of selling off older properties, including all of the chain's downtown hotels in the smaller cities, began. Gone were the Sheraton-Belvedere in Baltimore, the Sheraton-Lincoln in Indianapolis, and the Sheraton-Fontenelle in Omaha. Pruned down and reoriented to the motel market, the company was sold to the International Telephone and Telegraph Corporation (ITT) in 1968, becoming a subsidiary of that firm. ITT already owned six Sheraton franchises through another subsidiary, the Airport Parking Company of America. In the ensuing two years, with an infusion of ITT capital, some 160 new hotels and motor inns were opened in fourteen countries, including 92 franchised properties.[17] Unlike Hilton, Sheraton sustained its international operation.

In 1979 the Sheraton brand was attached to 240 properties in the United States, the highest density being in the Northeast and Florida. Nearly every large urban center was represented (see Fig. 5.6). Sheraton offered no standardized architectural designs. Indeed, in the tradition of the hotel, the firm sought to exploit the characteristics of particular locations. In a 1971

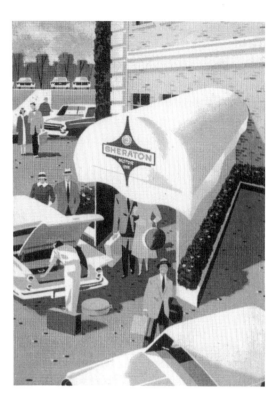

FIGURE 5.5 Postcard advertisement for the Sheraton Motor Inn, Buffalo, New York, circa 1955. The postcard reads: "Located on tree shaded Delaware Avenue convenient to the New York State Thruway."

Locations by county
- • 1
- ✳ 2-4
- ▲ 5-9

n = 332

FIGURE 5.6 Sheraton Hotels and Inns, 1979. The leading counties were Cook (Chicago) in Illinois, with 6 properties; and Allegheny (Pittsburgh) in Pennsylvania, Cuyahoga (Cleveland) in Ohio, and New York County (Manhattan) in New York, with 5 each. The chain was headquartered in Boston.

interview, Irving Zeldman, president of ITT Sheraton, speculated about Sheraton's future: "I think we're going to see more of what I call the 'deluxe' or 'in-between' inn. It's a 200 roomer with meeting rooms, perhaps an indoor pool and, as a matter of fact, many of the facilities of a conventional hotel, but on a smaller scale."[18] The firm was continuing to divest itself of old hotels, even its flagship giants, given the "astronomical investments" that would be required to refurbish them. Like Hilton, Sheraton was emphasizing airport as well as peripheral suburban locations in the nation's cities. However, it was less committed to the new convention centers. ITT Sheraton, like Albert Pick, operated supply subsidiaries that sold not only its own hotels but to other hotel and motel firms as well.

In the late 1970s ITT Sheraton sold off more than 80 of its aging properties, making the average age of motor inns only eight years. The firm operated in 41 countries at 403 locations with a total of 99,230 rooms.[19] It categorized 216 of its operations as highway inns, 47 as airport inns, and 114 as resorts. The franchise division added another 320 properties worldwide, and Sheraton's total sales topped $1.2 billion in 1978. In 1990 the company's brand was attached to 321 facilities in the United States, including 136 hotels, 31 resorts, 153 inns, and 1 suite hotel.[20] The company had "defranchised" some 250 hotels and inns over the previous four years. Known abroad for luxury accommodations, Sheraton had become déclassé back home, the result of an inability to fully control renovation and upgrading among franchisees. In 1993 the chain was reduced further to 152 properties, with the largest concentration in the Northeast (see Fig. 5.7).

MOTEL ASSOCIATIONS

The Depression of the 1930s placed the hotel industry in jeopardy. Substantially overbuilt, especially in the large cities, and facing a much reduced market for hotel services, some two-thirds of the nation's hotels went into receivership. The Roosevelt administration, faced with reversing the nation's economic fortunes, turned to regulating production and prices through the National Recovery Act. The National Recovery Administration strengthened the role of nationwide trade organizations and prompted the formation of such organizations where none had previously existed. Whereas the hotel industry was well represented by the American Hotel Association (AHA), the motel industry had no comparable institutional structure. The need was made acute when the AHA sought to bring tourist homes and tourist courts under its purview expressly to control what hotel owners and managers defined as unfair competition. In 1933, therefore, the National Tourist Lodge and Motor Court Trade Association

(NTL-MCTA) was organized, with J. C. Stevens, operator of a cottage court in Jacksonville, Florida, as its president.[21]

The NTL-MCTA changed its name to the International Motor Court Association (IMCA) in 1937 at a meeting in Monterrey, Mexico, the thinking being that the association would ultimately serve motel owners across North America. At the same time, the *Tourist Court Journal,* launched by Robert Gresham at Temple, Texas, was designated as the organization's official publication. The purposes of the association were to (1) gather and disseminate information of value to its membership, (2) protect members against unfair trade practices, (3) publish guides to member establishments, and (4) promote state and regional associations. Individual motel owners were accepted for membership in the IMCA through their local organizations. Although the NRA had been declared unconstitutional by the Supreme Court and the threat of the AHA had been removed, still the seed of a mutual, cooperative benefit association had been sown.[22] A. C. Hanson, of the Travelers Motor Court of Santa Barbara, California, served in a voluntary capacity as the IMCA's first president.

Ideally, trade associations were nonprofit, voluntary groups of business competitors organized to assist each other with mutual business problems.[23] They were also intended to operate as lobby groups to set or influence legislative agendas. The driving purpose of most associations was the collection and desemination of information. Associations sponsored

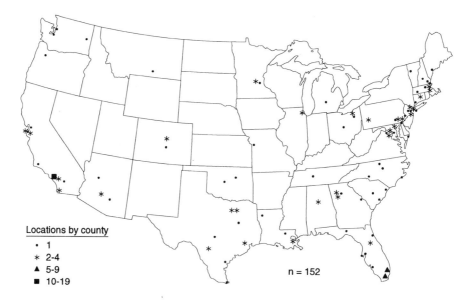

FIGURE 5.7 Sheraton Hotels, 1993. The leading counties were Los Angeles in California, with 11 properties; and Broward (Fort Lauderdale) and Dade (Miami) in Florida, with 5 each. ITT Sheraton was headquartered in Boston.

meetings, published trade journals, and generally promoted group interests. In 1941 the IMCA became the American Tourist Court Association. Rent control and gasoline rationing associated with World War II were major concerns at its annual meeting that year. In 1944 the name American Motor Hotel Association was adopted. Among its other services, the AMHA published an annual directory listing its members. In 1946 an affiliated group was organized as the American Roadside Service Association to include the owners and operators of gasoline stations, drive-in restaurants, souvenir and curio shops, and drive-in theaters, among other roadside businesses.

Other motel trade associations were organized, but most enjoyed only short lives. The American Motel Association was organized in 1936 to operate less as a volunteer association than as a business offering subscribers the services of a trade association. In 1949 its "approved" motels were concentrated along the tourist routes between New York City and Florida (see Fig. 5.8). Its annual *Motor Guide* listed both tourist homes and tourist courts. Regional trade associations also organized, some oriented to single highways. For example, the Main Streets of America Courts Association promoted the motels on U.S. 66 between Chicago and Los Angeles.

In 1962 the American Hotel Association became the American Hotel and Motel Association (AHMA), effectively putting an end to the national motel organizations, which had proven as weak as they had been ephem-

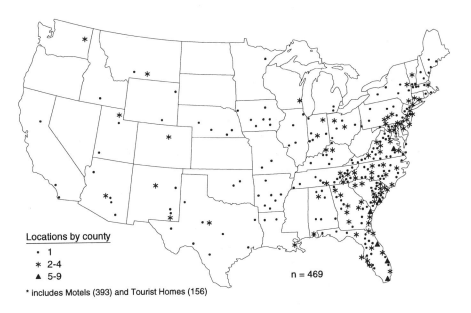

Locations by county
- • 1
- ✳ 2-4
- ▲ 5-9

n = 469

* includes Motels (393) and Tourist Homes (156)

FIGURE 5.8 American Motel Association approved members, 1949. The AMA was headquartered in Newark, New Jersey.

eral. In 1985 the AHMA was a federation of some 70 lodging associations in the United States and 33 foreign countries. Its membership consisted of managers representing more than 8,900 lodging facilities around the world. For the United States, members represented some 53 percent of the existing guest rooms, rooms that generated some 82 percent of total room revenue for the lodging industry.[24] Originally formed in 1910 to serve only hotel interests, the AHMA now represented the entire lodging industry.

MOTEL RECOMMENDATION SERVICES

The directories published by motel associations, while useful to tourists, did not—indeed, could not—rate or otherwise recommend one motel over another. The American Automobile Association developed a nationwide rating system and published its hotel and, later, its motel recommendations in annual directories for each region of the country. Founded in 1902, by 1960 the AAA comprised more than seven clubs and branches in both the United States and Canada.[25] Personal services rendered to member-subscribers included emergency car service, license and title service, personal accident and car insurance, travel information, and ticket booking. Hotels and motels recommended by the AAA were periodically inspected and rated for quality. Criteria of assessment included size, nature of facilities, services provided, management policies, level of maintenance, and fire-safety provisions. This AAA service existed (and continues to exist) not so much for hotel and motel operators as for the motoring public. Travelers are able to form expectations. Hotels and motels approved by the AAA, however, enjoy important validation as having succeeded in meeting customers' standards.

Another important recommendation service was initiated in 1929 by Emmons Walker, of Dover, Massachusetts, whose guidebooks rating hotels and motels were published annually for some forty years. The lodgings listed were located primarily along the Atlantic seaboard, from Quebec to Florida. In 1960 Emmons Walker, Inc., promoted itself as "the oldest referral group for America's Independent Motels."[26] The firm introduced the Best Eastern brand, with its logo, the Little Sleepyhead, an outline of a child in a nightcap carrying a candle. What began as a recommendation service turned into a referral chain before it faded in the face of better-financed and more aggressive operations.

Dozens of other recommendation companies were spawned, most to fade after a season or two. An emulator of Emmons Walker was Ray A. Walker, of Haverhill, Massachusetts, who published *Cabin Trails: A Dependable All Year Service for Discriminating Motor-Vacationists* (see Fig. 5.9). The Travelers, "A Division of the System," located in New York

City, published an "official directory," *Approved Travelers Motor Courts.* The 1938 guide listed 178 motels concentrated largely in the Northeast, especially in northern New England, but spread as far afield as California and Florida. The idea was to provide auto travelers motel guides (for a fee) and also to direct them to motels, restaurants, and tourist attractions from downtown and roadside information offices. In 1938 such offices were open in New York City, Miami, St. Petersburg, and Los Angeles as well as in suburban Los Angeles and suburban Washington, D.C. The company also maintained a kiosk at the Georgia-Florida state line, north of Jacksonville on U.S. 17. Curtailment of highway travel during World War II put an end to "the System."

The *Approved Federal Hi-Way Guide to America's Better Motor Courts and Tourist Homes* was first published in Minneapolis. It credited itself with consolidating four predecessor guides, the oldest dating back to 1926.

FIGURE 5.9 Cover of the 1939 *Cabin Trails* directory.

The 1950 guide listed nearly 1,000 lodgings, including 440 motels. Beginning in 1944 the American Travel Association published motel directories that not only approved individual motels but rated them on a five-point scale. Abridged editions were distributed free, but enlarged, "deluxe" versions were sold. In the 1950s, Duncan Hines moved from simply recommending restaurants to recommending hotels and motels as well. In recent decades, travel guides published by the Mobil Corporation (with their one- to five-star hotel, motel, and restaurant ratings) provide a similar service. Such recommendation systems operate independently of motel operators to benefit travelers as consumers.

A form of indirect recommendation came through the advertising of national manufacturers. Motels took discounts in the purchase of mattresses, television sets, air conditioners, and even soaps and other supplies when they allowed manufacturers to place their logos on motel signage. The emblems themselves were usually rented. National brands served to assure travelers of motel quality through association. For example, in the 1950s the Simmons Company maintained an extensive signage program for its Beautyrest brand. The program involved placing brand emblems on motel entrance signs and on small roadside billboards. Full-page color ads in such magazines as *Life* and the *Saturday Evening Post* alerted the consuming public to the program. Procter and Gamble similarly promoted "This is an Ivory Motel" signs; Motorola placed signs that read, "Just Like Home. Motorola TV in Your Room"; and the International Swimming Pool Corporation's offering read, "Come In And Enjoy Our Esther Williams Swimming Pool."

OWNERSHIP MOTEL CHAINS

True place-product-packaging first emerged in the motel industry with small ownerships chains. These were chains owned by a single person or corporate entity in which all the units had the same name, the same architecture, and the same interior room decor and offered the same range of services. Although its history is developed fully in chapter 4, Alamo Plaza Hotel Courts deserves mention here since it was the largest and perhaps the most visible of the early ownership chains. Begun in Waco, Texas, in 1929 by E. Lee Torrance and D. W. Bartlett, the chain grew to four units in 1938, all designed in pseudo-mission style with strong Spanish associations achieved through ornamentation. By 1959 the chain numbered twenty-three units (see Fig. 5.10). Here was a clear symbol by the American roadside, sign, building, and services all representing a distinctive corporate entity in the promotion of convenience, comfort, and quality in overnight accommodation.

Perhaps the oldest motel chain is Treadway Inns. Originated in 1912 by L. G. Treadway, the chain initially managed former New England coaching inns remodeled and reoriented to the automobile traveler.[27] The flagship unit was the Williams Inn at Williamstown, Massachusetts. Treadway turned to motels after World War II, becoming a small chain of thirty motels by 1971, when it was purchased by a New Jersey company, itself an owner of bowling alleys and the even smaller Mohawk Inns motel chain. Consolidating its motels under the Treadway logo, the firm turned to franchising as a means of expansion, its distinctive logo the outline of a colonial innkeeper pointing with cane in left hand, lantern held high in right. Today the company is a management firm, its owned motels operated under various franchise brands. Only one Treadway Inn, located at Batavia, New York, was operating in 1994.

Small ownership chains cropped up across the country as investors parlayed profits or bank credit into multiple ownerships. When the repetition of architectural design combined with distinctive color schemes, identical naming through signage, and consistency in the packaging of services, place-product-packaging was at work. Most chains contained only two, three, or four motels, individual units thriving variously as a function more of location and local management than of chain affiliation. Most of these chains simply dissolved when they became unprofitable, obsolete and/or deteriorated units being sold off piecemeal. A very early example was the Dutch Mill Tourist Camps, operated in Nebraska, Iowa, and

FIGURE 5.10 Alamo Plaza Hotel Courts, 1959. The chain was headquartered in Dallas.

FIGURE 5.11 Postcard advertisement for the Blue Top Courts and Lodges, circa 1950.

Missouri by the Dutch Mill Service Company. B. H. Gholson, a motel operator at Omaha, anchored his facility there with a gasoline station and restaurant built to look like a Dutch windmill. Gholson had the plan copyrighted and then licensed it to others.[28] In this instance an unusual building type drove the chain idea.

Some chains died aborning, their architecture and other elements, although designed to be visually attractive, proving disappointing. Traveltown, a would-be chain initiated in the late 1930s, opened two motels, one in Virginia and the other in Tennessee. The intention was to locate lookalike motels at 250- to 300-mile intervals, the approximate distance of a day's drive.[29] Some chains, on the other hand, had units located within a single locality. The Blue Top Courts and Lodges, with their distinctive blue rooflines, were all located in and around Dallas (see Fig. 5.11). The National Autohaven Company announced plans in 1931 for a chain of one hundred "motor inns" in the Middle West, centered in Chicago. The first, located south of the city on the Dixie Highway, may have been the only unit actually built. Many schemes, like National Autohaven, were intended more as stock speculations, the promise of the motel industry more a means to an end than an end in itself.

REFERRAL CHAINS

Motel associations were open to all, which made it difficult, if not impossible, to maintain standards, let alone raise them. Consequently, small groups of motel owners began to cooperate in upgrading properties, the idea being to create networks of high-quality motels through which busi-

FIGURE 5.12 Cover of the *Deluxe Motor Courts Guide,* circa 1939.

ness could be referred. Each member of a system was pledged to maintain agreed-upon standards and to display the group's identifying emblem. One of the earliest of the referral chains was the Deluxe Motor Courts, administered initially from Los Angeles (see Fig. 5.12). Promoters drove major highways to identify appropriate motels and sell owners on the benefits of affiliation. Deluxe Motor Courts were located primarily in California, Oregon, and Washington, although in 1936 salesmen added motels along U.S. 70 and U.S. 80 in Arizona, New Mexico, and Texas in anticipation of that year's Texas Centennial Exposition at Dallas (see Fig. 5.13).

United Motor Courts

United Motor Courts was the most successful of the early referral chains. Organized in 1933 in California, its membership grew rapidly. The group guaranteed clean rooms, quality beds, and good service from motel to motel.[30] Its 1936 directory claimed: "You will find in United Motor Courts a new and unparalleled achievement in combining comfort and economical luxury with the convenience of first floor accommodations made necessary by our present mode of automobile travel. United Motor Courts is a group of independent owners, comprising only those motor courts which come up to the highest standards in comfort, quiet atmosphere, and courteous service." The original membership, located mainly in California and Arizona, formed a western division. In 1937 the Tourist Cottage Owners' Association affiliated with the group, becoming its eastern division. Their "Follow the Wheel" logo was adopted by the larger organization, although it soon gave way to the United Court shield, patterned after the new markers of the federal highway system (see Fig. 5.14). A central division, centered in Texas, was also organized.

In 1937 United Court members were located from the Pacific Coast across the southern tier of states eastward to the Gulf and Atlantic Coasts (see Fig. 5.15). Over the next fifteen years the density increased in these areas, with the Middle West and the Northeast substantially underrepresented. Each motel in the chain retained its own name but displayed the United Court emblem, sometimes in combination with other emblems. For example, the Ocala Motor Court in Florida displayed both the United Court and the AAA emblem and advertised, on the back of its postcards, Beautyrest mattresses as well. After World War II the unwillingness of the chain's leadership to expel motels that failed to upgrade their facilities led to widespread disaffection. In 1947 forty motels withdrew to form Quality Courts United, and other members went on to form the American Motor

FIGURE 5.13 Deluxe Motor Courts, 1939. The chain was headquartered in Los Angeles.

FIGURE 5.14 *United Motor Courts Directory, Eastern Division,* circa 1940.

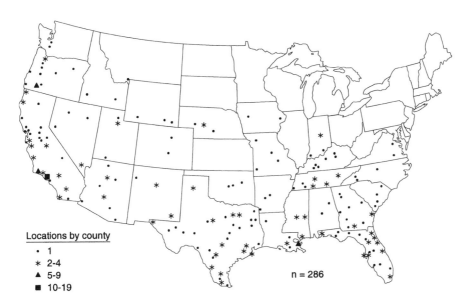

Locations by county
- · 1
- ✳ 2-4
- ▲ 5-9
- ■ 10-19

n = 286

FIGURE 5.15 United Motor Courts, 1937. The chain was headquartered in Gulfport, Mississippi.

Hotel Association. Although active into the 1950s, United Courts faltered in competition with chains that were more dedicated to quality control through constant innovation and upgrading.

Best Western

By far the most successful of the referral chains has been Best Western, whose operations are now worldwide (see Fig. 5.16). Best Western was founded in 1946 by M. K. Guertin, a Long Beach, California, motel operator. Guertin had long been involved as an organizer in the motel industry. He had been co-organizer in the 1920s of the first motel association, the Southern California Auto Court Association, and the first state association, the California Auto Court Association.[31] In addition, he had been an officer with the A-Plus Auto Court Association, the Standard Motor Court Association, and the Best Courts Association—all early referral chains—as well as United Motor Courts. Unlike previous cooperatives, Best Western was run as an incorporated business; Western Motels, Inc., headquartered initially in Long Beach, was the group's business arm, and Guertin was its manager. Promoters drove the major western highways to solicit members. In 1951 a map of the cooperating motels virtually outlined the nation's western highway system: U.S 101 and U.S. 99 in parallel along the Pacific Coast, U.S. 50 and U.S. 30 following the route of the old Lincoln Highway, U.S. 66 from Los Angeles to Chicago, and U.S. 70 and U.S. 80 in the Southwest (see Fig. 5.17).

FIGURE 5.16 Postcard advertisement for the Best Western Motels, circa 1955.

In the early 1960s, Best Western offered its members many benefits. It printed and distributed travel guides, listing motels according to the nearest major highway. Potential customers had only to read up or down from page to page to find the next Best Western motel on their route. The company bought advertising in national magazines, major newspapers, and AAA directories. Best Western operated a paid-in-advance reservation system. It offered group purchasing of motel furnishings and supplies, passings savings on through discounted prices. It provided members with group insurance, and it offered affiliation with several credit-card companies. The national headquarters also provided design and accounting expertise.

The chain's original logo was "The Nation's Friendliest Motels." Two salaried field representatives inspected the system's motels; in addition, each member was required to inspect three other member motels each year. Some 15 percent of the members were dropped each year for not meeting the chain's standards.[32] In 1963 members were assessed $250 on the first twelve units (the chain did not accept motels with fewer than twelve rooms) and $15 for each additional unit up to 49 units; larger motels were assessed on a sliding scale.[33] Each year members met in convention to elect officers, draft changes in their constitution as needed, and, generally, share information. Besides controlling quality, it was the chain's responsibility to develop marketing programs and decrease members' operating costs through bulk purchasing, shared-risk insurance, credit-card discounts, and training programs. Members, for their part, were required to maintain facility and service standards.

Through the 1950s, Best Western Motels concentrated west of the Mississippi River, leaving the remainder of the country to Quality Courts, the two chains advertising in one another's brochures. During the early 1960s a second brand, Best Eastern Motels, came to the fore, eventually to be subsumed under the Best Western label. In 1965 the chain had penetrated the Middle West, and established beachheads in the Middle Atlantic States and Florida (see Fig. 5.18). Each motel, being independently owned, operated under a separate name, but the Best Western sign was always prominently displayed (see Fig. 5.19). Members were required to purchase a range of furnishings carrying the Best Western logo, such as soap bars, shower curtains, and so on.

First at Long Beach and then later at Phoenix the chain maintained display rooms with sample bedroom arrangements. Carpets, drapes, table lamps, pillows, wastebaskets, linens, blankets, and, indeed, everything else to outfit a motel room could all be purchased there. In 1969 teletype machines were installed in the chain's 1,100 motels, and an instant reservation service was offered. Previously, cooperating motels had charged customers

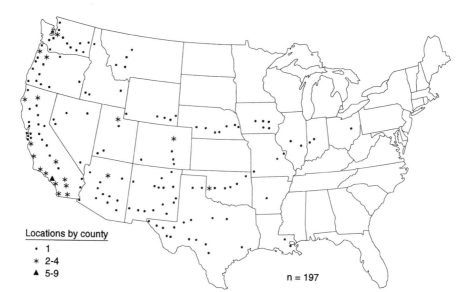

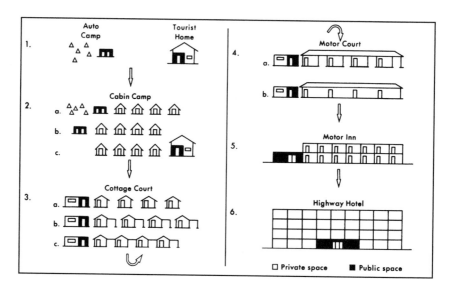

FIGURE 5.17 Best Western, 1951. The leading counties were Los Angeles in California, with 5 properties; and Humboldt, Monterey, Riverside, and San Bernardino Counties, also in California, Tillanook County in Oregon, and Salt Lake County in Utah, with 3 each. The chain was headquartered in Long Beach, California.

FIGURE 5.18 Best Western and Best Eastern, 1965. The leading counties were Los Angeles in California, with 16 properties; Cook (Chicago) in Illinois, with 9; and San Luis Obispo in California, with 8. The chain was headquartered in Long Beach, California.

FIGURE 5.19 The Colorado Lodge, Salida, Colorado, circa 1960.

for telephone calls placed to secure reservations. The group advertised itself first as "the world's fastest growing lodging chain" and then as "the
world's largest lodging chain." By 1976 the organization had 1,718 members offering 102,624 guest rooms in the United States, Canada, the Ca-
ribbean, Australia, and New Zealand.[34] Although the chain remained a
referral chain, its trappings were more like those of a franchise chain operation. The average property contained 78 rooms. Eighty-five percent had
swimming pools, 61 percent had restaurants, and 38 percent had cocktail
lounges.[35] There were no chain-owned or franchised properties, so the organization could focus exclusively on the needs of its membership. Rather
than making money *from* its members (as franchise operations did), Best
Western prided itself on making money *for* them.

In 1980 Best Western charged a 100-room property a $6,000 initiation
fee for chain membership; and it took an annual royalty fee of $2,370, an
advertising fee of $4,745, and a reservations fee of $3,650. These fees were
among the lowest in the industry. Fourteen quality-control inspectors
were employed full-time, inspecting approximately 30 percent of the
chain's 2,600 motels each year. The reservations center in Phoenix employed some 900 reservationists, who handled 5.6 million telephone calls
and booked about 6 million room nights, worth more than $200 million.[36]
Best Western operated three subsidiaries in 1980: Best Western Financial
Services (property management, brokerage, valuation, and consultation),
Best Western Supply (bulk purchasing of supplies), and the Best Western

Advertising Agency. The organization remained a nonprofit entity, with members electing their own leaders, a board of directors to guide the organization, and regional governors, whose duty it was to keep in touch with every property within their territory.

In 1990, 1,869 North American properties were augmented by 1,398 international properties. The chain was especially well represented in Europe through affiliation with preexisting national and regional hotel referral chains there. The total system represented 259,958 guest rooms worldwide in thirty-eight countries.[37] In the coterminous United States, Best Western operated at 1,822 locations in 1993 (see Fig. 5.20). Member-driven, affiliation was not a commodity that could be bought and sold like a franchise. Members that agreed to standards and abided by association rules were welcomed; those that did not were dropped. Memberships were renewed annually. Motels who chose to drop their affiliation had only to take down and return leased signs and refrain from otherwise using the Best Western logo. Best Western's primary rationale remained the referral of business across its network, a responsibility facilitated by increasingly sophisticated, state-of-the-art telecommunications.

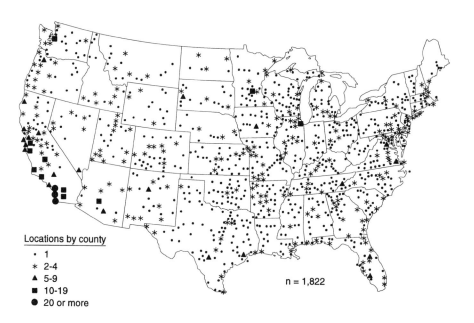

Locations by county
- • 1
- * 2-4
- ▲ 5-9
- ■ 10-19
- ● 20 or more

n = 1,822

FIGURE 5.20 Best Western, 1993. The leading counties were Los Angeles, Orange, San Diego, and Monterey in California, with 49, 25, 24, and 16 properties, respectively; and Cook (Chicago) in Illinois, with 14. The chain was headquartered in Phoenix.

FIGURE 5.21 Cover of the *Superior Motels Complimentary Directory*, 1964.

Superior Motels

Best Western was not the only referral chain, but of the early pioneers it alone has proven durable. Other referral chains popular in the late 1940s and early 1950s either failed or have been converted to franchise operations. The Superior Motel referral chain was one that failed. The organization stopped renewing memberships in 1979, although some its residual advertising, especially its distinctive cloverleaf emblems, still survives along American highways at former Superior Motel locations (see Fig. 5.21). In 1985 Best Value (with 38 motels), Magic Key (240), and Superior (44) combined to form USA Inns.[38] Best Value, for its part, was the successor to Budget Motels and Motels of America, two other franchise chains. Such was the nature of trademarks or brands. Even weakly established ones had value, if only for their limited name recognition.

At Superior's peak in the mid-1960s its logo identified more than 500 motels, mostly along the Atlantic seaboard from Maine to Florida (see Fig. 5.22). Originally called Superior Courts United, the chain was organized in 1950 with headquarters in Hollywood, Florida. It absorbed a number of lesser organizations, including the Eastern Motels Association, a referral group of inexpensive New England resorts and tourist courts. Superior Courts attracted more moderately priced motels, especially those less willing or unable to meet the inflating standards of Best Western and the franchise chains. In 1967 fees were set at $300 for the first year and $200 plus $1 per unit per month every year thereafter. Annual dues were not to exceed $776. Motel owners were required to purchase the Superior Motels sign, which was priced at approximately $1,000 in the late 1960s.[39] That signs were owned and not leased partially explains the brand's persistence as residual highway signage.

Budget Host and Independent Motels of America

The niche vacated by Superior Motels has encouraged the development of at least two recent referral chains, each focused on the "economy" market. Budget Host was organized in 1976, with 57 members controlling nearly 3,000 guest rooms.[40] The chain's brown and yellow logo features the outline of an old-fashioned gas lamp and the name Budget Host in bold

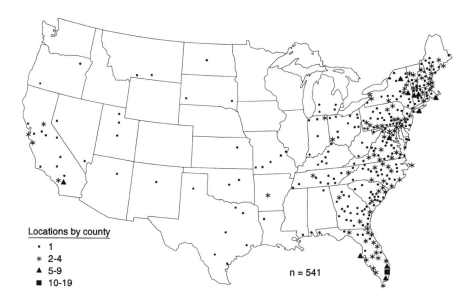

Locations by county
- • 1
- * 2-4
- ▲ 5-9
- ■ 10-19

n = 541

FIGURE 5.22 Superior Motels, 1964. The leading counties were Broward (Fort Lauderdale) in Florida, with 11 properties; and Hampden in Massachusetts, with 8. The chain was headquartered in Hollywood, Florida.

letters. The chain started in Missouri and Kansas and spread both east and west. In 1993 it had 156 members, with New England, the South, and the Pacific Coast noticeably underrepresented. The purpose of the organization, like that of Best Western, was to give independent operators brand identification. The referral-chain idea continues to attract promoters. Independent Motels of America (IMA) organized only in 1982. "Friendly, Clean, Comfortable" was the chain's slogan. Its logo comprised a yellow outline map of the coterminous United States with "IMA" in bold red lettering. Headquartered at Winner, South Dakota, the chain is currently concentrated in the northern Great Plains and the northern Middle West, although recent promotion has focused on California.

Chains were promoted in the hotel industry before the benefits of place-product-packaging were recognized and understood. Both individual and corporate pride were expressed in the early hotel chains as entrepreneurs built business empires that included several cities. These chains were made up of individual hotels, each promoted for its own individuality. The Statler and Hilton chains were the first to move toward place-product-packaging through naming, architecture, a mix of services, and promotion. In the motel industry, early chains, like Alamo Plaza Hotel Courts, reflected the same impulse. Sharing the same name, logo, architecture, and services, the chain operated as a system. The whole was conceived of and promoted as greater than the sum of its parts. Unfortunately, the limited scale of operation at Alamo Plaza precluded full benefit from the place-product-packaging commitment. Customers easily recognized Alamo Plaza by the roadside, but their small number precluded real advantage for the company.

Motel associations and recommendation services dominated a transition period in the 1930s, when locally based motel owners and operators began to appreciate the benefits of cooperation. Setting standards as a means of enhancing business was ingrained in the motel industry. Referral chains blossomed in the 1940s to offer limited aspects of place-product-packaging, but on a scale that translated into measurable advantage for participating motel operators. Motels affiliated with referral chains benefited from instant brand recognition and the implicit assurances of quality control. Independent operators achieved in concert what none could achieve on their own. Best Western would dominate the referral field through aggressive promotion and capable management. Independent operators, who were committed to growth and improvement in their local markets, found in Best Western important linkage, a referral system through which degrees of independence could be maintained along with the benefits of international brand recognition.

6

Motel Franchising – Part 1

In 1962 fewer than 2 percent of all motel establishments were affiliated with referral and franchise lodging chains. By 1987, however, 64 percent of the country's motels were part of these lodging networks. Chain-affiliated establishments accounted for nearly three-quarters of the total revenues earned in the lodging industry. More than half of America's motel and hotel rooms were owned or managed by the twenty-five largest lodging chains, the top five chains providing nearly 30 percent of the nation's rooms.[1] With the exception of popular resort communities, chain-affiliated motels and hotels continue to dominate the most lucrative market areas, such as those located near major airports, suburban mini-cities, highway interchanges, and central business districts. Their momentum has been further enhanced through the practices of important players in the travel industry. Travel agents routinely book their clients into reliable chain hotels, and popular lodging guidebooks, such as those published by AAA and Mobil, clearly favor chain establishments. Although many people associate chain establishments with mass-produced mediocrity and the cold-hearted corporate control of American life, they also represent remarkable success in the history of business. The growth of lodging chains since the late 1950s provides a good illustration of how corporate organizations have come to dominate the service industry in the United States.

The needs of both consumers and purveyors of lodging have strongly influenced the development of organized systems of distribution. For both business and leisure travelers, overnight accommodations represent a major portion of their expenses. Unlike roadside restaurants and gas stations, where the risks and encounters are limited to several dollars and a couple of quick stops, a stay at a motel involves a relatively considerable investment of money and time. At the end of a long day of meeting customers, driving along congested highways, or visiting with difficult relatives, the last thing a traveler wants to do is pay a lot of money for and spend an entire evening in a poorly kept, uncomfortable motel room. For motel owners, marketing is continually a significant problem. Because their properties usually are not known to potential customers prior to their first visual encounter, independent motel owners have relied on factors of presence—exposure, convenience, attractiveness, timeliness—to fill their rooms. Tools such as highway billboards and brochures can be used to announce a motel's existence and thus increase the chances that potential guests will consider them. Yet nothing is certain. Whereas restaurateurs and gas station operators can build a local base of customers, motel owners are much more dependent on attracting passing strangers each and every day.

It is thus not surprising that both travelers and motel owners have embraced lodging chains. With broad networks of member properties, rudimentary assurances of quality control, the ability to provide details on the locations and amenities of destinations down the road, chains relieve travelers from some of their uncertainties. And motel owners who join chains can more efficiently make their property's presence known to potential customers across the country, so that their uncertainties also are alleviated.

While the inherent needs of travelers and entrepreneurs prompted the formation of motel chains, the entrance of experienced, well-capitalized businessmen to the lodging industry accelerated the process. Although the referral chains had the advantages of quality control and recommendation services, they comprised mostly independent, often undercapitalized ownership. Chain standards and procedures were difficult to enforce, and systemwide changes were not easy to execute. As a result, the early chains were not particularly consistent, despite many of their members' best efforts. These problems were solved to a certain degree when established businessmen such as Howard Johnson, Kemmons Wilson (Holiday Inn), and Scott King (TraveLodge) developed motel chains that were financed through complex co-ownership or franchise arrangements. The motel properties themselves featured standardized building designs and were managed by people who were contractually obligated to follow strict operational procedures dictated by the chain's home office. Through these and other practices they gained the loyalties of American travelers and thus the majority of the total lodging market.

In this chapter and the next we continue the stories of America's major lodging chains. In contrast to the referral systems and associations detailed in the previous chapter, many of these chains were products of growth-oriented corporate enterprises that employed relatively sophisticated business strategies, including franchising and market segmentation.

FRANCHISING AND SEGMENTATION

Place-product-packaging in the lodging industry has come to embrace what students of marketing now call business-format franchising. With product franchising an agent or franchisee contracts to sell a franchisor's branded product or service. With business-format franchising the franchisee not only sells the product or service but also adopts a distinctive business strategy that embraces accounting, management, quality-control, training, and/or advertising functions. For the franchisee, business-format franchising represents a means of going into business for oneself, but not by oneself. In the 1980s, business-format franchising thrived in some three dozen different retail sectors, from hardware stores and real estate offices to printing and copying shops and bookstores. In 1990, sales of goods and services by franchise outlets were estimated at $716.3 billion, or 34 percent of all retail revenues.[2] Business formatting represented more than 70 percent of this franchise activity.[3]

Under the terms of most business-format franchise agreements a franchisor grants to franchisees the right to market a product or service (or both) using the trademark and business system developed by the franchisor. The contract imposes obligations on both parties in that the franchisor must provide the product or service, a proven business format, and management and marketing support, while the franchisee must provide local financing, management skill, and a determination to operate a profitable business. For the company with a successful product or service line, franchising offers a cost-effective strategy for achieving rapid expansion with minimal direct involvement at the local level and a minimal financial commitment. For franchisees, a franchise represents a proven business system with a reduced financial risk. For customers, franchised products and services offer predictable and reliable guarantees of satisfaction.

Franchising also has its disadvantages. For the franchisor, there is a lack of involvement at the point of final sale and a potential loss of quality control. For the franchisee, there is a loss of independence, since only the prescribed product or service and the related business format can be adopted. For the customer, the enhanced predictability that standardization brings becomes monotonous. Customer choices are circumscribed as fewer and fewer corporations come to dominate each retail sector through business-format franchising. Along the American roadside, the same brands of gasoline, fast food, and motel services appear over and over.

Most motel franchisees have traditionally involved four types of fees: an initial franchise fee, a royalty fee, an advertising or marketing fee, and a reservation fee. The services provided by franchising companies have var-

TABLE 6.1 Typical Motel Lodging Franchiser Services

Development
  Site identification
  Site acquisition
  Prototype plans and specifications
  Architectural programming- and
  -plan review
  Purchasing discounts
  Interior-design plans

Sales and Marketing
  Network of sales locations
  Trade-show representation
  Group sales activity
  Group- and tour-rate directories
  Governmental- and military-rate
  directories
  Corporate-rate directories
  Direct-mail programs
  Telemarketing and telesales
  programs
  Preferred credit-card discount sales

Advertising
  Television and print advertising
  Travel trade and meetings
  publications
  Travel directories

Communications
  Property public-relations
  consultation
  Assistance with press releases
  Familiarization trips for trade and
  consumer press
  Publicity with charities and public-
  interest groups
  Internal-systems publications

Quality Assurance
  On-property operational consulting
  Standards inspections
  Upgrading and refurbishing assis-
  tance and consulting

Training and Education
  Managers' and owners' orientation
  program
  Housekeeping, front-desk, maintenance, and supervision training
  seminars
  Video instruction tapes
  National and regional educational
  programs

Reservations
  Monthly activity reports
  Special package sales
  Yield management
  Twenty-four-hour terminal
  maintenance

Graphic Design
  Specification of logos, brochures, directories, stationery, billboards, and
  rack cards

Corporate Identity
  Design of all exterior signage
  Coordination of approved signage at
  all locations

Source: Adapted from Joseph E. Lavin and Dallas S. Lunceford, "Franchising and the Lodging Industry," in *Encyclopedia of Hospitality and Tourism,* ed., Mahmood A. Khan, Michael D. Olsen,
and Turgut Var (New York: Van Nostrand Reinhold, 1993), 370.

ied, but generally they have been those outlined in Table 6.1. Some franchisors have made territorial guarantees, reserving to specific franchisees
specific trade territories in which a corporate brand could be used exclusively. Other chains have not. The reservation system has proven to be
the most important service extended to motel chain members. By 1980,
35 percent of the typical Holiday Inn's business came through reservations.

The percentages varied between 10 and 20 percent for such chains as Sheraton and Marriott.[4]

Although franchising proved to be a highly successful growth strategy for lodging companies, it was not their only tool for expansion. In the 1980s and early 1990s, chains adopted market segmentation to maintain, if not accelerate, their rate of growth. Formally defined, market segmentation is the process undertaken by a firm's managers to conceptually divide a heterogeneous market into relatively homogenous market segments and then create (or acquire from competitors) products or services designed to meet the particular needs of targeted segments. The division can be based on a number of factors, such as geography (region, city size, climate), demography (age, gender, ethnicity, income), and psychography (social class, personality traits, lifestyle practices). Many major producers of such goods as automobiles, beer, cigarettes, laundry detergent, and magazines have used segmentation to dominate entire markets for decades.

Market segmentation in the lodging industry is a relatively recent phenomenon. Although Holiday Inn and Sheraton tried to create new lodging chains in the 1960s, the major players in the industry did not make significant use of segmentation until the early 1980s.[5] The first serious attempt to employ segmentation came in 1981, when Quality International introduced Comfort Inn to facilitate that company's expansion into the "luxury-budget" motel market segment. Six years later it bought the Clarion Hotel chain to penetrate the mid-rate and first-class hotel segments, developed Quality Suites to compete in the mid-rate all-suite market, and created the Sleep Inn brand to cover the economy motel market. In 1990 the firm acquired the Econo Lodge, Rodeway Inn, and Friendship Inn franchise systems to further consolidate its presence in the economy and luxury-budget markets. Appropriately enough, Quality International changed its name to Choice Hotels International during that year. Other companies that had begun as motel chains, such as Holiday Inn and Ramada Inn, followed suit during the 1980s. Hotel companies, including Hilton and Marriott, got into the act by developing motel and all-suite chains of their own.

Market segmentation in the lodging industry was more than a way to better meet the increasingly complex needs of the traveling public. It was also a strategy employed by the country's larger chains to overcome the effects of their own success. By the mid-1970s several of the big companies in the lodging industry—Holiday Inn, in particular—had begun to encounter problems associated with the size of their systems. After two decades of vigorous expansion, they had begun to "saturate" major market areas in different parts of the United States. They had reached the point where if they developed new properties in these market areas, they would be in danger of taking business away from their established properties. Consequently, expansion into new or underserved market areas was becoming increasingly difficult. Furthermore, as motel chains built or acquired hotels and hotel chains built or acquired motor lodges, they compromised the identities on which they had built much of their original success. Although growth through the addition of different forms of lodging increased system coverage and profit making, physical and operational consistency was the foundation of their franchises. From a marketing perspective, it was difficult to have it both ways.[6]

By forming new brands, however, these chains were able not only to reorganize their properties into more consistent sets but also to reenter markets their original chain brands had saturated and to venture into market areas that previously had been unsuitable. Marriott Corporation's line of full-service hotels, for example, were restricted to major metropolitan markets because of their inherent requirement of high volumes of upscale business and leisure traffic. Through their development of Fairfield Inn, a limited-service, luxury-budget motel brand, Marriott gained access to hundreds of additional market areas across the country without cutting into any of its existing hotel business. From its inception in 1988 Fairfield Inn had grown to a major national chain comprising more than 210 properties by 1995.

Just as chains were embraced by travelers and independent motel owners, new lodging brands spun off by Holiday Inn, Choice, Marriott, Promus, and other firms were well received by investors and lodging franchisees. By 1992 more than 1,900 properties and 230,000 rooms were affiliated with lodging chains created after 1980.[7] Ironically, the segmentation strategy may have created more problems than it solved. Because the major chains extensively developed and acquired existing motels and built new ones in the 1980s, many of the country's metropolitan market areas had become seriously overbuilt by the early 1990s. The resulting low occupancy rates, along with high levels of debt accrued through aggressive building and acquisition programs and an economic recession, put a number of formerly venerable chains into financial jeopardy and some into bankruptcy proceedings. Moreover, as lodging companies have continued to develop more new chains, the distinctions between them are increasingly difficult for consumers to perceive.[8]

CO-OWNERSHIP CHAINS

Co-ownership chains in the motel industry followed the lead of restaurateur Howard Johnson. By 1940 Johnson had opened 130 restaurants, more than half of them jointly owned with local operators on 50 percent shares. Thus the company was able to inflate the number of outlets established during a time of limited available capital. Because most bankers in the 1930s considered highway-oriented retail structures to be "specialty buildings" inappropriate for reuse by other kinds of enterprise in event of business failure, they were reluctant to finance them. In addition, Johnson could place local operations in the hands of owner-managers, who, because they held vested interests, could be counted on to be attentive to business. Local co-owners, for their part, bought into both brand identity and a business system.[9] Initially, two motel chains were closely associated with co-ownership financing and operations—TraveLodge (now a brand of the Forte Hotel chain) and Imperial 400.

Forte Hotels—TraveLodge

TraveLodge originated in 1935 when Scott King, a building contractor, opened King's Auto Court in San Diego. During that year's world's fair the motel was fully booked, a positive enticement for King to reorient his construction firm to the building of motels. Over the next five years King built twenty-four motels in various Southern California locations, most on contract to various investor groups.[10] The word *Travelodge* (the letter *L* was later capitalized) was created, and investors were given the right to use the name for ten years. The original TraveLodge was opened in San Diego in 1940, and the name was adopted for the firm in 1946, when King resumed peacetime construction activities. During World War II his firm constructed barracks and other buildings on San Diego's naval, marine, and army bases. An astute marketer and builder, King developed the "Sleepy Bear" logo, which served TraveLodge through the 1980s (see Fig. 6.1).

TraveLodge was the pioneer of the co-ownership method of operation in the motel industry. Owner-managers and the company shared equally in payments for lease rental or mortgages. In most instances, the co-owner managed the motel property, taking 10 percent of gross room revenues as a management fee. Profits before depreciation were divided equally. Most TraveLodges were built on leased land near downtown business districts, adjacent to peripheral shopping centers, or on major arterials connecting city downtowns with suburban retail centers (see Fig. 6.2). By 1961 there were 157 TraveLodges, only 15 of which were owned by the company alone (see Fig. 6.3). The bulk of the chain was located in California, with 18 properties in San Diego County and 14 in Los Angeles County. Only in California, Oregon, and Washington could the company claim substantive market penetration.

In 1965 TraveLodge formed a franchise division intended to push rapid expansion eastward across the United States both by converting already

FIGURE 6.1 Postcard advertisement for TraveLodge, circa 1960.

existing motels to the TraveLodge brand and by encouraging the construction of new properties. The last co-ownership contracts were issued in 1970, after which all expansion was driven by franchising. Franchisees paid a startup fee of $100 per room (up to a maximum of $10,000), and 10¢ per rented room per night. They contributed 3 percent of their gross income to the company's advertising fund, and entrance signs were leased at $100 per month.[11] TraveLodge franchise holders were given discounts through the firm's supply subsidiary, the Balboa Supply Company. A nationwide telephone reservation service was established.

TraveLodge maintained its own design and construction departments, clearly a holdover from King's construction business. Thus TraveLodges tended to look very much alike because of their common use of certain building materials (especially cement block), color schemes, signage, and building prototypes. The company expanded into large towns and small cities as well as focusing on major metropolises. A rule of thumb was that any community that could support a J.C. Penney store could also support a TraveLodge, and the firm quietly promoted itself as "the J.C. Penney of the motel business."[12] TraveLodge sought to offer moderately priced accommodations without frills but with "the essence of dependability, comfort, cleanliness and cordial hospitality."[13]

FIGURE 6.2 Postcard advertisement for the TraveLodge in Omaha, Nebraska, circa 1960. Located on the property was a twenty-four-hour Toddle House Restaurant.

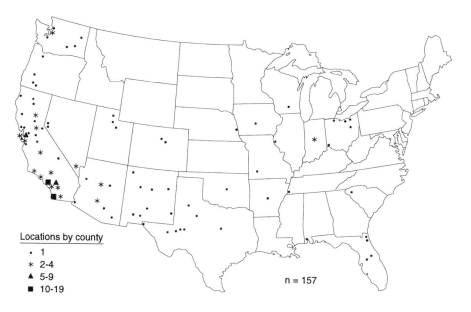

Locations by county
- • 1
- ✳ 2-4
- ▲ 5-9
- ■ 10-19

n = 157

FIGURE 6.3 TraveLodge, 1961. The leading counties were San Diego, Los Angeles, and San Bernardino in California, with 18, 14, and 8 properties, respectively. The chain was headquartered in San Diego.

In 1968 the firm was acquired by TL Management (a consortium of companies which included TraveLodge Australia Ltd., Trusthouse Forte Ltd., and Western International Hotels), but by 1976 Trusthouse Forte owned 95 percent. Trusthouse Forte had been formed in 1970 through the merger of Trust House and Forte Holdings Ltd.; in 1984 it owned more than 800 properties with some 76,000 rooms in forty-four countries.[14] Trust House dated back to 1903, when it was formed to promote the restoration of Great Britain's old coach inns. Forte Holdings Ltd., founded by Charles Forte in 1935, had quickly become a leading hotel management and food-service company in Great Britain. In 1990 Trusthouse Forte claimed to be the world's largest hotel-owning company, the fourth largest restaurateur and contract caterer, and the European market leader in airline in-flight catering.

Besides TraveLodge, the firm operated various hotel chains (Exclusive, Excelsior, Grand, Heritage, Viscount), purchasing the Strand, Knott, and Crest Hotel groups over the years. Among the noted hotels operated by Forte were the Grosvenor House in London, the George V in Paris, and the Westbury in New York City. In 1991 the company's name was changed to Forte PLC.

TraveLodge itself absorbed other firms. In 1987 it purchased and con-

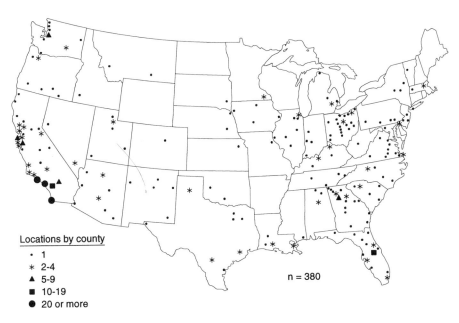

Locations by county
· 1
∗ 2-4
▲ 5-9
■ 10-19
● 20 or more

n = 380

FIGURE 6.4 TraveLodge, 1993. The leading counties were Los Angeles, San Diego, Orange, and Riverside in California, with 30, 27, 20, and 10 properties, respectively. The chain was headquartered in El Cajon, California.

verted Skylight Inns of America, and in 1990 it acquired the Lodge-Keeper Group (LK and Country Hearth Motels), both acquisitions enhancing market coverage in Ohio. A new logo was adopted—a navy-blue rectangular field with *Travelodge* spelled out in white lettering, the *L* once more lowercased. The company also promoted a new budget brand, Thriftlodge, the name spelled out on a red field. Many of the older, smaller Travelodges were converted to Thriftlodges. Newly built Thriftlodges were of a modular, back-to-basics construction. In 1993 there were 380 Travelodges in the United States (see Fig. 6.4). Still reflecting its origins, the company considered itself to be the major motel chain in California, where it sought deep market penetration in the major metropolises. Los Angeles, San Diego, Orange, and Riverside Counties in Southern California had 30, 27, 20, and 10 properties, respectively. Like many national chains, today's Travelodge reflects its geographical origins.

Imperial 400

Travelodge's success with co-owners prompted imitation. In 1959 Bernard Whitney, an attorney and certified public accountant, launched from Los Angeles another nationwide chain, Imperial 400, with investment capital supplied by the General Tire Credit Union, the Franklin National Bank of New York, and the Union Bank of California. The firm established locations by financing and constructing motel properties and then entering into partnership arrangements with local owner-operators. During its first year of operation Imperial 400 opened a new property roughly every ten days. Each motel shared a distinctive two-story design featuring a gull-shaped roof over the front portion of the motel containing the office and the manager-owner's apartment. The roof profile was repeated in the company's sign, prominently displayed at the motel entrance (see Fig. 6.5). Imperial 400 adopted as a logo the figure of a Scottish bagpiper "king" dressed in plaid, and its motto was, "Aye, royal accommodations at thrifty rates." Like TraveLodge, Imperial 400 provided limited service, restaurant and other facilities being omitted. Most Imperial 400 Inns were located near city or town centers on leased land. Also like TraveLodge, Imperial 400 was oriented to both the commercial traveler and the vacationer.

With its co-owners, Imperial 400 sought to combine the benefits of mom-and-pop operations with those of a chain. Co-owners invested in a fully operational motel. They had a spectrum of corporate services to fall back on in maintaining and amplifying their investments. A 1962 promotion read: "As a member of the 'clan' you benefit from these programs: scientific site location, advanced mortgage and construction financing,

FIGURE 6.5 The Imperial 400 Motel, Albuquerque, circa 1970.

Locations by county
- • 1
- ∗ 2-4
- ▲ 5-9

n = 82

FIGURE 6.6 Imperial 400 Motels, 1978. The leading counties were Los Angeles and San Bernardino in California, with 5 and 3 properties, respectively. The chain was headquartered in Arlington, Virginia.

national advertising and public relations, referral systems and advance reservations, training in the latest and most efficient methods of motel operation, centralized accounting and many more."[15] All members of the chain were expected to operate in exactly the same way. For example, all maids were to follow a seventeen-step daily room-cleaning system. The existence of owner-managers increased the likelihood that such precise operations would be achieved. Place-product-packaging had come fully to the fore; building design, signage, the mix of products and services, and the business format were all carefully orchestrated.

Expansion was perhaps too rapid. Forced into bankruptcy in 1965, the company was reorganized and its headquarters was moved to Englewood Cliffs, New Jersey, closer to its principal investors. In 1970 the company began to acquire the interests of its co-owners, and for several years expansion came primarily through enlarging and modernizing its fully owned properties. In 1978 the chain, then headquartered in Arlington, Virginia, owned and partnered in some eighty-two motels, the largest concentration still being located in California (see Fig. 6.6). In 1985 the company shifted from co-ownership to franchising as a means of expansion but enjoyed relatively little success. In 1987 it was purchased by a Luxembourg investment group, Interpart S.A., and a series of ownership changes that were highly destructive to the chain followed.[16] At one point Imperial 400 was made a pawn in the leveraged buyout of the MGM Grand Hotel in Las Vegas.

REFERRAL CHAINS CONVERTED TO FRANCHISING

Referral chains found it increasingly difficult to maintain standards among its participants. Dissatisfaction among the more progressive members of various cooperatives led to persistent splintering during the 1940s, the progressives moving off to found new referral chains with higher standards. Out of the United Courts organization, for example, came Quality Courts United. Tax-law changes in the 1950s revolutionized motel financing by allowing accelerated depreciation on properties. Absentee investor groups encouraged franchising. Many referral chains converted from cooperative associations to franchise corporations. Prime among them was Quality Courts United, the foundation for today's Choice Hotels, Inc.

Choice Hotels

QUALITY COURTS AND QUALITY INNS

Quality Courts United was created in 1941 when seven motel owners representing some 100 rooms banded together in a new referral cooperative. They hoped to raise standards and thus promote business for each other through cooperation, although as early as 1945 they seriously considered reorganizing as a franchising company.[17] Through the late 1940s, Quality Courts United restricted its operations to the eastern United States, leaving the trans-Mississippi West to Best Western. In 1950 a purchasing division was established, and a new central office was located in Daytona Beach, Florida. Management and architectural services supplemented the long-established directory and reservation programs. Advertisements soliciting chain membership in 1968 emphasized the following services: professional site planning, standard motel plans, financial counseling, central-purchase savings on furnishings and supplies, assistance in personnel training, national advertising, and advance-reservation facilities.[18]

Property inspection was an important central-office concern. Between 1959 and 1963 the chain's membership increased from 340 to nearly 600. But in those same four years some 250 affiliates resigned or were dropped, largely over quality-control issues.[19] All member motels were required to have air conditioning, telephones, swimming pools, paved driveways, and wall-to-wall carpeting, among other amenities. Increasingly, ownership of the chain's motels shifted from mom-and-pop operators to corporate investor groups, and more and more they were managed by management companies. In 1963, members of Quality Courts United agreed to convert their cooperative into a profit corporation. Members were extended stock options in a new company, and a public stock issue was promoted. Capital raised was directed toward motel purchase and new construction on behalf of the new firm.

When the company-owned properties constituted 40 percent of the total membership, the new corporation was authorized to absorb the original nonprofit organization. Members were then required either to take a franchise or drop out of the chain.[20] Franchises, of course, could be sold along with motel properties. Previously the Quality Court sign had returned to the cooperative whenever motel ownership changed (see Fig. 6.7). Franchising had profound implications for motel saleability. Through the mid-1960s, Quality Court United members had had difficulty retrieving equity in their properties at the time of sale. Usually, sellers obtained only a small percentage of a motel's worth in cash, the rest being tied up in long-term mortgage arrangements with buyers. With the referral chain's reorganization came the promise of a new market for motel properties whereby stock in the new company, or stock and cash, could be obtained.

The company's personality evolved through several changes of ownership. In 1968 Quality Courts Motels, Inc., was acquired by Park Consolidated Motels, and the chain's headquarters was moved to Silver Spring, Maryland. Park Consolidated was renamed Quality Courts, Inc. This firm

FIGURE 6.7 Murphy's Motel, a Quality Courts United Motel, Strongsville, Ohio, circa 1960. Prominent in this postcard is the chain's "sunburst" logo.

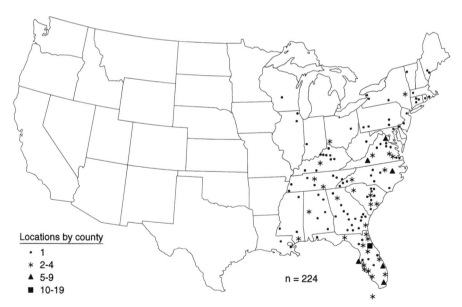

Locations by county
- • 1
- ✳ 2-4
- ▲ 5-9
- ■ 10-19

n = 224

FIGURE 6.8 Quality Courts United, 1951. The leading counties were Volusia (Daytona Beach) and Dade (Miami) in Florida, with 11 and 9 properties, respectively. The chain was headquartered in Ocala, Florida.

had been a franchisee operating Quality Courts in Maryland, Michigan, and Virginia. This would not be the last instance of a franchise holder purchasing a parent franchise company. Also acquired was the Revere Furniture Company, enhancing the chain's supply function. In 1972 the name of the chain was changed once again, to Quality Inns International, and the name of the parent holding company was changed to Choice Hotels International. In 1990 the organization was acquired by Manor Care, Inc., an owner and manager of nursing homes and other properties. Robert C. Hazard, chairman of the board and chief executive officer of the chain, launched a major expansion program. Marketing now under the name Choice Hotels, the firm moved vigorously into market segmentation. Royal Inns, a West Coast co-ownership chain of upscale, luxury motels, had been purchased in 1979; Quality Royale would be the company's first move into all-suite hotels.

The changing geography of the Quality Inn brand reflected the various corporate reorganizations and changed corporate objectives. In 1951 the chain's membership was concentrated heavily in the Southeast. Market penetration was strongest in Florida, where, for example, Volusia County (Daytona Beach) and Dade County (Miami) had eleven and nine members, respectively (see Fig. 6.8). By 1963 the chain had expanded into the Northeast and the eastern Middle West (see Fig. 6.9). And by 1993 the Quality Inn brand existed nationwide save for the northern Middle West and the northern Great Plains states (see Fig. 6.10).

COMFORT INNS

Quality Inn remained the company's primary brand through the early 1980s, when attention turned to the newly created Comfort, Clarion, and Sleep brands. The company also purchased Friendship Inns, Rodeway Inns, and Econo Lodge. Comfort Inns were introduced in 1981 to appeal to value-conscious customers, especially family vacationers, commercial travelers, and senior citizens. In eight years this chain numbered 860 properties; indeed, the chain enjoyed a 32 percent expansion in 1989 alone.[21] Choice hoped that Quality's image would "rub off" on the downscale Comfort brand.[22] Actually, the reverse probably occurred. Many of the Comfort Inns were newly constructed, and properties converted from other brands were usually extensively renovated. The Quality Inns, on the other hand, suffered from obsolescence. Between 1981 and 1993 more than half of the original Quality Inns were eliminated because they failed to meet the chain's standards.[23] In 1993, there were 850 Comfort Inns, compared with only 390 Quality Inns. Comfort Inns were located throughout the lower forty-eight states, with the highest concentration in Southern California (see Fig. 6.11).

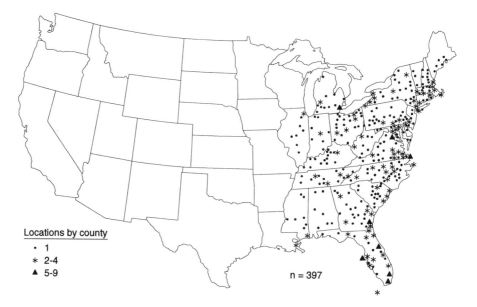

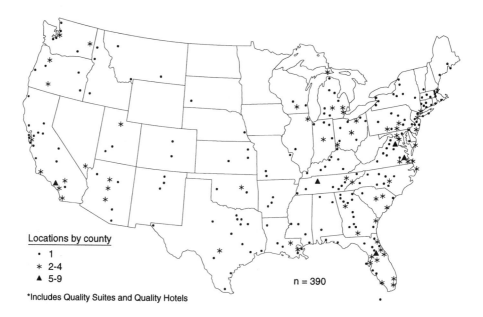

FIGURE 6.9 Quality Courts United, 1963. The leading counties were Pinellas (St. Petersburg) in Florida, Essex (suburban Boston) in Massachusetts, and Chesapeake (Virginia Beach) in Virginia, with 8, 7, and 6 properties, respectively. The chain was headquartered in Daytona Beach, Florida.

FIGURE 6.10 Quality Inns, 1993. The leading counties were Los Angeles in California, Orange (Orlando) in Florida, and York (Williamsburg area) in Virginia, with 6 properties each. The chain was headquartered in Silver Spring, Maryland.

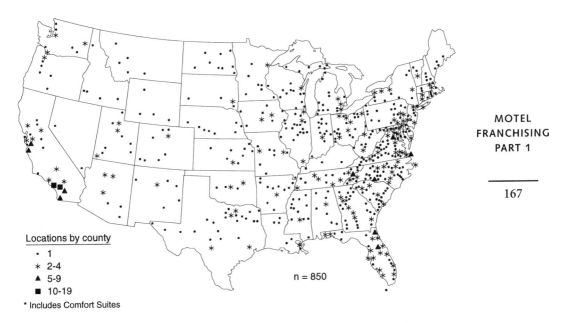

Locations by county
- • 1
- * 2-4
- ▲ 5-9
- ■ 10-19

* Includes Comfort Suites

n = 850

FIGURE 6.11 Comfort Inns, 1993. The leading counties were Los Angeles, Orange, and San Diego in California, with 17, 10, and 8 properties, respectively. The chain was headquartered in Silver Spring, Maryland.

CLARION INNS

Clarion Inns were introduced in 1987. Clarion originated with the Associated Inns and Restaurants Company of America (AIRCOA), a hotel management company that joined with Choice to promote Clarion Inns as a joint venture. Both AIRCOA's properties and Choice's Royale Inns were rebranded as Clarion Inns or Clarion Suite Hotels. Clarion focused on the upscale market. Hotels and resorts featured gourmet restaurants, lounges, meeting facilities, recreational facilities, and other amenities found in larger, full-service hotels. Clarion Carriage House Inns were smaller boutique hotels and country inns marketed for their historical associations and other unique qualities of place. In 1993 there were fifty-two Clarion Inns nationwide.

SLEEP INNS

The Sleep Inns chain was launched in 1988 under the McSleep label and focused on the economy end of the motel market. "The concept is just like McDonald's," claimed Robert Hazard. "A guy making $150,000 a year can eat there and feel comfortable and a guy making $10,000 a year can eat there and feel comfortable because he knows what he's getting—consistent quality."[24] That the McDonald's Corporation objected, perhaps not so much to the analogy as to the trademark infringement, re-sulted in the simplification of the chain's name following court litigation. Sleep Inns were to be built according to a single prototype featuring standard twelve-by-sixteen-foot rooms. A new federal program helped launch the chain. The Small Business Administration's 7A Program provided guaranteed market-rate financing in a second-mortgage arrangement for investor syndicates.[25] By 1993, however, only thirteen Sleep Inns had been established.

FRIENDSHIP INNS

Choice International purchased the Friendship Inns brand in 1990. Friendship originated in 1961 as a referral chain headquartered in Salt Lake City, Utah. It attracted as members the owners of older motels who were less concerned with upgrading their properties than they were interested in the advantages of chain affiliation. The cooperative's logo was a heraldic emblem symbolizing travel and overnight hospitality (see Fig. 6.12). From 32 inns in 1963 the chain increased to 771 properties in 1974 (see Fig. 6.13). This rapid growth reflected the low costs of joining and sustaining membership. In 1967 the annual membership fee was set at only $10 per guest room. The Friendship Inn sign could be leased or purchased outright for a mere $487. Members were required to meet minimum AAA standards and to be listed in AAA tour guides. The company provided a reservation service, centralized buying, national advertising, and nationwide distribution of chain directories.[26] In 1971 the Vagabond Inn chain joined Friendship Inns, to be known as Friendship Inn Vagabonds.

Friendship Inns was converted into a franchising company when Alfred Olshan bought the company from its founder, J. Richard Williams, in 1985, relocating its headquarters to North Bergen, New Jersey. The chain

FIGURE 6.12 Advertisement from the *Friendship Inns Directory*, 1974.

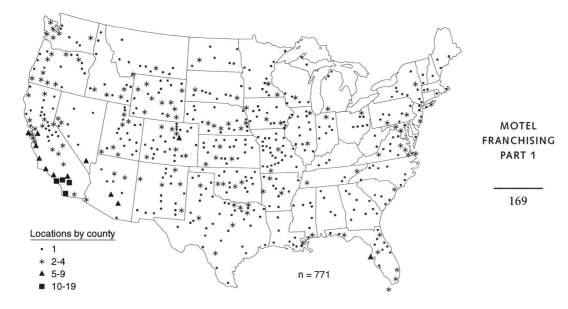

FIGURE 6.13 Friendship Inns, 1974. The leading counties were Los Angeles, Orange, Riverside, San Diego, and San Bernardino in California, with 12, 12, 10, 10, and 9 properties, respectively. The chain was headquartered in Salt Lake City, Utah.

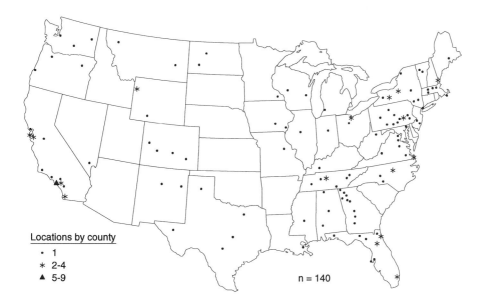

FIGURE 6.14 Friendship Inns, 1993. The leading counties were Los Angeles in California and Chesapeake (Virginia Beach) in Virginia, with 5 properties each. The chain was headquartered in Silver Spring, Maryland.

was overloaded with outdated, substandard properties. A corporate image and a new style of management seemed appropriate. Sold a year later, the company became Friendship Inns Franchising Corporation, only to be sold once again in 1989 to Econo Lodges of America, the number of its properties down to 129. In 1990 Econo Lodges, in turn, was acquired by Choice Hotels. In 1993 there were only 140 properties in the Friendship Inns system (see Fig. 6.14). Like Econo Lodge, Friendship Inns represents one of Choice Hotels budget brands. More importantly, it also demonstrates that brands once widely established can persist, valued for their name recognition.

ECONO LODGE

The Econo Lodge brand emerged in 1972, when Mid-Atlantic Builders of Norfolk, Virginia, a construction company, changed its name to Econo Travel Motor Hotels Corporation. The firm's intention was to emphasize motel construction, but from the beginning the company was a business-format franchiser. The firm took a "package approach" to buildings, furniture, supplies, and its systems of management, bookkeeping, accounting, and controls.[27] The standard two-story design contained forty-eight rooms, requiring a lot with front footage of only 150 feet and a depth of only 250 feet. Each room contained two beds, two wall-unit headboards, two nightstands, a chest of drawers, a desk, a luggage bench, a clothes rack, a television, and a telephone, in addition to bathroom facilities. Rooms were designed to be cleaned rapidly and repaired efficiently. Properties were built primarily for absentee owners, managers intended to be husband-and-wife teams, especially retired couples. The buildings had only electric utilities, so each room could be heated or air-conditioned only as use demanded. As its name suggested, Econo Travel was a budget chain. Like Friendship Inns, the chain adopted the figure of a Scotsman as its logo in order to emphasize value for low price. "Spend a night, not a fortune," was the chain's slogan.

In 1983 the company was sold to the Charlotte, North Carolina, real estate investor Ben Douglas. The Econo Lodge name was adopted, and plans were made to expand the chain from an East Coast regional operation to a national one. Three years later the firm was sold to New Image Realty, Inc., also of Charlotte, following a financial reorganization. In 1985 the company acquired, in turn, the Memphis-based Lagniappe Inns as part of a renewed expansion strategy. Four years later the company purchased Friendship Inns but maintained it as a separate chain. In 1990 Econo Lodges of America's franchise division was sold to Choice Hotels, enabling Choice to position itself firmly at the economy end of the motel market. New Image Realty retained property-management and -development functions. In 1993, there were 744 Econo Lodges nationwide, with the highest concentration along the East Coast (see Fig. 6.15).

RODEWAY INNS

One month before selling out to Choice Hotels, New Image Realty purchased the Rodeway chain; thus the Rodeway brand also entered the Choice stable of brands. Organized in 1962 in Phoenix, Rodeway Inns of America had been acquired by the Vantage Company of Dallas in 1971. The Prudential Life Insurance Company participated in a joint venture with Rodeway to finance inns, which were then managed by the company.[28] The Rodeway logo featured a traveler lying back in a rocking chair, his shoes off, a cat asleep at his feet, and a newspaper open in his lap. The idea behind the chain was, again, to offer independent operators the advantages of big-chain identity. By 1973, 136 inns were operating primarily in the Southwest and the central South. Perhaps the company's most ambitious project was the nineteen-story, 267-room cylindrical tower built in downtown St. Louis in 1970. Originally an owner and operator of its inns, after 1976 the company focused solely on franchising and quickly divested itself of all property ownership.

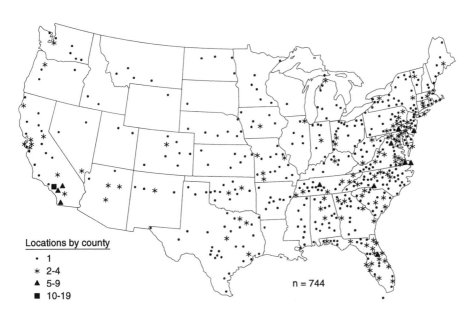

Locations by county
- · 1
- * 2-4
- ▲ 5-9
- ■ 10-19

n = 744

FIGURE 6.15 Econo Lodges, 1993. The leading counties were Los Angeles in California; Chesapeake (Virginia Beach), Fairfax (suburban Washington, D.C.), and Surrey (suburban Norfolk) in Virginia; and Orange (Orlando) in Florida, with 13, 9, 8, 8, and 7 properties, respectively. The chain was headquartered in Silver Spring, Maryland.

In 1985 the Rodeway brand was purchased by the Ladbroke Group, the British hotel, real estate, and retailing giant. Ladbroke sold the chain to Ramada Inns of Phoenix two years later. (Ladbroke, in turn, then purchased Hilton International from the Alleges Group, then the parent company of United Airlines, Hertz Rental Cars, and Weston Hotels.) In 1990 Prime Motor Inns, the new owners of Ramada, sold Rodeway to Econo Lodge. Here was a motel brand that, rather like Friendship Inns, had suffered from a lack of strict quality control, in part because of the quick succession of owners speculating in the company. In 1993, 102 Rodeway Inns were operating, the majority located in California and the Southwest. Franchising invited speculation not only at the level of the franchise but in the franchising companies themselves.

Choice Hotels International considered itself to be the world's largest hotel franchise company. Worldwide its various brands were attached to more than 2,700 properties with some 256,008 rooms.[29] It operated two divisions, or franchise groups, in the United States. The Sunburst Group (named for the original Quality Courts United logo) included Clarion Inns (upscale hotels, all-suite hotels and resorts, and boutique properties), Quality Inns (mid-priced, full-service motels and hotels and limited-service all-suite hotels), Comfort Inns (upper-economy, limited-service inns and all-suite properties), and Sleep Inns (limited-service economy inns). The Economy Group included Friendship Inns (lower-economy, limited-service motels), Econo Lodges (limited-service, mid-priced economy motels), and Rodeway Inns (limited- and full-service, upper-priced economy motels). Choice was the first corporation to fully embrace market segmentation as a marketing device.

Congress Inns

The history of Choice Hotels International may suggest a kind of historical progression whereby brands never fade, but always succeed to some extent. The history of the Congress Inn brand suggests otherwise. Here was a referral chain that, like Quality Courts United, converted to a franchise operation. But Congress Inns had no white knight to rescue and resuscitate its trademark (see Fig. 6.16). Founded in the early 1950s in Santa Monica, California, the Congress of Motor Hotels was a referral group formed as a membership cooperative. It was run very much like Best Western and Quality Courts United, except that greater emphasis was placed on motel financing. The chain was backed by Congress Enterprises, Inc. A 1960 advertisement read: "Congress Enterprises, Inc. was formed to finance motor hotels—in purchasing, upgrading, remodeling, enlarging, or new construction, under Congress's lease-back program."[30]

FIGURE 6.16 The Congress Inn, Santee, South Carolina, circa 1960. Featured were seventy-eight fully carpeted, air-conditioned rooms, a restaurant, two swimming pools, and a "space-age" playground. (*Source:* Brooks Photographers, Tracys Landing, Maryland 20779.)

Congress Inns International was the corporate entity that promoted franchising. A 1961 advertisement read: "Ask the average person to name a food store, a variety store, a service station and 99 times out of 100 you'll get a nationally known chain-name—Safeway, A & P, Woolworth, Kresge, Texaco, Shell. In almost every type of business today, the BRAND NAMES stand out. The motel industry is no exception. Why is it that chain-name motels are enjoying 9 percent more occupancy, on the average, than comparable 'local name' independents?"[31] Congress therefore represented another means by which the independent motel owner could convert to a nationally recognized brand. Unlike Best Western and Quality Courts United, however, Congress extended its members and franchisees territorial rights.

Congress offered motel owners three different franchise packages: a full franchise, which used the Congress Inn name exclusively; a modified franchise, which combined the Congress Inn logo with the local motel name, the former emphasized; and a limited franchise, which also combined both names but emphasized the local name.[32] Sold to Gulf American Land Corporation in 1963, the company moved its headquarters to Miami Beach, Florida. In 1964 the chain had 172 properties spread from coast to coast (see Fig. 6.17). Plagued by quality-control problems—there were perhaps too many options—the Congress Inn brand faded during the 1980s.

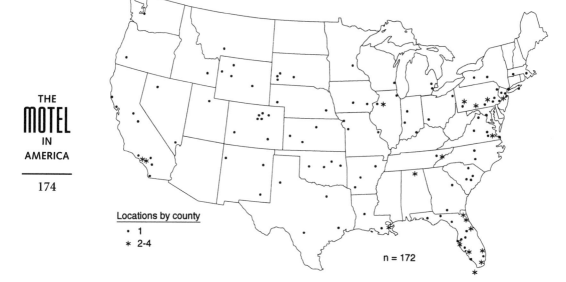

Locations by county
- • 1
- * 2-4

n = 172

FIGURE 6.17 Congress Inns, 1964. The chain was headquartered in Miami.

FRANCHISE CHAINS

Ownership chains dominated hotel networking early in the twentieth century. In the 1930s, trade associations and then referral chains provided independent motel operators with important networking. Regional referral chains, several of which had become national organizations by the 1950s, represented the beginnings of large-scale place-product-packaging in the motel industry. Nonetheless, the 1950s were a decade of transition marked, for example, by the rise of co-ownership chains. More importantly, the 1950s also saw referral chains converting to franchise operations. New tax laws and new sources of investment capital made the absentee investor syndicate primary in motel financing. The era of the small independent operator was coming rapidly to an end. One company emerged to set the standard. It was the company to which referral chains, like Quality Courts United and the Congress of Motor Hotels, felt obligated to respond competitively. That company was Holiday Inn.

Holiday Inn

Holiday Inn was so important in the reconfiguration of the motel industry that we devote chapter 9 to it. Here we limit our discussion to a historical overview, comparing it with other evolving chains. Holiday Inn has become one of the great business success stories of America. How

Kemmons Wilson, the Memphis house builder, struck on the Holiday Inn idea, built his company through franchising, and integrated vertically, moving into such diverse areas of operation as furniture manufacturing, food service, and even steamship-line operations, has become the stuff of legend. Wilson might stand in a pantheon beside the likes of Henry Ford and Ray Kroc. He has become symbolic of fundamental change in the nation's twentieth-century economy.

Holiday Inn began in Memphis in 1952 with the opening of 3 inns, each guarding a major highway approach to the city. By 1958 there were 79 properties concentrated in the Southeast within a day's drive of Memphis (see Fig. 6.18). In 1964, however, there were 531 inns spread from the Atlantic Coast to the Rocky Mountains and beyond (see Fig. 6.19). In 1993 there were 1,498 properties nationwide, the heaviest concentrations decidedly in the Northeast, Florida, and California (see Fig. 6.20). These maps reflect not only new additions to the chain but the effects of disenfranchisement, the dropping of properties that failed to renew franchises and the franchises that were dropped for failure to meet evolving standards. Vividly portrayed, however, is the rise of a national chain from a decidedly regional operation to a national powerhouse dominant in the industry through the 1960s and 1970s.

Franchising was Holiday Inn's method of expansion. Local investors were invited to participate in a marketing system worked out during the early years of managing company-owned properties. Franchises were sold individually and in bulk lots. An Oklahoma investor syndicate established

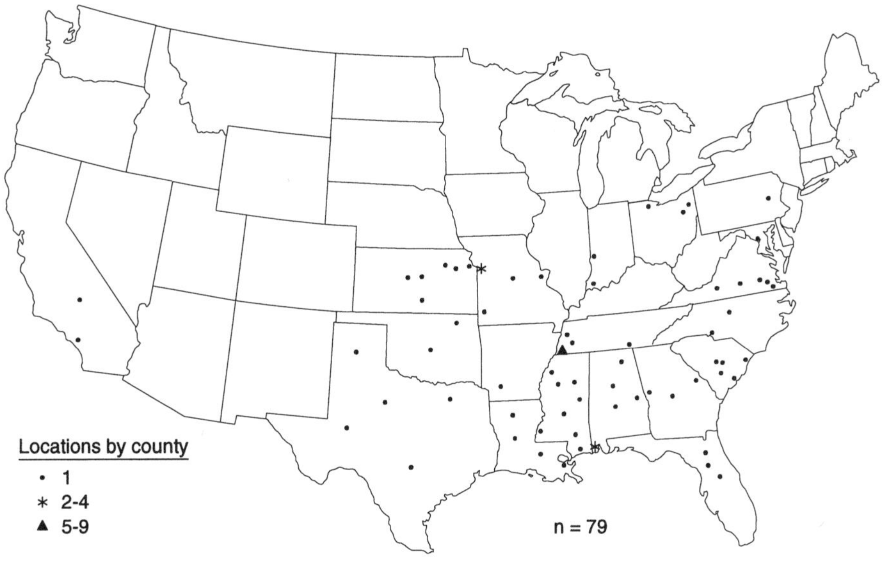

FIGURE 6.18 Holiday Inns, 1958. The chain was headquartered in Memphis.

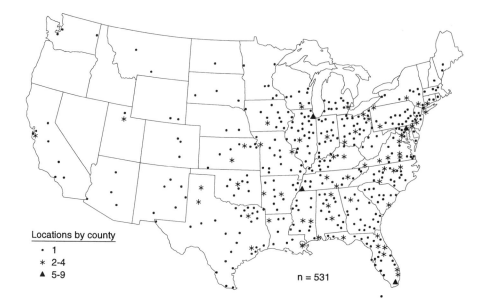

FIGURE 6.19 Holiday Inns, 1964. The leading counties were Shelby (Memphis) in Tennessee, Cook (Chicago) in Illinois, and Dade (Miami) in Florida, with 9, 6, and 6 properties, respectively. The chain was headquartered in Memphis.

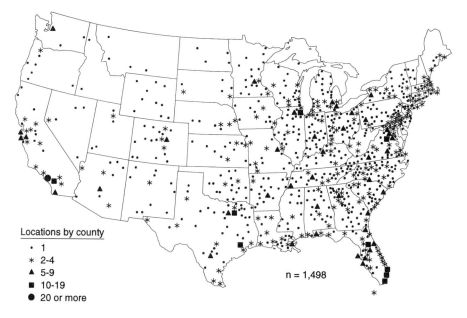

FIGURE 6.20 Holiday Inns, 1993. The leading counties were Los Angeles in California, Harris (Houston) in Texas, Cook (Chicago) in Illinois, Orange (Orlando) and Dade (Miami) in Florida, and Orange in California, with 24, 16, 15, 13, 12, and 11 properties, respectively. The chain was headquartered in Atlanta.

14 inns oriented to that state's new turnpikes in the early 1960s. In 1970 American Motor Inns, Inc., of Roanoke, Virginia, operated 31 inns from Maine to North Carolina. Topeka Inn Management, Inc., operated 50 inns in fifteen states, from Florida to California (see Fig. 6.21). Thus Holiday Inn encouraged the rise of "chains" within the chain. Topeka Management, for example, was the twelfth largest motel-hotel ownership group in the United States in 1974 (see Table 6.2).

In the early 1970s Holiday Inn could advertise: "We build a new room in the time it takes most people to find one. Twenty-two minutes to be exact." The ad continued: "We don't mean just a room. We mean first-rate rooms. And people everywhere are reserving them as fast as we can build and open Holiday Inns (a new one opens somewhere every 52 hours)." That year the chain received on average 130,000 reservation requests daily.[33] As "the Nation's Innkeeper," Holiday Inn offered year-round air conditioning, a swimming pool at every inn, free advance reservations, a telephone and television in every room, meeting facilities for all occasions, baby sitters and house physicians on call, baby beds, free ice, food service, valet laundry service, free kennels for dogs (and free Ken-L-Ration), and credit-card privileges. Children under twelve stayed with parents free.

In 1956 Richard Brown and an associate purchased a five-acre tract midway between Birmingham and Bessemer in Alabama. Then for $500 they purchased a Holiday Inn franchise. For this fee and the small monthly

TABLE 6.2 Largest Lodging Chains in the United States, 1974

Rank	Organization	Properties	Rooms
1.	Holiday Inns	1,703	270,173
2.	Best Western	1,300	90,000
3.	Friendship Inns	1,087	70,000
4.	Ramada Inns	669	91,000
5.	Howard Johnson's	531	50,000
6.	TraveLodge	468	30,000
7.	Sheraton	370	94,248
8.	Quality Inns	327	33,700
9.	Red Carpet / Master Hosts	236	30,050
10.	Rodeway Inns	155	19,200
11.	Hilton Inns	150	56,650
12.	Topeka Inn Management	76	12,123
13.	International Hotels	67	25,752
14.	Hyatt Corporation	62	19,100
15.	Hilton International	61	23,263

Source: Donald E. Lundberg, *The Hotel and Restaurant Business* (Boston: Cahners, 1976), 26.

FIGURE 6.21 The Holiday Inn, Lawrence, Kansas, circa 1965. Topeka Inns Management began with a string of Kansas Holiday Inns before spreading nationwide as one of Holiday Inn's largest franchisees.

payments that followed they received a set of plans for motel construction, counseling service on financing their inn, the benefits of a national advertising program, rights to purchase discounted supplies through a central purchasing office, access to chain credit-card agreements, and access to Holiday Inn's personnel-training program. The Memphis office reserved the right to make regular quality-control inspections and kept control of the giant Holiday Inn sign. By 1964, however, the cost of initial licensing had increased to $10,000. The royalty fee was 15¢ per unit per night or 3 percent of the gross room revenue, whichever was greater. The royalty fee included a charge of 8¢ per unit per night for national advertising.[34] Holiday Inn had come of age.

In 1980 Holiday Inns of America purchased Harrah's Corporation, the operator of gambling casinos in Nevada, and began development of its own casino hotel in Atlantic City, New Jersey. In 1984 the company entered the luxury and all-suite hotel markets with its new Crowne Plaza and Embassy Suites brands. It also acquired the California-based Granada Royale Hometel chain and created a wholly new subsidiary, Hampton Inns, in order to target the upper end of the limited-service market. In 1985 Holiday Inn purchased Residence Inn to target the extended-stay business traveler, only to sell the chain to Marriott two years later. And in 1989 Holiday Inn created Homewood Suites.

The Promus Companies

The British brewing and food products giant Bass PLC acquired Holiday Inns International in 1990. However, the Embassy Suites, the Homewood Suites, and the Hampton Inns brand, as well as the company's gambling casinos, were first spun off as the Promus Companies. Thus Bass in effect acquired only the Holiday Inn brand. Holiday Inn's headquarters was moved to Atlanta, but the Promus Corporation remained in Memphis. The name Promus (pronounced "promise") is from the Latin word *promus,* meaning "one who serves." The company's annual revenues shrunk from $1.6 billion to $1 billion. Its operations, however, were more focused. Eighty-five percent of its revenues now came from gambling.[35] Besides casino hotels, the company also operated gambling boats in Illinois and Louisiana.

THE EMBASSY SUITES

Originally dubbed Holiday Inn Guest Suites, Embassy Suites was launched in 1983. But it was not until 1985, when the newly acquired Granada Hometel properties were relabeled Embassy Suites, that the chain truly took off. Many properties were built around a multistory atrium complete with fountains and lavish indoor plantings. The exterior façades reflected a narrow design template, a high degree of similarity from one property to another. Suites had separate living room, bedroom, and dining/work areas and were provided with a refrigerator and wet bar as well as the traditional bathroom. There were 103 Embassy Suites nationwide in 1993 (see Fig. 6.22). More than half were managed by the company, and the remainder were operated by franchisees. In 1991 the Embassy Suites Division acquired the Florida-based Park Suites hotel chain.

THE HAMPTON INNS AND HOMEWOOD SUITES

The Hampton Inns were launched in 1984. These limited-service highway hotels were designed to serve markets not served by the parent Holiday Inns, especially economy-minded business travelers. Its standardized format featured free in-room movies, free local telephone calls, and complimentary continental breakfasts. Properties did not contain large public spaces, restaurants, or lounges. Room rates were 20–40 percent below those of the parent chain. A standard architectural format quickly emerged. Building exteriors sported dark bronze metal roofs, canopied entrances, and off-white masonry façades for easy maintenance (see Fig. 6.23). Like the Embassy Suites, the Hampton Inns attained place-product-packaging more fully than even the look-alike Holiday Inns.

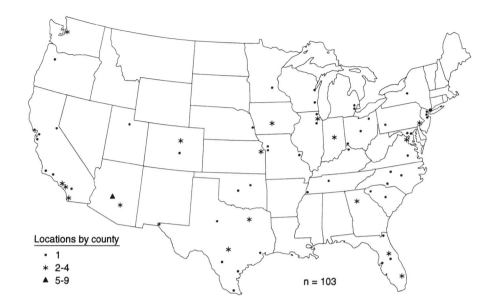

Locations by county
- • 1
- ∗ 2-4
- ▲ 5-9

n = 103

FIGURE 6.22 Embassy Suites, 1993. The leading counties were Mariposa (Phoenix) in Arizona, with 5 properties; and Denver in Colorado, Fulton (Atlanta) in Georgia, and Los Angeles in California, with 4 each. The chain was headquartered in Memphis.

By 1989 the Hampton Inns chain had grown to 200 properties, an average of 45 hotels added in each of the previous five years.[36] The Hospitality Capital Group of Atlanta provided much of the expansive energy. Promus held a one-third stake in Hospitality Capital, the remaining two-thirds being held by Japanese investors. Some $75 million in investment capital was funneled into Hampton Inns construction at a time when the cost of a new 130-room motel (including land and furnishings) ran to approximately $5 million.[37] Eighty percent of the chain's properties were franchised. Inns were typically developed and then syndicated, with Hampton Inns, Inc., managing the properties and maintaining an ownership percentage. Unlike most other chains, therefore, Hampton Inns expanded almost entirely through new construction, retaining substantive control over operations.

In 1993 there were 353 Hampton Inns, concentrated mainly in the eastern United States (see Fig. 6.24). The company had come to emphasize metropolitan and small-city locations, preferring suburban sites. In 1992 Promus merged the 22 Homewood Suites into the Hampton Inns operation. In 1994 the Hampton Inns brand was expanded to provide suites as well as standard rooms. The Promus operation represented an old firm under a new name, a firm committed to continued innovation and change commensurate with changing market conditions. But rather than target all

FIGURE 6.23 The Hampton Inn North, Ann Arbor, Michigan, 1993.

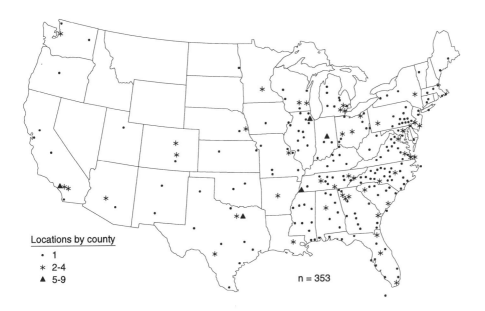

Locations by county
· 1
∗ 2-4
▲ 5-9

n = 353

FIGURE 6.24 Hampton Inns, 1993. The leading counties were Cook (Chicago) in Illinois and Shelby (Memphis) in Tennessee, with 7 and 6 properties, respectively. The chain was headquartered in Memphis.

segments of the emerging hospitality field, Promus chose to market only in those segments of the industry that promised the most rapid growth. Whereas Choice Hotels had entered virtually all segments of the hospitality field, Promus focused, enabling the company to profit more from the financing, construction, and management aspects of new business growth.

Hospitality Franchise Systems, Inc.

Among the giant motel conglomerates formed was Hospitality Franchise Systems, Inc. In the 1990s this umbrella organization franchised five established brands, each with its own distinctive history: Ramada Inns, Howard Johnson's Motor Lodges, Days Inns, Super 8 Inns, and Park Inns. Here again market segmentation was promoted. Initially, it involved not so much the creation and purchase of brands carefully targeted to specific market segments (as with Choice Hotels and, as we will demonstrate in the next chapter, with Marriott) as the collection and resuscitation of tarnished brands. Hospitality Franchise Systems has proven to be an able rehabilitator of chains once plagued by age and obsolescence, overly rapid expansion, or indifferent management.[38]

RAMADA INNS

Ramada Inns originated in 1954 as a small chain of motels centered in Flagstaff, Arizona. In 1959 the name Ramada, the Spanish word meaning "a shady resting place," was adopted.[39] The firm was reorganized in 1963 as a public stock company to own, manage, and franchise under the Ramada Inn brand. In 1967 a company franchise cost $12,500 and carried an annual fee of 2.5 percent of gross sales. Eight cents per room per day was assessed for national advertising.[40] As at Holiday Inns, the following services were made available to franchisees: site evaluation, architectural and engineering advice, discounted purchasing of furnishings and supplies, an advertising program, and reservation services. Through 1960 the company operated primarily in the Southwest (see Fig. 6.25). Nonetheless, it adopted an eastern architectural motif (see Fig. 6.26). Licensees were required to adopt a standard "Williamsburg" design when undertaking new construction. Two-story buildings veneered in red brick and topped by gable roofs, often punctuated with cupolas, sported large porte-cocheres supported by white pillars. Most Ramada properties contained a restaurant, a cocktail lounge, meeting rooms, and a swimming pool. For its logo Ramada adopted the image of a carriage footman blowing a horn from which draped a banner reading "Ramada Inn Roadside Hotels." The chain's slogan was "Luxury for Less."[41]

Locations by county
· 1
* 2-4

n = 24

FIGURE 6.25 Ramada Inns. 1960. The leading county was Maricopa (Phoenix) in Arizona, with 3 properties. The chain was headquartered in Phoenix.

FIGURE 6.26 The Ramada Inn, Springfield, Missouri, circa 1975.

By 1971 there were 79 company-owned inns and 224 franchised properties. The company had branched out into campgrounds oriented to recreational vehicles (Outdoor Ramada Parks) and had purchased several hospitals. Financing for chain expansion came from major banks, including the Continental Bank of Chicago. By 1975 there were 515 inns, 113 of them company-owned; by 1979 there were 644 properties, of which 128 were company-owned.[42] When the chain was twenty-five years old, it began the first of several refurbishing programs, the company acknowledging the need for more intensive quality control. Expansion and diversification had been emphasized at the expense of maintenance and the upgrading of existing properties, prompting one business magazine to call Ramada "the sick man of the U.S. lodging industry."[43] The renaissance idea took hold in the name of a new brand—the Ramada Renaissance Hotels, a top-end, luxury product. By 1983 some $350 million had been spent in renovation and 20 percent of the inns had been dropped for not meeting the enhanced standards.[44] Gone were the shag rugs and the dime-store art. The focus on the vacation traveler was replaced by a new concern for the business client.

In 1990 Prime Motor Inns, one of Ramada's largest franchisees, took control of Ramada Inn's domestic franchising when New World Hotels, a company based in Hong Kong, acquired Ramada International. Prime Motor Inns also came to control the Rodeway Inns and the Howard Johnson's chains. Thirty Ramada Renaissance Hotels, Ramada Hotels, and Ramada Inns remained with Ramada International, as did the ownership and franchising rights to 110 hotels in 36 foreign countries.[45] Domestic control of the Ramada Inn brand then passed to the Blackstone Group, an investment banking firm based in New York City. Blackstone established Hospitality Franchise Systems, Inc., as the parent of both the Ramada Inns and Howard Johnson's franchise operations. The Rodeway Inns brand was sold to Choice Hotels. Hospitality Franchise Systems licensed the Ramada name from New World and assumed oversight for Ramada Inns. New World's Ramada International Hotels and Resorts continued to market the Ramada Renaissance properties.[46] A new economy-oriented brand, Ramada Limited, was emphasized in the 1990s. In 1993 there were 626 Ramada Inns, with the highest density decidedly along the East Coast (see Fig. 6.27).

HOWARD JOHNSON'S MOTOR LODGES

Howard Johnson was a pioneer of place-product-packaging along the American roadside. Taking over a variety store in Wollaston, Massachusetts, in 1925, Johnson began to manufacture his own brand of ice cream.

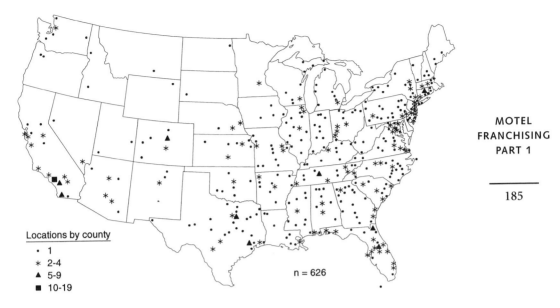

Locations by county
- · 1
- * 2-4
- ▲ 5-9
- ■ 10-19

n = 626

FIGURE 6.27 Ramada Inns, 1993. The leading counties were Los Angeles and San Diego in California, Davidson (Nashville) in Tennessee, and Orange in California, with 15, 9, 8, and 8 properties, respectively. The chain was headquartered in Parsippany, New Jersey.

The success of several roadside stands led to development of a 125-property restaurant chain spread across New England, New York, and New Jersey, with outliers in Florida, in the years immediately prior to World War II. Again, Johnson relied heavily on the co-ownership concept, retaining half-ownership in all franchised outlets. Howard Johnson's Restaurants were built according to carefully contrived design guidelines. Buildings sported orange porcelain tiled roofs crowned with ornamented cupolas, white walls, and turquoise shutters and trim. In 1971, at the peak of their popularity, there were 871 restaurants in operation, 575 of them under co-ownership. Most were located east of the Mississippi River, with the highest density in the Northeast.

In the late 1940s Howard Johnson's began to encourage motel development in conjunction with its restaurants, the restaurant and motel functions being seen as complementary. At Danville, Virginia, the Wayside Motor Court and the Howard Johnson's Restaurant were developed simultaneously but under different ownerships (see Fig. 6.28). In 1954 Howard Johnson's entered directly into the motel business as a franchiser. Five years later 71 properties had been established in the trade area served by the company's restaurants (see Fig. 6.29). Design Incorporated of St. Louis developed a set of prototypes, called "trademarks in color," that carried forward the orange and turquoise motif of the restaurants.[47] Motel build-

FIGURE 6.28 The Wayside Motor Court and Howard Johnson's Restaurant, Danville, Virginia, circa 1955.

FIGURE 6.29 Howard Johnson's Motor Lodges, 1959. The leading counties were Hudson (suburban New York City) in New Jersey and Montgomery (suburban Philadelphia) in Pennsylvania, with 3 properties each. The chain was headquartered in Boston.

HOWARD JOHNSON'S MOTOR LODGE

SPRINGFIELD, MISSOURI

FIGURE 6.30 The Howard Johnson's Motor Lodge, Springfield, Missouri, 1970. The message on the back of this postcard reads, in part: "The largest motel we have ever stayed in—and expensive, but extremely nice."

ings sported gabled roofs and, of course, exaggerated ornamentation born of the earlier restaurant cupolas. Exaggerated A-frame structures built as "gatekeeper" offices doubled as a kind of sign (see Fig. 6.30). Motels and restaurants, although complementary, were under separate franchise agreements and therefore separate management.

Bought in 1980 by the British tobacco and food conglomerate Imperial Group PLC, the Howard Johnson's motel and restaurant chains were sold to the Marriott Corporation in 1985. Marriott retained the company-owned restaurants but sold the motel and restaurant franchising operations to Prime Motor Inns, Inc. Formed in 1968, Prime was a public franchising company that owned and managed motels under the Ramada, Sheraton, Holiday Inn, and Howard Johnson's labels. The company's motels all targeted the commercial traveler in large urban areas. The Howard Johnson's chain, like the Ramada chain, suffered from obsolescence and lack of strict quality control. Previous managements had disinvested properties in a heavy profit squeeze. Strictly highway-oriented in their locations, Howard Johnson's motels and restaurants had assumed a "turnpike" image.[48] Turnpikes initially symbolized the modernism of automobility, but highways had come to connote noise, dirt, and traffic congestion.

Prime's management introduced a new logo, weeded out low-performance properties, and moved to promote strenuously the Hojo and Plaza-Hotel brands introduced earlier by the Imperial management. Wellesley Inns and AmeriSuites, two new brands, were established, and the Pickett

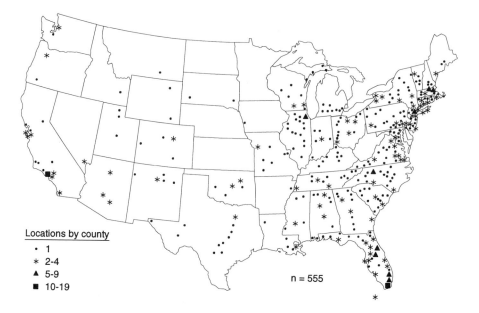

FIGURE 6.31 Howard Johnson's Motor Lodges, 1993. The leading counties were Dade (Miami) in Florida, Los Angeles in California, and Orange (Orlando) in Florida, with 11, 10, and 7 properties, respectively. The chain was headquartered in Parsippany, New Jersey.

Suite Hotel Company, which operated Guest Quarters Suite Hotels, was purchased. In 1990 the Howard Johnson's chain was sold once again. Acquired by the Blackstone Group, it was integrated into Blackstone's Hospitality Franchise System. Largely shorn of their orange roofs, turquoise ornamentation, and gatehouse image, there were 555 Howard Johnson's Motor Lodges across the country in 1993 (see Fig. 6.31). A substantial East Coast concentration remained, a clear reflection of the chain's origins and early vigor.

DAYS INNS

Founded by Cecil B. Day in Atlanta in 1970, Days Inn brought several innovative ideas to the hospitality field. Days Inn was created as a budget, full-service chain offering most of the Holiday Inn product and service line, but at discounted prices (see Fig. 6.32). One of the first chains to extend discounts to senior citizens as an important marketing emphasis, Days Inn was also one the first chains to emphasize interstate highway interchanges, not in the bigger cities, as Howard Johnson's did, but in peripheral suburban and small-town locations. Growth was rapid, the chain doubling in size every year through 1975. In 1982 there were 295 Days Inns, the vast majority arrayed along the major interstates of the Southeast (see Fig. 6.33). Especially evident on the 1982 map are I-75 and I-95

FIGURE 6.32 The Days Inn, Naples, Florida, circa 1980. Featured were cable TV, direct-dial telephones, and a twenty-four-hour restaurant.

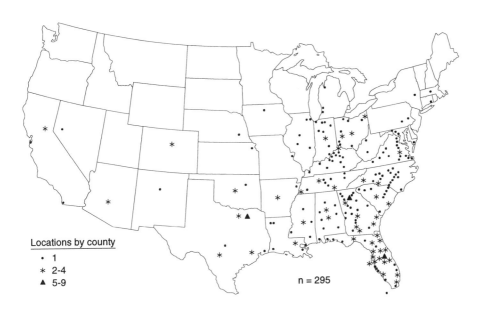

Locations by county
- • 1
- ✳ 2-4
- ▲ 5-9

n = 295

FIGURE 6.33 Days Inns, 1982. The leading counties were Orange (Orlando) in Florida, Dallas in Texas, and DeKalb (suburban Atlanta) in Georgia, with 8, 7, and 7 properties, respectively. The chain was headquartered in Atlanta.

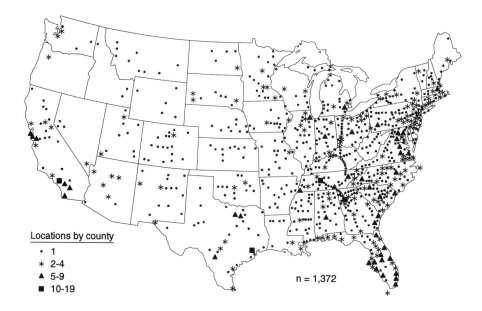

FIGURE 6.34 Days Inns, 1993. The leading counties were Los Angeles in California, Davidson (Nashville) in Tennessee, Fulton (Atlanta) in Georgia, Orange in California, and Orange in Florida, with 15, 13, 10, 9, and 9 properties, respectively. The chain was headquartered in Parsippany, New Jersey.

properties built to service Florida-oriented vacation travelers. Whereas other chains were reorienting to the commercial client, Days Inn remained unabashedly dedicated to the tourist. The vast majority of the Days Inns were franchised.

After Cecil Day's death in 1984 the Days Inns chain was sold to the Reliance Capital Group, a holding company with interests in real estate, insurance, supermarkets, and distribution of liquefied petroleum gas, among other enterprises. Reliance then set about to strip the company of assets prior to reselling the chain. Some 120 company-owned properties were sold to franchisees and investor syndicates for around $500 million (almost $142 million in cash and the rest in assumed debt or Day's Inn notes).[49] Reliance continued to hold management contracts on many of the properties sold, taking annual revenues of 5 percent plus management-incentive fees. From franchised properties Reliance also took a 6.5 percent franchise fee plus an advertising fee. In 1984 the investment firm of Tollman-Hundley acquired the Days Inn operation, selling it a year later to the Blackstone Group, which then added Days Inns to its Hospitality Franchise Systems subsidiary. The Thrifty Scot and Sunwood Inns chains were also acquired and added to the Days Inn group. As with the other Hospitality Franchise System brands, the chain's headquarters was moved to Parsippany, New Jersey.

Days Inns expanded primarily through conversions. Defrocked Holiday Inns, Ramada Inns, and properties from other older chains came to sport the Days Inn sunburst logo. The chain also aggressively marketed outside the Southeast and became one of the fastest-growing national brands during the late 1980s. In 1993 there were 1,372 Days Inns nationwide (see Fig. 6.34), many of them along interstate highway interchanges.

SUPER 8 MOTELS

Super 8 Motels was acquired in 1993, the purchase placing Hospitality Franchise System firmly in the budget or lower-economy segment of the market. Here was an instance of a small regional brand that successfully developed a place-product-packaging scheme directed at a specific market niche and then drove that program forward until its coverage was nationwide. Founded by attorney Dennis Brown in Aberdeen, South Dakota, in 1973, the company's 115-property chain of budget motels had spread across the entire northern Great Plains by 1981 (see Fig. 6.35). Critical to the chain's success was the place-product-packaging strategy worked out around a set of "Tudor-style" building prototypes that could be rapidly and cheaply erected and efficiently managed and maintained

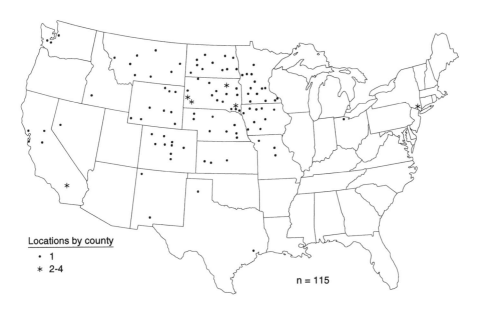

Locations by county
· 1
* 2-4

n = 115

FIGURE 6.35 Super 8 Motels, 1981. The leading county was Orange County, New York, with 3 properties. The chain was headquartered in Aberdeen, South Dakota.

FIGURE 6.36 The Super 8 Motel, Albuquerque, 1993. This Super 8 was located north of the city's business district in a cluster of motels at the intersection of I-40 and I-26.

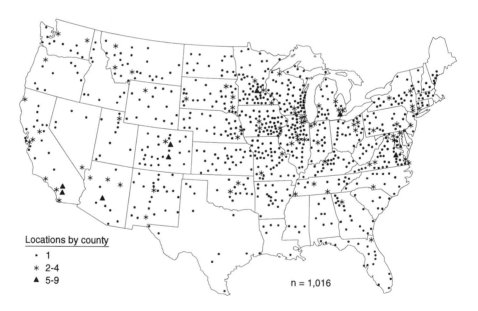

Locations by county
· 1
∗ 2-4
▲ 5-9

n = 1,016

FIGURE 6.37 Super 8 Motels, 1993. The leading counties included Riverside in California, Arapaho (suburban Denver) in Colorado, Hennepin (Minneapolis) in Minnesota, and San Bernardino in California, all with 6 properties each. The chain was headquartered in Parsippany, New Jersey.

(see Fig. 6.36). Super 8 buildings became a readily identifiable roadside sign, the name and the chain's logo derived from the initial room price, $8.88. Here was place-product-packaging at its most efficient.

Associated Contractors of America, a subsidiary, facilitated property development for investor syndicates. Growth accelerated. The chain opened a new property every forty days in 1976, every eighteen days in 1977, every fifteen days in 1978, every five days in 1984, and every ninety-seven hours in 1986.[50] Conversions constituted only 10–15 percent of the new additions. In essence, here was a chain built totally from scratch. Franchises were sold in wholesale quantities to selected investor groups. For example, Motels of America, Inc., based in San Diego, was a major Super 8 franchisee, with 45 properties. Thus franchising, which had started out as a means of bringing independent motel operators into national marketing systems, continued to mature as a device engendering "chains" within chains. In 1989 Super 8 began to experiment with economy suites, but its business remained "cheap sleep"—no-frills budget motels aimed at vacationers and business clients traveling by interstate highway. Secondary and tertiary urban markets remained the focus, first across the Middle West, then in the Northeast and the Far West, and finally in the South. In 1993 there were 1,016 Super 8 Motels nationwide (see Fig. 6.37). As with Days Inns, linear arrays of interstate highway locations are clearly evident on the map.

PARK INNS

Hospitality Franchise Systems acquired Park Inns in 1993. This small chain was founded in Dallas in 1988 by Robert L. Brock, an early Holiday Inns franchisee, a partner in Topeka Inn Management, and later the creator of the Showbiz Pizza Palace chain of restaurants. Brock had pioneered Holiday Inn's Holidome concept. The Park Inns chain expanded slowly, primarily, like Days Inns, through the conversion of older motel properties from other brands. In 1992 there were fifty-seven Park Inns scattered across the United States.

Franchising changed substantially. Between Quality Courts United's conversion from a referral chain and Super 8's overnight expansion along the nation's interstates, business-format franchising had come of age in the hospitality industry. In the first instance, franchising was marketed as a means of networking independent operators within national systems of place-product-packaging. In the latter instance, it was promoted more as a means of enticing investors speculating in real estate. Franchising had evolved from a mere option for those developing new motels to a necessity. Networking under the umbrella of an established brand reassured bankers, savings and loan officers, insurance company portfolio managers, and others who held the purse strings of investment capital. Networking through a chain promised sustained business generated through chain reservation systems. Chain affiliation required adherence to standards and provided absentee owners and their financiers with performance guarantees. A business system was critical to absentee ownership.

7

Motel Franchising – Part 2

IN THIS CHAPTER WE CONTINUE THE STORY OF PLACE-PRODUCT-PACK-aging in the motel industry, contrasting the rise of national chains with that of smaller regional companies. We then focus on the specialty brands targeted to budget, all-suite, and luxury hotel markets. We also explore the drift back to ownership chains during the 1980s and 1990s, as well as the evolving strategy of retaining management contracts for motel properties developed. Thus we visit the management company, an increasingly important component of the hospitality industry. We also acknowledge the unsuccessful chains, those that thrived only briefly along America's roadsides, and ask what undermined those attempts at place-product-packaging. Finally, we grapple with the process of rebranding, a strategy by which motel owners reposition themselves in a changed motel market.

The common modes of franchising were revised in the 1970s and 1980s as companies experimented with other means of chain expansion and operation. Management contracts, lease agreements, limited partnerships, joint ventures, and an outright return to ownership chain operations were among the means adopted. Quality control had always been franchisors' major difficulty in maintaining brand integrity. The inability or the unwillingness of franchisees to adhere to business formats and otherwise maintain standards was a problem for even the best-managed chains. Properties that violated standards damaged the whole. Chains, after all, were only as strong as their weakest members.

Hospitality International

Hospitality International (not to be confused with the larger Hospitality Franchise Systems) came to promote a number of motel brands targeted at

the budget end of the limited-service market. Its Red Carpet Inns, Scottish Inns, and Passport Inns have largely been newly constructed, located near interstate highway interchanges. Its Master Hosts and Downtowner brands, on the other hand, have comprised motels remaining from once vigorous franchise companies. Hospitality International is a study in brand persistence, the value of its brands sustaining the enterprise despite numerous changes in corporate ownership and management style.

RED CARPET INNS

Red Carpet Inns of America, founded by a former president of Quality Courts United, became a motel franchiser in 1969. Headquartered in Daytona Beach, Florida, the firm operated two subsidiaries, the Red Carpet Construction Company and Red Carpet Financial Services, Inc. Among its early franchisees was Candyland, Inc., of Jesup, Georgia, which built and operated 14 Red Carpet Inns along interstate highways across the South, each motel including a Candyland Restaurant. In two years the chain grew to 29 properties, with another 131 franchises sold.[1] The chain numbered 124 properties in 1993, many of them along interstate highways, especially I-75 in Georgia (see Fig. 7.1).[2] Although the chain operated a reservation service, much of its patronage came from "windshield" decision making, customers selecting Red Carpet Inns based on their appearance and accessibility. The chain's red signs featured the outline of a burning candle.

FIGURE 7.1 Red Carpet Inns, 1993. Interstate highway locations in Georgia and Florida are especially apparent on this map. The chain was headquartered in suburban Atlanta.

FIGURE 7.2 Master Hosts Motor Hotels, 1966.

Locations by county
- • 1
- * 2-4
- ▲ 5-9

n = 246

MASTER HOSTS INNS

The Master Hosts Motor Hotels Association was formed as a nonprofit referral chain in 1952. It was very much the Cadillac of the referral chains movement, accepting only members with luxury-end properties. Each motel offered its customers a full range of hotel services, and maintenance standards were very high. This Fort Worth–based network had 246 members by 1966 (see Fig. 7.2). In 1969 the chain was acquired by International Industries, Inc., and converted to a franchising company, its name changed to Master Hosts Motor Hotels. Members were given stock in the new company and extended an option to either purchase a franchise or retain referral membership. In 1971 Red Carpet Inns of American purchased the Master Hosts chain, then down to 200 properties.[3] The Red Carpet and Master Hosts logistical operations were combined, although each brand survived to designate separate chains. The Master Hosts chain lost momentum as properties aged and ownerships changed; in 1993 only 7 were still operating.

SCOTTISH INNS

Scottish Inns of America was organized in the late 1960s at Kingston, Tennessee, expressly to build an ownership chain using modular construction. Like Imperial 400, the company adopted the Scottish themes of thriftiness and value in developing its image. Modules were constructed and shipped to motel sites from plants in Tennessee and Florida. Rooms, produced at a rate of one per hour in 1972, could be installed for as little as $6,000, perhaps the lowest cost per room in the industry.[4] The company did not operate motels itself; rather, it leased motels to independent operators in return for half of the room revenues. Scottish Inns paid financing costs, taxes, and insurance costs and assumed responsibility for building repairs. A franchise operation was also begun, a separate organization owned jointly by Services Concepts International, Inc. (a group of former Kentucky Fried Chicken executives), and Scottish Inns of America.

In 1973 Scottish Inns reversed its leasing policy and assumed the management of all but a handful of its owned properties. The company was reorganized in 1978 through absorption of its largest franchisee, Southern Scottish Inns of New Orleans, and its headquarters was moved to Nashville. In 1982 the chain comprised 75 properties concentrated mainly in Southeast. In 1993 there were 148 properties, still located in the same region. Like the Red Carpet Inns, most of these motels were located along interstate highways. Red Carpet Inns absorbed Scottish Inns in 1985 to form Hospitality International, headquartered first in Biloxi, Mississippi, then in Tucker, Georgia, a suburb of Atlanta.

DOWNTOWNER MOTOR INNS AND PASSPORT INNS

Organized in 1958, the Downtowner Corporation of Memphis sought a specific market niche. Building and operating its own motels, as well as franchising the Downtowner brand, the company targeted business-district locations in small and large cities (see Figs. 2.35 and 7.3). Specifically, Downtowner Motor Inns were located near large downtown hotels in order to benefit from the spillover of convention and other hotel business. One of the chain's earliest properties was located across the street from the Hotel Peabody in Memphis. Journalist Seymour Freedgood wrote in *Fortune:* "It might be called the downtown 'leeching market.' The Downtowner strategy, which is now emulated by all the chains in some degree, is simple in the extreme. 'The idea'. . . is to throw up a hundred or so rooms across the street from the big convention hotel in town and operate them without frills."[5] Such facilities then "leeched" off hotel traffic. A new brand, Rowntowner Motor Inns, was introduced in 1967 to promote expansion in suburban locations.

As central business districts declined in American cities, so also did downtown hotels and, consequently, the Downtowner chain. The decline precipitated a string of ownership changes. The Aetna Life and Casualty Insurance Company refinanced the company in 1971, taking part ownership. Perkins Pancake House acquired the chain in 1972 and moved the company headquarters to Las Vegas. There were in that year 78 properties in the chain, 29 of them company-owned and 20 franchised.[6] In 1973 the

FIGURE 7.3 The Downtowner Motor Inn, Florence, South Carolina, circa 1965.

chain was purchased by Dynamic Motel Management, Inc., of Nashville, which sold it to Hotel Systems of America, Inc., of Memphis, in 1975. At the same time, Hotel Systems of America bought the newly created Passport brand. In 1985 the company was sold once again, this time to a Nashville investor syndicate, which, in turn, passed the two company's two brands on to Hospitality International. In 1993 there were only two Downtowner Inns (in Hot Springs, Arkansas, and Athens, Georgia). There were 17 Passport Inns, most of which were located at I-75 interchanges in Georgia.

Marriott

Marriott is one of the oldest names in franchising, both as a franchisee and as a franchiser. In 1926 J. Willard Marriott bought the A&W root beer franchise for Washington, D.C., which led to a successful restaurant chain, the Hot Shoppes. In 1937 Marriott began catering flights out of Washington's National Airport for both Eastern Airlines and Capital Airlines. During World War II the company's food services were extended to industrial plants, hospitals, and governmental offices. By 1976 the Marriott Corporation claimed to be the world's largest food-service organization, with 150 Hot Shoppes and airline commissaries at twenty major airports.[7] The company also owned Big Boy Restaurants of America, the franchiser of the Big Boy coffee shops in some six hundred locations nationwide. In 1967 the Roy Rogers Western Roast Beef franchise chain was acquired, and all of the service and control functions of the Marriott Company were consolidated into a new central commissary division, Fairfield Farm Kitchens, headquartered in Prince Georges County, Maryland.

The company's first motel, the luxury Marriott Motor Hotel, was opened near National Airport in 1956. Promoted as the world's largest motel, the property contained 370 rooms in eleven buildings, a restaurant (operated by Hot Shoppes), a gift and convenience store, barber and beauty shops, a swimming pool, and a children's play area. Bellboys on bicycles escorted guests from the registration area to parking spaces adjacent to their rooms.[8] By 1966 additional motor inns had been opened in Dallas, Philadelphia, and Newark. Two years later the company expanded into full-service hotels through purchase of the Essex Hotel, overlooking New York City's Central Park. Various Marriott motels were made members of either the Quality Courts United or the Master Hosts referral chains. However, the company determined, after Quality Courts United became a franchise company, to promote its own Marriott brand. By 1974 the Marriott Company owned 37 motels, 5 resorts, 2 condominiums, 3 cruise ships, and 2 theme parks (the Great America Parks, in Illinois and California).[9]

MARRIOTT HOTELS AND RESORTS

In 1969 Marriott established a franchise division but chose to manage all the properties it franchised. Marriott developed properties and then sold them to investment syndicates, retaining management contracts. In 1980 there were 493 Marriott hotel and motel properties with more than 126,000 guest rooms.[10] Through the 1980s the Marriott organization vigorously embraced market segmentation, targeting brands at certain customer groups. At the top of the company's hierarchy of products stood Marriott Hotels and Resorts. Next came Residence Inns, Courtyard by Marriott, and Fairfield Inns, properties packaged as motels. In 1992, 211 hotels, resorts, and all-suite hotels operated under the Marriott name, the highest concentrations located in and around the major northeastern cities from Boston to Washington, D.C. (see Fig. 7.4). Included were the two flagship Marriott Marquis Hotels, in New York City and Atlanta.

RESIDENCE INNS

Residence Inns began as the Brock Residence Inn Franchise System, headquartered in Wichita, Kansas. Purchased by Holiday Inns in 1985, the chain was then sold to Marriott in 1987. From the beginning, Residence Inns were promoted as "extended-stay," all-suite motels targeted at business people attending conferences, temporarily assigned away from home, or moving residences in the context of job transfer. Rooms were large and organized into separate functional areas, following the all-suite concept. Each suite included a fully equipped kitchen (see Fig. 7.5). In 1992 there

Locations by county
- • 1
- ∗ 2-4
- ▲ 5-9

n = 211

*Includes Marriott Suites and Resorts

FIGURE 7.4 Marriott Hotels, 1992. The leading counties were Fairfax and Arlington in Virginia, Harris (Houston) in Texas, and Los Angeles in California,
with 7 properties each. The chain was headquartered in Washington, D.C.

FIGURE 7.5 Advertising from the 1992
Marriott directory depicting Residence Inn
room prototypes.

MORE LIKE AN APARTMENT THAN A HOTEL

With several spacious room layouts to choose from,
depending on location, you feel more like you're at home
than on the road.

STUDIO

Our over-sized Studio offers you all of the conveniences
and comforts of home– including a fully-equipped kitchen.

PENTHOUSE SUITE

The spectacular two-story Penthouse Suite gives you a
flexible floor plan with twice as much space as a conventional

FIGURE 7.6 Residence Inns, 1992. The leading counties were Orange in California, with 7 properties; and King (Seattle) in Washington and Los Angeles in California, with 5 each. The chain was headquartered in Washington, D.C.

FIGURE 7.7 Courtyard Inns by Marriott, 1992. The leading counties were Dallas in Texas, with 7 properties; and Cook (Chicago) in Illinois, DeKalb (suburban Atlanta) and Fulton (Atlanta) in Georgia, Fairfax and Arlington in Virginia, and Orange in California, with 5 each. The chain was headquartered in Washington, D.C.

were 179 Residence Inns nationwide, located primarily in medium to large urban markets, preferably near suburban office parks (see Fig. 7.6).

COURTYARD BY MARRIOTT

Courtyard by Marriott was launched in the early 1980s following years of market research and prototype testing in the Atlanta market.[11] Each 125- to 150-room, two-story motel was developed around a courtyard, which lent a domestic ambiance, each property simulating a suburban luxury apartment or condominium complex. Targeted was the discerning guest who wanted "an attractive, comfortable, functional room; a relaxing, secure environment; a relatively simple restaurant; helpful friendly staff; and an affordable price."[12] Courtyard properties were extensively landscaped, designed to resemble country inns. And the central courtyard contained a swimming pool. Most Courtyards by Marriott were located in suburbs of major cities, near airports, major shopping centers, or office parks. In 1992, 198 Courtyards were in operation, the largest concentration between Boston and Washington, D.C. (see Fig. 7.7). Marriott's upscale motel product has generated much imitation: Club House Inns of America, Wyndham Garden Hotels, Quality Inn's Benchmark Inns, and Hil-Crest by Hilton. The term *clubcourt* has been coined to describe this distinctive motel package.

FAIRFIELD INNS

The Fairfield Inns brand was launched in 1986 to target the economy, limited-service segment of the hospitality market. By the end of 1988 the chain had 18 properties in operation, and by the end of 1992, 119, concentrated largely in the Middle West (see Fig. 7.8). Rooms were small and accessed, in most properties, by means of outside stairways and balconies. Most Fairfield Inns were located near interstate highway interchanges in suburban locations. The chain, like Marriott's food-service commissary, was named after the family's forty-five-hundred-acre Fairfield Farm in Virginia. Like the company's Residence Inn and Courtyard chains, the Marriott name is closely linked through signage and advertising with the Fairfield name. The hope was that the reputation of the prestigious Marriott Hotels and Resorts would enhance the reputation of the corporation's lesser products.

In 1985 Marriott purchased the struggling Howard Johnson's Company and then broke it up into separate units, selling the motel business to Prime Motor Inns and keeping the restaurants. In 1990 Marriott was second only to Pepsico in total food and beverage sales.[13] But Marriott also continued to be a major player in the hotel and motel business even

without the Howard Johnson's motels. In 1987 one of every three new hotels built in the United States was a Marriott hotel.[14] In 1990 the company
controlled an estimated 4 percent of the U.S. $50 billion lodging mar-
ket and had begun to call itself the world's largest "hotel operator."[15] In
1994 the company was divided into two separate corporations: Marriott
International was to provide management and contract services for 139
owned properties among 762 hotels and motels carrying the Marriott
name; Host Marriott was to inherit ownership of those 139 properties and
14 retirement communities and to operate airports concessions and the
restaurants.[16]

The reorganization plan involved a spin-off of some $2.8 billion in debt
to Host Marriott. At bottom was the decision to emphasize management
rather than ownership, with Marriott International intended to be the
principal corporate successor. The plan suggested that Marriott valued
its lodging interests most. Indeed, the company had come to the conclusion that the restaurant divisions should be sold. The restaurant industry was characterized as mature and thus not conducive to rapid growth.
Michael Porter, in his book *Competitive Strategies,* suggests that an industry exhibits the following characteristics when it makes the transition
from growth to maturity: "impending market saturation, customers' being able to choose among a selection of leading brands, limited product

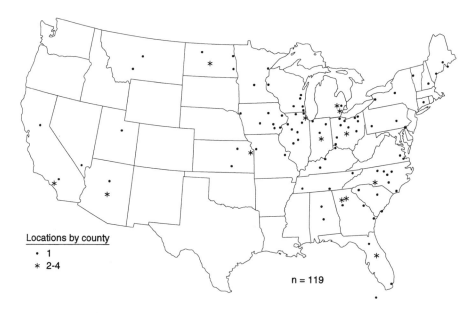

FIGURE 7.8 Fairfield Inns, 1992. The leading counties were Cook (Chicago) in
Illinois and Fulton (Atlanta) in Georgia, with 3 properties each. The chain was
headquartered in Washington, D.C.

FIGURE 7.9 The La Quinta Motor Inn, San Antonio, Texas, circa 1970. (Photo by Frank Whaley, P.O. Box 8557, Corpus Christi, Texas 78142.)

differentiation among competitors, competition waged through mass advertising, players' engaging in price competition and dealing, shakeouts of major players, strong cyclicality of revenue streams, generally falling prices, and lower profits and margins for all players."[17]

La Quinta Motor Inns

Sam and Philip Barshop's La Quinta Motor Inns began as Barshop Motel Enterprises, the largest franchisee of Rodeway Inns. Reorganized as LQ Motor Inns in 1973, the company focused on the La Quinta Inns concept developed five years earlier to accommodate visitors to San Antonio's World's Fair. By 1980 the La Quinta chain comprised 95 properties, 81 company-owned and the remainder licensed as franchises.[18] La Quinta Motor Inns, which targeted the business traveler, had 100 to 125 rooms and were located at interstate highway interchanges near airports, medical centers, or office parks in metropolitan areas with at least 100,000 population. Inns were clustered, with none located more than three hundred miles from another. Prices were 25 percent lower than those of competing Holiday Inns.

The name La Quinta comes from the Spanish word *quinta*, meaning "villa," and so inns were designed according to a Spanish or Mediterranean architectural vocabulary (see Fig. 7.9). Buildings were standardized through the use of precast concrete panels. Bathrooms were prefabricated. Restaurants, most of which were built by La Quinta, were located adjacent to most motels and leased to national restaurant operators such as Sambo's or Denny's. Properties were managed by husband-and-wife teams, who received free lodging in a one-bedroom apartment, food discounts at the adjacent restaurant, free laundry and local telephone services, and a monthly car allowance.[19]

The company grew through massive infusions of capital from the Prudential, Metropolitan, and New York Life insurance companies as well as from investors, such as BNL Development Corporation, a subsidiary of the Burlington Northern Railroad. All of these companies entered into joint venture agreements with La Quinta. Thus the Barshops turned away from franchising and relied instead on limited partnerships and other devices. The company discontinued domestic franchise licensing in 1977, although it continued to franchise in Mexico. Motel quality was difficult to control through franchising, a lesson La Quinta had learned earlier as Rodeway Inn's exclusive franchisee in several southwestern states. In 1990 La Quinta began an extensive renovation and remodeling program, in the process adopting a modified sign. The company also began to rebrand older motels, often from other chains, and give them the La Quinta name. In 1993 there were 112 La Quinta Inns, the majority concentrated in Texas and the Southeast (see Fig. 7.10). The chain was notably absent from the nation's northernmost states.

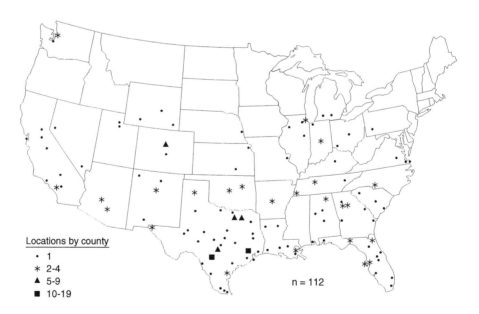

Locations by county
- • 1
- * 2-4
- ▲ 5-9
- ■ 10-19

n = 112

FIGURE 7.10 La Quinta Inns, 1993. The leading counties, all in Texas, included Harris (Houston), with 16 properties; Bexar (San Antonio), with 11; and Tarrant (Fort Worth), with 8. Dallas County in Texas and Denver County in Colorado had 7 each. The chain was headquartered in San Antonio.

FIGURE 7.11 The Budgetel Inn, Effingham, Illinois, 1993.

Marcus—Budgetel

The Marcus Corporation of Milwaukee is rooted in the theater business. Through the 1930s and 1940s Benjamin Marcus built a chain of movie houses across Wisconsin, and in the 1950s his company concentrated on drive-in theaters. Having branched out into film distribution, vending, and real estate development, Marcus turned to building a chain of restaurants, buying the Big Boy franchise for Wisconsin, Minnesota, and Iowa and rights to Kentucky Fried Chicken for selected Big Boy locations. In 1970 more than twenty Marc's Big Boys and twenty-one separate Kentucky Fried Chicken stores were in operation.[20] Next established was the Captain's Joynt restaurant chain, the first two in rebranded Howard Johnson's buildings. By 1979 the number of company-owned theaters had grown to 83, and the number of restaurants to 109.[21]

The firm entered the hotel business in the 1960s, first in Oshkosh and then in Milwaukee, where two large downtown hotels, the Pfister and the Sheraton Schroeder, were renovated, the latter renamed the Marc Plaza. The company also managed the new Sheraton Mayfair. Two Guesthouse Motor Inns were opened in Appleton and Manitowoc, Wisconsin, respectively. But a new idea, Budgetel, conceived as a limited-service, discount-priced motel chain, was launched by Steven Marcus, heir to the company's management. The first property opened in Oshkosh in 1973. Initially the firm planned to own and operate half of its new inns, franchising the remainder.[22] Accordingly, a prototype building was designed in 1984 to enhance franchise sales (see Fig. 7.11). Long, linear, three- or four-story boxes sheathed in precast concrete slabs, the Budgetels had a distinctive appearance. By 1987 fifty-seven inns had been opened, only four of them franchised.[23] Each Budgetel featured oversized guestrooms and spacious hallways for inside entry. "Luxury for less" was the motto. In 1993 there were ninety-eight Budgetels in the Middle West and the Southeast, approximately one-quarter of them franchised (see Fig. 7.12).

ELS—Knights and Arborgate Inns

Like Budgetel, the Knights Inns had a distinctive architectural program. Knights Inn was a division of Cardinal Industries, the latter firm founded in 1954 in Columbus, Ohio, as a housing prefabricator using modular, assembly-line construction. Cardinal specialized in apartments and condominiums and in the early 1970s developed a modular motel room. The first Knights Inn opened in 1973, and by 1979 the chain had twenty-two properties.[24] The inns were extensively landscaped, and the decor was "Tudor," with roughly sawn cedar beams, decorative wall murals, and a color scheme of "royal" blue, red, and purple. Double walls reduced heat loss. Single-story construction meant less noise and facilitated parking immediately adjacent to rooms. The chain's logo featured the outline of a

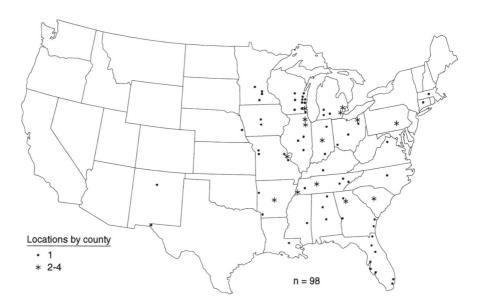

Locations by county
• 1
* 2-4

n = 98

FIGURE 7.12 Budgetel Inns, 1993. The leading counties were Davidson (Nashville) in Tennessee, with 4 properties; and Cook (Chicago) in Illinois, Fulton (Atlanta) in Georgia, Milwaukee in Wisconsin, and Wayne (Detroit) in Michigan, with 3 each.

FIGURE 7.13 A Knights Inn advertising promotion, circa 1975. The postcard reads: "The only 2nd story at Knights Inn!" Initially the company's motels were built with prefabricated, modular units, all of a single story, replicating the more traditional motel.

crenelated castle (see Fig. 7.13). Arborgate Inns, a complementary brand, also featured the same prefabricated units, but their design was contemporary. Knights "Stop" and Knights "Court" brands were later additions.

Like Scottish Inns, Knights Inns and Arborgate Inns were factory-built and shipped to motel sites on trucks. Rooms were 98 percent complete" on arrival and included all furnishings, even linens, towels, ashtrays, and drapes. Most Knights Inns were franchised, but Cardinal Industries, through limited partnership agreements, acted as the managing partner. Thus the company built and managed all properties, the franchise merely serving as an investment instrument for local investors. In 1989, Cardinal's lodging division was made a separate corporation following Chapter 11 bankruptcy. ELS (for Economy Lodging Systems) now operates the motels as an affiliate of Hospitality Management Services (HMS). Previously, HMS had been a management company operating Comfort Inns, Travelodges, Econo Lodges, Days Inns, and a Holiday Inn, all in Ohio or Illinois.

In the 1990s ELS stepped away from strict use of Knights Inn building prototypes. This move was prompted by the rebranding of many Knights Inns not owned by the company (conversions to Motel 6, Travelodge, Days Inns, and other brands) and by the company's purchase of other motels for rebranding. Nonetheless, the company successfully sued in the

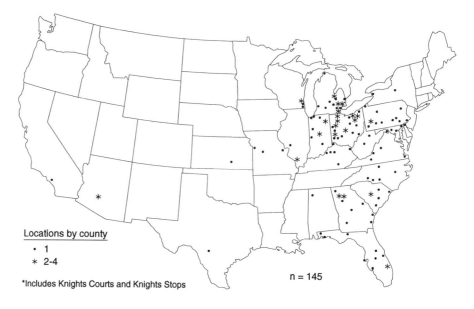

Locations by county
- • 1
- * 2-4

*Includes Knights Courts and Knights Stops

n = 145

FIGURE 7.14 Knights Inns and Arborgate Inns, 1992. Interstate highway locations predominated, especially along I-75 in Ohio and Michigan. The chain was headquartered in suburban Columbus, Ohio.

courts to require the new owners of old Knights Inns to completely alter the look of their properties. According to the court ruling, ELS retained the "trade dress" or "total image and overall appearance" of the Tudor prototypes.[25] New owners had not only to resign their properties but to change their physical appearance through "deidentification." In 1992 there were 145 Knights Inns and Arborgate Inns in the Middle West and the Southeast, with the highest concentration in Ohio, along the I-75 and I-71 interchanges (see Fig. 7.14).

BUDGET CHAINS

We have already discussed several brands that were either launched as or developed into economy, limited-service products—Super 8, Econo Lodge, and Friendship Inns. Absorbed by larger corporations, these brands targeted the economy segment of the hospitality market. Here we focus on the independent budget brands. In 1990, fourteen chains in the United States offered rooms priced at less than $25.00 (see Table 7.1). "No-frills" operations with prices set well below the market average were encouraged. Both the budget-conscious vacationist and the business traveler were targeted. Several chains grew into national operations, but most have remained regional in implication.

TABLE 7.1 Largest Budget Motel Chains in the United States, 1990

Rank	Brand	Properties	Single-Occupancy Rooms	Lowest Room Rate
1.	Super 8	672	42,200	$22.88
2.	Econo Lodge	560	44,606	20.00
3.	Motel 6	522	59,900	17.95
4.	Red Roof Inns	204	22,700	23.96
5.	National 9 Inns	137	7,400	24.00
6.	Friendship Inns	120	6,000	20.00
7.	Allstar Inns	73	7,800	20.00
8.	Regal Inns	53	5,500	24.88
9.	Vagabond Inns	43	3,700	20.00
10.	E-Z 8 Motels	34	3,300	19.88
11.	Family Inns	34	3,100	15.77
12.	Excel Inns	28	3,200	24.00
13.	Travelers Inns	26	3,500	20.00
14.	Economy Inns of America	22	2,500	19.90

Source: Daniel W. Daniele, "Budget Chain Breakdown," *Hotel and Motel Management* 205 (April 30, 1990): 1, 43–44, 46, 50, 56, 58–62.

Note: Motels included are those in which the lowest single-occupancy room rate is less than $25.00.

Accor S.A.—Motel 6

Home builders William Becker and Paul Greene launched Motel 6 in Santa Barbara, California, in 1962, initially charging $6.60 for a single room. They bought materials in bulk and built to the same basic blueprint in each new location (see Fig. 7.15). Rooms came with only the bare necessities. Pay phones were available at the office, and television sets were coin-operated. To keep labor costs low, rooms were designed for minimal maid service, and repairs were handled by teams of maintenance workers dispatched from the central office. Business was conducted on strictly a cash basis. Because "through-the-windshield" decision making accounted for most customers, the firm was slow to develop a reservation system. All properties—145 in 1973—were owned and managed by the company (see Fig. 7.16).

In 1985 the chain was acquired by the Motel Holding Company through a leveraged buyout arranged by Kohlberg, Kravis, Roberts, and Company. The new owners began to upgrade the company's motels by adding such amenities as telephones, free color television, and credit-card acceptance. The chain began to experience "amenity creep," the offering of more and more extras, but always at a budget price. In 1987 the chain

FIGURE 7.15 Motel 6, Bakersfield, California, circa 1970.

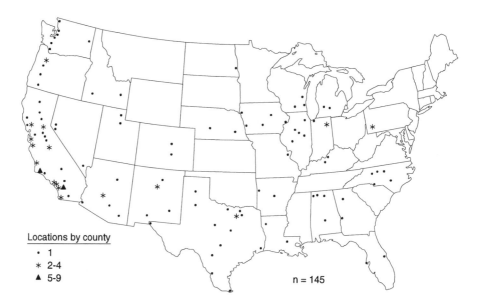

FIGURE 7.16 Motel 6, 1973. The leading counties, all in California, were Santa Barbara, with 6 properties; Riverside, with 5; and Los Angeles, with 4. The I-5 locations in California, Oregon, and Washington were important, as were the Route 99 locations in California. The chain was headquartered in Santa Barbara.

opened an Atlanta office and begin extensive expansion in the East, partly through the purchase of small regional chains. A year later the corporate headquarters moved to Dallas. Perhaps, no other motel company benefited more from radio advertising, specifically Tom Bodett's "And we'll leave the light on for you" radio spots, which developed something of a cult following in the early 1990s. In 1991 Motel 6 acquired some 50 Regal 8 properties from Tollman-Hundley Hotels, strengthening the chain in the Middle West. In 1991 Paris-based Accor S.A., then the world's largest lodging holding company, acquired Motel 6. In 1993 there were 738 Motel 6s nationwide, with the highest concentration in California (see Fig. 7.17). As Figure 7.17 shows they were linearly arrayed along interstate highways.

Other Budget Chains

Like Motel 6, the Red Roof Inns chain is company-owned and -operated. Headquartered in suburban Columbus, Ohio, it spread first across the Middle West and then into the Northeast and the Southeast. The first motel opened in 1973; 69 properties were in operation by 1982, and 206 by 1993 (see Fig. 7.18).[26] The company was acquired by the Morgan Stanley Real Estate Fund in 1993. Its distinctive, red-roofed prototype building is readily identifiable. Inns are located near interstate interchanges but rarely at them, which helps keep real estate costs down. Red Roof Inns are deliberately situated near the properties of other chains in order to enjoy a "spillover" effect, customers being diverted from other motels by Red Roof's equally attractive presence and lower prices.

Microtel is another budget chain of note. Launched specifically to fight "amenity creep," this company introduced a prototype building with guest rooms designed for maximum operating efficiency. Rooms were a mere 192 square feet, compared with 275 square feet for the average motel room.[27] Furnishings were built-in to minimize maintenance. Microtel also engaged in "parasite marketing," drawing customers from the nearby properties of better-known chains. Lehigh Hotel Properties, owner of the chain, contracted management to a subsidiary, the Hudson Hotels Corporation. Here was place-product-packaging of a high order. Indeed, the system was successfully defended in the courts against the infringement of Choice Hotel's Sleep Inn design.[28] Nonetheless, in 1993 there were only eleven Microtels.

Unlike Red Roof Inns and Microtel, which are latter-day ownership chains, Budget Host Inns revives the old referral chain idea. Established in 1976, Budget Host was intended to link older, independent, full-service motels that wanted to target the budget market.[29] One of the chain's

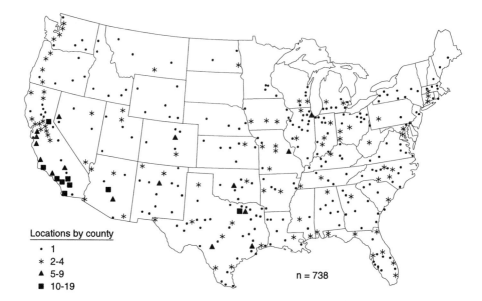

FIGURE 7.17 Motel 6, 1993. The leading counties, all in California, were San Bernardino, with 19 properties; and Los Angeles and Riverside, with 18 each. Maricopa County (Phoenix) in Arizona had 14 properties; and San Diego, Orange, Sacramento, and Santa Barbara Counties in California had 12, 11, 10, and 10, respectively. The chain was headquartered in Dallas.

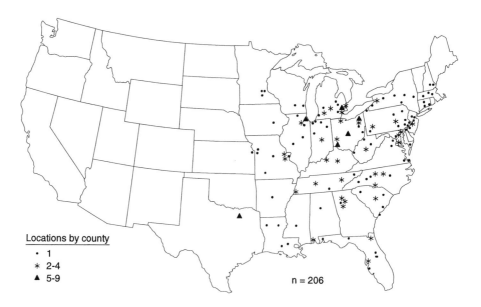

FIGURE 7.18 Red Roof Inns, 1993. The leading counties were Franklin (Columbus) in Ohio, with 7 properties; Cuyahoga (Cleveland) and Hamilton (Cincinnati), also in Ohio, with 5 each; and Cook (Chicago) in Illinois, Dallas in Texas, and Oakland (suburban Detroit) in Michigan, also with 5 each. The chain was headquartered in suburban Columbus, Ohio.

founders, Ray Sawyer, was previously editor of *Motel/Motor Inn Journal*. Originally called the *Tourist Court Journal*, this trade magazine long promoted the interests of the industry's independent operators. In 1993 there were 156 participating Budget Host members. Budget Host served to complement the Best Western chain, accepting independent motels that were unwilling or unable to meet the requirements of the much stronger referral system. Budget Host provided independents with a mechanism for confronting the Motel 6s, the Red Roof Inns, and the Super 8s.

REGIONAL MID-PRICED CHAINS

Important also are the mid-priced regional chains. Their treatment, as well as discussions of the all-suite hotel and luxury hotel chains which follows, allows a sense of completion—a full coverage of the hospitality industry through to the threshold of the twenty-first century.

The Northeast

New England and the Middle Atlantic States have been extensively covered by the major chains. Several national companies originated in the Northeast (Sheraton, Howard Johnson's), and one is headquartered there today (Hospitality Franchise Systems). No national chain can afford not to have a major presence in the Northeast, which perhaps explains the general lack of strictly regional brands operating there in contrast to other parts of the country. One regional player—Susse Chalet—deserves comment. Organized in 1967, the company pursued a place-product-packaging scheme built around Swiss architectural themes. Since the words *Swiss* and *Suisse* could not be trademarked (no place name can be copyrighted), the name *Susse* was contrived. The company constructed its own motels using precast and prestressed concrete techniques. Franchising was dropped in the early 1970s in favor of company-owned properties, and in 1977 there were only twenty-three units in the Susse Chalet system. During the 1980s the company built inns primarily to sell or refinance to investor syndicates.[30] In 1993 there were thirty-six Susse Chalets, most of them in New England.

The Middle West

Regional chains abound in the Middle West, which has also proven to be fertile ground for the incubation of several national chains (Super 8, Budgetel, Carlson, ELS). In 1993 Best Inns of America, headquartered in Marion, Illinois, operated twenty-five properties, largely in Illinois,

FIGURE 7.19 The Cross Country Inn, west of Columbus, Ohio, on I-70. The photo shows the drive-through reception "desk."

Indiana, and Missouri. Another chain, Cross Country, originated as a construction company. Expanding on the building of apartments in 1983, in ten years Thomas Benadum created a twenty-five-property motel chain situated in the Columbus, Cleveland, Cincinnati, Toledo, and Detroit areas. Distinctive buildings with drive-in registration facilities came to clearly signify Cross Country Inns at its locations at interstate highway interchanges (see Fig. 7.19). Excel Inns, of Madison, Wisconsin, operated twenty-eight properties in Wisconsin, Minnesota, Iowa, and Illinois in 1993. Also having roots in apartment-building construction, Excel Inns developed not only a distinctive prototype building but an innovative construction technology that involved stacking masonry blocks without mortar and then covering them with stuccolike bonding. Like Best Inns and Cross Country Inns, Excel Inns also owns and manages its properties.

Heartland Inns of Waterloo, Iowa, operated nineteen properties, largely in Iowa, in 1993. Lees Inns of North Vernon, Indiana, operated seventeen motels, most of them in the Indianapolis area. Select Inns of Fargo, North Dakota, operated thirteen motels in the Dakotas and Minnesota. Signature Inns of Indianapolis operated twenty-nine properties from Iowa in the west to Ohio in the east, although the majority, like the Lees Inns, were concentrated around Indiana's capital city. Dillon Inns, managed by Vista Host, Inc., operated some sixteen motels from Nebraska and Oklahoma in the west to Indiana and Michigan in the east; however, in 1993 the organization rebranded its properties, converting most of them to Hampton Inns. A decade earlier the company's president spoke of the chain's "recognition problem." Dillon Inns had to be located at "visible, accessible sites" where the architecture could be perceived as distinguishing.[31] Indeed, failure to achieve strong visibility, even in a limited regional market, led many small chains, including Dillon Inns, to rebrand their properties.

One middle western regional, the St. Louis–based Drury Inns, in the 1990s appeared well positioned for sustained growth. Like most of the other regionals, Drury Inns was rooted in the residential construction business, in this instance a plastering company. Like many other companies, Drury Inns developed a prototype building to give the firm a distinctive image across its trade territory. The chain comprised forty-one properties in 1993, concentrated mostly in Missouri, but there were some properties in Colorado and Texas (see Fig. 7.20). A chain of eleven budget-oriented Thrifty Inns had also been established, largely through the conversion of older motel properties rather than through new construction.

The Southeast

Admiral Benbow illustrates the fate of most small regional chains that have evolved over decades. Lacking a threshold in its chosen territory, many properties became part of more visible, national brands. Founded in 1961, the company became a subsidiary of the Morrison Cafeteria chain

Locations by county
· 1
* 2-4

n = 41

FIGURE 7.20 Drury Inns, 1992. The leading counties were Bexar (San Antonio) in Texas and St. Louis in Missouri, with 3 properties each. The chain was headquartered in suburban St. Louis.

Locations by county
· 1
* 2-4

n = 60

FIGURE 7.21 Shoney's Inns, 1993. The chain was headquartered in Gallatin, Tennessee.

seven years later. Twenty-three properties were operating in 1975, most of them located near airports or at interstate highway interchanges.[32] When the chain was sold to Universal Development Management, Inc., a large Days Inn franchisee, in 1981, it was down to only five properties, all franchised. When it was sold again in 1986, to an investor syndicate based in Marietta, Georgia, plans were laid to revive the franchise operation. But in 1993 there were only nineteen Admiral Benbow Inns, primarily in Georgia and Tennessee.

The Family Inns chain is also franchised, but all but one of its sixteen licenses are located in eastern Tennessee. The Innkeeper Inns chain, which operated only in North Carolina and Virginia, had nineteen properties in 1993. The largest of the southeastern regionals was the Shoney's Inns chain, with sixty properties (see Fig. 7.21). Like Marriott and Marcus, Shoney's Inns were rooted in a successful Big Boy restaurant franchise. Alexander Shoenbaum launched his chain of eighteen hundred restaurants (now located in thirty-six states) from Charleston, West Virginia, in 1951. The company sold its Big Boy franchise to Marriott in the mid-1970s, its restaurants thereafter operating only under the Shoney's name. Shoney's Lodging, Inc., was launched in 1976 and had grown to number fifty-six properties in 1990, when its was purchased by one of its largest franchisees. Sholodge, as the company is now called, owns a half-interest in Prime Motor Inns' AmeriSuites franchising operation. Finally, Kemmons Wilson, Holiday Inn's founder, returned to motel franchising in the early 1980s. In 1993 there were sixteen Wilson Inns, all located, as the earliest Holiday Inns had been, within an easy day's drive of Memphis.

Several major motel chains originated in the Southeast and remain headquartered there today: Choice, Holiday Inn, Hospitality International, Marriott, Promus. Choice and Hospitality International achieved much of their early expansion by absorbing regional chains. The Southeast has been a fertile ground for the development of new chains. Not only was the motel relatively more important there in the early years of automobile travel (in comparison with the Northeast and Middle West especially) but the region has enjoyed vigorous economic growth through recent decades (again in contrast to the Northeast and Middle West). Florida, of course, remains a major tourist destination and is one of the nation's fastest-growing states. Florida-oriented tourist traffic is stimulus to motel construction in most of its neighboring states.

The West

National 9 Inns of Salt Lake City owned and franchised sixty-eight properties 1993, most of them located in California, Utah, and Colorado. Red Lion Inns of Vancouver, Washington, owned fifty-two properties located primarily in Washington, Oregon, and California (see Fig. 7.22). Red

Locations by county
• 1
* 2-4
▲ 5-9

n = 52

FIGURE 7.22 Red Lion Inns, 1992. The chain was headquartered in Vancouver, Washington.

Lion has built new full-service properties as it has expanded, whereas National 9 has relied more on the rebranding of older motel properties, both those of independents and those formerly owned by other chains. National 9 develops properties and sells them to investor syndicates, holding on to management contracts. Shilo Inns of Portland, Oregon, operated forty-five properties located for the most part in Oregon, Idaho, and California. Travelers Inns, headquartered in Brea, California, operated at thirty-two locations from California in the west to Oklahoma and Texas eastward. Vagabond Inns of San Diego operated forty properties in 1993, largely in California. Numerous national chains originated in the West (Best Western, Friendship Inns, La Quinta, Ramada Inns, Travelodge), a reflection of the early relative importance of motels as a form of lodging there. The West continued to be a generator of new motel brands, a function of the region's expansive economy up through the 1980s.

ALL-SUITE HOTELS

We have touched previously on the all-suite concept as an alternative to the mid-priced, full-service motel. We have treated Embassy Suites (originally a Holiday Inns brand, now operated by Promus) and Residence Inn (a Marriott brand). Embassy Suites and Residence Inns were the two largest all-suite chains in 1990 (see Table 7.2). The Comfort Inn, Days Inn, Marriott Hotel, and Radisson Hotel brands also had all-suite alternatives. Of the "stand-alone" brands, those not linked to other brands, Guest Quarters was the largest. Guest Quarters Suite Hotels originated in Atlanta

TABLE 7.2 Largest All-Suite Motel Chains in the United States, 1990

Rank	Brand	Properties	Suites
1.	Residence Inn by Marriott	148	17,000
2.	Embassy Suites	99	24,000
3.	Radisson Suite Hotels	23	4,700
4.	Lexington Hotel Suites	22	3,300
5.	Days Inn Suites	19	2,500
6.	Comfort Suites	18	2,000
7.	Guest Quarters Suite Hotels	17	3,800
8.	Hawthorn Suites	9	1,100
9.	Inn-Suites International	8	1,000
10.	Marriott Suite	8	2,000
11.	Woodfin Suites	8	1,200

Source: Daniel W. Daniele and David J. Tarr, "All-Suites: Are They Hot or Not?" *Hotel and Motel Management* 205 (February 26, 1990): 30.

FIGURE 7.23 The Guest Quarters Hotel, Austin, Texas, 1993.

in 1972. In 1990 the Ohio-based Pickett Suites chain was absorbed, and it was later rebranded under the Guest Quarters label (see Fig. 7.23). Owned by Holiday Inns, the chain was acquired by a subsidiary of General Electric in 1992. Next in size, Lexington Hotel Suites and Inns, launched at Grand Prairie, Texas, in 1961 lays claim to being the first all-suite chain. Originally Lexington Apartments and Motor Inns, the company quickly grew to comprise fifteen properties spread across Texas and Oklahoma. Although the first all-suite motels appeared in the 1960s, it was an idea that required time to mature. Tax laws allowing liberal deductions for business-related entertainment provided a major boost to the all-suite concept.

LUXURY HOTEL CHAINS

Motels originally emerged along America's roadsides as an alternative to the full-service, downtown hotel. As the motel industry matured, its product became increasingly hotel-like, especially in the form of the motor inn and the highway hotel pioneered by Holiday Inn, among other chains. Today the hotel and motel industries are merged as a single "hospitality" field. Many hotel companies anticipated the inevitability of this merger and moved to establish motel chains to complement their hotel operations. The Hotel Corporation of America was one such firm. Opening its first Charterhouse Inn in Kittery, Maine, in 1957, the Hotel Corporation of America was to follow a design prototype created for the company by architect-planner Victor Gruen. By 1989, 12 Charterhouse Inns from New England to Virginia augmented the company's hotels, which included the Plaza Hotel in New York City and the Mayflower Hotel in Washington, D.C. The Hyatt Corporation of America followed a similar pattern with Hyatt Chalet Motels, initially a co-ownership chain, begun in 1960.[33] In 1990 Hyatt was a builder and manager of hotels with 105 properties, all managed for local investor groups. Hawthorne Suites Hotels was the firm's all-suite product.

Other companies, many of them survivors from the hotel building boom of the early twentieth century, remain primarily hotel-oriented, having never embraced the traditional motel concept. The Doubletree Hotels Corporation is essentially the survivor of the earlier Canadian Pacific Hotels; the railroad still owns a controlling interest, and the Chateau Frontenac in Quebec City remains one of its flagship properties. Doubletree, like Hyatt, is essentially a development and management company, although the firm did share ownership in several of its 57 hotels in 1991. Doubletree acquired Guest Quarter Suites Hotels in 1995.

The Carlson Companies' Radisson Hotel chain enjoyed very rapid growth during the 1970s and 1980s, again as a developer and manager of properties. The company has hotels, including the Radisson in Minneapo-

FIGURE 7.24 Radisson Hotels, 1993. The leading counties were Los Angeles and San Diego in California, with 6 properties each; and Hennepin (Minneapolis) in Minnesota, with 5. The chain was headquartered in Minneapolis.

lis, from which the chain takes its name. The Radissons are seen as forming a "collection" of unique properties, an apparent voidance of the place-product-packaging idea.[34] Yet, paradoxically, emphasis on unique design and decor, hotel to hotel, uses this very diversity to produce a clear chain image. In 1993 there were 174 Radisson properties nationwide (see Fig. 7.24). Carlson has experimented over the years with a number of "clubcourt" and other motel products under the Country Hospitality Inns and Pierre Radisson names.

Ritz-Carlton is one of the oldest names in the hotel business, and it was the first to be syndicated. Its popularity goes back well into the nineteenth century. Cesar Ritz, a Swiss restaurateur, created a chain of unrivaled luxury hotels in Lucerne, Paris, London, and New York; quite like most of today's hotel companies, Ritz only managed the various hotels for local investor groups. The current chain operated twenty-five properties in 1992, primarily in large metropolitan markets. Stouffer Hotels and Resorts, now owned by the Nestle Company, grew out of an Ohio-based restaurant chain that specialized in downtown metropolitan locations. In 1990 only seven of its thirty-four hotel properties were company-owned; the remainder were operated under management contracts. Westin Hotels (originally Western International Hotels) has been sold and resold frequently (owners have included United Airlines' Allegis, Ladbroke, Robert Bass, the Aoki Corporation of Japan, and, most recently, DSC S.A., a Mexico City–based conglomerate). Westin operated thirty-five hotels and resorts in the United States in 1993, again mainly in major metropolitan markets. Finally, the Omni Hotel chain operated forty-five owned and franchised hotels in 1993, mostly in the urban eastern United States.

MANAGEMENT COMPANIES

Important in the corporate structuring of the hospitality industry are the management companies that decline to operate under their own brands, operating instead under labels copyrighted by other firms. In 1992, twenty-two firms managed 30 or more properties (see Table 7.3). The Hong Kong–owned Richfield Hotel Management, Inc., operated 126 hotels and motels with more than 20,000 rooms under eight different brands. Motels of America, based in Des Plaines, Illinois, operated 87 properties, most of them under the Super 8 logo. The New Jersey–based Prime Hospitality Corporation, briefly the owner of the Ramada Inns and Howard Johnson's franchises, operated 78 properties under six different labels. Some management firms evolved after faltering in the development of their own individual brands; Treadway and Admiral

TABLE 7.3 Largest Motel-Management Companies in the United States, 1992

Rank	Company and Brands	Properties	Rooms
1.	Richfield Hotel Management Best Western Comfort Inns Days Inns Embassy Suites Hampton Inns Hilton Hotels Holiday Inns Radisson Inns	126	20,430
2.	Motels of America Cricket Inns Super 8 Inns	87	6,842
3.	Prime Hospitality Corporation Holiday Inns Howard Johnson's Marriott Hotels Radisson Hotels Ramada Inns Sheraton Hotels	78	14,280
4.	Larken, Inc. Doubletree Hotels Holiday Inns Hilton Hotels Radisson Hotels Ramada Inns Sheraton Hotels	75	14,250
5.	Winegardner & Hammons, Inc. Comfort Inns Embassy Suites Hampton Inns Holiday Inns Homewood Suites Quality Inns Radisson Hotels Ramada Inns Residence Inns	60	12,826

Source: "Top Management Companies," *Lodging* 18 (August 1992): 69–70.

Benbow are examples already mentioned. Most firms, however, evolved in the 1970s, when insurance companies, banks, and other lenders found themselves reluctant owners of failed properties. Management companies offered not only operational expertise but strategies for returning properties to fiscal solvency.[35]

MOTEL CHAIN PERSISTENCE

Numerous motel brands or trademarks were copyrighted from the 1930s on. Table 7.4 lists some of the brands that enjoyed only limited use. Among the more original were ABC—America's Best Choice (would not the name be listed first in directories?), Chain of Inns (was that not the essence of place-product-packaging?), and the St. Christopher System of Motels (why not invoke the patron saint of travelers?). Inns of America developed a prototype building and signage system with substantial promise (see Fig. 7.25, showing a postcard advertisement, the reverse side of which reads: "Inns of America furnishes gracious living in modern units, each equipped with air-conditioning, telephones, free television, radio and muzak. Enjoy the Panoramic View from our Swimming Pool in the Sky"). The motel's name had fundamental appeal as a descriptor, yet the brand atrophied almost immediately.

It was difficult to know what would capture the public's imagination and loyalty or what would attract investment capital. Even brands already well developed in some other industry could fail. Neither Horne's Motor Lodges nor Stuckey's Carriage Inns, which derived from the popular restaurants and pecan stores popular on the roadsides of the Southeast, survived. Some chains may have been doomed from the start. Milner Hotels, the operator of older, second-class hotels (and, indeed, the nation's largest hotel chain in the 1950s), launched Milner Lodges in the 1960s; a negative halo effect quickly stunted the operation.

What was it that garnered success in the building of hotel and motel chains? Brand image was important. Persisting brands all enjoyed easily remembered names that could be associated readily with value in travel (Best, Budget, Comfort, Econo, Embassy, Holiday, Residence, Rodeway, Sleep, Travelodge), with personalities synonymous with roadside hospitality (Hilton, Howard Johnson's, Marriott), or with memorable logos as signatures (Motel 6, Red Roof, Super 8). Other brands involved names from the American cultural mainstream to which status implication easily attached (Hampton, Sheraton, Radisson). But a name was not enough; signage, architectural design, service mix, management system, and pricing, all variously perfected and coordinated across chains, was critical. Effective place-product-packaging was essential.

Additionally, chains had to reach certain size thresholds to thrive. There had to be sufficient market presence to engender brand consciousness and brand loyalty; otherwise the costs of maintaining the brand as a marketing system could not be justified. Access to investment capital was critical. Banks, insurance companies, and other major investors capitalized the successful chains, in turn driving local investor syndicates, which amplified investment. Successful packaging of the motel product and successful capitalization went hand in hand. Where the two could not be linked, chains faltered and brands disappeared. Independent owners turned increasingly to national brands from the 1960s onward. Owners of multiple properties converted instead of sustaining their own brands. Often they adopted different brands for different targeted market niches. Dependence on a spectrum of brands spread investor risk across several place-product-packaging systems.

The largest hospitality companies active in the 1990s embody the essence of successful place-product-packaging. Table 7.5 lists the twenty

TABLE 7.4 Selected Brands Active in the United States between 1940 and 1980

Brand	Headquarters
ABC—America's Best Choice	Camp Hill, Pa.
American MoteLodges	Salinas, Calif.
American Travel Inns	Salt Lake City, Utah
Budget Inns	Indianapolis, Ind.
Camera Inns	Bristol, Tenn.
Chain of Inns	Las Vegas, Nev.
Chief Econo Inns	Columbus, Miss.
Econ-O-Tel	Fargo, N.D.
Friendly Inns	Boiling Springs, Pa.
Heart of America Motels	Raleigh, N.C.
Hickory House Motor Inns	Popular Bluff, Mo.
Homeplace Inns	Angleton, Tex.
Horne's Motor Lodges	Bayard, Fla.
Inns of America	Johnson City, Tenn.
Latch Key Inns	Dallas, Tex.
Leisure Inns	Billings, Mont.
Mark Twain Inns	Dallas, Tex.
Pacemaker Inns	Atlanta, Ga.
Porter House Motels	Phoenix, Ariz.
Prestige Inns	Seattle, Wash.
Rebel Motor Inns	Memphis, Tenn.
Regal Motels	Los Angeles, Calif.
Spirit of '76 Inns	Columbus, Ohio
Stuckey's Carriage Inns	Eastman, Ga.
St. Christopher System of Motels	Palm Beach, Fla.
Scot's Inn	Columbus, Ohio
Suburban Haus, Inc.	Muncie, Ind.
Thrift Courts of America	Elkhart, Ind.
Totels International	El Segundo, Calif.
Tudor Inns of America	Gastonia, N.C.
United Motor Inns	Dallas, Tex.

GRACIOUS LIVING IN THE HEART OF JOHNSON CITY, TENNESSEE

FIGURE 7.25 The Inns of America, Johnson City, Tennessee, circa 1960.

largest chains in the United States in 1992, giving the number of properties branded and the number of rooms contained in those properties for each firm. The table also gives the total number of properties represented for each brand. In 1992 Hospitality Franchise System was the largest domestic lodging organization, with 2,291 properties and 283,697 rooms variously branded (Days Inns, Ramada Inns, and Howard Johnson's/Hojo, in descending order of importance). Next came Choice Hotels International (Comfort Inns, Econo Lodge, Quality Inns, Rodeway Inns, Clarion Inns, and Sleep Inns), Best Western International, and Holiday Inn Worldwide. Super 8 became part of Hospitality Franchise Systems in 1993, inflating that company's first-place standing. The Marriott Corporation, Motel 6, Travelodge, and the Promus Companies came next. Hospitality International, Sheraton, Hilton, the Carlson Group, La Quinta Inns, Red Roof Inns, the Economy Lodging System, National 9, Hyatt Corporation, Budgetel, and Preferred Hotels rounded out the top twenty list.

The largest chain was Best Western. The Best Western sign appeared on more domestic motels and hotels than any other—1,800 properties nationwide. Holiday Inns (1,398), Days Inns (1,217), Super 8 Motels (887), and Comfort Inns (764) followed. Thus the nation's predominant referral chain and its most vigorous franchise chain topped the field. Co-ownership chains had all but disappeared. Ownership chains and management-contract chains were of very modest size. A snapshot in time such as the one provided in Table 7.5 masks one very important development of the

TABLE 7.5 Largest Lodging Chains in the United States, 1992

Rank	Organization and Brands	Properties	Total Rooms
1.	*Hospitality Franchise System*	*2,291*	*283,697*
	Days Inns	1,217	
	Ramada Inns	575	
	Howard Johnson's/Hojo	499	
2.	*Choice Hotels International*	*2,158*	*195,953*
	Comfort Inns	764	
	Econo Lodge	695	
	Quality Inns	390	
	Friendship Inns	134	
	Rodeway Inns	107	
	Clarion Inns	51	
	Sleep Inns	17	
3.	*Best Western International*	*1,800*	*185,000*
4.	*Holiday Inn Worldwide*	*1,398*	*269,489*
5.	*Super 8 Motels*	*887*	*57,806*
6.	*Marriott Corporation*	*690*	*150,000*
	Marriott Hotels	212	
	Courtyard by Marriott	200	
	Residence Inns	179	
	Fairfield Inns	99	
7.	*Accor/Motel 6*	*671*	*76,145*
8.	*Forte/Travelodge*	*500*	*39,050*
9.	*Promus Companies*	*444*	*71,253*
	Hampton Inns	314	
	Embassy Suites	102	
	Homewood Suites	23	
	Harrah's Casino Hotels	4	
10.	*Hospitality International*	*305*	*20,206*
	Scottish Inns	148	
	Red Carpet Inns	112	
	Passport Inns	22	
	Master Hosts Inns	21	
	Downtowner Inns	2	
11.	*ITT Sheraton*	*281*	*83,737*
12.	*Hilton Hotels*	*265*	*96,172*
13.	*Carlson Hospitality Group*	*242*	*52,119*
	Radisson Hotels	171	
	Colony Hotels	40	
	Country Lodging	31	
14.	*La Quinta Motor Inns*	*213*	*27,057*
15.	*Red Roof Inns*	*209*	*23,261*
16.	*Economy Lodging System*	*271*	*19,500*
	Knight's Inns	170	
	Arborgate Inns	9	

TABLE 7.5 *continued*

Rank	Organization and Brands	Properties	Total Rooms
17.	*National 9 Inns*	*163*	*8,224*
18.	*Hyatt Corporation*	*103*	*55,557*
19.	*Budgetel Inns*	*91*	*9,624*
20.	*Preferred Hotels*	*66*	*16,019*

Source: The Chain Report, *Lodging Hospitality* 48 (August 1992): 59–62.

1980s and 1990s: the conversion boom. For example, in the years 1988, 1989, and 1990, 244, 331, and 393 properties, respectively, changed from one brand to another (see Table 7.6).

When a franchise agreement expires, an owner must assess his or her market position. Careful thought must be given both to the costs of chain affiliation and, more importantly, to the changing market context. A change in brand may enable a motel operator to target a more appropriate market niche and affiliate nationally at a lower cost. Motels initially developed as full-service, mid-priced properties might, with age, be more appropriately targeted at the limited-service, economy-minded customer, especially if newer, upscale properties have come to compete in the locality. Repositioning through brand conversation is a clear sign of industry maturation.

The maturation of place-product-packaging has involved a spectrum of chain-building devices. Not counting the trade associations (which functioned mainly as lobbying groups), referral chains were the first to network independent motel operators. Following the example of the hoteliers, small ownership chains, such as Alamo Plaza Hotel Courts, also were initiated but paled in comparison with referral organizations like Best Western and Quality Courts United. Co-ownership chains, led by Travelodge, enjoyed a brief popularity until they were overwhelmed by the successes of full franchising, epitomized by the Holiday Inn, Choice, and Hospitality Franchise brands. In recent years the franchise chains have been challenged by renewed reliance on the ownership chain and by the rise of the management chain, two strategies for maintaining quality among networked motels and hotels. In successful place-product-packaging, every place of business must function like the others, competitive advantage accruing from system integrity. Ownership and management would seem to offer the strongest guarantees for such integrity. As in most industries, competition has narrowed the hospitality field to fewer and

TABLE 7.6 Lodging Chain Conversions, 1988–1990

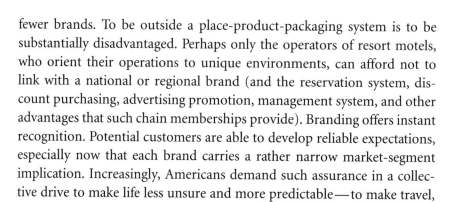

Type of Conversion	1988	1989	1990
Chain to chain	244	331	393
Independent to chain	221	262	372
Chain to independent	232	273	250
Total	697	866	1,015

Source: Edward Watkins, "Do Conversions Make Sense?" *Lodging Hospitality* 47 (November 1991): 34.

fewer brands. To be outside a place-product-packaging system is to be substantially disadvantaged. Perhaps only the operators of resort motels, who orient their operations to unique environments, can afford not to link with a national or regional brand (and the reservation system, discount purchasing, advertising promotion, management system, and other advantages that such chain memberships provide). Branding offers instant recognition. Potential customers are able to develop reliable expectations, especially now that each brand carries a rather narrow market-segment implication. Increasingly, Americans demand such assurance in a collective drive to make life less unsure and more predictable—to make travel, more specifically, less of a travail.

8
The Changing Motel Room

How have motel rooms been packaged over time? what has constituted typicality in room size, shape, decor, and furnishings from decade to decade? In segmenting the market, motels have always spoken to class, status, and lifestyle associations in setting customer expectations. In recent decades, major chains have amplified the resort connotation implied in spending the night away from home.[1] Accordingly, motel room accoutrements increasingly have been adopted in home bedroom configurations, the differences between home and away-from-home blurred. The television in the bedroom, the mirror and vanity outside the bathroom, even the telephone in the bathroom, had their roots in the motel.

In this chapter we assume the lodger's point of view, seeking to show what motel customers encountered as the motel industry matured. Our method is descriptive although no specific typology is offered. This is a highly personalized study in material culture. We do not attempt to provide a historical ledger of key designers and builders. Our purpose is far less to explore the political exchanges between the final arbiters of a room's look—entrepreneur and designer, construction contractor and designer, motel maids and manager—than to give a sense of what motel rooms have looked like over time.

A caveat is necessary. Our knowledge of past "room geography" comes from trade literature aimed at improving practice by lauding selected examples and occasionally by repeating the principles espoused by interior decorators. Such materials rarely dwell on what was wrong in specific cases; this must be inferred from the solutions offered. Rarer still are descriptions of common practices that were deficient only in being viewed as mediocre by those who were more forward-looking. Postcards remain a prime document for those who wish to see what motel rooms actually looked like, but this source too is idealized rather than representative to the extent that postcard art was composed and retouched to amplify visual impressions.[2] In our attempt to accurately portray conditions in what was an industrywide quest for "more and better" rentable space over time, we thus discount overstated claims.

THE 1920s AND 1930s

Early automobile travelers were satisfied to find roadside lodging under dry cover (a tent in some places), sufficient bedding, bathing facilities, and personal security. The fifty cents to two dollars charged per night for these first commercial lodgings through the 1920s and 1930s was a considerable bargain.[3]

Travelers' standards for overnight lodging were based on their own homes or their expectations for them. Americans in the early twentieth century wanted efficiency and technology in the home. As convenience became possible through the introduction of central heating, electricity, and refrigeration, rising construction costs were compensated by smaller house size. Gwendolyn Wright claims that the floor plan for the average-sized home in early-twentieth-century Chicago contained three first-floor rooms and minimal second-floor space. Partitions became less common as rooms were unified through open floor plans. Function had long defined spaces, but spaces became multipurpose. Framing became lighter. Insulation became thinner, and thus claims to soundproofing diminished. Building plans became increasingly standardized, resulting in less varied final products. Plainness was valued in furnishings. The concurrent aim was a comfortable house for every family. By the mid-twenties, popular magazines arbitrating interior style favored small houses furnished comfortably and simply.[4] This trend was largely reflected in the early motels.

Motels from the outset honored the hegemonic value of a separate house for each family. Communal bathing and toilets existed in some early roadside lodgings, but they soon came to be regarded as unpleasant and undesirable. The *Tourist Court Journal*'s first advice about room geography was in a 1937 article about how to cheaply but effectively construct private tiled shower stalls.[5] As in residential architecture, privacy underlay the dominant motel model, which was a freestanding house that shared no facilities with others unless the occupant preferred otherwise. Prescriptive trade literature and motel advertising were preoccupied with furnishing a surrogate private home on the road. No alternatives were given serious consideration. Barracks, for example, were an eccentric house type whose exterior appearance served to arrest the potential customer's attention-ment; the interior space, however, was divided for separate occupancy (see

Fig. 8.1). At many motels, porticoes, window boxes, and a private walk to one's car echoed their counterparts in permanent residences, as did room geography (see Fig. 8.2).

It may well be that privacy was the area in which the motel, and especially the motel guest room, first and most significantly satisfied the upper-middle-class values that shaped the motel trade from its inception. Elizabeth Cromley has demonstrated well that people seeking to demonstrate their improving rank on the social ladder desired privacy in their bedroom at home and yet, in many ways, found it difficult to realize that privacy.[6] Alternatively, in a motel people were removed from routine ties, even when they were accompanied by their families, and the motel room itself, unlike the bedroom at home, in no way connoted the rank of its occupants. Perhaps we should not find it surprising, then, that families spoke of enjoying travel, with its nightly stays in motel rooms. Nor, perhaps, should we be surprised that single as well as married business people willingly stayed in motel rooms on their nights away from home. Motels, and especially motel rooms, theoretically satisfied the dominant appetite for "getting away," as long as home's perceived advantages were available at the motel.

Roadside lodgers were transient by definition, but many owners attempted to attract long-term roadside lodgers from the first.[7] Some Depression-dogged families even found it cheaper to reside in roadside cabins than in regular housing.[8] A tendency soon developed to anticipate or stimulate consumer demands. In 1933 the *Architectural Record,* which had a professional interest in helping to generate more elaborate or architect-designed interiors, for example, illustrated floor plans for a sixteen-by-fourteen-foot "family cabin" at Coronado Tent City, Coronado Beach, California, with separate spaces for dining, living, sleeping, bathing, and cooking. Open windows banded with canvas strips provided ventilation.[9] Although Clara Keyton's description of the Cozy Corner Camp Ground in Arizona, run by her and her husband, dates from 1925, eight years earlier than the "family cabin," Keyton probably gives a more accurate view of the interiors that prevailed through the early 1930s: "Our first four cottages—really were four rooms—had either a spring built on a frame, or a sanitary cot for a bed. A second-hand mattress with doubtful character, a home built table, two-hole monkey stove for heat and cooking, two chairs, a bench, and an electric light, constituted the furnishings. There was just one large window to each room, with neither a shade nor a curtain. All water was carried from a faucet at the service station." A nearby competitor grudgingly added mattresses, but with unbleached muslin covers that were exceedingly hard to keep clean. Perhaps typical of some motel owners, Keyton's competitor classified her lodgers as "dirty tourists."[10] Traveling

FIGURE 8.1 The Bunkhouse Motel, in Rapid City, South Dakota, anticipated lodgers' expectations for a vacation in the West not only in its name and outward appearance but also by featuring "gentle western saddle horses in season." However, "private tile baths, tub and shower combination," were also assured.

FIGURE 8.2 With their wallpaper, small dresser, and mirror, rooms at the George-Anna Cottages, in Jackson, Tennessee, during the late 1930s looked very similar to bedrooms in local homes.

for pleasure remained a somewhat dubious activity in the minds of many who were not yet attuned to the emerging consumer culture. And there would always be those owners who provided poor-quality lodging. Some owners thus counterweighed others' push for quality roadside lodging.

Finding a room for the night was an adventure at first. The rapid turnover among owners might mean that a motel that only a short time before had passed an exacting inspection to be listed in a directory of reputable motels might have fallen into a state of disrepair under new management.[11] Room layout and size also varied considerably in the early years.[12] Octagonal was the shape one motel owner recommended for his patented "knockdown house," named for its collapsibility and portability. An advertisement for the kit featuring homey decorations belied its utilitarian structure (see Fig. 8.3). Thus, roadside accommodations varied widely, so that it was customary to rent a room only after inspecting it.[13]

Throughout the market's vast middle ground there were numerous motels to choose from. A 1935 *Popular Mechanics* article aimed at owners building their own cabins mentions some of the earliest choices. One plan the magazine offered was for a ten-by-twelve-foot cabin with a bed, chair, folding table, and a bench to hold a camp stove. Windows at all four corners were lumberyard stock originally intended for barns. Wire screens replaced windows and the front door to keep out pests in warm weather. While the outside was to be painted, the fact that neither interior painting nor inside walls nailed to the studs were mentioned implies they were absent in this traveler's "special." A second choice, which presumably rented for more, was no larger than the first but had other features characteristic of home: a built-in cabinet for the folding table and interior wallboard. Electricity was advised for both alternatives.[14]

Adornments were generally out of the question in these minimalist rooms. Yet some owners decorated them for no apparent reason other than their own satisfaction. For example, although Nelson's Dream Village, at the edge of the small town of Lebanon, Missouri, had electricity when it opened in 1934, fireplaces complemented the cabins' "English" style.[15] Illustrative also were the idiosyncrasies reported in one California motel, which had "dainty festoons of pink and blue crepe paper decorating the unpainted plank ceiling and cigarette and soap ads completely papering the walls."[16]

Unarguable values and varying financial calculations combined to determine the final look of the room as well. For example, being cool was an important consideration, which contributed to the *Architectural Record*'s promotion of one set of as-built plans for cabins at Wilton, Connecticut: "Open air space between roof and ceiling has been successful insulation

A COMPLETE HOUSE »» $195⁰⁰

(UNFURNISHED)

Ideal for Tourists, Seaside, Commercial and Industrial Uses

EXTERIOR

INTERIOR

In an effort to supply the great demand for a complete tourist or seaside house at a low price, we have created the Lighthouse Tavern. It comes to you in knocked down form, and can be easily erected by you within a few hours. Receive the house in the morning and rent or occupy it that night. The only tools necessary in erection are a wrench and a screw driver, and two men can handle any one part with ease.

Each house contains four pairs of casement windows which give 100 per cent ventilation. All windows are complete with ready hung screens, and all hardware is in place. There is one glass top door with night latch. The roof is slate composition, and an exceptional grade of Southern pine is used throughout. They may be easily heated in winter by gas or oil, and the roof is ventilated with a metal vent which can be closed at will by a damper. Each house is painted one coat before shipment, and enough paint is sent for another coat both inside and out. Standard colors are ivory with brown trim outside and light green walls and ivory ceiling inside, but we can supply any colors desired.

We know from our experience that a competing house cannot possibly be built by local carpenters for anywhere near the price of the Lighthouse Taverns. Only our experience, equipment and buying power make it possible for us to do so.

The floor space is approximately 125 square feet, the smallest inside dimension being 12 feet by 12 feet. The octagonal (eight side) design makes them extremely staunch and wind resisting and also provides the maximum of floor space as all dead square corners are eliminated. The house can be made longer, windows, doors or solid panels substituted at will, as all are interchangeable. We also manufacture bath rooms, kitchens, and dining nooks which can be attached at any time. When used for refreshment stands, more windows can be substituted.

The standard house (without furniture) with one door, and four pairs of casement windows, complete as described above, which can be shipped by truck or rail, at only

$195⁰⁰ F. O. B., Houston, Texas.

«««   »»»

"LIGHTHOUSE TAVERNS"

(Patent applied for)

Manufactured by

LIGHTHOUSE MANUFACTURING COMPANY

Office: 3103 Main St.   HOUSTON, TEXAS   Phone Hadley 1107

FIGURE 8.3 Ewart H. Lightfoot's kit was advertised as a "Lighthouse Tavern" approximately 125 feet square with "hung screens," "glass top door with night latch," and a ventilated roof. It came painted ivory with brown trim on the outside, with light green walls and ivory ceilings on the inside.

against the hot sun." [17] The potential profit from this comparatively novel technique would have been self-evident to owners who were sensitive to the needs of the proverbially hot and tired traveler. Cabins' limited space and problematic ventilation induced outdoor sitting, a leisure activity common for Americans when they were not traveling. Passing the time outside with travelers in neighboring cabins added a social rationale in

FIGURE 8.4 At Wigwam Village Number 2 in Cave City, Kentucky, sitting and talking after a hard day's drive was encouraged by a well-maintained kind of center stage around which the cabins were situated. Its communal function was also assumed in weekend croquet matches between local people.

which early reporters of the motel phenomenon found verification of America's classless society, for people of various backgrounds seemed to stay at motels. "America Hobnobs at the Tourist Camp," read a headline in the *New York Times Magazine* in 1934.[18] Compensating, perhaps, for perceived interior inadequacies but surely appreciating the profits to be made from extended stays and return business, owners like Frank Redford, at Cave City, Kentucky, meticulously landscaped and maintained a communal area as part of their motel (see Fig. 8.4).

Might this integration of outside and inside have been both a concession to building costs and unwitting compliance with the period's conservative esteem for the frontier experience?[19] Here perhaps persisted the antimodern impulse Belasco discovered in early auto camping, although it was evident mainly among devotees of the house trailer by the late 1930s.[20] As time passed and greater expendable wealth made possible the inclusion of more amenities, room geography became a realm of owner-contrived private delights for lodgers. The shift added impetus to America's general tendency toward privatization. In the future, people would spend time at motels with close friends or family for social entertainment, often indoors. Did the stark simplicity of early room geography, with its promise of comfort through amenities, also reflect a common ambivalence on the part of lodgers about high-style modernism? Motel owners altered materials for crass ends, but functionalism reigned, nonetheless, albeit expressed in carpentry and not stated ideologically.

Economic depression brought new influences. Architects were quick to offer their services, but small entrepreneurs tended to plan and, in some cases, even to build their own motels. Architects with an existing practice in motels would seem to have had an advantage in gaining the business of the frugal and wary small entrepreneur. An example was Houston architect Tom E. Lightfoot, whose father was a builder who had gone into the motel trade, patenting the "knockdown house," owning a motel, and helping organize the International Motor Court Association. Son Tom started his architectural practice at fifteen years of age and was a lifelong consultant to the *Tourist Court Journal.* Chester Liebs has speculated that architects became more influential as time passed. He points convincingly to their designs of picturesque cabins on manicured lawns, which helped stimulate the popular appetite for privacy in suburban housing. Considerable inroads, however, were made quickly by manufacturers of household goods. The Simmons Company was one of the most aggressive, judging from the frequency of printed advertising, especially for mattresses.[21]

Consumers and owners quickly sorted through options to formulate a common room geography by the end of the 1930s. The case of kitchens is illustrative. Whereas a "community kitchen" and central dining room could be recommended to lodgers who did their own cooking in 1931,[22] it was considered "logical progress" by 1934 that many motels offered both a restaurant and some rooms with "kitchenettes," complete with cooking utensils, dinnerware, and dishes.[23] In 1935 the *New York Times* found wide rationale for rapid standardization: "Now intensified competition, plus the insistent demand of the tourist—particularly the woman tourist—for better accommodations, for 'all the comforts of home,' has brought about the general improvement."[24] Labor-saving devices seemed to be even more urgent on the road than at home, where their justification was to free one's time for personal pursuits.[25] Why, after all, work during one's vacation? But roadside restaurants began to spring up, and kitchenettes became outmoded in the many motels that catered to the passing tourist, though they remained popular in motels patronized by the long-term lodger. The percentage of travelers who did their own cooking plunged from 80 percent to 12.5 percent in the decade ending in 1936.[26] While many new and remodeled motels omitted cooking facilities, those aimed at an upscale clientele, such as the Grande Vista Tourist Homes in St. Joseph, Michigan, or the Alamo Plaza chain, might include kitchenettes

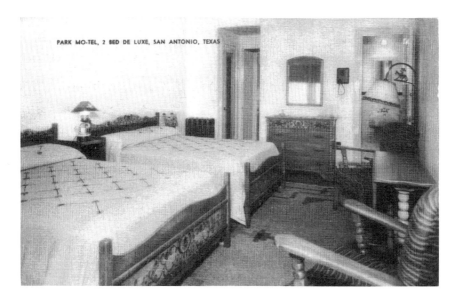

PARK MO-TEL, 2 BED DE LUXE, SAN ANTONIO, TEXAS

FIGURE 8.5 This room at the Park Mo-tel in San Antonio, Texas, offered two double beds, a ceramic-tile bathroom, radiator heat, and a wall speaker that connected the lodger with the front desk. A high-quality motel room of the 1930s, its ambiance derived from upper-middle-class notions of what was desirable in a home. The hyphenated word *mo-tel* indicates that the basic nomenclature was immature at the time.

in all rooms (with an additional fee if used) or only in more expensive rooms.[27]

Despite the Depression, motel rooms began to function as display rooms for consumers shopping for their homes. Motel rooms could be observed as possible settings for individual furnishings. New products and arrangements could be introduced to lodgers, and it provided wary consumers a chance to overcome their hesitations regarding products they had pondered purchasing. Staying in a motel thus was akin to visiting department store displays and, at least by 1925, viewing photographs of model rooms for milady's residence in the widely circulated monthly magazine *Good Housekeeping*. Motel rooms played a pivotal role in American home decoration because they began to be more fully furnished at the very time when consumers were being encouraged to break with the past and remodel for the new age. Many commodities insinuated by this means also led to values founded in Depression relief: newness for its own sake and verification of newness by superficial look versus functional improvement. Thus, multiplying motel rooms provided a new mainspring for the consumer culture.[28]

The forward-looking room geography of the 1930s is exemplified in the Park Mo-tel in San Antonio (see Fig. 8.5) and the Tourist-Traveltowns, an incorporated chain. Twelve of the Park Mo-tel's fourteen cabins had two double rooms, and two had three double rooms. Each room measured approximately twelve feet by twelve feet. Closets, rather than wardrobes or racks, distinguished each room. Partitions separated the washbowl, toilet, and shower in the twelve smaller cabins, and running water and baths were available only in the two bigger cabins. All had three windows for ventilation, electric heaters when needed, varied color schemes (green, white, yellow, and mahogany), a writing table, twin beds, and wall lamps. A poll had found chandeliers, bureaus, and double beds to be undesirable.[29] Diversification characterized room geography, as Americans on the highway sought to satisfy their individual tastes.

FROM THE 1940s TO THE 1960s

By the early 1940s the interests of those who that would thenceforth determine room geography were already in existence, despite the wartime construction moratorium, which halted their full interplay. As these interests repeatedly interacted with one another, impulses that had been felt in the past became principles guiding the future. In the reciprocal process of offering and expecting specific room geographies, all interests pushed harder to influence the outcome. Tensions yielded ever-changing room geographies as wits sharpened, including those of the consumers, in the search for satisfying combinations of service, decor, and spatial arrangement. From diverse interests, sometimes collaborating and sometimes colliding, patterns emerged that were common throughout the consumer culture.

"Comfort and convenience" became the clearly articulated rationale. Apparently, a room geography emerged in response to consumer demands; but, in fact, owners largely honored their contrary commitment to economy. Luxury may have been advertised, but it was no longer the product of owners' trying to provide the very best in order to attract lodgers, only later to figure profits and losses. Owners increasingly shared information by watching and calculating, and this resulted in efficient rooms on which the minimum amount was spent to obtain maximum profit. Consumers contributed powerfully to these dynamics. Although their comfort and convenience was integral in calculations of profit, their taste for novelty was apparent. The latest in technologies—lighting and cooling, for example—became a test of quality among lodgers. Either brand names such as General Electric or Carrier air conditioners were mentioned in trade magazine articles about individual motels or brand manufacturers advertised the testimonials of individual motel owners. Stories of enduring motels in the trade literature invariably included lessons learned about the necessity of constant improvement.[30] Consumers also thwarted novelty by expecting low room rates.

Government and the recommendation services had a hand in determining room geography too. At the municipal and the state level, codes were passed in the name of public health. Often the spokesmen were self-interested. California's hotel industry, for example, had been the first to lobby successfully for legislation that eventually induced higher-quality motels beginning in the 1930s. Although the American Automobile Association required motels to have hot water, a shower and tub, chairs, a dresser, a clothes closet, baggage stands, a writing desk, and lighting for inclusion in its early directories, it was admitted that approval depended on the inspector's subjective opinion. Later AAA listings distinguished several classifications based on "physical design" (e.g., number of stories) and "major services" (e.g., presence of a swimming pool).[31] A means of objectivity was thereby achieved.

Changes in room geography ultimately came from within the industry. M. K. Guertin, long an officer of Best Western Motels, for example, replaced many furnishings in his own motel to increase profit, and his colleague Bob Gresham sought him out for a detailed case study on the subject of "upgrading," as it was known in the trade vernacular, in the *Tourist Court Journal*. Bill Edmundson, another forceful leader in the motel business, wrote his own appeal for upgrading in the *Journal*. Edmundson used the example of the twenty-five-year-old Rex Plaza Motor Court at Tupelo, Mississippi, to support his claim that he had found "dramatic proof of what can be done in room up-grading" by replacing metal furniture with wooden furniture, window air-conditioning units with central air conditioning, and painted walls with brick (on the front and side walls) and wooden paneling (on the rear wall).[32]

It was, after all, principally the market forces of supply and demand that determined the look of the motel room. No government code forced into use materials, technologies, or services that lacked other incentives for their adoption. Motels could find a market niche, albeit a less prestigious one, without published ratings. The suppliers cleverly hazarded changes for increased profit, and consumers eagerly yet discriminatingly selected from the offerings. After the early 1940s the major difference in the changing room geography was that the latest styles and technologies were more quickly adopted, suggesting a radically different look with each subsequent change. This was what both owners and consumers desired.

World War II briefly halted the repetitive cycle of the deliberately new succeeding the old. A representative "deluxe" motel to be built in early 1942 in Phoenix, Arizona, was featured in the May 1942 issue of *Tourist Court Journal*. Each 22-by-13-foot unit was to have three separate

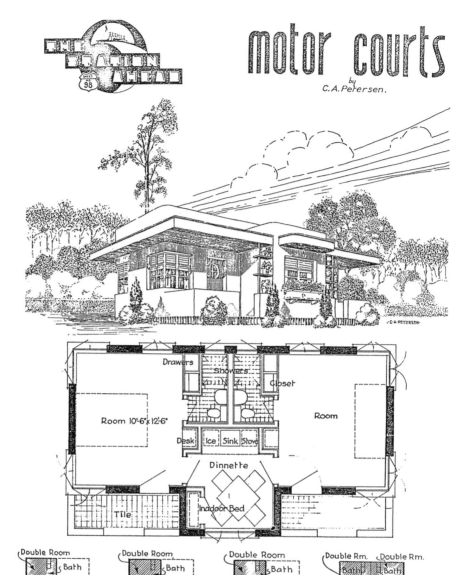

FIGURE 8.6 C. A. Petersen, Pure Oil's chief architect, privately sought opportunities in the post–World War II era by designing a tourist court with "flexibility." At the foot of a page in his privately published *The Station Ahead* (1952), Petersen illustrated that "by merely opening or closing doors and with no sacrifice of space two, three or five occupants can be accommodated."

rooms—a living room–bedroom, kitchen, and bath—its own forced-air furnace, air conditioning, and carpets. In a different article for the *Journal,* Tom Lightfoot outlined more common lodging to satisfy the booming wartime demand. Each unit (measuring either 20 feet by 13 feet or 17.5 feet by 13 feet) comprised a living room–bedroom, bath, and closet and was located adjacent to a unit of the same size. A passage joining the two could be made into a single room in the event that a large family was lodged. Versatility became a plus (see Fig. 8.6). The color scheme in the rooms was to vary. The owner's challenge, however, was to pick colors that cost no more than white. Wartime necessitated that a "victory tourist court" be built quickly and inexpensively.[33] The advice would be repeated in peacetime.

Comfort and convenience could be achieved with improved lighting, argued another wartime author in the *Journal.* "As a purely utilitarian art, proper lighting enables motel management to attain a home-like atmosphere that every guest appreciates, atmosphere that provides a degree of comfort and satisfaction that results in continued patronage."[34] Enter lighting tools developed for the war, including cool fluorescent in daylight and a range of colors combined with familiar incandescent lights for spot-lighting and auxiliary lighting at night.[35] Lighting was no longer intended only to aid vision; it was to enhance the object seen. Fluorescent lighting was credited, as a result, with permitting women to apply more flattering makeup. Things could be made to be more than they were. Again, illusion was preferred to reality in this consumer culture. The provision of better lighting drove up prices. Additional wall outlet plugs would be necessary for the best lighting. "It would be better to use the double head type, which only costs a few additional pennies over the single type," the *Journal* reported. Americans learned to pay more for their fantasies, which were facilitated by the automobile and its appurtenances. And the present was forgotten in the look forward to the promise of tomorrow. "Now is the time to foresee the future!" the *Journal* article concluded.[36]

The wartime building moratorium only slowed the move toward futuristic room geography. A report on a tourist court in Springfield, Illinois, built during the war, seemed almost quaint in its assurance that "guests like to gather in the afternoons and evenings to visit" in the well-landscaped courtyard. The inside of each cottage was a place of splendid seclusion, with throw rugs on hardwood floors, knotty pine walls, good insulation in the walls and ceilings, and heated water for bathing and heating.[37]

Room geography became a special province of designers and some architects and interior decorators, but more often it was the activity of suppliers of plans and furnishings for the motel trade alone. Efficient calculation by these experts yielded rooms that had a sparer appearance than in the past yet replete with the latest technological devices, as consumer appeal and owner expense meshed. An instructive article in the *Architectural Record* in 1950 described the desirable room as being no larger than in the past decade, between fourteen by fourteen and sixteen by eighteen, but making more obvious use of metal. Windows, which among architectural details so singularly convey an impression, were to be metal, "with aluminum recommended to save painting (avoid flimsy sections)." Furniture was to be of the "standard flush-metal" type and to have "rustproof glides." Headboards disappeared as fixtures of the beds themselves, to be replaced by permanent fixtures on the wall. The best beds were thought to be the "dolly or Hollywood type of bed with no footboard"; their casters made movement easier for housekeeping. Easier daily cleaning and greater durability reduced labor and maintenance costs.[38]

The effect was less homelike. Tall bureaus were to be replaced by lower, multipurpose "vanity-desk with two drawers." Luggage racks were introduced. Plate glass was recommended for protecting any remaining wooden surfaces from "acetone-type nail polish removers." There was no mention of wooden floors; the preference was for asphalt tile or wall-to-wall carpeting, which were cheaper to maintain. About trim, the *Architectural Record* advised: "Asphalt tile cove base is neat, durable and requires no paint. Narrow, flush metal door and window trim reduces maintenance and gives desirable simplicity." Kitchenettes were out altogether; owners were advised to have at least a coffee shop. In bathrooms, tile and wing walls on shower stalls instead of shower curtains made sense because of the heightened attention to maintenance. Lounges became the appropriate setting for social exchanges, both increasing cost and bringing indoors activity that had been fashionable outdoors.[39] New heating technologies added space inside rooms; at the same time, they permitted individual lodgers control. Convection heating recessed beneath the picture window of each room was a notable feature in the U.S. Grant Motel in Mattoon, Illinois, according to a 1953 article in the *American Motel Magazine*.[40] And a 1951 article in the *Tourist Court Journal*, "Yording's Hides the Heat," praised the panel heating in the concrete floors of another motel.[41]

Swimming pools became popular in the 1950s but were never considered to be extensions of the room space, latter-day counterparts of earlier landscapes for sitting and talking. Some small owners privately admitted that the pool, which often was situated beside the highway to attract lodgers, was a relatively expensive bit of advertising that was too little used by lodgers (see Fig. 8.7).[42] Owners of larger motels, for example, the Sands Motel on Chicago's North Side, also felt pressured to have a swimming pool (see Fig. 8.8). Here the atmosphere of a rural resort was replicated near the heart of the city.

FIGURE 8.7 The 82-unit George-Anna Motel added a pool out front as part of its post–World War II remodeling in 1954.

FIGURE 8.8 The swimming pool of the 250-unit Sands Motel was the subject of this advertisement postcard.

Experts set forth broad principles and devised formulas based on quantified behavior. Janet Smith, whose byline for a 1954 article on the "usable room" proclaimed that she held a doctorate and was employed at Florida State University, posited that "space for furniture-in-use is the key." She deduced that a chair measuring twenty-one inches by twenty-eight inches required at least fifteen additional inches in front for a footrest zone, while a lounge chair required twenty-four inches; chairs required a walkway measuring at least two feet between them; and a night stand's lampshade must be at least sixteen inches wide. Numerous measurements were prescribed for the relationship between other elements, including light for personal grooming and clothes storage.[43] Her advice was for owners who wanted to help design their own motels.

Clare A. Gunn, a professor at Michigan State University's School of Hotel, Restaurant, and Institutional Management, distilled his room geography for would-be owners in two publications, the first of which started with the prime command, "To develop the most convenient, comfortable and attractive room at the lowest cost of construction and upkeep."[44] Room geography was at the heart of Gunn's command, because the room was where most lodgers spent most of their time. The principle to "plan from the inside out" informed Gunn's several different room types. Building on Smith's "usable room" concept, Gunn reasoned that one should determine first what furniture was needed, then add space for movement, and finally let circulation patterns dictate proportion as well as size. Gunn also counseled designers to consider what the lodger would see from within the room and perhaps enclose a patio with a picture window or door in "deluxe units."[45] Room geography was no longer derived from predetermined dimensions with houselike features made to fit. Room geography was the expression of logical installments with little reference to the home. Generalizations drawn from "scientific" observations further diversified room geographies. Gunn declared that "business travelers usually prefer the studio-type room (one which appears as a living room by day). Tourists and vacationists are usually busy elsewhere during the day and standard beds are well accepted"[46] (see Fig. 8.9).

Since the room was the principal focus for motel design, motels began to emerge as demonstrably unique landscape forms. No longer was home the standard. Colors were to be "striking" and "gay," not "homey and restful." In the bathroom, both tubs and showers were desirable, a concession to what untutored owners learned from lodgers despite the experts' longstanding recommendation for showers only. Striking diversity stemmed from the desire to satisfy as many lodgers as possible, in this case by providing a combination of bathing facilities not yet to be found in many

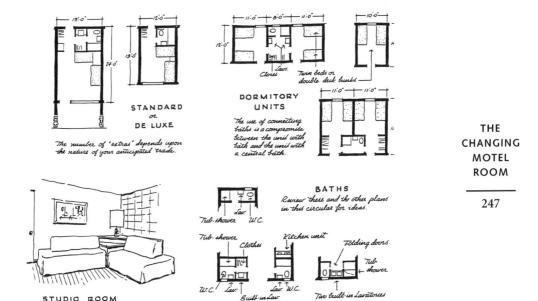

FIGURE 8.9 Clare A. Gunn sketched a model studio room and variations on other features for his general audience (*Source:* Gunn, *Motels and Resorts.*)

houses. Some lodgers also wanted kitchenettes, which had been out of fashion for a while in motels. Hence Gunn recommended that kitchenettes be returned, but he advised that they be manufactured as units easily installed and locked against travelers who expressed no interest in them.[47]

The *Architectural Record* editors' *Motels, Hotels, Restaurants, and Bars,* published between 1945 and 1953, and Geoffrey Baker and Bruno Funaro's *Motels* (1955), two guides to motel design that were more widely available than Gunn's, were the collaborations of architectural presses that reinforced the consensus among professional designers on the essential points of room geography. Distinguished by high-quality photography with brief legends about fine Sun Belt examples, the former illustrated the increased use of window glass to unite the motel room with the outside in a "motel style" resort in California (see Fig. 8.10). Another California example was praised for its departure from traditional motel design: the owner-designers' "theme was a zip not associated with quiet home life, which shows in extemporaneous innovations and economies thoroughly acceptable in architectural circles."[48] Baker and Funaro agreed that the size and shape of rooms should be determined by the furniture and the equipment the rooms would be required to contain, plus their use and maintenance, and that showers with tubs satisfied the widest possible

FIGURE 8.10 The legend accompanying these photographs in *The Architectural Record* reads: "Outdoor and indoor space merge so completely that in these photographs it is difficult to find the line of enclosure. Views through the glass wall are from the owner's living room toward covered patio. Note same brick inside and out." (*Source: The Architectural Record*, 7.)

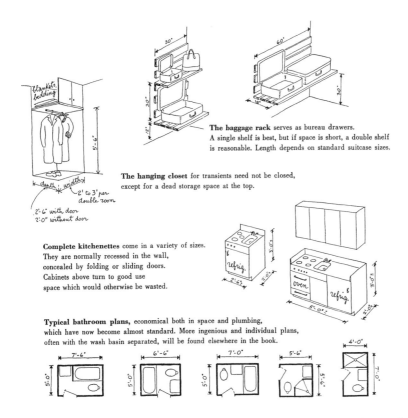

The baggage rack serves as bureau drawers.
A single shelf is best, but if space is short, a double shelf
is reasonable. Length depends on standard suitcase sizes.

The hanging closet for transients need not be closed,
except for a dead storage space at the top.

Complete kitchenettes come in a variety of sizes.
They are normally recessed in the wall,
concealed by folding or sliding doors.
Cabinets above turn to good use
space which would otherwise be wasted.

Typical bathroom plans, economical both in space and plumbing,
which have now become almost standard. More ingenious and individual plans,
often with the wash basin separated, will be found elsewhere in the book.

FIGURE 8.11 Sketched details in Geoffrey Baker and Bruno Funaro's *Motels* illustrate the motel's distinctive room geography by the 1950s. (*Source:* Baker and Funaro, *Motels,* 211.)

range of lodger preferences; most importantly, they asserted the distinction between the house and the motel: "Typical small house furnishing plans do not apply successfully to the motel; the needs are different, and so is some of the furniture (e.g., the baggage rack replaces the chest of drawers)."[49] They included a composite drawing that gave suggestions and underscored the distinction between a motel and a house (see Fig. 8.11).

Just when the motel left the house behind as the model for room geography is debatable. Clearly, motor inns and motor hotels had long modeled their upper-scale rooms after plush hotels.[50] Figure 8.12 shows a postcard from the Home Ranch Motel, close to the Harrisburg East interchange of the Pennsylvania Turnpike, advertising its room amenities at the end of the 1950s. Big investors began flooding the market in the 1950s with visions of hotel-like amenities as the best means for making a profit. But not all people in the motel trade agreed. Baker and Funaro, for example, doubted the wisdom of increased services that blurred the distinction between the motel and hotel: "In a way room telephones may

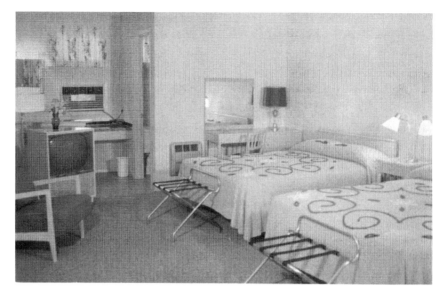

FIGURE 8.12 "'Air-conditioned'—Wall to Wall Carpeting—Television—Thermostatic Heat" were highlighted advantages of the Home Ranch Motel.

be the most typical example of progress in the wrong direction." They enumerated at length the financial detractions of room telephones and tried to jar the motel owner into remembering that the motel's considerable investment advantage over the hotel was in its lesser but sufficient services.[51]

FROM THE 1960s TO THE PRESENT

Big investors did lead the trend toward room packaging in the 1960s because of their desire to delineate a geographical market and establish their business within it by the use of trademark architecture. Eventually, the inside as well as the outside of a chain's motels took on a particular corporate image. These new economic factors reinforced prevailing ones. The centrality of room geography to overall motel design, the look of institutional blandness, the reinforcement of the motel as a special place, the reckoning of the look in terms of maximum profit for minimal cost, the frenetic replacement of older with newer technologies in the name of lodger comfort and convenience—all of which place-product-packaging utilized—continued to combine to make rooms into visible corporate domains.

Howard Johnson's was the first to fully package motels, emphasizing engineered room geography. The company's design team (Carl Koch and associates, architects; Rufus Nims, architect; R. H. Dwinell of Howard

Johnson's; and John Woodard of Contract Interiors, interior decorators) developed and articulated the principles. Exterior and interior motifs were integrated in a total design concept launched in the late 1950s. Regarding room geography, the team came to several conclusions based on their own aesthetic sense, what they thought typified lodger behavior, and their discussions with motel owners. The team agreed that first impressions in a room were just as critical as first impressions from the highway in drawing the lodger. Since lodgers went through a room in a particular sequence—first to the luggage rack, then to the dressing area, then past the bed and sitting area to look at the view from glass doors or windows—it was important to briefly arrest their attention in order to impart that positive, first impression. For this the team designed a partial screen to focus attention on furnishings and the distant, large patio window. Later in his stay the lodger was intended to find that the screen gave privacy without blocking light and air. The architects were also satisfied that the screen helped organize the interior by function without confining the lodger in separate rooms (see Fig. 8.13). Immediately upon entering, then, the lodger could easily locate the luggage racks, coat closet, and shelves or drawers, shelves being favored "since most travelers live out of their suitcases and may leave behind things stowed away in the drawers." All but one room type included a dressing area, a large mirror, a counter, and two lavatories. To distinguish itself from its competitors, Howard Johnson's provided two shower heads (the higher for men, the lower for women) and two lavatories. Like Torrance more than twenty years earlier, Howard Johnson planned his chain to flash elegance yet rent for moderate rates.[52]

Having no previous business experience in lodging, the Howard Johnson's team was not bound by distinctions that previously had divided the motel from the hotel trade. While motel people often preferred wooden to carpeted floors, believing the maintenance was cheaper, hotel men counseled carpeting and Howard Johnson's installed it. Although hotel people warned that low beds would wear out faster because lodgers would use them as seats, the chain's design team recommended low beds to help impart an impression of space.[53]

The distinctive room interiors of Howard Johnson's helped orient the industry to prepackaged room modules. Holiday Inn was challenged, even adopting a prefabricated, four-room unit of "junior" rooms (a 140-square-foot room, the chain's standard room measuring 250 square feet) beginning in 1963. Holiday Inn's rooms were indistinguishable from those of many motels through the 1950s and 1960s.[54] Holiday Inn's rooms were typical of the spare place-product-packaging (see Fig. 8.14). Sameness pervaded the rooms of many referral chains (see Figs. 8.15, 8.16, and 8.17).

FIGURE 8.13 Howard Johnson's established industrywide state-of-the-art room geography beginning in the late 1950s and early 1960s. Included here are several innovative features, including a wall-hung counter for personal belongings, a lavatory wall *(right)* concealing the sleeping area from the entrance, and the use of timber to impart a sense of shelter. Rufus Nims and John Woodard provided this experimental design for a Howard Johnson's Inn at Little Rock, Arkansas. (Photo courtesy of Alexander Georges.)

Sameness may well have played a role in satisfying the conflicting urges felt by lodgers dealing with culture's constraints. In an age given to accepting professional preachments as superior to personal inclinations, there may nonetheless have been a vernacular reaction to motel room geography based on the best-designed rooms. On the one hand, for example, professional designers grumbled that generic motel designs that made no reference to the special qualities of each locale were dysfunctional.[55] Professional designers also described the home bedrooms as the rooms most fitting for expressing their occupants' special personalities.[56] On the other hand, with the weight of professional advice for designing rooms ironically dictating against individual choice as wrongly eccentric, especially at home, where people spent most of their time, was the motel room's very lack of distinctiveness a rejection of the stiflingly systemic control many felt was the hallmark of modern life? Was the motel room's very lack of distinction a temporary respite on the road consistent with the overall escapism attributed to automobile travel? In look-alike motel rooms people could perhaps shrink for a brief time from the burdens of confining roles, especially those of gender, symbolized in their bedroom design and decoration at home.[57] More certainly the sameness of motel rooms strongly testified to the culture's well-articulated business values, seeking to win profit partly by minimizing operating costs through mass replications.

It was a short step from look-alike room geography in the name of efficiency to prefabrication of rooms, which were then transported to a construction site for assembly.[58] Thus returned the kits marketed in the 1920s and 1930s for the small owner's construction. This time, however, the tide flowed with the prefabricators, whose widely replicated rooms enabled them to exercise authority over their own expanding empires. Had they taken a clue from the lucrative prefabricated housing of the postwar era?[59] Certainly Kemmons Wilson's first partner, Wallace Johnson, was known as the Henry Ford of the housing industry before he switched to motels.[60] Standardization was in fashion.

FIGURE 8.14 Holiday Inn's reputation was built in part on reliably common room geography. Pictured here is a view of a reconstructed original room. (Photo courtesy of Kemmons Wilson Companies.)

FIGURE 8.15 Little differentiates this room, from a privately owned motel near Chicago in the early 1950s, from those shown in Figs. 8.16 (early 1960s) and 8.17 even though all were created by small operations.

FIGURE 8.16 A room in an individually owned motel near Rochester, New York, in the early 1960s.

FIGURE 8.17 A small chain in Indianapolis, Indiana, started with rooms like this in the early 1990s.

Holiday Inn led the way among chains developing their own design and commodity supply companies. Its Inn Keepers Supply Company so dominated from its founding in 1957 that it sold not only to other motel chains but also to other institutions, including apartment complexes, hospitals, and schools.[61] Best Western followed beginning in the mid-1960s. At its headquarters in 1965, Best Western set up three model bedrooms separated by dividers. Across from these were displayed various furnishings from selected suppliers of such items as carpets, drapes, table lamps, pillows, wastebaskets, and linens. To maximize control, Best Western determined the furnishings' arrangement rather than leaving it to the furnishers, as was done at trade shows.[62] By 1970 a new headquarters included Beswesco, a new wholesale supply division that had four model rooms and a display area for selected suppliers, as well as a design studio, where staff worked with individual motel owners. Beswesco's director said: "It's almost like a supermarket for motel owners, plus expert assistance in design and color selection."[63] It was 1980, when Holiday Inn stopped supplying competitors, however, before Best Western perforce established its own supply division, Best Western Supply, for "expendables" such as soap and housekeeping items. For furniture and decorative items, Best Western turned to three "contract houses" serving different regions.[64]

Sources multiplied, but the results were homogeneous. The Southern Cross Motor Hotel, for example, adopted a spray-on wall tile so that the new motel would have "'hospital clean' interiors."[65] "Contract houses" supplied furnishings as well as plans for arrangement. Some motel owners competed with them. Portel, an obvious play in name on the portability of prefabricated motel rooms, was the company of a motel owner of thirty-five years (see Fig. 8.18).[66] Another entry into prefabrication was a manufacturer of housing components, Cardinal Industries, whose Knights Inn division was created in the early 1970s. Four basic room types were created for its reproduction (see Fig. 8.19).[67] Even the *Tourist Court Journal,* with its audience of mom-and-pop entrepreneurs, who represented diversity, if only for their laggard remodeling, by 1971 was calling attention to modular construction as worthy of consideration.[68]

Calculation of the most efficient room geography led not just to prefabrication, but to prefabrication based on design-behavior analysis. The drive to understand every factor in a motel operation and regulate it for a single, quantifiable goal led some in the motel trade to try to develop a virtual calculus of room geography. Regal 8's property manager in the 1970s, for example, determined "normal usages" per room per rental: 2 books of matches; 1.5 to 2 plastic cups; .1 box of Kleenex; .1 roll of toilet tissue; 1.5 to 2 bars of soap; .2 to .3 oz. window cleaner; .2 oz. room deodorizer; .4 oz. toilet bowl cleaner; .05 can of cleanser; .8 oz. laundry soap; and .03 oz. sour. Applying these figures, the property manager was able to project a yearly profit-and-loss statement for the chain according to various occupancy rates.[69]

With the advent of high finance, with its dialogue on efficiency and behaviorist designing, the motel remained more than ever a distinctive kind

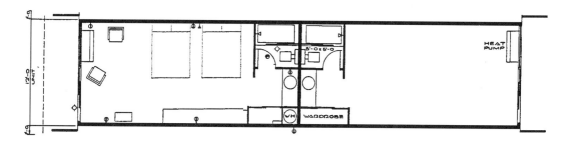

FIGURE 8.18 The legend accompanying this drawing in the September 1962 *Tourist Court Journal* reads: "Portel units may be arranged up to three stories high. Double unit shown here is typical installation. Floor plan shows unit opening to left with furnishings and unit opening to right without furnishings. Two bedroom sizes are manufactured. Each unit has own self-contained hot water heating and air conditioning. Individual walls, floor, and ceiling seal each unit from its neighbor to reduce noise factor and to improve insulation quality, thus reducing fuel costs." (*Source:* "Here Are the Newest Factory-Built Units," 56.)

FIGURE 8.19 The Knights Inn's "Tourister" room was distinguishable by two extra-large beds. Assuring the lodger of the room's corporate pedigree, however, was the logo emblazoned on the wall.

of lodging. Most investors sought a higher percentage of return on their investment in motels than in hotels, with the result that relatively expensive elements were omitted from motel planning. Interior designer Henry End lamented motel owners' tendency to bypass professional architects as being too costly.[70] End further affirmed that since the period's chase after hotel-like quality, recent motel owners "are returning the motel industry to its original concept: an inexpensive place to spend the night along the highway without all the frills of a hotel."[71]

Even with the vast range of room geographies that developed in the 1980s as the result of the coincidence of a glutted market and a growing consumer taste for individual expression, the motel retained its generic character. *Fortune* magazine tabulated "what you get in the bathroom" as a means to distinguish the six motel market segments. Three examples suffice. In a room costing less than thirty dollars a night, the budget lodger could expect to find two small bars of soap, plastic or paper cups, and two bath towels. In a mid-priced room, one costing less than sixty dollars a night, the lodger could expect two medium-sized bars of soap, shampoo, glass cups, two plush bath towels, and occasionally more than one toilet. At the scale's upper end, the luxury lodger could expect fresh flowers, pot-pourri, designer soaps (a small, glycerin bar at the sink, a large bar at the bath), baskets or trays of grooming aids (bath gel, talcum powder, shampoo, hair conditioner, cotton balls, Q tips, emery boards, nail-polish remover, and mouthwash), glass tumblers, kits (shaving, manicure, and sewing), shoehorns, shoeshine mitts, tissue dispensers, lighted makeup mirrors, shower caps, terry robes, beach and terry bath towels, a bath rug, a portable hair dryer, a bath scale, a retractible clothesline, a telephone, a TV, marble fixtures, double sinks, heating lamps, and often separate tubs, showers, and toilets—all for one hundred dollars and up for a night.[72] Luxury's role in the segmentation strategy notwithstanding, the planners still pulled downward to the least common yet profitable denominator, *Fortune* warning that "coddling customers may fill more rooms, but the price is high, putting profits under pressure."[73]

While the newest providers of room geography created several least common denominators in the segmented market, habitual opponents cried out against declining sensibilities in a mass culture, citing roadside commerce as a major culprit. Both sides actually seemed benignly compatible in this cultural tug of war. On the basis of room geography alone, one entrepreneur established a niche in Memphis's chain-dominated motel trade in the late 1960s by appealing to the appetite for diversity. "No two rooms—even those with the same color scheme—are exactly alike," Neil Griffins of the Lamplighter Motor Inn declared.[74] Mom and Pop persisted (see Figs. 8.20 and 8.21). Elitists proclaimed their own superiority in tasteful, architect-designed motels.[75] The very sameness of mass material

FIGURE 8.20 At a motel in Richmond, Indiana, a trapezoidal shape maximized room space in an irregularly shaped site plan. Shelves were built onto the walls adjacent to the bed to compensate for the lack of space for a night stand.

FIGURE 8.21 Here is the opposite end of the room shown in Fig. 8.20. The wall-mounted TV increases the available floor space in the tiny room.

culture seemed to generate an antithetical need in some for diversity, diversity of motel room geography included.

Entrepreneurs, managers, accountants, furnishings dealers, building contractors, room prefabricators, motel designers, architects, recommendation-service inspectors, and government code inspectors converged on motel rooms to determine their geography. Their influence differed from place to place, and some, such as government code inspectors, were only indirectly influential since even ungraded motels often responded to the competition from their graded rivals. Clearly, many of these forces influence the look of the lodger's habitation for the night; however, the anticipated lodger influences the choices made by these forces.

Finding the room geography that will be most attractive to the lodger has been a difficult task, as the technologies with which rooms are stocked and decorated are soon outmoded, and the expanded motel market presently tries to appeal to almost every pocketbook and taste. Nonetheless, some general historical principles explain room geography's complexity. Lodgers sought comfort and convenience, and owners tried to offer these qualities in the most efficient way. Underlying both lodger demand and owner supply were upper-middle-class taste and fashions at any particular time. Despite the distinctiveness for which upper-middle-class taste was revered, motel rooms ended up looking more alike as the motel became a generic kind of place. Ceaseless searching for the right combination in room geography helped spur the constant flux of modern living. In the process, however, novelty for its own sake quickly came to certify the owner's ability to stay abreast of the changing times, and cosmetic changes supplanted fundamental changes in yielding the all-important consumer goods.

Place-product-packaging has emerged as the dominant effect in room geography to date, but this is not an obvious consequence evolving from the past. Investors looking for big profits have implemented place-product packaging during the last forty years at most. Smaller investors have consistently offered distinctive-looking rooms from the outset. Lodgers thus have been presented with diversifying room geographies for a long time. These diversifying geographies have been second only to the home as highly private places of profound public meaning. Interposed between what the public wants and the host of calculating contributors, motel room geography has been perhaps one of the most influential commonplaces in determining what people expect and receive from the consumer culture.

9

The Nation's Innkeeper

IN THE HISTORY OF AMERICAN BUSINESS CERTAIN COMPANIES STAND AS legends. They are the companies that revolutionized their respective industries by creating innovative products, production methods, or marketing schemes. They are also the companies that have managed to remain leaders despite the rise of imitators and episodes of internal and external difficulty. In the automobile industry, for example, Americans credit the Ford Motor Company with having put "America on wheels." In computers the leader is IBM; in software, Microsoft; in photographic film, Kodak; in restaurants, McDonald's. And in the lodging industry it is Holiday Inn.

Certainly other companies have had an important part in the history of the American lodging industry, such as Hilton, Howard Johnson's, Marriott, and, more recently, Motel 6. But Holiday Inn led the motel industry's transformation from an aggregate of independent, largely disorganized, and inconsistent local businesses to a set of standardized properties dominated by internationally oriented corporate networks over the past forty years. Through the development of a superior facility, adoption of a franchise system, implementation of quality-control standards, acquisition of supply firms, investment in an advanced computer reservation system, and other practices, Holiday Inn built what became the single largest lodging chain in the United States within only a matter of years. In essence, Holiday Inn became the motel of America.

In this chapter we examine Holiday Inn's success by presenting a history of the company. In contrast to our study of the Alamo Plaza chain, the emphasis here will be less on the motel properties built by Holiday Inn than on the strategies enacted by the company's management since the early 1950s. As noted above, the Holiday Inn facility was indeed a superior product in many ways. Yet it was only one element contributing to the company's quick ascendence. What also moved Holiday Inn to the top was the implementation of property development and marketing concepts *before* they became standard industry practices. Holiday Inn's leaders never really invented anything; they simply adopted, refined, and fielded strategies in a more progressive and aggressive fashion than their competitors. The current general perception that a stay at a Holiday Inn holds no unpleasant surprises—that the chain's facilities, standard rooms, reservation system, and free ice are run-of-the-mill—is actually a testament to the company's success. Many of the designs, services, and pricing policies applied by Holiday Inn have been borrowed and in some cases improved upon by both chain and independent operators over the past forty years. Hence, for better or for worse, the contemporary world of look-alike, feel-alike motels has been molded by the people of Holiday Inn.

KEMMONS WILSON AND THE BEGINNINGS OF HOLIDAY INN

The first Holiday Inn opened in 1952, but the story of the company really begins several decades earlier, during the formative years of its founder, Kemmons Wilson. Born in 1913 to Kemmons and Ruby "Doll" Wilson of Osceola, Arkansas, Wilson had a challenging childhood. His father died from what was thought to be Lou Gehrig's disease only months after Kemmons Jr. was born; his mother subsequently moved to Memphis, Tennessee, where she took a low-paying job as a dental assistant. Young Kemmons held various part-time jobs to help support his mother and himself and, through observation and experience, learned the art of profit making. At age seven he organized a team of twelve boys to sell the *Ladies' Home Journal* from door to door at a dime a piece. As their agent, Wilson kept one penny out of the three-cent-per-copy commission and cleared as much as three dollars a week. Through the Depression years, Wilson found other ways to glean profits out of modest investments. In the early 1930s, for example, he bought a popcorn machine on credit and sold popcorn to moviegoers at the Memphian Theatre as a freelance concessionaire with the manager's permission. When it became apparent that Wilson's operation was making more money than the theater was making from ticket sales, the manager forced him to sell out and took the popcorn operation over for himself. Wilson then parlayed the money received from the sale of his popcorn machine into a pinball machine–leasing operation.

So successful was the pinball venture that within several years Wilson had pulled his mother and himself out of poverty. In 1933, a year when many Americans were in deepening financial trouble, he was able to spend his pinball profits on a new house for his mother at a cost of twenty-seven hundred dollars. A year later Wilson managed to obtain a sixty-five-hundred-dollar loan against the house for a business distributing Wurlitzer jukeboxes. The discovery of real estate's extraordinary power in providing financial leverage prompted Wilson to enter the homebuilding trade. Between the mid-1930s and the early 1950s Wilson became one of Memphis's largest residential and commercial building developers and the owner of several movie theaters in the region.[1]

In 1951 Wilson discovered a new real estate and business opportunity. During a vacation trip with his wife and five children from Memphis to Washington, D.C., Wilson was disappointed by the roadside accommodations along the way. As he explained in a 1968 speech to the Newcomen Society, "It didn't take us long to find out that most motels had cramped, uncomfortable rooms—and that they charged extra for children. Few had adequate restaurants and fewer still were air-conditioned. In short, it was a miserable trip."[2] The aspect that most riled him was the surcharge of two dollars per child: "Our $6 room became a $16 room. . . . I told my wife that I didn't think this was fair. It wouldn't encourage people to travel with their children. I told her I was going to build a chain of motels, and I was never going to make a charge for children as long as they stayed in the same room as their parents."[3]

Always on the lookout for opportunities to make a profit, Wilson deduced on the trip that the motel industry was the "greatest untouched business in the country."[4] Immature and inconsistent, yet facing an increasing demand from business and leisure travelers crossing the country by automobile, the motel industry was ripe for organized, well-financed development. Wilson, who was already experienced as a tract-housing developer, tied into Memphis's world of money and marketing, and a near millionaire by the early 1950s, was suitably poised for the challenge. He boldly proclaimed to his wife that his motel chain would comprise four hundred properties before he was finished.[5] Using a tape measure he always kept handy, Wilson measured the motel rooms he encountered on the trip and sketched out room and site plans. When he returned to Memphis, he submitted his drawings to draftsman Eddie Bluestein, who then produced a formalized motel design. Bluestein, who had watched a rerun of a Bing Crosby movie while working on the project, wrote the words "Holiday Inn" across the bottom of the plans. Wilson liked Bluestein's renditions—and the name—and thus began work on building his first motel.[6]

Wilson obtained a $325,000 loan from a local bank and selected a lumberyard he owned on Summer Avenue (U.S. Highway 70) at Memphis's eastern edge as the construction site. In August 1952 the first Holiday Inn Hotel Court opened at a cost of approximately $280,000.[7] The facility included all the amenities Wilson had missed at motels on his Washington

FIGURE 9.1 Aerial view of a first-generation Holiday Inn, Memphis, Tennessee, circa 1955. The early Holiday Inns were one-story brick complexes with room segments built in barracks-like rows.

FIGURE 9.2 Kemmons Wilson and the Great Sign, circa 1955. The famous sign stood nearly 50 feet high and was constructed of 1,500 feet of neon tubing, 500 light bulbs, and 10,000 pounds of steel.

trip—a swimming pool, air conditioning, an on-premises restaurant, in-room telephones, free ice, dog kennels, and free parking (see Fig. 9.1). The motel also provided a babysitting service and, true to his vow, allowed children to stay in the same room as their parents for no extra charge.[8] The first version of the celebrated Great Sign, featuring the neon star, yellow-bulbed directional arrow, green field, scripted lettering, and large white marquee, was placed prominently at curbside (see Fig. 9.2). The striking green and yellow colors were selected by Wilson's mother, who also designed the motel's guest-room decor.[9] Over the following eighteen months Wilson built three additional properties at other Memphis entrance points.

The success of the Memphis motels encouraged Wilson to pursue his dream of creating a national lodging chain. Having established a solid design concept, he went on to the formidable tasks of organizing and financing an expansion scheme. Wilson made two key moves. First, he recruited fellow Memphis tract-housing developer Wallace E. Johnson to his company. Johnson was a prominent officer of the National Association of Home Builders and thus had numerous contacts with other major housing developers across the country. Second, Wilson adopted the increasingly popular idea of franchising, which would shift the costs and risks of motel construction to franchisees, who would pay Wilson for the rights to use his facility design, operational concepts, and the Holiday Inn name. In 1954, Wilson and Johnson formed Holiday Inns of America, Inc., and developed a plan whereby investors could become franchisees by making a $500 cash payment and signing a contract obliging them to pay a royalty of 5¢ per room per night and a national advertising fee of 2¢ per night. The partners invited seventy-five prominent homebuilders from across the country to become Holiday Inn franchises, but, to their disappointment, only three joined the chain.[10] The following two years were somewhat bleak for the company, at least in retrospect. By December 1955 Holiday Inns of America was $37,500 in the red, operating from an abandoned plumbing shop donated by Johnson, and barely able to meet its payroll. A year later the company Christmas bonus consisted of a greeting card and an I.O.U.[11]

Frustrated by their inability to substantially expand the chain and hampered by their growing debt, Wilson and Johnson concluded that they needed a dynamic individual who could more effectively manage the company. In January 1956 they hired William B. Walton, a Memphis attorney who had been working for the local Home Builders' Association, as Holiday Inn's new executive vice president. Under his leadership, the company changed its franchise recruitment strategy. Instead of trying to attract housing developers, the company approached doctors, lawyers, and other professionals who had relatively large sums of cash available for investment and who had a yearning to directly participate in a new business. The company also sent out two franchise salesmen, Jack Ladd and Barney McCool, to solicit franchises in an old station wagon formerly used for farm work. In an attempt to enhance the image of a franchise's apparent value, the company increased the amount of the required cash payment to $1,000.[12] In 1957 the company's cash-flow woes were addressed when the company managed to find underwriting for a stock offering. The decision to go public was a major turning point. The first offering of 120,000 shares priced at $9.75 per share sold out in the first day.[13] The infusion of cash and the solid performance of existing properties allowed the company to attract new franchisees and investors. By 1960 more than one hundred Holiday Inns were in operation; in December 1962 the four-hundredth Holiday Inn—Wilson's initial goal—was built in Vincennes, Indiana; and by 1964 the company was receiving an average of one franchise application every three days (see Fig. 9.3).[14]

While Holiday Inn demonstrated to the lodging industry how franchising could work as a financial arrangement to facilitate growth, it also showed how franchising could be operated as a consistent, quality-oriented business relationship. One of the first steps the young company took was the formation of an organization designed to structure operative links between the management in Memphis and franchisees. In 1955 the National Association of Holiday Inns (NAHI) was established. As an advisory body made up of both company executives and franchisees, NAHI was given the power to set the rules of property operations and to devise national advertising recommendations. NAHI also became the channel through which franchisees could suggest improvements and express complaints.[15] Holiday Inn's management also maintained the strength and attractiveness of the franchise concept by rigorously enforcing quality standards and by encouraging franchisees to develop strong ties with their respective communities. In its attempt to gain the valuable loyalties of travelers who were frustrated by the unpredictable conditions of the nation's motels, Holiday Inn developed comprehensive operational standards ranging from the details of the building design and materials, to the cleanliness of the restaurant, to the ways front-desk personnel were to handle guests.[16] The company also saw local loyalties as crucial to each property's success and, ultimately, to the success of the entire chain. As members of a national chain, Holiday Inn properties were always in danger of being perceived as interlopers within their respective locales. To counter this, franchisees were encouraged to hire local firms to serve various needs, either during the phases of construction or for daily operations. Additionally, the managers of properties—"Innkeepers"—were required by the company to make at least 365 personal visits per year to individuals

FIGURE 9.3 Warren Spahn and Kemmons Wilson, 1964. The legend Holiday Inn publicists attached to this promotional photograph reads, in part: "Warren Spahn, famed southpaw of the Milwaukee Braves, is shown signing a franchise agreement for a Holiday Inn in Belle Glade, Fla., with Kemmons Wilson, chairman of the board of Holiday Inns of America, Inc. Mr. Wilson said he was delighted that Spahn was becoming a member of the Holiday Inn family which now numbers more than 500 in 44 states, Canada, and Puerto Rico. Spahn, whose baseball career spans two decades and who has won more games, 356, than any other active pitcher, is enthusiastic about the future of Belle Glade. . . . Spahn anticipates that the area will become popular with vacationers and tourists."

and organizations to solicit their business and recommendations. The Great Sign's marquees were also put to use, as Innkeepers displayed personalized greetings to such people and groups as newlyweds, fraternal organizations, and local sports teams. Such strategies not only fostered loyalty in the property's community but also enhanced the image of the chain as a whole. Residents of a town with a well-respected Holiday Inn were more likely to consider staying at one of the chain's properties when they themselves took to the road.

The company also gained early success by developing the "Roadside Holiday Inn" design concept. When the first Holiday Inns were designed, the plans called for a series of barracks-like rows of single-story brick buildings. The pool often was situated at the edge of a site, as were the

FIGURE 9.4 The Holiday Inn, Wildwood, Florida, circa 1970. Beginning in the late 1950s, most new Holiday Inns were two-story structures with room and service building segments organized around a central recreational courtyard.

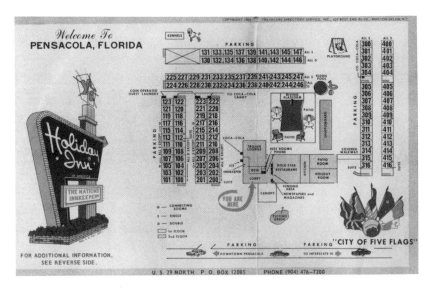

FIGURE 9.5 A property-facilities map distributed to guests of the Pensacola, Florida, Holiday Inn, 1965. Holiday Inns featured an array of amenities designed to meet the needs of families, business travelers, local organizations, newlyweds, and others.

FIGURE 9.6 The "glass wall" design is exemplified here by the Holiday Inn in Mayfield, Kentucky, 1996. Large panels of glass give the typical Holiday Inn Roadside a bright, modern appearance.

lobby and restaurant buildings (see Fig. 9.1). In 1956, however, the company contracted the services of William W. Bond, a Memphis architect, to develop the chain's new properties.[17] In 1958 Holiday Inn unveiled its now classic design, in which two-story, flat-roofed room segments formed a U- or L-shaped courtyard (see Fig. 9.4). Dubbed "U-2" by executives in the company, this design featured a centrally situated public space with a large swimming pool, recreational facilities, and perimeter landscaping. A building containing a lobby, restaurant, and meeting rooms closed the courtyard (see Fig. 9.5). The site layouts, number of guest rooms, meeting-room capacities, and other features differed from location to location because of land-parcel configurations and franchisees' expectations for guest demand. Because Holiday Inn was careful to maintain design and amenity consistency across the chain regardless of location, franchisees' demands were always scrutinized and often negotiated. To lower construction costs, provide brighter rooms, and present a strikingly modern appearance, the exterior walls of the guest-room segments were made almost entirely of large glass panes, with metal-sheathed doors and metal frames (see Fig. 9.6). Construction specifications also called for walls made of concrete block and floors made of concrete slabs to reduce the risk of fire (and thus the costs of insurance) and also to mitigate the spread of noise between rooms.[18] Although the design had its flaws—the oversized windows leaked energy and noise, the bathrooms were minuscule, the flat roofs allowed snow and rainwater to accumulate, and the concrete-slab foundations of the second floors conducted vibrations — it brought a new level of sophistication and modernity to the motel industry. In contrast to the multitude of low-slung, brick or wooden independent motels of the late 1950s and early 1960s, the sleek two-story metal, concrete, and glass Roadsides, with their inviting courtyards and amenities, became places of distinction. In many of the smaller towns where Holiday Inns arrived — where existing motels often were at best modest affairs and the old hotels had become run-down or been closed — they also became the nicest places for people to stay.

Just as important as the facility design of the Roadside Holiday Inn was which road, and which side of the road, the Holiday Inn was located on. Before a potential franchisee's application would be approved by the Memphis head office, Kemmons Wilson had to personally sanction the proposed site location. Up to 1962 Wilson traveled to the community where the proposed site was located to determine whether the site was truly suitable. In most cases, he would fly his private plane over the proposed site at different times of the day to assess how well the site fit into the local geography. Among the criteria used in evaluating locations were regional commuting patterns, traffic counts, and proximity to major "draws" (e.g., manufacturing plants, universities, stadiums, conference centers). In addition, convenience for out-of-town travelers was a consideration. Locations at the outer edges of communities, on major highways, and on the righthand side of inbound lanes were preferred. Wilson and his staff also helped franchisees find sites with high growth potential. During the late 1950s and early 1960s this meant obtaining information about where interchanges in the new Interstate Highway System would be built and buying up choice interchange sites before property values soared.[19]

THE YEARS OF RAPID EXPANSION AND DIVERSIFICATION

After going public in 1957, Holiday Inns of America grew not only in terms of the number of properties but also as a corporate enterprise. In 1957 the Inn Keepers Supply Company was formed as a subsidiary to order, stock, and ship a standardized inventory of goods and equipment used by all of the motels in the system. By the late 1960s, Inn Keepers handled more than ten thousand different items, which it sold not only to Holiday Inns but also to apartment complexes, hospitals, schools, universities, other institutions, and even competing motel chains around the country. The concept was expanded in 1967 with the opening of the Institutional Mart of America (IMA), a three-hundred-thousand-square-foot exposition center where hundreds of manufacturers displayed products for institutional buyers. In addition to providing a central showcase, IMA provided comprehensive marketing services for its vendors. Other companies Holiday Inn created or acquired after 1957 included the Holiday Press (to print chain directories, magazines, office forms, restaurant placemats and menus, and other items), the Holiday Inn Construction Division (to build motels for franchisees and the company), the General Innkeeping Acceptance Corporation (to help franchisees finance furnishings and equipment), the Nat Buring Packing Company (to produce and distribute meat for the restaurant operations), the Phenix Carpet Mills (to manufacture rugs and carpeting), Holiday Industries (to manufacture plastic furniture components), Artes de Mexico and the Johnson Furniture Company (to manufacture guest-room, lobby, and restaurant furnishings), Hi-Air, Inc. (to provide executive aircraft sales, service, and pilot instruction), and Holiday Inn Records (to produce promotional recordings and syndicated radio shows).[20] These diversification efforts were capped in 1969 with acquisition of TCO Industries, which operated both the Continental Trailways intercity bus system and the Delta Steamship Lines.

The investment that made the most enduring contribution to Holiday Inn's success, however, was the Holidex Reservation System. Intrigued by the possibilities that computers could serve in managing Holiday Inn's rapid growth and increasingly complex operations, Kemmons Wilson investigated various alternatives in the early 1960s. In 1964 he negotiated an $8 million agreement with IBM to develop and install a centralized computer reservation system through which customers could instantly book guest rooms at any property in the country. The Holidex went on-line in the summer of 1965; at that time it was the world's largest commercial computerized communication system and far exceeded the capabilities of all other lodging reservation networks. In addition, the Memphis-to-property computer linkages set up for Holidex also allowed the company to quickly upload data on nearly every aspect of the chain's operations, ranging from room availability, to inventory levels, to cash flow. In later versions of the Holidex system, Innkeepers could order supplies from the Holiday Inn subsidiaries; front-office personnel at individual properties could take interactive training courses with the central computer; and employees could send e-mail messages to any other Holiday Inn in the world.[21] Despite the technological advancements achieved through the Holidex, part of the new system's success also came from old-fashioned front-line sales techniques. When the system was first installed and relatively unknown, front-desk personnel were instructed to ask guests who were checking out if they wished to make that night's reservation through the Holidex. Not only were guests introduced to the capabilities of the system but their patronage was further maintained.[22] Although the Holidex system now stands as one of the most successful and most influential innovations in the lodging industry, at the time Wilson considered it a major gamble. In a 1985 interview with *Memphis Magazine* Wilson said that the multimillion-dollar investment could have ruined the company if the system had failed. It was an immediate success, of course, and as Wilson noted, "From then on . . . it wasn't a question of trying to sell franchises— it was a question of allocating them." During the late 1960s the popularity of Holiday Inns among both customers and investors was such that a new Holiday Inn was built every two and a half days, a new room every twenty minutes.[23]

The mid-1960s also marked the beginning of Holiday Inn's expansion into downtown, international, and small-town markets. Until then the company and franchisees had developed properties along major highway thoroughfares at the edges of America's cities and larger towns. Careful to protect these locations from intrusion by new properties, yet eager to maintain system growth, Holiday Inn saw the big-city downtowns as prime venues for expansion. Moreover, the chain's growing reputation among cost-conscious business travelers, the company's ability to market and manage more sophisticated properties, such as downtown hotels, and the declining quality of competing hotels in many of the country's cities (already battered by the popularity of suburban Holiday Inns and other motels) made the move a viable strategy. In 1963 a fourteen-story, 254-room hotel with a revolving rooftop restaurant in Baltimore became the first of many downtown properties. At about the same time, and for many of the same reasons, the company opened resort hotels in the West Indies and Barbados, which were followed by properties in Canada, Mexico, Western Europe, North Africa, Central and South America, and Southeast Asia. Accompanying this move overseas was a change in slogan: Holiday Inn became "The World's Innkeeper."[24]

A rare misstep occurred in the company's efforts to expand into smaller American communities that could not support a traditional 120-room Holiday Inn and into the "economy" market segment. At the time that the company was moving into downtown and international markets, it was also developing a new no-frills chain called Holiday Inn Junior. Kemmons Wilson explained: "There was a trailer manufacturer [in Pine Bluff, Arkansas] which went bankrupt. I heard about it and went to the auction and bought the thing [in 1962]. I then designed a four-room module in a fifty-foot trailer where the rooms were twelve and a half by roughly twelve feet. It was a pretty nice little room, and I thought that it would go."[25] As compact properties without such amenities as swimming pools, restaurants, and dog kennels, Holiday Inn Juniors offered rooms at nearly half the rate of those at traditional Holiday Inns. The costs of construction and furnishings—about $1,000 per trailer—were an even better bargain for the company and its franchisees, especially compared with the costs of a typical Roadside Holiday Inn. Plans called for one thousand company-owned and franchise Holiday Inn Juniors, but only about one hundred were ever developed. Wilson now admits that his idea was "a flop"; he concluded that guests "just didn't want to be in that small of a space . . . even at half-price." [26]

A PERIOD OF TRANSITIONS

By 1970 the Holiday Inn system comprised approximately 1,300 properties and well over 175,000 rooms worldwide. Nearly 30 million shares of common stock valued at as much as $50 per share had been issued. Now renamed Holiday Inns, Inc., the company generated $708 million in gross revenues, with a net income of more than $42 million by the end of the year (see Table 9.1).[27] The Holiday Inn system far exceeded the nearest competitor in the mid-market lodging segment, Ramada Inn, by more than 100,000 rooms. In the early 1970s the company continued its aggressive overseas expansion, developed the Trav-L-Park chain for recreational vehicle campers, and opened the eighty-eight-acre campus of Holiday Inn University in suburban Memphis, designed to host training seminars for the growing legions of managers running the company-owned and franchise operations. In June 1972 Kemmons Wilson's portrait appeared on the cover of *Time* magazine.[28]

Yet, despite the decade's promising start, the 1970s turned out to be an unsettled, transitional period for the company. Sources of instability included the 1973 OPEC oil embargo and the ensuing economic recession of 1974. Rapidly increasing gasoline prices, spot gasoline shortages, high inflation rates, and lower business revenues resulted in a net reduction in automobile travel by both vacationers and business people. At the same time, construction costs were rising sharply, quality across properties was becoming uneven, and new economy motel chains were beginning to chip away at the chain's leisure-travel customer base. The financial consequences of these changes were significant. Between 1973 and 1974, Holiday Inn, Inc.'s annual net income fell from $41.7 million to $27.5 million (34.1 percent) despite an 11.9 percent increase in total revenues. More striking was the drop in the price of its common stock. In 1972, common stock prices had reached a high of $55.875 per share, but they plummeted to a low of $4.25 per share two years later. The highest price attained in 1974 was only $18.375 per share.[29]

For a company that had become accustomed to nearly continuous

TABLE 9.1 Financial and System Growth of Holiday Inn, 1956–1988

Year	Total Revenues (millions $)	Net Income (millions $)	Inns Systemwide (#)	Rooms Systemwide (#)	Average Rooms per Inn Systemwide (#)
1956	1.6	0.2	26	2,107	81.0
1957	2.0	0.4	51	4,000	78.4
1958	2.5	0.4	76	6,123	80.6
1959	5.5	0.5	105	9,085	86.5
1960	12.2	0.7	162	15,249	94.1
1961	17.5	1.2	196		
1962	30.1	1.8	300		
1963	49.3	2.5	415		
1964	57.1	2.9	493		
1965	71.2	4.1	587	69,880	119.0
1966	100.8	7.1	728	93,283	128.1
1967	319.2	19.5	882	114,093	129.4
1968	404.9	27.3	1,015	133,730	131.8
1969	539.8	32.6	1,164	158,887	136.5
1970	604.6	37.5	1,271	179,364	141.1
1971	707.9	42.1	1,371	200,464	146.2
1972	775.2	42.0	1,470	221,113	150.4
1973	808.8	41.7	1,591	246,913	155.2
1974	905.1	27.5	1,688	267,032	158.2
1975	917.0	41.9	1,714	274,969	160.4
1976	965.6	38.8	1,713	278,064	162.3
1977	1,035.3	52.7	1,700	278,957	164.1
1978	935.8	62.8	1,718	286,579	166.8
1979	1,112.6	55.9	1,741	296,251	170.2
1980	1,533.8	108.3	1,755	303,578	173.0
1981	1,765.1	137.4	1,751	308,113	176.0
1982	1,425.3	72.0	1,744	312,302	179.1
1983	1,585.1	124.4	1,707	310,337	181.8
1984	1,759.8	131.0	1,696	314,032	185.2
1985	1,804.5	150.0	1,688	317,628	188.2
1986	1,648.7	103.4	1,641	317,038	193.2
1987	1,664.8	108.1	1,599	314,001	196.4
1988	1,596.6	87.6	1,592	314,127	197.3

Sources: Moody's Bank and Finance Manual (New York: Moody's Investors Services, 1958, 1960, 1962, 1964, 1966, 1968, 1970, 1972, 1974); *Moody's Industrial Manual* (New York: Moody's Investors Services, 1976, 1980, 1982, 1984, 1986, 1989); *Holiday Inns, Incorporated, 1981 Annual Report* (Memphis: Holiday Inns, 1982); *Holiday Corporation 1988 Annual Report* (Memphis: Holiday Corporation, 1989).

growth since going public in 1957, these financial setbacks were cause for alarm. The company's first response was to reorganize its executive management team, the most important changes being the naming of Roy E. Winegardner to the post of first vice chairman and L. H. Clymer to the post of president. While Kemmons Wilson and William B. Walton both maintained top-level positions, Winegardner and Clymer essentially took over the operations of the company. Under their leadership, Holiday Inn management took on a multifaceted recovery strategy. In 1975 the company adopted a plan to divest all manufacturing and food-processing subsidiaries, and by 1978 all but four of twenty-six divisions had been sold.[30] In 1976 the firm phased out its construction company, and in 1978 the Trav-L-Park recreational campground chain was sold to outside investors. One year later it unloaded the increasingly troublesome Continental Trailways bus line and its affiliated operations. The company's new leadership also began to revamp the marketing and management of its food and lodging business. As Executive Vice President Clyde H. Dixon argued in 1974, "the days when we could build an inn, plug into Holidex, light up the sign, swing open the doors, and watch the guests come flooding in are gone. Now it's marketing, marketing, marketing all the way."[31]

Accordingly, a number of marketing and operational strategies were either refined or introduced during the latter half of the 1970s. In order to better stabilize its business through economic recessions, the company began to favor lodging locations that could more effectively serve "multiple markets." While the chain had achieved its remarkable success by building Holiday Inns within cities and towns located near highway interchanges, the new management sought out rapidly growing suburban sites that would serve a more diverse (i.e., more business-oriented) base of customers.[32] Accompanying this multimarket location strategy was an updated identification scheme and marketing approach aimed at "niche markets." As it developed and built new properties at airport, downtown, resort, suburban minicity, and other locations, it also allowed properties to take on forms, amenities, and pricing structures suitable for their particular environments (see Fig. 9.7). As Holiday Inn began to reduce the importance of the traditional family-on-vacation market by diversifying and segmenting the chain, it redirected its marketing sales campaigns toward corporate America. For example, it negotiated agreements to install Holidex terminals in travel agencies and corporate travel offices; it also worked on getting the Holidex system linked into airline reservation computers so that air carriers' agents could book both flights and rooms for their passengers in an efficient manner.[33]

While much of the company's energy was directed toward capturing a larger share of the lucrative corporate travel and meeting markets, the leisure market was also pursued in at least two ways. First, Holiday Inns expanded its Family Plan in 1974 by raising the age under which children could stay in their parents' room at no extra charge from twelve to eighteen at participating inns. Second, it developed the Holidome design concept, which featured a large interior public area containing a festive variety of amenities. As in the center courtyard of the Roadside design, a swimming pool acted as the core attraction of the Holidome. Often, other features, such as a miniature golf course, a dining patio, and a bar, were integrated into the facility. The Holidome was designed to generate business in several ways. With its climate-controlled environment, it encouraged family-oriented travel during the months when the weather was too cold for swimming and other outdoor activities. Whereas competitors' outdoor recreation and public areas were essentially useless in cold weather, Holidomes were open and inviting. Holidomes made it possible for Holiday Inns to accommodate family weekend getaways as never before. Even during the summer months Holidomes guaranteed parents a safe place for their children to release their energy should the weather become inclement. Holidomes also helped a property's conference and banquet

FIGURE 9.7 Cover of the *Holiday Inn Directory* for January–May 1976. Holiday Inn promoted its array of diverse lodging facilities and its presence across the country and throughout the world as part of its larger effort to reduce its vulnerability to economic fluctuations. The ubiquitous Roadside Holiday Inn *(bottom left)* was now just one of many types of properties in the chain.

trade by providing an attractive facility where meeting participants could stroll comfortably during breaks and after sessions. Lastly, Holidomes offered the traveling public rooms with a variety of entrance and view options. In contrast to the typical Roadside Holiday Inn, which had exterior corridors facing either the courtyard or the parking lot, the Holidome offered rooms with exterior or interior corridor exits and proximity to recreation areas, restaurants, conference facilities, or parking. By 1977 more than 60 inns had been built as or converted to Holidome properties. An additional 180 Holidomes were in operation by 1987, the majority located in the Middle West.[34]

By 1979 Holiday Inns, Inc., focused increasingly on the upscale hospitality markets. Gross annual revenues were over $1.1 billion, and the number of rooms was only several thousand shy of the 300,000 mark (see Table 9.1). Yet, while Kemmons Wilson was pleased with the performance of his company and had become a very wealthy man, he had gradually lost control over his creation and perhaps some of his interest in his job. Since the inception of Holiday Inn he had maintained an active, powerful role in the company. The crises of the early 1970s, the ascendancy of a new management team, the disposition of the companies Wilson had created or bought, and the sheer size and complexity of the Holiday Inn empire had finally taken their toll on his effectiveness as a leader.

Wilson's diminishing power over Holiday Inn reached the critical point in the summer of 1979. In June he suffered from a heart attack and had to have open-heart surgery. While he was recovering, the company's board of directors voted to acquire the Perkins' Cake & Steak family-style restaurant chain. "I was in a hospital bed and I called [the board]," relates Wilson. "I had a speaker put on the phone and told them that I didn't want them to buy Perkins because I thought it was a terrible mistake. But they bought it and I said, 'I guess I don't control the company anymore.' So I decided I was going to retire. I was 65 at that time, and it was certainly time to retire, but I probably wouldn't have done it except for [the Perkins decision]."[35] Wilson thus tendered his resignation as chairman of the board and left the company. At about the time that Perkins' was acquired, the company bought a 40 percent interest in River Boat Casino, Inc., which operated adjacent to the Holiday Inn–Center Strip in Las Vegas, Nevada. The company also was in the midst of negotiating the full acquisition of casino and gaming giant Harrah's. The casino deals also forced other transitions in the Holiday Inn's top management: Wilson's longtime friends and partners William B. Walton and L. M. Clymer resigned from the company in protest for moral or ethical reasons, gaming being highly repugnant to them.[36]

NEW CHAINS, NEW SUCCESS, NEW OWNERS

As Holiday Inns, Inc., entered the 1980s, the Wilson style of management quickly became a thing of the past. In a 1982 *Memphis Magazine* article on the company's status after thirty years of operation, Judy Ringel
wrote of the contrast:

> Unlike the loosely-run organization put together by Kemmons Wil-
> son . . . the affairs of this billion-dollar enterprise are now being tightly
> controlled by a group of professional corporate managers. Under their
> leadership, whims and hunches have no place, and speculative deals
> with good-ole-boy cronies are a thing of the past. Instead, decisions
> are now based on a million-dollar-a-year customer research program,
> meticulous attention to cost control, and clearly defined long-term
> goals. In short, for Holiday Inns' new generation of corporate man-
> agers, acting on impulse or taking on uncalculated risk would be as
> unthinkable as showing up for lunch in the executive dining room
> without a coat and tie.[37]

Holiday Inn's new top management team, led by Michael D. Rose, who
had joined the company in 1974 as Roy Winegardner's protégé, continued
strategies initiated in the mid-1970s. In 1980 it completed the acquisition
of Harrah's and other casino hotels in Nevada and in Atlantic City, New
Jersey. By 1983 the company's casino and gaming operations were contributing nearly $592 million (37.3 percent) of the company's total gross
revenues and $115.7 million (39.7 percent) in operating income. By 1988
the revenues brought in by the company's hotel and casino segments were
nearly even.[38] The company sold its Delta Steamship Lines division in
December 1982, which essentially completed its divestitures of the non-
hospitality-related companies acquired by Wilson during the firm's first
two decades. The final and most symbolic break with the Wilson era came
when the company officially replaced the Great Sign with the current rectangular green sign featuring white script and a yellow-orange starburst
(see Fig. 9.8). The Great Sign's colors, lighting, size, and design were too
expensive, too garish, and just too old-fashioned for a management team
that was trying to streamline and modernize their company's costs, operations, and image.

Holiday Inn's management worked to further maintain its dominance
in the mid-market lodging segment by upgrading or discarding its older
Roadside properties and guiding continued expansion into the rapidly growing suburban areas of big cities. Beginning in the mid-1970s, the
top management concluded that it would have to more proactively remedy the problems associated with properties that were substandard or los-

FIGURE 9.8 Holiday Inn, Mayfield, Kentucky, 1996. The Great Sign was replaced in 1982 by the current design. In an advertisement in the December 26, 1982, *Holiday Inn Directory* the company explained, "We changed our sign because signs are an outward symbol of the product they represent . . . and our hotels have changed significantly since our first sign was designed."

ing money. Increasing competition from rapidly growing regional mid-market and budget chains such as La Quinta, Motel 6, Red Roof Inns, and Super 8, which featured consistent building designs, relatively newer properties, and highly competitive pricing, forced Holiday Inn to impose stricter operational standards upon its franchisees. The company both pressured its innkeepers and marketed its quality-maintenance program with its famous "The Best Surprise Is No Surprise" national advertising campaign of the late 1970s and the subsequent "'No Excuses' Room Guarantee," initiated in 1981. Through the latter program, Holiday Inn promised guests that their rooms would be clean, all fixtures and devices would work properly, and there would be an adequate supply of towels, soap, blankets, and other necessities. If a property's personnel could not keep the promise, the night's stay would be free.[39] Holiday Inns with poor performance records and persistent problems were inspected by representatives from Memphis as often as every thirty days. If repairs failed to solve matters or if a franchisee refused to cooperate, the property would lose its affiliation with the chain when its franchise license expired.[40] Because of the strict standards imposed during the post-Wilson era, the number of properties carrying the Holiday Inn banner actually decreased through most of the decade of the 1980s, while the total number of rooms gradually increased (see Table 9.1).

Yet, while the company was continuing to refine its Holiday Inn proper- ties by redefining them, it was also preparing a number of new lodging brands designed to effectively compete in market segments where an aver- age Holiday Inn could not. The first to debut, the Holiday Inn Crowne Plaza hotel chain, was the company's attempt to more effectively penetrate the metropolitan upper-tier lodging market. Unlike most of the original Holiday Inns in the system, Crowne Plazas offered a variety of "luxury" amenities and services, including concierge floors, separate arrival and de- parture desks, complimentary breakfasts, and relatively elegant furnish- ings.[41] The growth of this chain, which was based on conversions of exist- ing Holiday Inn hotels and new construction, proved rather lackluster, however. When the chain was launched in 1983, the company predicted that about sixty properties would be opened over a five-year period.[42] By the summer of 1988, however, only twelve were operating in the United States, and another fifteen in cities and resort areas in other parts of the world. By 1992 the domestic total had increased by only three. In late 1994, in an attempt to strengthen the brand's identity, the company announced that it was stripping "Holiday Inn" from its name and would more actively pursue the lucrative convention and conference markets. Renamed and revitalized, the chain comprised thirty-nine domestic and seventy-two foreign properties by mid-1995.[43]

The two chains introduced shortly after Crowne Plaza's debut were much more successful. In its bid to enter the fledging all-suite segment of the lodging market, Holiday Inns, Inc., created Embassy Suites in 1983 as a wholly owned subsidiary. Originally conceived in the late 1970s when the company initiated research in the all-suite concept, Embassy Suites was a response to a rising yet largely underserved demand among the country's growing legions of frequent business travelers for rooms that could serve a wider variety of functions.[44] Unlike a standard hotel room, suites allowed guests to host coworkers and clients in relative comfort and with an ap- pearance of professionalism; the guest's clothes, luggage, and other per- sonal belongings could be concealed in a separate bedroom. At the same time, the suite allowed the convenience, privacy, and intimacy unavailable at restaurants, offices, or other meeting venues. The impetus for a new brand also came from inadequacies of existing Holiday Inn properties to adopt the all-suite concept. Conversion of standard rooms to suites was not cost-efficient, the addition of suites to existing Holiday Inn properties would confuse consumers, and the Holiday Inn name was not prestigious enough to attract executive clientele. Hence, Embassy Suites was launched, with the first property opening in suburban Kansas City in the spring of 1984. To speed up the chain's growth, enhance its geographical presence, and eliminate competition, Holiday Inns, Inc., bought the small Granada

Royale Hometel chain later that year for $106 million (while also assuming more than $63 million in liabilities). By 1990 the Embassy Suites chain had 99 properties and approximately 24,000 suites in operation across the country.

During the period when Embassy Suites was being developed, the company was also working on the creation of Hampton Inn. The Hampton Inn concept was developed in response to a number of actual and anticipated changes in both supply and demand. First, as many of the older Roadside Holiday Inns were being upgraded or discarded in the late 1970s and early 1980s, the company opened up territory within the economy lodging segment in various market areas. As a limited-amenity product line, Hampton Inn acted as the company's "replacement product." Second, Holiday Inns, Inc.'s executives anticipated the gradual aging of the country's population, which, in turn, would affect the composition of the lodging industry's consumer base and the national labor market. Although an older population would mean a greater number of affluent baby boomers and retirees in the total lodging market, it would also, in effect, create a shortage of younger workers who would be willing to take jobs in the traditionally low-paying lodging industry. The Holiday Inn management believed that Hampton Inns, being competitively priced and providing relatively high-quality accommodations and limited services (e.g. free continental breakfasts, free local telephone calls, in-room movies, and swimming pools), could capture a large portion of its intended market segment. At the same time, they could potentially mitigate the problems of labor shortages and increasing wage levels by not including labor-intensive operations such as restaurants, lounges, and catered meeting facilities.[45] Space-efficient guest rooms and standardized facility designs also were incorporated into the Hampton Inn concept in order to reduce land-acquisition and construction costs. The first Hampton Inn was built in Memphis in 1984. By 1990 the Hampton Inn chain comprised 220 properties and more than 27,000 rooms. As discussed in chapter 6, Holiday Inn also briefly experimented with the Residence Inn and Homewood Suites brands during the 1980s.

At the same time that the company was developing its new chains, it was also busy restructuring its finances in several ways. First, in 1984 the Holiday Corporation was incorporated to act as the parent organization for the dozens of hotel, casino, and property-development subsidiaries controlled by the company. Holiday Inns, Inc., itself became one such subsidiary of the corporation in the following year. Second, the new corporation also activated a high-stakes plan to protect itself from takeover attempts by corporate raiders such as Donald Trump. In 1985, the Holiday Corporation's board of directors authorized its management to repurchase 2.5 million shares of its own stock; within two years the amount had risen to 12 million, resulting in a near doubling of the price of its shares. In 1987 the company took the "poison pill" by initiating a major recapitalization plan in which it distributed a special $1.55 billion cash dividend ($65 per share) to shareholders. This dividend, based on borrowings of $1.64 billion, raised the Holiday Corporation's debt level to as high as $2.8 billion and thus discouraged attempts by raiders. Third, the corporation sold off selected assets in order to pay off the debt accrued through the recapitalization scheme and to position the company more as a franchise and property manager and less as a hotel and motel owner-operator. The purpose of this strategy was to further defer the costs and risks of property development and operation to franchisees, to conserve capital for additional opportunistic acquisition of its own stock, and to improve its return on equity. In order to raise some of the cash it needed for the stock repurchase and recapitalization plans, the Holiday Corporation sold entire or major portions of its interest in a number of subsidiaries. Among the deals made was the sale of all of its properties outside of North America and a group of thirteen U.S. hotels to the British brewing conglomerate Bass PLC for $475 million in 1988.

The end of the 1980s also marked the end of American ownership for Holiday Inn. In January 1990 Bass purchased the entire Holiday Inn chain for $2.23 billion. Left behind in the acquisition, however, were the Embassy Suites, Hampton Inn, and Homewood Suites franchise systems, as well as the Harrah casino and gaming operations. These subsidiaries were sold to a new lodging group, The Promus Companies, founded by Michael D. Rose and Holiday Corporation managers who did not want to work under Bass. While Promus remained in Memphis, Bass moved its newly acquired lodging division, Holiday Inn Worldwide, to Atlanta, Georgia, explaining that it needed a more cosmopolitan city with the "resources and infrastructure" required to build a globally oriented, competitive firm.[46] Holiday Inn Worldwide's new chief executive officer, Bryan Langton, also noted that the move was a way to shed the old company's cumbersome bureaucracy, establish a more productive ethic among its staff, and provide a more attractive setting for executives the company wanted to recruit. By 1992 only 300 of the 2,450 Holiday Corporation employees were working for Holiday Inn Worldwide at its new Atlanta offices.[47]

Not content with having just the Holiday Inn and Holiday Inn Crowne Plaza chains to work with in an increasingly complex and segmented lodging market, Bass financed the development of new brands. In 1991 it created Holiday Inn Express as its "streamlined version" of the standard Holiday Inn property and competitor to such lines as Hampton Inn, Comfort Inn, and Fairfield by Marriott (see Fig. 9.9). This chain was

FIGURE 9.9 Holiday Inn Express, Paducah, Kentucky, 1996. Holiday Inn developed the Holiday Inn Express chain to compete with Promus's Hampton Inn, Choice's Comfort Inn, Marriott's Fairfield Inn, and other luxury-budget lodging brands.

formed by converting older, smaller Holiday Inn properties, where excess amenities such as restaurant and meeting facilities were removed from the total configuration. Soon, however, the company expanded the chain through new construction. The targeted markets were, and still remain, cost-conscious business travelers and leisure travelers who are willing to do without the on-site dining rooms and lounges.[48] Holiday Inn Worldwide was aggressive in building the chain from the outset; two hundred Holiday Inn Express properties were in operation within only three years of the chain's inception. Other brands created during the period were Holiday Inn Crowne Plaza Resort and Holiday Inn Sunspree Resort to compete in the luxury leisure market. And in 1994 the company announced development of the Holiday Inn Select and Holiday Inn Hotel and Suites brands. Holiday Inn Select, intended to be a group of the chain's best Holiday Inn properties, is designed for the upper-middle market, comprising mostly business travelers. The Hotel and Suites brand is designed to simultaneously cover the suites and first-class hotel segments.[49]

In the contemporary world of look-alike, feel-alike service and retail establishments, Holiday Inn seems to be just another middle-of-the-road chain operator. Its rooms are usually reasonably clean and comfortable, the restaurants are about average, the employees are adequately polite and efficient, and the prices are usually somewhere between those of budget motels and full-service hotels. A frequent business traveler would probably describe Holiday Inns as being not the worst, not the best, but pretty good overall.

Yet upon examination of its forty-plus history, Holiday Inn stands out as one of the most important companies in the history of the American lodging industry. Many of the aspects of the motel that are taken for granted were developed and, more importantly, maintained as standard features by the company in the early 1950s as a way to create a competitive advantage. In contrast to the independent motels of the era, which reflected the tastes, whims, and financial wherewithal of their respective owners, Holiday Inn guaranteed every guest free ice, air conditioning, telephones, televisions, doctors and chaplains on call, family-oriented rates, pools, on-site restaurants, and other amenities at every location all of the time. Travelers discovered and accepted Holiday Inn's consistent value through the 1950s and 1960s. Competitors, independents and chain operators alike, adopted many of Holiday Inn's strategies during this period. In the 1990s most people now *expect* the features that once made the Holiday Inn chain special wherever they stay.

The company also contributed to American lodging in other ways. Through the development of the Roadside Holiday Inn motel design, for example, it brought a new, modern look to the commercial landscape. Whereas many motels in the late 1950s and early 1960s were low-slung, neon-clad affairs stretched along the roadside, new Holiday Inns were glassy-bright two-story structures poised by Interstate highway interchanges. The focus of the facility was inward, toward a public yet private recreational courtyard. And unlike many of the motels of the era, the Roadside Holiday Inn was built to last. Today a significant number of the old Roadsides continue to prosper as Holiday Inn franchises, as members of other chains such as Best Western and Days Inn, or as upscale independent motels.

Just as enduring as the structures has been the Holidex computer reservation system. Through his $8 million gamble on Holidex, Kemmons Wilson revolutionized the lodging industry. Holidex not only made making reservations a much more certain and speedy process for travelers; it became the instrument through which a corporate empire could be efficiently integrated. Regardless of location, every Holiday Inn was in constant touch with the Memphis headquarters, and vice versa. Computer links with the company's supply divisions and with other firms, such as airlines and travel agencies, further enhanced a network that eclipsed the managerial and marketing capabilities of every other motel and hotel chain in the country for many years. Holiday Inn's current management is continuing to maintain the company's reputation as a leader in the adoption of computer technology. In June 1995 the company announced its newest location, a homepage on the "information superhighway." In addition to features such as an on-line chain directory, a meeting-facilities guide, promotional information for frequent guests, and company news releases, the Holiday Inn website has an interactive interface that allows individuals to directly book their own reservations through a personal computer. Although several other lodging chains had homepages before Holiday Inn, the company claims to be the first to offer an on-line self-service reservation system.[50]

The history of Holiday Inn also has significance beyond the sphere of lodging. It might be considered a classic case study of the rise and struggles of the American corporation. While the Holiday Inn room—the basic product—has not changed a great deal over the years, the company has been reinventing itself since the early 1950s. By becoming a franchise-based system, opening the company to the public by selling shares on the stock market, acquiring and creating dozens of subsidiaries, making changes in top management in the wake of financial crisis, locating properties at carefully chosen sites, developing contemporary facility designs, adopting segmentation as a marketing strategy, and, most recently, selling out to a foreign multinational conglomerate, Holiday Inn has evolved in ways not uncommon to corporations in other industries. As competitor motel chains have tried to imitate Holiday Inn, aspects of the company's history have been replicated within the lodging industry. As a result, the average motel in America is no longer a simple mom-and-pop operation along the roadside but, instead, a small component of a large, complex multinational corporate enterprise with a dynamic history.

10

The Motel in Albuquerque

IN PREVIOUS CHAPTERS WE DISCUSSED HOW THE MOTEL IN AMERICA HAS
developed over time in terms of its architectural and interior design, ownership, operations, and marketing. In this chapter we examine the motel's
evolving occupation of urban space. This aspect is important because the
motel's success in capturing an ever-increasing share of America's lodging
market has been accomplished not only through progressive improvements to its form, function, and management but also through effective use of location within urban markets. As the geography of America's
cities and the demands of the lodging market have changed over the past
seventy years, motel owners and investors have been quick to respond.
They have taken advantage of the construction of new highway networks,
the economic maturation of suburbia, the growth of business travel, the
increasing importance of air travel, and the rise of middle-class tourism
by building new properties near emergent nexuses of consumer demand.
Moreover, motel owners and investors have come to design lodging facilities that match the combination of site characteristics and the demands
of certain locations. Proximity to highway interchanges, airport terminals,
industrial parks, tourist attractions, regional shopping malls, and even
other motels has come to affect the types and locations of new motels. In
contrast, the traditional hotel, tied to downtown locations by the inertia
related to the high costs and risks of building at other metropolitan locations, has not been so significant a participant in America's lodging
revolution.

Here we examine the historical geography of the lodging industry in Albuquerque, New Mexico, to illustrate how the motel has played an integral
part in urban development. Although literally every city in the United
States has experienced the geographical evolution of lodging over the

decades, Albuquerque, a popular overnight stop for motorists traveling the legendary U.S. Route 66, gained a national identity based on its
exceptionally large inventory of motels. When Route 66 was near its peak
in 1960, for example, motorists could choose from more than one hundred motels along the highway's fourteen-mile course through the city.
Tourists' impressions of Albuquerque were further enhanced by the distinctive names and appearances of the city's lodging establishments. The
adoption of regional place and cultural names gave motels a southwestern
identity. Signs announcing such roadside accommodations as the Zia
Motor Lodge, the Coronado Lodge, and La Hacienda Court told visitors
that they were not only in the Desert Southwest but also in the unique cultural milieu of New Mexico. Many of the city's motels featured Pueblo Revival stucco façades and were painted in the traditional earth tones to
manifest images suggested by their names. Undoubtedly, through magni-
tude and packaging, the motels of Albuquerque provided their guests a
special sense of place.

We selected Albuquerque for two more substantive reasons as well.
First, the city possessed what could be considered an ideal environment
for the development and evolution of the motel. For example, because of
Albuquerque's mild climate, the motel, with its relatively light construction, was acceptable to guests year-round even before the widespread use
of air conditioning. The city's fortuitous position on Route 66 also encouraged the motel's development there. South of the snowbelt and high
and dry enough to enjoy rather pleasant summers, the New Mexico portion of Route 66 was recognized as the best all-season highway connecting
the Middle West and the Pacific Coast. Albuquerque, the largest city between Oklahoma and California along Route 66, became a destination for
cross-country motorists. Not only did its merchants offer an array of
goods, services, and stores that other, smaller towns along the way could
not support or offer but it possessed a uniquely attractive cultural and
natural landscape. As a result, Route 66 provided Albuquerque an ever-
growing flow of potential customers searching for gas, food, lodging, and
other products and services. Additionally, Albuquerque's motel industry
has been boosted by the city's virtually unabated economic and population
growth since the 1880s. With a continual increase in new businesses, research facilities, government agencies, and residents, motels in turn have
enjoyed steady growth from the nontourist market. Lastly, motel entrepreneurs have benefited from a consistently pro-growth, pro-business political environment over the years. Zoning ordinances and strict building
codes, which could have stifled the volume and forms of motels in Albuquerque, have never been unduly imposed by city or county governments.

The second reason we selected Albuquerque is the city's structural typicality. Some authors, for example, have argued that Albuquerque's pro-growth leaders have wasted the city's rich cultural heritage and attractive natural setting by not imposing restrictions on the pace and forms of its economic development. As a result, Albuquerque has, in their opinion, grown up to become just another sprawling, generic Sunbelt boom town.[1] Indeed, its historical and economic geography fits a familiar pattern. It began as an agricultural and trade settlement along a major river and then grew rapidly upon the arrival of the railroad. Effective local boosterism brought new industries, federal projects, and people to town. The rush of newcomers prompted the construction of dozens of tract-housing developments and a grid of commercial strips. Upon the advent of the Interstate Highway System, freeways were cut through the city, and towns that once had been isolated farming communities became suburbs. In the 1990s, city leaders have been confronted with problems of socioeconomic and ethnic segregation, high crime rates, pollution, and water shortages. While this scenario has Albuquerque as its basis, it could just as well be applied to Denver, El Paso, San Antonio, Tucson, Wichita, and many other places both larger and smaller in size. Altogether, what we see in Albuquerque is the opportunity to observe the progress of the motel within a context both special and representative. Albuquerque may or may not be a typical American city, but the processes of change typical to American urban places have certainly played out there.

BEFORE THE MOTEL

Albuquerque occupies the Middle Valley of New Mexico's Rio Grande. The city is flanked on the east by the rugged Sandia and Manzano Mountains. To its west is a somewhat steep rise from the Rio Grande floodplain to the plateau of an extended mesa. Although Albuquerque is commonly thought of as one of the country's newer cities, it is actually one of North America's oldest continuously inhabited settlements. Believed by scholars to have first been settled in about A.D. 500 by pithouse dwellers, the area in which modern-day Albuquerque is situated has hosted a succession of cultures. Around the thirteenth century the Anasazi of both the Four Corners region of present-day northwestern New Mexico and the Mogollon Mountains of southwestern New Mexico migrated to the Middle Valley. After a century of settlement they had developed a network of some forty villages and an extensive irrigated agricultural complex. The Spanish effectively colonized New Mexico by the early 1600s, but in 1680 a violent revolt by the region's pueblo nations forced their temporary retreat. In 1706 the colonial governor of the reclaimed territory founded the villa San Francisco de Alburquerque on the site of a hacienda that had been destroyed during the revolt.[2] Thirty-five families moved in, restored the area's farmlands, and established trading enterprises to serve the increasing flow of traffic along the Camino Real, which ran from Mexico City to Santa Fe.[3] In the ensuing years Albuquerque was defined by its productive farms, its plaza of small businesses, and its Catholic church. Despite subsequent conflicts and changes in political control over New Mexico—the Mexican Revolution in 1821, the Mexican-American War in 1845, and the Confederate invasion of the territory during the Civil War—Albuquerque remained a rather prosperous but tightly knit, slow-growing settlement.

The event that truly transformed Albuquerque's economy and society was the extension of the Atchison, Topeka & Santa Fe Railway (AT&SF) southward into the area in April 1880. Built on undeveloped land several miles east of the town plaza, the railroad spurred the rapid development of a new town consisting of a depot, a rail yard, warehouses, other businesses, residences, and, of course, a hotel. The boom was further supported a year later when the AT&SF was extended to Deming, in the southwestern part of New Mexico, where it connected with the Southern Pacific main line to Los Angeles. In 1883 the Atlantic & Pacific Railway, an AT&SF subsidiary, completed its line from Albuquerque to Needles, California, where it joined Southern Pacific's route to San Francisco. As one of AT&SF's major centers for locomotive servicing and freight transfer, Albuquerque grew at an unprecedented rate.[4]

Since the 1880s the city's economic expansion has been unabated. The transferral of the county courthouse from the town of Bernalillo in 1878; mining booms in other parts of New Mexico; the growth of the lumber-processing, livestock-marketing, and wool-processing industries; and the continued role of farming all boosted Albuquerque's fortunes through the first decades of the twentieth century. Another major contributor to Albuquerque's growth in the early 1900s was tourism. Like many of the industries noted above, tourism was facilitated by the railroad as it made New Mexico and points west more accessible to travelers from the East and the Middle West. What initially made tourism a particularly successful enterprise in Albuquerque and northern New Mexico, however, was the Alvarado Hotel (see Fig. 10.1). Built as an integral part of AT&SF's station depot complex, it was, as New Mexico historian Marc Simmons describes, the "shining jewel" among the railway's entire network of facilities:

> Built at a cost of $200,000 alongside the tracks facing First Street, it was touted as the finest railroad hotel on earth. The design adhered to the California Mission style, which made use of towers, balconies, and arcades supported by arches. Inside, carved beams, massive fireplaces, and black oak paneling in the dining room lent an elegant tone to the

southwestern theme. On May 11, 1902, the press announced that the newly completed Alvarado opened in "a burst of rhetoric, a flow of red carpet, and the glow of myriad brilliant electric lights." Instantly, it became the social center of Albuquerque.[5]

Managed under contract by Fred Harvey, the guest accommodations and food services at the Alvarado were presented with unusual quality and panache to railway travelers, who were given relatively long layovers at Albuquerque. Harvey's son-in-law, John Frederick Huckel, recruited Navajo and Pueblo craftsmen to demonstrate weaving and jewelry making to visitors at the station complex in order not only to entertain them but also to invoke interest in return trips. Through AT&SF's marketing campaigns, efforts by Albuquerque's business community to develop bus tours to regional points of interest, and positive word-of-mouth communications, the flow of tourists making northern New Mexico a destination rather than a required stop increased through the following decades. As the effective point of entry to New Mexico, Albuquerque and its growing number of downtown hotels, all built within a few blocks of the train station, greatly benefited from this increase.[6]

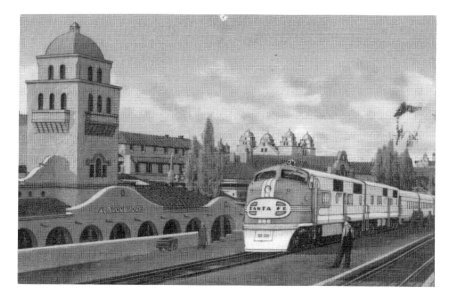

FIGURE 10.1 The Atchison, Topeka & Santa Fe Railway's mission-inspired Alvarado Hotel, Albuquerque. The railway's transcontinental trains had relatively long layovers at Albuquerque, which allowed artisans from nearby pueblos ample opportunity to sell their wares to train passengers and other visitors. This introduction to the region's arts and culture helped foster New Mexico's tourism industry.

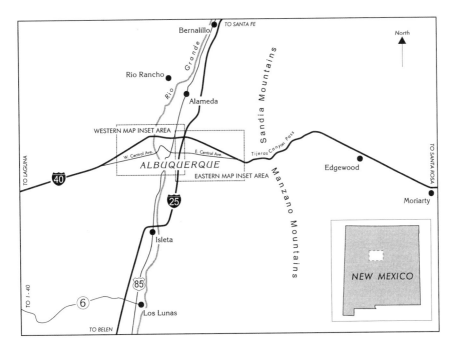

FIGURE 10.2 The Albuquerque, New Mexico, area.

THE EMERGENCE OF THE ROADSIDE TOURIST CAMP
IN THE 1920s

At the time when Albuquerque's passenger rail traffic was beginning to
near its peak, highway development in and near the city was just getting
started. Prior to the Great Depression, the only major highway through
Albuquerque was U.S. Highway 85, which ran through the state from
Trinidad, Colorado, to El Paso, Texas (see Fig. 10.2). Although U.S. 85
served cross-country motorists who chose to take a southerly route
around the Rocky Mountains, much of the east-west traffic in the state was
handled by U.S. Highways 60, 70, and 80.[7] Nevertheless, Albuquerque was
the state's largest and most important city and thus received its share of
visitors. Accordingly, it was along U.S. 85 (Fourth Street), which paralleled
much of the old Camino Real, that the city's first automobile-oriented
businesses were established. The motel's predecessor, the open-air tourist
camp, was no exception. During the 1920s virtually all of Albuquerque's
tourist camps were built along U.S. 85, and all but two were clustered
along a thirteen-block stretch of North Fourth Street between Menaul and
Mountain Roads, north of the central business district (see Fig. 10.3).[8]

Although tourist camps were not exactly a high form of service, their

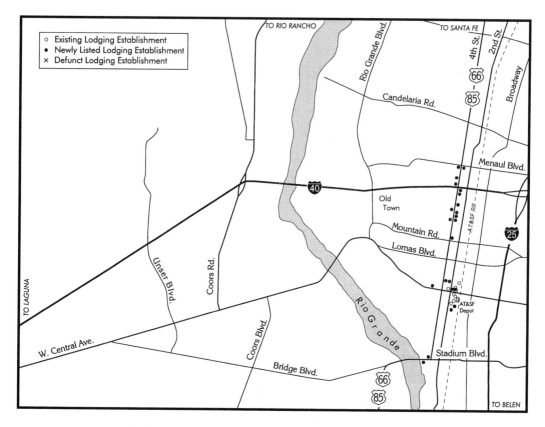

Newly Listed Lodging Tourist Camps and Motels : 1921 - 1930

<u>U.S. 85 (north)</u>

Albuquerque Auto Court
Bill's Barbeque & Tourist Camp
Green Haven Tourist Park
Highway Auto Camp
King's Rest Tourist Courts
Kozy Kamp
Mountain View Auto Camp
National Old Trail Camp
Open Air Camp
Paramount Camp
Pueblo Plaza Camp
Shady Nook Camp
Sunshine Tourist Camp

<u>U. S. 85 (south)</u>

DeLuxe Camp Grounds
First American Camp

miles

U.S. 66 and U.S. 85
shared same route
through city. Interstates
25 and 40 not yet
constructed during this
period.
Establishment locations
are approximate.

FIGURE 10.3 Lodging in the western half of Albuquerque, 1930. North of the central business district, on Fourth Street, evolved the city's first motel strip during the Depression years.

owners avoided locating in the impoverished and industrial areas south of downtown. Rather, they acquired vacant land not far from reputable businesses that could meet the needs of the traveling public. Guests of the various tourist camps also generated enough demand to support the establishment of new commercial enterprises geared to the needs of automobile-based visitors as well. Thus, because of the preexisting environment and the purchasing power of tourist-court travelers, Albuquerque's first "strip" developed along North Fourth Street. In the 1600 block of North Fourth (six blocks north of Mountain Road), where both the Paramount Camp and the Pueblo Plaza Tourist Camp were situated, for example, a general store, two cafes, a hardware store, a barbershop, a bakery, two drugstores, a warehouse, a grocery, and a curio shop also did business. Further up and down the street were other establishments, such as automobile repair garages, service stations, and dairies. Schools and residences were interspersed along that segment of the highway as well.[9] As Franklin McCann, a sociologist writing in 1942, observed, many of these early tourist camps were built just north of the Albuquerque city limits. In this regard, the tourist-camp owners' site selections were purely cost-cutting measures. Outside of the city, land was cheaper, taxes were lower, and zoning regulations were much less restrictive.[10] Tourist-camp operators also wanted to get a "first crack" at the visitors entering the city from points north, who might otherwise be tempted to stay at a downtown hotel. Already well established by the 1920s and thriving off passenger rail traffic, the downtown hotel trade was growing just as vigorously. During the decade, the number of hotels nearly doubled; virtually all were located in the city's small central business district.

U.S. ROUTE 66 AND THE AUTO COURT COME TO TOWN IN THE 1930s

Despite the important presence of U.S. 85, Albuquerque was not the most accessible city by car prior to the mid-1930s. Its relative position within the Desert Southwest's major highway network changed, however, with the construction and improvements to what was to become America's most famous highway, Route 66. Before 1935 the highway took a rather circuitous route across New Mexico, running from the Texas–New Mexico border to a point about twenty miles west of Santa Rosa. From there the highway went northwestward, where it joined with U.S. 85 and went through Santa Fe and Albuquerque to Los Lunas. At Los Lunas the highway separated from U.S. 85, went up to Laguna, and proceeded westward to Gallup and the Arizona border (see Fig. 10.2). Considerable

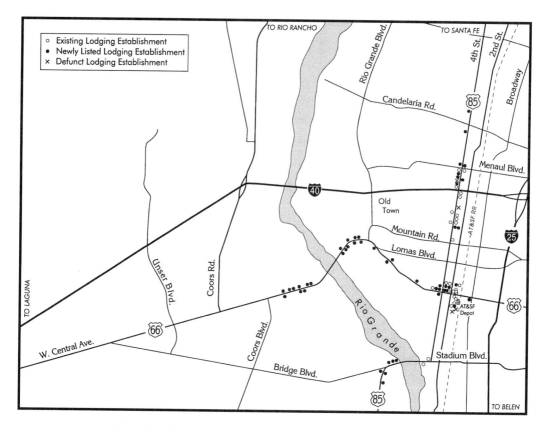

Newly Listed Tourist Camps and Motels : 1931 - 1940

U.S. 85 (north)

Albuquerque Auto Court
Coffee Camp
Court John
85 Court
Grande Camp
La Casa Camp
La Posada Courts
Lendick Trailer Park
Orange & Black Auto Court
Spanish Gardens Court

U.S. 85 (south)

Goldacre Camp
Mission Camp
O. K. Camp
Texhoma Court
West Side Camp
Windmill Camp

U.S. 66 (west)

Auto-Tel Courts
Central Park Tourist Court
Country Club Auto Court
Duke's Cabins
El Rancho Court
El Vado Court
Haller's Court
Meehan's Tourist Home
Monterey Court
Motel Court
Pueblo Bonita Courts
Sandia Cottages
Silver King Court
66 Court
Stop-In Court
Texas Ann Court
Tower Court
White Way Court
Wigwam Court
Will Rogers Highway Lodge
World Court

0   1
miles

North

Interstates 25 and 40
not yet constructed
during this period.

Establishment locations
are approximate.

FIGURE 10.4 Lodging in the western half of Albuquerque, 1940. With the re-configuration of U.S. 66, Central Avenue emerged as the dominant motel row.

amounts of money and highway engineering were required to overcome the obstacles that prevented a more direct route, namely, the rugged Sandia and Manzano Mountains between Santa Rosa and Albuquerque and a somewhat steep and extended slope onto a mesa several miles west of Albuquerque. However, as a result of effective lobbying efforts by Albuquerque's business community, federal and state funds were allocated toward the shortening and reorienting of Route 66. In 1935 the Laguna Cutoff, a segment extending from Albuquerque to Correo, was opened. At the same time, highway engineers had developed an efficient method by which construction crews could literally blast a roadway through Tijeras Canyon Pass, between the Sandias and the Manzanos. Thus, in 1937 the Santa Rosa Cutoff, extending from Santa Rosa to Albuquerque, was completed. A year later both the Laguna and Santa Rosa Cutoffs were completely paved.[11]

Over the following three decades, intra- and interstate traffic through the city increased dramatically. Accordingly, Albuquerque thrived as an overnight stop for motorists making their way across the long, seemingly empty stretches of the Desert Southwest. As the largest city between Oklahoma City and Los Angeles, as a place with a pleasant climate, a beautiful physical setting, and a distinctive cultural milieu, Albuquerque became a choice layover destination for travelers on Route 66. The improvements to Route 66 also contributed to a profound shift in the direction of the city's physical growth. Prior to the highway's arrival, Albuquerque was expanding along the north-south axes of U.S. 85 (Fourth Street) and the AT&SF tracks. As the construction of Route 66's cutoffs was being completed, the boulevard that would handle the east-west traffic through the city, Central Avenue, was undergoing improvement. Lane additions to Central Avenue and other major east-west boulevards, construction of the Central Avenue viaduct beneath the AT&SF tracks, and the extension of utility lines guided the expansion of commercial and residential development in completely new directions.[12]

Auto courts were among the first businesses to colonize the eastern and western edges of the city, and during the 1930s they did so in force. On West Central Avenue more than twenty courts opened during the decade; east of downtown another nine were built in clusters near the University of New Mexico campus and the south gate of the new state fairgrounds, just outside of the city limits (see Figs. 10.4 and 10.5). Among the nine establishments on East Central was the De Anza Motor Lodge, constructed in 1938 midway between the present-day intersections with Carlisle and San Mateo Boulevards (see Fig. 10.6). The De Anza was the creation of Charles Garrett Wallace, a well-known trader of Zuni jewelry and crafts. Like Holiday Inn's founder, Kemmons Wilson, Wallace was motivated to

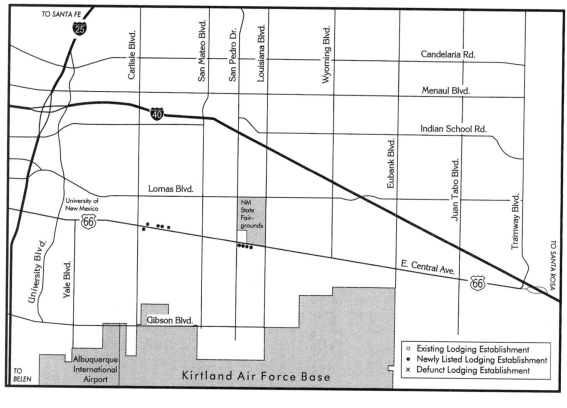

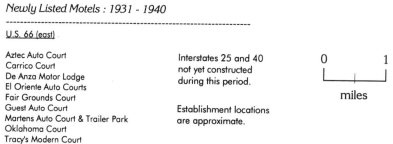

Newly Listed Motels : 1931 - 1940

U.S. 66 (east)

Aztec Auto Court
Carrico Court
De Anza Motor Lodge
El Oriente Auto Courts
Fair Grounds Court
Guest Auto Court
Martens Auto Court & Trailer Park
Oklahoma Court
Tracy's Modern Court

Interstates 25 and 40
not yet constructed
during this period.

Establishment locations
are approximate.

0   1
miles

FIGURE 10.5 Lodging in the eastern half of Albuquerque, 1940.

build the De Anza because he experienced an unmet demand for the motel firsthand. Unlike Wilson, who was driven to improve roadside accommodations for family vacationers, however, Wallace's perspective was that of a well-traveled, inventory-laden salesman. In an 1985 interview with the *Albuquerque Tribune,* Wallace recollected the basis for his decision: "I was selling my Indian goods around the country and [at] every hotel I stopped at, I had to haul my rugs and jewelry up and down the stairs. I saw the need for motels. Didn't have to walk up and down those stairs. Park right at your door. It was a miracle."[13] When the De Anza was opened in the late 1930s, it was located more than two miles from the city limits, in open desert. Not only was it on the eastern edge of the city's built environment but it was on the cutting edge of motel design and quality, if not several decades ahead of its time. Wallace's motel was probably the most lavish motel in Albuquerque. At a time when motel lobbies were modest affairs, the lobby at the De Anza was more like that of a resort lodge. It featured a sitting area surrounding a burl table made from an Arizona Ponderosa pine, fire-cured log ceiling beams, a large pueblo-style fireplace, and Native American jewelry, rugs, and furniture. The floor of the adjoining coffee shop was constructed from two hundred pounds of turquoise gathered from mines located across the southwestern United States. The guest-room segments were constructed of sturdy materials, and the walls were thickly insulated. The rooms were relatively well furnished and paired with individual garages. Even the interior wall baseboards were considered in the design, curved at the corners to make cleaning easier.[14]

Like the De Anza, many of Albuquerque's auto courts took on a southwestern identity from the start. Although the tourist camps established in the 1920s had attractive names (e.g., Sunshine Camp, Mountain View Auto Camp), the auto courts of the 1930s tended toward more exotic, culturally flavored names. In an early attempt at market segmentation, several places tried to attract refugees from the Dust Bowl who were in search of friendly surroundings with such names as Oklahoma Court, Will Rogers

FIGURE 10.6 The De Anza Motor Lodge. Built by Charles Garrett Wallace in 1938, the De Anza was one of the first motels on East Central Avenue and employed Pueblo Revival architectural treatments. The motel remains open in the mid-1990s.

FIGURE 10.7 The Zuni Motor Lodge, 1946. Like the De Anza, the Zuni Motor Lodge played on regional themes, following the original example of the Alvarado Hotel. (Photo 1980.184.061, Albuquerque Progress Collection, courtesy of The Albuquerque Museum, donated by Sunwest Bank.)

FIGURE 10.8 A room at the King's Rest Tourist Park, 1935. Motel owners also used pueblo furnishings to give their properties a southwestern accent. At the King's Rest, pictures, rugs, and baskets gave the room interiors a distinctive sense of place. (Photo 1978.152.169, Brooks Studio, courtesy of The Albuquerque Museum, donated by Channell Graham and Harold Brooks.)

Court, and Texas Ann Court. Wordplay was used by the owners of the Royal Courts and the Auto-Tel Court. And other owners took a more generic approach, giving their courts such names as Guest Auto Court, Stop-In Court, and Motel Court. But travelers were most frequently reminded that they were in the heart of New Mexico by names such as Aztec Court, Pueblo Bonito Courts, El Rancho Courts, and El Vado Court. Pueblo Revival architecture, as expressed by adobe or stucco façades and earth-tone color schemes, bolstered the images evoked by the names (see Fig. 10.7). Guest rooms furnished with southwestern decor completed the place-product packaging (see Fig. 10.8).

The emergence of the auto court signaled the beginning of the end of the tourist camp as the favored overnight accommodation for cost-conscious automobile travelers. In Albuquerque the transition was subtle in that only two camps had gone out of business during the 1930s. In fact, several more had opened, most notably along the southern segment of U.S. 85, near the Barelas Bridge, an area considered to be the city's slum, and on U.S. 85 well north of town. Nevertheless, seven new auto courts were built on North Fourth Street, most of them near the existing tourist camps south of Menaul Road (see Fig. 10.4).

Despite the competition from the auto courts, hotels were still doing a strong business and continued to be built at a vigorous rate in the downtown area. The most notable addition was the new Hilton Hotel, which opened in 1939 at the corner of West Central Avenue and North Second Street. Conrad N. Hilton, who had grown up in the village of San Antonio, New Mexico, about 90 miles south of Albuquerque, and who had previously assembled a small chain of hotels in Texas, took special pride in his first hotel in his home state. In his autobiography, *Be My Guest,* Hilton recounted that when he first visited Albuquerque as a boy, he never dreamed "that one day the Albuquerque Hilton would stand right in the middle of it all, tall enough to cast a shadow on the railroad station and even outshine the old Alvarado, pride of the Fred Harvey system." According to Hilton, the hotel was "an instant success" and marked the beginning of the first major expansion of his fledgling hotel empire.[15]

THE BOMB, BOOM YEARS, AND THE EXPLOSION OF THE MOTEL INDUSTRY IN THE 1940s

Wars, both hot and cold, were good to Albuquerque. From World War II through the Cold War era, federal defense projects provided major sources of economic growth. At the Albuquerque Army Air Depot (later named Kirtland Air Force Base), which was developed on a large desert mesa southeast of the city in 1941, military and civilian engineers designed nuclear-warhead delivery systems for aircraft and rockets. Personnel at the base also contributed to atomic-weapon detonation tests in Nevada and in the Pacific. At neighboring Sandia Laboratory, other scientists worked on the H-bomb. And at Manzano Base, located just southeast of both facilities, the military stored what was estimated to be the world's greatest concentration of nuclear weapons. After World War II, tourism gave the city an additional boost. The onset of the baby boom, a rapidly growing middle class, the growing popularity of automobile-based cross-country vacations, and even the Hollywood-led national fascination with the old American West made Albuquerque an increasingly popular stop for traveling Americans.

The resulting boom during the latter half of the 1940s was in the city's motel industry. Between 1940 and 1950 more than seventy new motels were added to Albuquerque's already relatively large stock of accommodations. Demand and competition were such that some owners invested in the expansion and modernization of properties built in previous decades (see Fig. 10.9). By 1948, motels and tourist courts accounted for 35 percent of the city's lodging receipts.[16] Central Avenue (Route 66) was clearly the boulevard of choice for new development. On West Central most of the new construction took place on the undeveloped lands west of the Rio Grande. Major portions of the street were almost entirely dominated by small, low-budget motels. Between the present-day 2400 and 5000 blocks of West Central Avenue, for example, eleven of the twenty-six commercial and residential addresses housed motels by 1950 (see Fig. 10.10). The east-

FIGURE 10.9 An addition to the Texas Ann Court under construction, 1946. Increasing demand for lodging after World War II encouraged owners of existing motels on Central Avenue to expand and improve their properties. (Photo 1980.184.021, Albuquerque Progress Collection, courtesy of The Albuquerque Museum, donated by Sunwest Bank.)

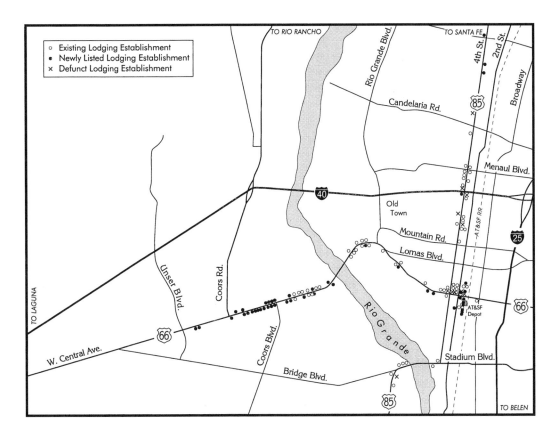

Newly Listed Tourist Camps and Motels : 1941 - 1950

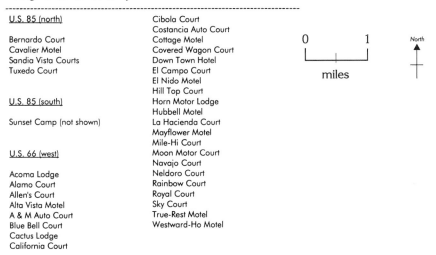

U.S. 85 (north)	Cibola Court
	Costancia Auto Court
Bernardo Court	Cottage Motel
Cavalier Motel	Covered Wagon Court
Sandia Vista Courts	Down Town Hotel
Tuxedo Court	El Campo Court
	El Nido Motel
	Hill Top Court
U.S. 85 (south)	Horn Motor Lodge
	Hubbell Motel
Sunset Camp (not shown)	La Hacienda Court
	Mayflower Motel
	Mile-Hi Court
U.S. 66 (west)	Moon Motor Court
	Navajo Court
Acoma Lodge	Neldoro Court
Alamo Court	Rainbow Court
Allen's Court	Royal Court
Alta Vista Motel	Sky Court
A & M Auto Court	True-Rest Motel
Blue Bell Court	Westward-Ho Motel
Cactus Lodge	
California Court	

0   1

miles

North

FIGURE 10.10 Lodging in the western half of Albuquerque, 1950.

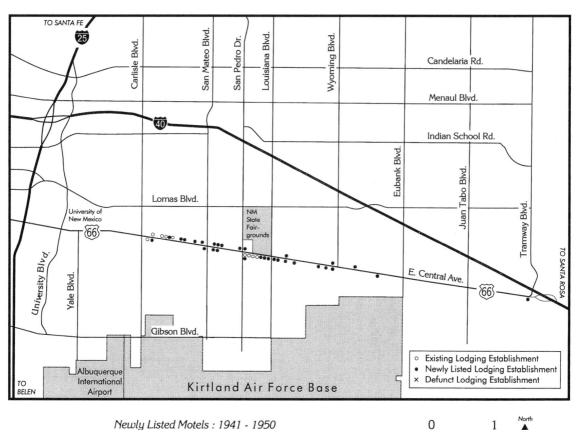

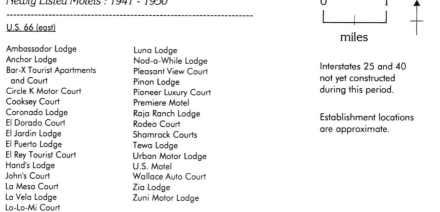

Newly Listed Motels : 1941 - 1950

U.S. 66 (east)

Ambassador Lodge
Anchor Lodge
Bar-X Tourist Apartments
 and Court
Circle K Motor Court
Cooksey Court
Coronado Lodge
El Dorado Court
El Jardin Lodge
El Puerto Lodge
El Rey Tourist Court
Hand's Lodge
John's Court
La Mesa Court
La Vela Lodge
Lo-Lo-Mi Court

Luna Lodge
Nod-a-While Lodge
Pleasant View Court
Pinon Lodge
Pioneer Luxury Court
Premiere Motel
Raja Ranch Lodge
Rodeo Court
Shamrock Courts
Tewa Lodge
Urban Motor Lodge
U.S. Motel
Wallace Auto Court
Zia Lodge
Zuni Motor Lodge

0   1   North

miles

Interstates 25 and 40
not yet constructed
during this period.

Establishment locations
are approximate.

FIGURE 10.11 Lodging in the eastern half of Albuquerque, 1950. East Central
Avenue exploded as the city's newest motel strip during the 1940s.

ern approach of Route 66 had become slightly more diversified in terms of its commercial mix, but motels and other roadside services, such as gas stations and cafes, occupied most of the built environment there as well (see Fig. 10.11). The emerging dominance of Route 66 over U.S. 85 is clearly evident when new construction is considered. On Fourth Street, both north of downtown and near the Barelas Bridge, little changed during the 1940s. Several of the older tourist camps were converted to used-car lots; only four motels opened further north on U.S. 85. New hotels also continued to appear downtown during the 1940s, although many of them served as temporary housing for workers and their families rather than as business- or tourist-oriented establishments (see Fig. 10.10).

Altogether in the late 1940s motel investors were extending eastward and westward to greet the burgeoning flow of visitors who entered the city

TABLE 10.1 Nomenclature Identifying Non-Hotel Lodging Establishments in Albuquerque, New Mexico, 1940–1990

Identification	Percentage of Establishments					
	1940 N=64	1950 N=116	1960 N=133	1970 N=115	1980 N=102	1990 N=86
Cabins	3.1	0.0	0.7	0.0	0.0	0.0
Camps	25.0	6.0	0.7	0.0	0.0	0.0
Courts	59.3	63.8	37.6	16.5	5.9	2.3
Cottages	1.6	0.0	0.0	0.0	0.0	0.0
Inns	0.0	0.0	0.7	7.8	12.7	20.9
Lodges	3.1	18.1	18.8	20.9	20.6	17.4
Motels	0.0	10.3	35.3	47.8	53.9	52.3
Motor hotels	0.0	0.0	3.8	7.0	5.9	4.7
Trailer camps/parks	4.7	0.9	0.7	0.0	0.0	0.0
Other	3.1	0.9	1.5	0.0	1.0	2.3
Total	99.9	100.0	99.8	100.0	100.0	99.9

Sources: For 1940, "Tourist Camps," *Hudspeth's Albuquerque City Directory* (El Paso: Hudspeth, 1940); for 1950, "Tourist Courts," *Hudspeth's Albuquerque City Directory* (El Paso: Hudspeth, 1950); for 1960, "Motels and Auto Courts," *Hudspeth's Albuquerque City Directory* (El Paso: Hudspeth, 1961); for 1970, "Motels," *Hudspeth's Classified Buyer's Guide of the City of Albuquerque* (El Paso: Hudspeth, 1971); for 1980, "Motels," *Albuquerque (Bernalillo County, N.M.) City Directory* (Dallas: R. L. Polk, 1980); and for 1990, "Motels," *Albuquerque (Bernalillo County, N.M.) City Directory* (Dallas, R. L. Polk, 1990).

Note: Nomenclature constructs include the following:
Cabins: *cabins*
Camps: *auto camps, camps, campgrounds, tourist camps*
Courts: *auto courts, courts, motor courts, tourist courts*
Cottages: *cottages*
Inns: *inns, motor inns*
Lodges: *lodges, motor lodges*
Motels: *motels*
Motor hotels: *motor hotels*
Trailer camps/parks: *trailer camps, trailer parks*
Other: Names without tags, e.g., The Sahara

via Route 66. Also in the 1940s, the term *motel* was adopted by a significant number of Albuquerque's lodging entrepreneurs. While the decade began without a single establishment dubbed as a "motel," twelve (approximately 10 percent of Albuquerque's nonhotel stock) had come into being by 1950. Employed in even greater numbers were the terms *lodge* and *motor lodge*. Between 1940 and 1950, the number of lodges and motor lodges increased from two (3 percent) to twenty-one (18 percent). The term *court* and its variants were still most favored, with seventy-four (nearly 64 percent) in operation by 1950 (see Table 10.1).

GROWTH AND INFILL IN THE 1950s

In 1950 Albuquerque's population was 96,815. By the decade's end it had more than doubled. Continued expansion of the research facilities at the military bases and Albuquerque's increasing domination as the state's commercial center brought yet another decade of solid growth. Although the motel industry reflected this growth, it did not enjoy the exaggerated boom of the late 1940s. The industry had reached maturation beyond its adolescent growth spurt. As noted above, motels and tourist courts accounted for 35 percent of all lodging receipts in Albuquerque in 1948; ten years later, however, their share had risen to 63 percent.[17] Yet, despite motels' increasing domination of the lodging market, changes in their location patterns were much less dramatic than in the previous decade. Twenty-five new motels were constructed on Central Avenue, but in contrast to the patterns of the previous decades, most were built on lots near or between preexisting establishments. Moreover, several of the older auto courts near the state fairgrounds were replaced by more profitable, nonlodging enterprises during the 1950s. On North Fourth Street, new construction was limited to four motels located between the 5900 and 7400 blocks, and several of the old tourist camps were converted to other uses (see Fig. 10.12). The only motel to open away from the well-beaten paths of U.S. 85 and Route 66 was The Sahara, on Gibson Boulevard near the Veterans Administration Hospital and Kirtland Air Force Base (see Fig. 10.13).

Toward the end of the 1950s there was a period when no new hotels opened and eight downtown properties shut down altogether. Hotel closure took place just as several new motels were providing more sophisticated services. In fact, it was during the 1950s that motel investors started to take serious aim at the hotel. Two ways were most evident. First, several investors chose sites on Central Avenue that flanked the downtown area. Appearing about three blocks west of the downtown district was the Desert Inn Motor Hotel, and several blocks further west was the new

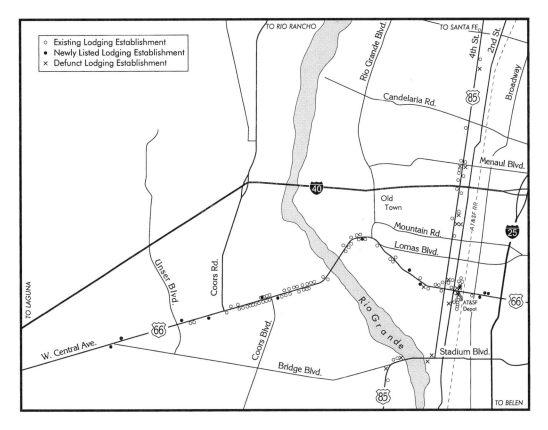

Newly Listed Motels : 1951 - 1960

U.S. 85 (north)	U.S. 66 (west)
El Camino Lodge (not shown)	Apache Lodge
Neldora Motel (not shown)	Belle Vista Motel Court
Scott's Motel (not shown)	Capri Motor Lodge
Taos Courts (not shown)	Desert Inn Motor Hotel
	El Don Motel
	Elms Court
U.S. 85 (south)	Grandview Motel
	Hi Way House Hotel
Dreamland Tourist Court (not shown)	Oasis Lodge
	Town House Motor Hotel
	TraveLodge
	West Mesa Motel

0   1
miles

North

Interstates 25 and 40
not yet constructed
during this period.

Establishment locations
are approximate.

FIGURE 10.12 Lodging in the western half of Albuquerque, 1960. Growth on West Central Avenue was much slower during the 1950s.

Capri Motor Lodge. Just east of the AT&SF tracks, the Hi Way House Hotel and the Town House Motor Hotel opened for business. One of the first franchise motels in Albuquerque, a TraveLodge, was built in the same block as the Hi Way House. By moving in closer to downtown, motels were beginning to challenge the territory once dominated by the hotels.

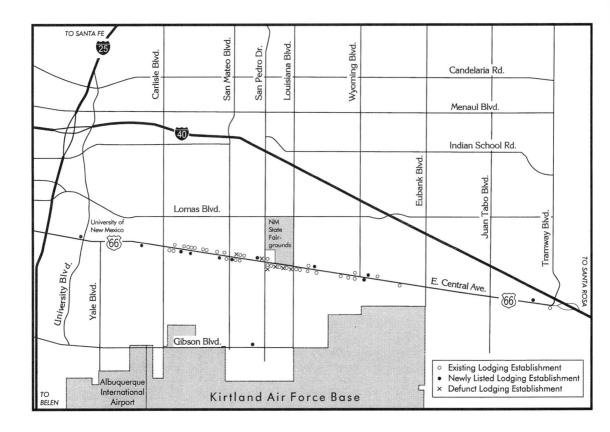

Newly Listed Motels : 1951 - 1960

<u>U.S. 66 (east)</u>

Bel-Air Motel
Canyon Motel
Chief Lodge
Comfort Lodge
Desert Sands Motor Hotel
Hiway House Hotel
Loma Verde Motel
Park Lane Hotel
Sundowner Motor Hotel
Trade Winds Motor Hotel
Tropicana Lodge

<u>Gibson Blvd.</u>

The Sahara

0   1 North

miles

Establishment locations
are approximate.

FIGURE 10.13 Lodging in the eastern half of Albuquerque, 1960.

Second, as these establishments' names suggest, investors were also looking to capture a greater share of the upscale lodging market in the city. In
contrast to the small, single-story courts consisting of a dozen to several
dozen rooms, many of the newer motels featured two-story complexes of
fifty or more rooms, heated swimming pools, large lobbies, adjoining coffee shops and lounges, and other amenities. Establishments such as the
Desert Sands Motor Hotel, the Sundowner Motor Hotel (see Fig. 10.14),

FIGURE 10.14 The Sundowner Motor Lodge of the 1950s promised "engaging entertainment, dancing, a cocktail lounge, epicurean dining, a swimming pool, and a patio" to lure a more upscale clientele.

and the Tropicana Lodge set new design and marketing standards within the local lodging community and posed serious competitive threats to both the older, smaller motels on Central Avenue and the aging hotels in the downtown area.

THE INTERSTATE AND NODAL DEVELOPMENT OF THE 1960s

In scores of towns and cities across the United States the construction of the Interstate Highway System profoundly changed how and where people traveled by automobile. Interstates often provided faster, safer routes for motorists commuting to and from work and for tourists attempting to minimize the time required to reach destinations. The efficiency of the interstate system was achieved, in part, by the limitations of access; travelers did not have to deal with problems such as cross-traffic and controlled intersections. This change in highway design, in turn, profoundly altered the geography of services and retailing across the country. Whereas the conventional commercial strip provided continuous access to commercial properties along its margins, interstates only allowed episodic access to properties at interchanges exits. This modification in highway design resulted in several new patterns. First, the form of new commercial development initially went from linear strips to interchange-defined clusters. Second, interstates—which usually ran parallel to older highways with

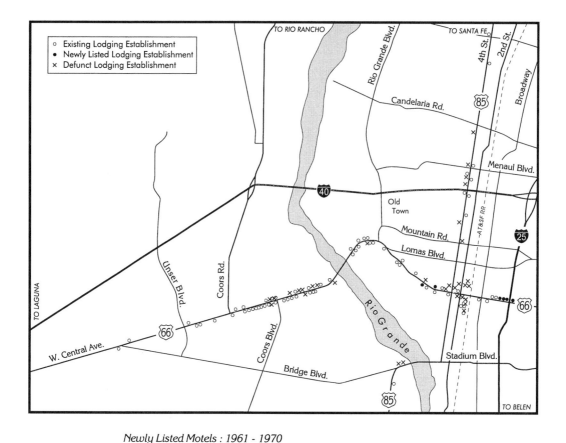

Newly Listed Motels : 1961 - 1970

U.S. 85 (north)

Vina's Motel (not shown)

I - 25 Interchanges

Cross Roads Motel
Imperial 400 Motel
Lorlodge Motel - East
Pan American Lodge

U.S. 66 (west)

Downtowner Motor Inn
Lorlodge Motel - West

0   1   North

miles

Interstates 25 and 40
under construction
during this period.

Establishment locations
are approximate.

FIGURE 10.15 Lodging in the western half of Albuquerque, 1970. The 1960s abandonment is clearly evident in the downtown area, on North Fourth Street, and on West Central Avenue.

mature commercial strips—facilitated the development of new, shorter strips set perpendicular to the older ones. That is, as land adjacent to interchanges filled up, new development spread along the thoroughfares crossing the interstate highway. Third, because interchanges necessarily created a scarcity of land with reasonable access to the freeway and thus concentrated the flow of traffic to specific points within a region, the value of land near interchanges was extremely high. Not only did persons or organizations who wished to buy or lease the land have to have considerable investment capital but the businesses they developed had to generate a substantive revenue flow. As we discussed in an earlier chapter, owners tried to solve this dilemma by associating their businesses with franchise chains in order to more effectively market their establishments and to generate greater volumes of business.

Thus the arrival of not one but two interstate highways in Albuquerque was accompanied by significant changes in motel development strategies and patterns. In the late 1960s, Interstates 25 and 40 were completed, replacing U.S. 85 and U.S. 66, respectively, as the primary highways through the city. Investors in new motel and other lodging properties responded accordingly. With the exception of several establishments, including the aptly named Downtowner Motor Inn at 717 West Central Avenue, new motels tended to be constructed at or near interchanges during the 1960s (see Fig. 10.15). Moreover, most of the new properties were affiliated with major chains. Between 1960 and 1970, for example, two Holiday Inns were built, one on Menaul Boulevard near the interchanges at the intersection of I-25 and I-40 and another several blocks west of the interchange at I-40 and Tramway Boulevard on East Central Avenue (see Fig. 10.16). Other chain establishments included an Imperial 400, two Lorlodges, a TraveLodge, a Rodeway Motor Inn, and a La Quinta Motor Inn. A notable exception was the independent White Winrock Hotel, designed as an integral part of the Winrock Center, an indoor shopping-mall complex located at the interchange at I-40 and Louisiana Boulevard. It eventually became a member of the Best Western chain.

The eventual completion of the interstate highways in Albuquerque did take its toll on lodging establishments, which were both isolated from the main flows of visitor traffic and deteriorating with age. Between 1960 and 1970 North Fourth Street lost six establishments, West Central Avenue, twelve, and East Central Avenue, eight. Only one motel was left near the Barelas Bridge on U.S. 85 in the south-central part of the city (see Fig. 10.15). Although the motel business had never been better in terms of total demand, the older motels marooned on the older commercial strips were beginning to find it difficult to compete with their better-equipped competitors. The demise of the downtown hotel was well on its way

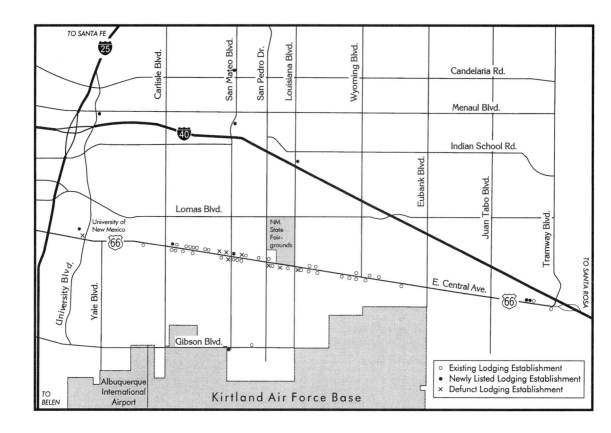

Newly Listed Motels : 1961 - 1970

U.S. 66 (east)

Rodeway Inn
TraveLodge - East

I - 25 Interchanges

Holiday Inn - Midtown

Gibson Blvd.

Bird of Paradise Motel

I - 40 Interchanges

Holiday Inn - East
La Quinta Motor Inn
White Winrock Hotel

Other Areas

The College Inn
La Mesa Inn
El-Mar Motel (not shown)

0   1   North

miles

Interstates 25 and 40
under construction
during this period.

Establishment locations
are approximate.

FIGURE 10.16 Lodging in the eastern half of Albuquerque, 1970. The 1960s abandonment of motels on East Central Avenue was balanced by new freeway interchange motels.

during the 1960s as well. During that decade, eighteen hotels in the downtown area closed. The hotel that had introduced visitors from across the country to Albuquerque and New Mexico, the Alvarado, was one of the victims. In 1970 the AT&SF demolished the hotel and replaced it with a gravel parking lot (see Fig. 10.17). Two years later the railway handed over its flagging passenger route through Albuquerque to Amtrak.[18]

FIGURE 10.17 The demolition of the Alvarado Hotel, 1970. With the completion of the Interstate Highway System and the gradual decline in passenger rail traffic through New Mexico, most of Albuquerque's downtown hotels were closed. (Photo 1991.003.014, Tracy Green Collection, courtesy of The Albuquerque Museum, donated by Rachel Moran.)

DISPERSAL AND DIVERSIFICATION IN THE 1970s AND 1980s

Between 1970 and 1990 Albuquerque continued to grow and mature. Its population increased from 245,000 to 385,000, making it the nation's thirty-eighth largest city by 1990. Like many Sunbelt boom towns of the period, Albuquerque enjoyed growth that was fostered, in part, by the relocation of corporate branch operations, the immigration of retirees from other parts of the country, and the expansion of governmental facilities and services. The city's attractive setting and climate, low cost of living, relatively cheap labor, accessibility to other places in its region, and pro-development atmosphere were among the incentives that led organizations and individuals to move there. The growth was manifested in familiar ways. Across the United States, many of the new corporate operations were constructed at "greenfield" sites, usually located near the edges of metropolitan areas and freeway interchanges. In Albuquerque, many of the larger branch plants and offices were built in newly developed office parks adjacent to I-25, just north of "The Big I" interchange, where Interstates 25 and 40 intersect. Retirees and other newcomers took up residence in housing developments built in the northeastern heights and in

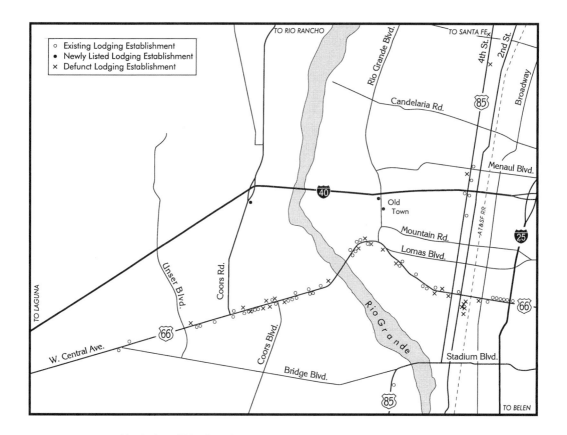

Newly Listed Motels : 1971 - 1980

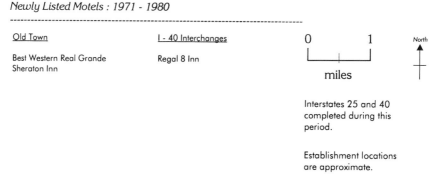

Old Town

Best Western Real Grande
Sheraton Inn

I - 40 Interchanges

Regal 8 Inn

0   1

miles

North

Interstates 25 and 40
completed during this
period.

Establishment locations
are approximate.

FIGURE 10.18 Lodging in the western half of Albuquerque, 1980. The motel abandonment continued.

the northwestern section of the metropolitan area. Rio Rancho, a mass-tract, middle-income suburb located northwest of Albuquerque, went from practical nonexistence in 1970 to New Mexico's seventh largest city by 1990.

In contrast, the downtown area languished as the city's economic energy was spreading northward. As historian Marc Simmons describes, it had lost its role as the social center of the city and become downright depressing by the 1970s. According to Simmons, downtown Albuquerque "stirred with some residual life during the day, [but] by night it lay deserted, utterly bereft of the noisy communal activity that had enlivened its streets in times past. Perhaps no other comparable city in the West experienced such a degree of lassitude after hours." City leaders unintentionally encouraged its demise by initiating urban-renewal projects that destroyed the downtown's historic structures, which in turn were replaced by faceless, intimidating office towers and parking lots. Moreover, Simmons adds, the architectural styles employed in new public structures were less than inspirational: "large-scale municipal projects like the Civic Plaza and a new City Hall, intended to symbolize Albuquerque's push-ahead commitment to modernization, came off instead as monuments to mediocrity."[19]

The city's lodging geography reflected these general development trends. Prior to the 1970s the majority of Albuquerque's motels were located along either Central Avenue or North Fourth Street, and hotels were clustered in the downtown district. By 1990, however, nearly half of the city's motels were located in nodes at or near highway interchanges across the northern half of the metropolitan area (see Figs. 10.18 and 10.19). The downtown area now had only two hotels, one being the new Doubletree Hotel, built adjacent to the convention-center complex.

A related trend that began in the 1970s was the construction of more diverse lodging facilities. Although hotels had all but disappeared from downtown Albuquerque by 1990, new ones were finally built in other parts of the city. During the 1970s the Four Seasons Motor Inn, an expansive, 350-unit hotel with elegant public areas and large meeting facilities, was built at the interchange at I-40 and Carlisle Boulevard. Several blocks south of the interchange at I-40 and Rio Grande Boulevard, in the Old Town district, a new Sheraton hotel was built as well.[20] Hilton also made the move to the interstate. In the late 1970s the company sold its downtown building (which is now the La Posada de Albuquerque) and constructed a 253-room high-rise tower in the northeast quadrant of the interchange at the intersection of I-25 and I-40, adjacent to the Holiday Inn—Midtown (see Fig. 10.20). Other lodging segments also were represented by new development. Motel 6 installed one property several blocks south of the new Hilton Inn and another at the interchange at I-40 and Tramway Boulevard, at the eastern entrance to the city. Additional budget-segment enterprises included a Regal 8 Inn, an American Family Lodge, and a Dollar Inn. Three mid-market motels—a Howard Johnson's Motor Lodge, a Ramada Inn, and a Kelly Inn—founded Hotel Circle at the I-40 and Eubank Boulevard interchange (see Fig. 10.21). The addition of

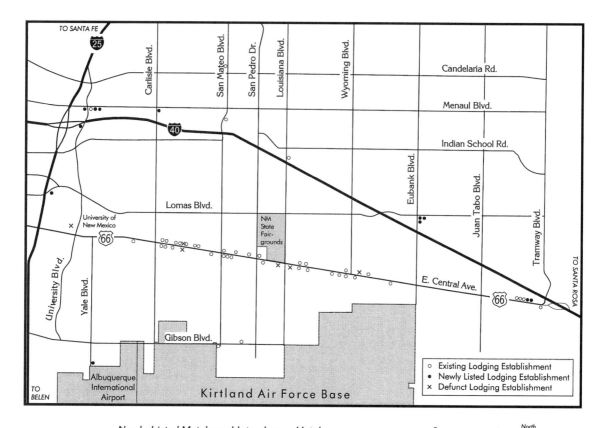

Newly Listed Motels and Interchange Hotels :
1971 - 1980

Albq. International Airport   I-40 Interchanges

AMFAC Hotel   Days Inn
                                    Four Seasons Motor Inn
I - 25 Interchanges   Howard Johnson Motor Lodge
                                      - Hotel Circle
American Family Lodge   Kelly Inn
Hilton Inn   Motel 6
Howard Johnson Motor   Ramada Inn
  Lodge - Medical Arts
Motel 6

0   1   North ▲

miles

Interstates 25 and 40
completed during
this period.

Establishment locations
are approximate.

FIGURE 10.19 Lodging in the eastern half of Albuquerque, 1980. The development of highway interchanges is clearly evident here.

motels and hotels at interchanges continued through the 1980s. While most of these facilities were built within gaps of already well-developed land along the Interstate 40 corridor, a number of properties were also constructed in areas that were gaining importance in the city. As Albuquerque International Airport became a more significant portal for visitors to the city and the region, five new motor hotels, with a total of more than 500 rooms, were built within a mile of the terminal complex. To the

FIGURE 10.20 The Albuquerque Hilton, 1993. This highway hotel anchors a cluster of motels at the junction of I-25 and I-40, northeast of downtown Albuquerque.

FIGURE 10.21 This "American Owned" motel from the 1970s, off I-25 north of Albuquerque's central business district, shown here in 1993, positions itself for the 1990s with a nativist appeal.

FIGURE 10.22 Albuquerque's Holiday Inn Pyramid Hotel at Journal Center, 1995. This highway hotel suggests that the motel industry has indeed come full-circle, replicating upscale characteristics of the traditional downtown hotel in a suburban office-park setting.

north, along Interstate 25, upscale facilities were opened to take advantage of the growth of new corporate office parks and light-industry facilities in the area (see Fig. 10.22).

The spread of large, upscale lodging facilities across the city during the 1970s and 1980s was accompanied by the continued attrition of the older motels on Central Avenue and Fourth Street. Albuquerque's west side suffered the greater loss. More than forty motels along Central Avenue closed during the period, and only three motels remained on Fourth Street by 1990 (see Figs. 10.23 and 10.24). The properties suffered mixed fates. Fewer than half became apartments or other forms of housing (e.g., halfway houses operated by charitable organizations). Many were torn down and replaced by parking lots or new businesses. Others were simply left vacant. Many older establishments on Central Avenue have maintained the appearance of motels by maintaining their names and signs, but in effect they have become low-cost efficiency apartment buildings for the city's transient population. At the once elegant Sundowner Motor Hotel, for example, portable barbecue grills stand outside the rooms of some long-term guests and the cars of some have been placed atop cinder blocks for major repairs. The de-evolution of Central Avenue can be seen most clearly on the strip west of the Rio Grande. The transitions that have taken

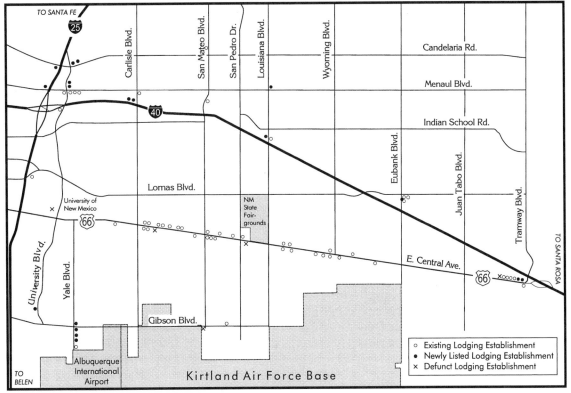

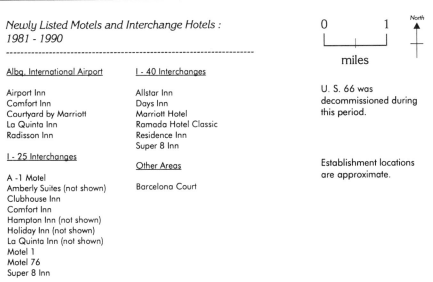

Newly Listed Motels and Interchange Hotels :
1981 - 1990

Albq. International Airport

Airport Inn
Comfort Inn
Courtyard by Marriott
La Quinta Inn
Radisson Inn

I - 25 Interchanges

A -1 Motel
Amberly Suites (not shown)
Clubhouse Inn
Comfort Inn
Hampton Inn (not shown)
Holiday Inn (not shown)
La Quinta Inn (not shown)
Motel 1
Motel 76
Super 8 Inn

I - 40 Interchanges

Allstar Inn
Days Inn
Marriott Hotel
Ramada Hotel Classic
Residence Inn
Super 8 Inn

Other Areas

Barcelona Court

0   1
miles

U. S. 66 was
decommissioned during
this period.

Establishment locations
are approximate.

FIGURE 10.23 Lodging in the western half of Albuquerque, 1990.

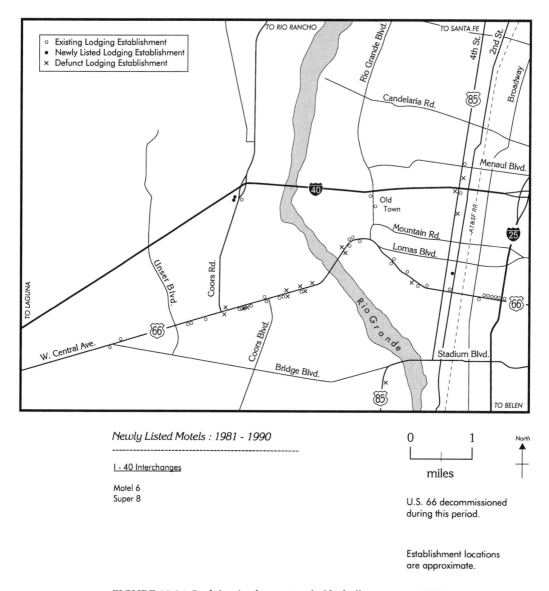

FIGURE 10.24 Lodging in the eastern half of Albuquerque, 1990.

place since 1950 can be seen in Figure 10.25. The five-block segment on West Central Avenue between the Rio Grande bridge and Coors Boulevard was at the western edge of Albuquerque in the late 1940s. By 1950 fifteen small motels, along with nineteen other commercial establishments, were in operation there. As newer motels built further west lured eastbound travelers in subsequent years, the older motels gradually declined. The arrival of Interstate 40 and competition from relatively modern motels at the interchanges eventually killed off all but three motels in the five-block segment by 1990. The remains of most of the properties have been cleared

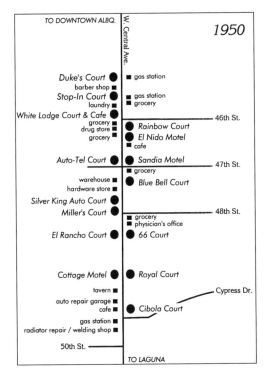

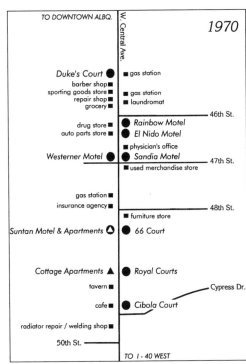

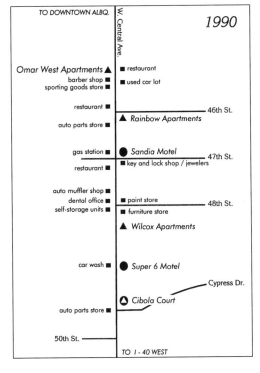

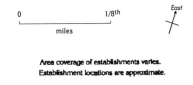

Area coverage of establishments varies.
Establishment locations are approximate.

FIGURE 10.25 Commercial establishments from the 4500 to the 5000 block of West Central Avenue. In 1950, this section of Route 66 was at the western edge of Albuquerque. Competition from motels further west and the arrival of Interstate 40 caused a gradual decline in business and in the number of motels in subsequent years.

● Motel　　○ Motel / Apartments　　▲ Apartments　　■ Commercial Establishment

FIGURE 10.26 The Monterey Non Smokers Motel, 1995. In order to survive on West Central Avenue, the Monterey has had to market itself to customers who would go out of their way to visit the motel.

away, and several, such as the Cottage Motel and the Auto-Tel Court, have been replaced with new businesses. Three have been converted into low-rent apartment complexes. The Cibola Court has taken on a dual role as a motel that takes on tenants.

Other operators have worked hard to maintain their aging structures and attract clientele. The El Vado Motel, located just east of the Rio Grande on Central Avenue, has attempted to capture part of the tourism resulting from nostalgia about U.S. Route 66 by keeping its 1930s-era appearance intact and well maintained. The nearby Monterey Motel, also built in the 1930s, has targeted the nonsmoker market segment (see Fig. 10.26). Several motel operators have also tried to counter the disadvantage of being located off the interstates by becoming part of national franchise chains so that they could lure guests through directory listings, telephone reservation networks, and the reputation of a brand name (see Fig. 10.27).

In order to become and stay a profitable enterprise, the motel has had to meet and anticipate the demands of the marketplace. This truism is particularly evident in the spatial patterns and general history of lodging in Albuquerque. The responses made by motel operators have taken on patterns as well. The example of Albuquerque suggests three stages of evolution in the geography of the metropolitan motel. The first stage began in the early 1930s, when roadside tourist camps were replaced by auto courts.

Taking advantage of the lower costs and absence of restrictions encountered on county land, auto courts colonized along main highways on the outer edges of town. The divisions in the lodging marketplace were clear: hotels served visitors who arrived by railroad, business travelers, and the more affluent segments of society, while auto courts met the needs of the automobile traveler. At the time, the niche occupied by the auto courts was not the most lucrative or most prestigious one, but it was a growing one.

A second stage began in the late 1940s, when auto courts evolved (in terms of both sophistication and name) into motels. After World War II, motel investors filled in the growing commercial strips and built new properties on undeveloped land even further from the center than previously. Motels gradually took on better forms as more demanding customers began to come their way. As more and more middle-class Americans took their vacations by car, as more business travelers switched from the train to the automobile, and as the built environment of the city itself matured, motels too became more sophisticated. Amenities such as swimming pools, air conditioning, on-premise full-service restaurants and lounges, and in-room telephones were built into facility and guest-room designs. It was also during this period that downtown hotels were experiencing serious financial trouble. Losing a share of their market to the motels, hurt by cutbacks by the passenger railroads (which were having their

FIGURE 10.27 The former Capri Motor Lodge at 1213 W. Central Avenue. In order to gain more customers, the owners made arrangements for the Bargain Inn to become affiliated with the Knights Inn franchise chain in 1994.

own problems competing with automobiles), and becoming very costly to maintain as they aged and needed renovation, hotels began to disappear from the city center. By the late 1960s, motels had much of the total lodging market to themselves.

The third stage arrived with the new Interstate Highway System in the late 1960s and early 1970s and remains in effect some twenty-five years later. Due to changes in the way motorists traveling on an interstate can actually enter the city, a new roadside service geography has developed. Service nodes have replaced the long commercial strips, resulting in episodic clusters of motels, gas stations, restaurants, and other automobile-oriented establishments. As major firms have also built new facilities near interchanges and as motels catering to business travelers have followed, the nodal pattern of development has strengthened. The third stage is also characterized by the emergence of the airport-oriented cluster, where motel investors have responded to the rising importance of air travel in local economic development. An important aspect of nodal development, either by the interstate or the airport, has been the phenomenon of franchise affiliation. Although motel franchisees appeared on old commercial strips before the arrival of the interstate, the competitive pressures of interchanges have prompted operators to link up with the chains. The pressures on the motels along bypassed commercial strips have been no less severe. As with the old downtown hotels of the previous decade, their customers have taken new routes and left them competing for fewer and fewer dollars. Lastly, the third stage has witnessed a comeback by the hotel. Using some of the strategies that made motels popular, hotel investors have finally ventured to the side of the highway to regain the customers lost between the 1950s and 1970s. In some cases, the distinctions between motels and hotels have become difficult to make.

What might the future hold for the urban geography of the motel? Given the case of Albuquerque, the 1990s would appear to be a period of both infill and expansion. New construction is taking place at interchanges in outer suburban and exurban areas, where upscale commercial and residential development is under way. Because new freeway construction comparable to the federal interstate highway program of the 1960s and 1970s is not likely in the foreseeable future, the availability of undeveloped land at existing interchanges is likely to decrease, which in turn may lead to a period of building renovation and same-site replacement. Moreover, as land becomes more scarce, more expensive, and taxed at higher rates, some interchanges may force out or repel budget motels. The currently diverse offerings that still coexist at many interchanges—from budget motels to hotels—may become less so as budget motels are outbid by land uses that promise to generate more money for investors. Consequently, new budget motels may be forced to locate further away from the interchanges on intersecting strips and to interchanges in parts of cities traditionally shunned by the lodging industry, such as those near the derelict edges of downtown, industrial-warehouse areas, and even low-income neighborhoods. Shortage of buildable space and higher land costs will also encourage the proliferation of present design trends—barracks-like motels with three or more levels, little or no landscaping, smaller rooms, total restrictions on tractor-trailer parking, and the elimination of pools, courtyards, and playgrounds. Altogether, the short-term future will most likely involve the continuation of these changes in motel facility design; the long-term future may involve the segregation of motels by market segments in developed areas of cities. Whatever occurs, motel investors will most likely waste little time in responding to new demands and new opportunities as cities continue to evolve. Albuquerque and other places across America will bear watching.

11
Conclusion

> The use of the automobile has changed many homes by turning them into something like tourists' camps reserved for individual tourist families. The house must provide quiet for rest and sleep, bathing facilities, a place to get a bite if one is too tired to dress to dine somewhere else and a place to store clothing and certain encumbrances human mortals have not yet been willing to shake off.[1]

With these words, Edith Louise Allen, a home economist with a penchant for social reform, began the concluding chapter of her book about how the conditions of American housing were perceived in the 1920s to be radically changed. The car had become an unsettling cause, and home life a disadvantaged consequence. The decline of the house as the domain for traditional family life was compensated by the emergence of the motel as a habitation attuned to the heightened mobility brought about by the automobile. The home took on the characteristics of the motel as a transitory stopping place.

The motel's intriguing diversity and manifold implications can be viewed in terms of a set of opposites—mobility versus immobility, cosmopolitanism versus parochialism, family ownership versus corporate ownership, homogeneity versus segmentation, control versus freedom, diversity versus sameness, change versus stability, safety versus danger, convenience versus inconvenience, formality versus informality, and work versus leisure. But only tentative conclusions are possible. Above all, we invite continued exploration of the American roadside through examination of the motel, a kind of place that is increasingly central to the American experience. What sorts of symbolic value accompany its functionality? What is the motel's significance in present-day America?

Complaints against the desensitizing nature of automobile travel are legion, disgruntlement today energizing the proponents of "blue highways," who advocated bypassing the bypass and the interstate for the more intense social interactions of the traditional roadside. Yet among the three primary roadside services—the motel, the gas station, and the fast-food restaurant—motels probably have most readily gratified, and continue to gratify, the yearning for contact with people along the road. In them the sights, sounds, and scents unique to localities can penetrate deeply. Motels are locales of sojourn. In them people spend proportionately more of their hurried travel than in the other two kinds of roadside haunt. Early motel owners intuited that the public places where lodgers might socialize with different kinds of people—before the cabin door, beside the driveway, beside the pool, in the lounges and coffee shops—were important (see Fig. 11.1). Only more recently has market segmentation fostered the illusion that one might be able to find either interaction with or privacy among one's own kind.

Motels have just as certainly helped satisfy the owner's, the manager's, and the staff's needs for interaction with others. The hospitality industry necessarily has been people-oriented. Stationary desk clerks, housekeepers, and repair persons—especially in cases where Mom and Pop performed many or all of these functions—counted it an intangible benefit of the developing motel trade to talk with lodgers and become at least superficially acquainted with people and ways otherwise unfamiliar to them.

The motel has also been readily experienced as a place of isolation, a means for guests to avoid contact with others. To many the room has loomed as a private place of retreat where loneliness or aloneness, variously indulged, is allowed its play. Thus the roadside can be made to mirror personal proclivities either toward or away from sociability.

Motel proprietors could fashion themselves as arbitrators of community mores. Fear of wild license along the pioneering roadsides—where different kinds of people might mix—suggested and sometimes demanded restraint. Demands grew not only for zoning, that is, for determining where certain kinds of businesses could operate, but for legally enforced standards regarding activities that could or could not take place at motels. For community leaders, civilizing the roadside meant populating the new roadside environment with "reasonable" beings, not transients with "loose" morals. The motel was a place that invited social interaction as well as regulation of that interaction.

The motel room is a carefully regulated setting. Imagine arriving at the motel of your choice and closing the door to your night's "home on the road" (see Fig. 11.2). The very phrase implies a promise, and one that is kept in most cases. But let something go awry and the tensions inherent in

FIGURE 11.1 The motel's principal public spaces were traditionally out-of-doors. By the 1950s, communal areas in most motels focused on the swimming pool. Concord, California's Concord Inn advertised itself as "a garden hotel with golf, swimming, cocktail, dining, and banquet facilities."

FIGURE 11.2 At the Stardust Motel near Disneyland in Anaheim, guests can enjoy a carefully screened patio as an outdoor extension of room privacy. "Designed and appointed for discriminating travelers," the postcard reads.

the promise become apparent. *Home* symbolizes security; *road,* the underlying uncertainty of travel. Your agreement at the registration desk for a night's lodging on the road assumes a complicated world of provisions taken for granted.

Even a few nondecorative aspects of the motel room's seemingly spare setting make this assumption obvious. You close the door behind you and prepare to relax in privacy only to notice the "rules of the house" posted on the door separating you from the outer world. Your life and property are in the motel's safekeeping—but only to a degree. First, the limits of liability for personal property are stated in lengthy legal jargon. You had best put valuables in the motel safe, but do not count on recovering their full monetary value if they exceed the amount stipulated on the notice. Second, printed advice in case of fire alerts you to a special evacuation route and procedure. You are obviously not in familiar surroundings. Third, safety is increased with a properly latched and locked door, you are reminded. Fourth, a printed layout of the motel and its grounds attempts to orient you to the rough configurations of your universe for the night. And, lastly, posted rates and checkout time remind you that the circumstances to which you have just oriented yourself apply only for a restricted time, after which you must move on to another setting or renew your agreement for this one. As if these provisions were not enough to dramatize the insecurities of the road, the blinking light on your phone may call your attention to some procedural detail at the desk or possibly some urgent news from home or office. The viewing port through the door allows you to decide whether to open the door to someone on the other side. The deadbolt guards your selection. Perhaps, a booklet offers suggestions for sightseeing, shopping, and restaurants in your new locality. Clearly, you are a stranger, a person from somewhere else.

The search for security simultaneous with adventure is a basic trait of modern consciousness. And the automobile-borne traveler seeking "home on the road" at a motel perhaps more commonly experiences this aspect of modern culture than anyone else. But motels also act on the culture. They are not merely passive mirrors of society. Motels are key factors influencing our automobile-related dependency on one another, our communities, and ourselves. In our eager fantasies of improving ourselves through motion (e.g., through vacations, new jobs, or new homes) we take encouragement from the reassurance of others. Motel architecture reassures. Subdued lighting, pastel shades, and a spacious lobby, for example, convinces us that we are on the threshold of a pleasant experience, even a playful one if we catch sight of a sign directing us to the pool. Location is an initial factor in attracting customers (see Fig. 11.3). Likely pulled to motels in constellation by an interstate exchange, we may reject possibilities along

FIGURE 11.3 The Candlelight Motel near Georgia's Fort Benning emphasized automobile convenience.

older traffic arteries as passé or possibly even dangerous. Place expectations develop in response to motel signage and layout, which are seen as symbols of anticipated satisfaction. Satisfactions obtained from the motel experience influence other aspects of life.

Group taste reigns supreme in the segmented motel marketplace. Individual preference, however, lurks as the logical focus of efforts to satisfy various tastes. Motels encourage such fragmentation. With emphasis on communication and the need to appreciate others in the "other-directed" society, motel service and decor play to individualized taste. The traditional hotels' comparative rigidity—principally admission through a formal lobby and tipping a hierarchy of attendants—lost out to the motels' comparative flexibility, and this did not go unnoticed by early motel operators. Elaborate testing of hospitality ideas led to the transformation of the tourist cabin into the modern motel. Customers are given what they want; however, the more they are given, the less certain they become of just what it is they want.

Localities desire motels not only because of the money travelers will spend when they stop to spend the night but also because of the contact they provide with the world beyond. Is parochialism threatened or enhanced by such encounters with an imagined cosmopolitanism beyond?

Motels also screen experience, separating travelers both from traveling and from one another. Owners' increasing desire to satisfy travelers often leads to deliberate contrivance. Owners try to give the illusion of a catered and a carefree "home on the road," while "reality" buzzes outside the room, on the highway. They try to communicate elegance (in the case of an Alamo Plaza) or escape (a Holiday Inn). Motels' successfully contrived "atmosphere" makes of the motel a kind of stage on which services are performed, seemingly denying the consumer a glimpse of the space "behind the scenes" where management figures and labor works. Nonetheless, hallways blocked by housekeepers' service carts stacked high with soaps and towels to replenish rooms for the next night's lodgers and managers trying to register incoming lodgers while phones ring with new requests jar the consumer into "reality." By trying to keep these workaday intrusions from interfering with the lodger's comfort, successively more clever illusions are created by the interplay between staff and lodger. Over time, has not the motel stay become one of the objectives of travel—splashing in the pool, playing in the game room, eating in the restaurant, attending a conference? Motels are self-contained environments, to a degree that neither the gas station nor the fast-food restaurant, the other two leading purveyors of roadside services, can ever be.

Seekers of "reality," which is denied in motels, may find fulfillment in backpacking and camping, activities that pretend to lack place management. The contrived campground, of course, may be no less orchestrated than the motel in the terms of the social interaction encouraged. Overtly, motels not only screen life within their walls but also focus experiences beyond their walls. As purveyors of local travel and entertainment literature, motels reinforce established definitions of what is fun and where and when fun is obtainable. As welcoming members of the local chambers of commerce or hosts, motel managers also contribute significantly to defining official tourist destinations. And in personal encounters, registration desk personnel will recommend local streets and leisure activities. The camper may not only commune more directly with "nature" as salvaged and spared in a locality but also avoid the engineered orchestration of attractions beyond "nature." But it is a release from direction, not a total avoidance thereof, discontent and reduced amenity substituting for motel tyranny.

Inconvenience is an unacceptable dimension of the very adventure a wide range of travelers seek on the road. Convenience remains a hallmark of all coveted roadside experience. If half the fun is supposed to be in *getting* there, many, perhaps most, would rather emphasize the destination, or *being* there. Motel and hotel lodgers have arranged an elaborate system of interdependent satisfactions well removed from the primitive. They promote motel convenience as inherently homelike, the ultimate form of destination. Motels are not alone in facilitating convenient travel, but they are primary mediums. Increasingly, they have become the destination in

FIGURE 11.4 The teepee and "Wyoming Howdy Wagon" dominating the entrance to Cheyenne's Downtowner Motor Inn assure lodgers that they have arrived at their intended western destination.

travel, substituting substantially for the larger sense of place beyond (see Fig. 11.4). They enable the traveler to be "at home" in a strange place.

Motels are neither suspended in space as place nor in time as context. Historian Michael Kammen, in his insightful study of modern America, despairs of manipulating collective memory in order to build consensus: "So it has been, so it is, so the pattern very likely shall continue. Americans will historicize the present in a somewhat facile, sometimes inadvertent way, and they will continue to depoliticize the past as a means of minimizing conflict." Kammen holds out faith that history-minded scholars can help rectify the problem.[2] What might study of the motel in America contribute? Class, gender, and race merit attention by scholars of the roadside. Highway and roadside history have too often read like a nostalgic romp in the carefree good old days, avoiding the harsh realities. As comfort and amenity providers, motels may invite nostalgic recollection. Nonetheless, the hard questions remain: What is the real significance of motels in the American experience? What do the social interactions in these places say about society and its institutions? Is the truth too harsh to reconcile with the escape fostered in advertising?

Who benefits from a night's lodging? Obviously, successful investors benefit more than anyone else. Vacationers and business travelers come second. And those reaping the smallest benefit are the poorer and less educated, who as housekeepers, launderers, and maintenance people run motels for owners and managers. Manual labor's plight is especially poignant along the roadside, as Richard Horwitz has revealed in his study of the highway strip motel.[3] There those with little hope of the affluence symbolized by the motel itself labor surrounded by the more affluent and the more powerful. The disparity is all too obvious. Perhaps no more striking tableau of labor's drain and leisure's fruits exists. The motel stands as a microcosm of the larger society beyond — controlling profiteers, consuming clients, laboring functionaries, languishing minorities.

Searching for acceptance based on talent, not category, blacks and Hispanics are largely underrepresented save in the menial labor category. The disproportionately low percentage of female owners and managers also needs underscoring.[4] Traditionally, motels have been created by and for the hegemonic white, male-dominated, middle and upper-middle classes. Exemplifying the discrimination against minorities are the anguished words of a mother of one of the young blacks killed in Detroit's infamous Algiers Motel incident of 1967: "You know what hurt me so bad again? Because they never was a white motel they could have, that the Negro police could come in and shoot it up like they did that Negro hotel, that they walk in out of the street and shoot an innocent guest like they did, and get turned loose. Tell me what would have happened if a Negro police had have walked into a all-white neighborhood and shot it up, like they shot up the Algiers Motel. They could not do it."[5] The geographical and historical dimensions of racial discrimination in relation to motels will require special attention in future research.

A less understood group, for some time including day laborers and those who were reclusive for various reasons but now including the recently impoverished as well, is the long-term residents, or "hidden homeless." These people are not mentioned in any motel trade literature, and so far they have not been treated in academic studies. The federal census does not include persons living in motels, although their plight is well known to some social workers and police and numbers seem significant to the few journalists who have reported the phenomena in studies of individual cities. Have the hidden homeless become a permanent group in American society, or are they a temporary group resulting from a temporary increase in poverty and a shortage of available housing? In Dallas, motels housing the hidden homeless are the older but not necessarily run-down motels close to the center of town, near bus lines, where the rent is cheap. Of twelve occupants in the Avalon Motel in Dallas several live on social security, several are disabled, several are transients, and one is the maintenance man. In suburban Westchester, New York, as well as in several southwestern cities and Los Angeles, a disturbing increase has been reported in the number of middle-class families whose declining incomes

CONCLUSION

———

331

make it necessary for them to live in motels. In the 1980s private charity in Tulsa sustained another variation, an old motel serving as a residence for people who otherwise would have been homeless. We have observed several cases of day laborers who, preferring an older motel's cheap rates and services to the responsibilities of a permanent home, such as real estate taxes, may reside at a motel on a weekly or monthly basis. Sporadic newspaper reports of arrests or deaths in motels remind us that many motel occupants are "unseen" because most of society and many of the occupants, especially drug dealers and prostitutes, prefer it that way. The most common references to the motel's sheltering anonymity are jokes about couples wealthy enough to briefly share a room in a "no-tell motel." Nudged into keener awareness, the critical landscape observer also will find certain regions where otherwise homeless take fleeting advantage of abandoned motels as homes; derelict motels along less-used highways in temperate coastal climes are an example.[6]

A newspaper report about one motel, regarded as a "public nuisance," on the eve of demolition describes the death rattle of many motels: "When workers arrived to bulldoze the weeds and debris Saturday morning, police roused a half-dozen vagrants who were living in the motel. They left behind shoes, hats, an umbrella and in one case, a can of deodorant. One man had been sleeping in a room crowded with mattresses, magazines and rubble. Above his bed was a small electric fan, hooked by jumper cables to a car battery. On the walls, pictures of the Dalai Lama and naked women were taped to newspaper food pages." An absentee-owned corporation had abandoned the property, and the local operator, behind on mortgage payments, had "walked away."[7]

Motels often experience a common life cycle. Launched optimistically as exciting new investments, in time they fall to owners who manipulate them exclusively as profit-making schemes. When traffic patterns almost invariably shift in the national culture of frenetic automobility, they rush to squeeze out the maximum profits from declining rates in expectation of short-term ownership. Motels that are not abandoned and do not fall into physical disrepair and social reprobation gain new life as housing for the elderly, small office space, or stores. A few invite the respectable, long-term occupancy of general residents. The economic system abhors idleness. Survivors secured against vandalism, strangely, wait in limbo (see Fig. 11.5). Conversely, where motel owners consider the land too valuable to support low-density use of the motel encouraged through historic preservation, pressure develops to raze and redevelop the property with a more profitable venture. These generalizations notwithstanding, future research is needed to explain such subjects as where, when, and in what form old motels are transmuted.

FIGURE 11.5 Abandoned motels like this one at Mattoon, Illinois, are problematic: should they be razed or adapted?

Motels have diverse uses. Business opportunities for the few, employment bases, travel facilitators for the many, and, in general, purveyors of temporary rootedness, motels are central to America's enhanced mobility. They are central to the American quest for new opportunity, but, paradoxically, they also represent a necessary anchor.

Americans seek stimulation in adventure on the highway yet gravitate toward security, as Warren Belasco has pointed out.[8] Not only customers but also entrepreneurs adhere to the road, with its tension between adventure and security; for out of the mom-and-pop enterprise first emerged corporate chains and franchising. The bulk purchasing and mass advertising that came with such linkages brought profits to owners, and travelers found comfort in the replicated patterns of amenities housed in similar-looking architecture offered regionally or nationally.

We have extended Belasco's concern to the years after World War II. In the process, however, we have identified a tendency to so guarantee security as to exceed by far the expectations for the motel industry in the years to 1945. Predictions on the eve of World War II were surely for motel growth and luxury, but within the context of small business. Sinclair Lewis had predicted in 1920 that someone would eventually build a chain of inexpensive and reliable motels.[9] But no one moved aggressively to put that idea into practice for another third of a century. Entrepreneurs and consumers alike were convinced that the homelike virtues of the motel could only be available from homelike providers; hence, the mom-and-pop enterprise was the dominant aspiration and practice. Even the most ambitious chain, Alamo Plaza, waited for opportunities to develop instead of trying to structure the market. This was true not only in terms of locations but also in terms of advertising: although Alamo Plaza beckoned in the name of hotel-like luxury for fifteen years, it did not stride forward to situate itself in the motor-inn niche before that niche developed in the 1950s. Kemmons Wilson, a homebuilder offering the qualities of mid-range housing for travelers, alone revolutionized the industry by thinking in terms of scale. Once the step toward an extensive financial empire was taken, however, place-product-packaging accompanied it as the means of aggrandizement. Place-product-packaging then functioned like an unquestionable truth, an immutable structure. Now it goes unchallenged by investors and seems to be instinctively sought by travelers.

American lifestyles are more regimented than might be expected among a people avowing individual freedom as a national characteristic to be maintained and occasionally even asserted internationally in foreign policy. Standardization not only eases the way to profits but also allays the insecurities of a people ideologically freed of social hierarchy. Individuals pursuing their own destiny by their own wits have substituted their own sustaining structures and myths. Freedom on the "open road" thus has led by this time not only to place-product-packaging but also to market segmentation. The uncertainties resulting from social atomization are resolved in America's materialistic culture by associating with one's social kin, either those who are equal to oneself or those aspiring to better. The hyper self-consciousness of American culture may well allow Americans to perceive the incongruity of aspiration and practice, with the consequence that motels may revert to the homogeneous motel pitched in advertising to the average man or woman. Or will Americans end up with a narrow range of highly segmented motel experiences? Is the resort motel assured a future or in decline? Surely marketing advantage will be sought in restlessly changing appeals. Maneuvering for advantage will persist. The relay race will probably continue between a succession of corporations subsuming their predecessors. Intellectuals may criticize the apparent tail-chasing of American culture, but, lacking historical perspective, most people derive pleasure in the chase and entrepreneurs are satisfied to profit from it. Furthermore, Americans have no absolute identity. If lost community is symbolized for elitists in the anonymous-looking motel, for example, they are reaching for an idealized past that never was. Community and individuality have strained in tension throughout the American past.

Americans seem to oscillate between the opposites listed at the outset of this conclusion. For example, in seeking excitement one may verge on the dangerous, yet satisfaction is sustained short of the dull. High formality puts many off, yet distinction is preferred even in the casual. The more leisure people enjoy, the harder they work in order to extend their leisure. Projecting future motel activity in terms of all the polarities listed above invites dedicated scholarly attention.

Studies of the motel in America to date have been subject to scholarly biases. The most obvious is the nearly complete avoidance of the motel as a serious subject. Two of the few exceptions are the academic realms concerned with "leisure studies" and hotel and motel management. Neither ventures far beyond the business concerns of increased profit making. Historic preservationists have explored the longer temporal and broader cultural contexts of the motel, examining it as a "resource" to be managed. Beyond its function as architecture, the societal significance of this distinctive place-type in America remains little contemplated. The motel's general absence from scholarly agendas may have to do with the pervasive presumption that as a feature of virtually every American locality it is to be taken very much for granted. In their commonplaceness motels seem to deserve little consideration. As architecture, motels are seen as little more than obvious design templates for obvious, largely functional, purposes. Architectural historians have deliberately avoided motels as being undeserving of study.[10]

Perhaps the ahistorical perspective of the motel business itself, which tends to be focused on the future, also discourages scholars. Few corporations have maintained a substantial archive of business records or photographs. If the past plays any role, it is as a slight marketing gloss, an occasional appeal to nostalgia, often through the use of old photographs, advertising, or decorations perhaps to trigger thoughts of a less troubled time. Similarly, architects clear their files on motel work perceived as pedestrian; and designers often do not count their work for motels as truly significant.

Yet research obviously is possible. Focus on the entrepreneur is certainly possible. Family-oriented businesses (especially the mom-and-pop motels) and corporations tantamount to them (wherein one or a very few individuals have been key) usually reward the curious scholar. There is usually sufficient information to document and interpret a single motel or a corporate proliferation of a motel chain. Here, however, the scholar can and must augment the record with an oral-history project, interviewing those whose decisions might otherwise be only inferred from the written record, which is often self-promoting, or forgotten altogether. Such research can be very time-consuming and expensive. Developing sufficient rapport with often far-flung retired personnel in order to understand the reasons for decisions that have been unknown to the public requires much patience and perseverance.

Thus, much remains to be addressed in future studies of the motel as a feature of the American landscape. Avenues for future inquiry include the following:

1. The development of the motel as an architectural ensemble comprising not only form but decoration and style.
2. The design work of those who molded the motel's central feature, the room.
3. The influences of those who have influenced designs, e.g., building contractors, reference services, code inspectors, zoning boards, and, of course, motel entrepreneurs as clients.
4. The motel's relationship to specific landscape contexts, e.g., highways, interstates, central business districts, military barracks towns, edge cities.
5. The segmentation of markets on the basis of social status.
6. The emergence of place-product-packaging concepts to assign known market segments.
7. The territorial competition between corporations in penetrating local, regional, national, and even international markets.
8. The preservation, reuse, and dereliction implicit in old motels.
9. The iconography of the motel in art and other discourses high and low.
10. The role of entrepreneurship in defining the motel as an institution.
11. The role of class, gender, and race as they relate to all of the above.

As authors we have tried to at least tentatively explore these various avenues. Our learning has been stimulated by constant reference to the kaleidescopic visions of landscape experience past and present. Especially striking is the motel's diversity despite its comparative novelty in the American experience. Place-product-packaging has remained our principal concept for bringing order to the diversity encountered. Corporate liveries are numerous, but the concept behind them, namely, to quickly make known a distinctive brand ahead on the roadside, and with it a known quality of services, seems to have been accepted. The independent motel suffers from the lack of such reinforcement, the prospective guest being left to examine other clues to quality and satisfaction, such as architectural form, level of maintenance, or suitability of landscaping. The chains establish certain expectations, the independents conforming or deviating from these engineered expectations. In our world of accelerated, changeful mobility, where temporary anchorage remains an absolute necessity, place-product-packaging is here to stay. Motels provide a place to pause on an occasional day, weekend, or extended vacation. They are contrived "homes away from home" that are depended upon by most Americans. Their structure and function speak as a vocabulary of belonging to a place. Their standardization facilitates our future as a society and culture. They must therefore be easily read as destination.

Motels are above all symbolic of two insatiable national appetites: for an upper-middle-class lifestyle and mobility. The room for the night away from home, the motel's raison d'être, reveals most clearly that upper-middle-class aspirations have captivated the imagination of owners, designers, and lodgers. From the very start, with the notion of a diminutive home replicated for transient habitation through the various amenities added (e.g., kitchenettes and televisions) and configurations (a single cubicle later subdivided into a sleeping room, a shower-bathroom, and a washroom–dressing room), room geography has led to increasing expense in pursuit of America's coveted highest standard of living. The yearning has not been aristocratic, that is, luxury for only a few. Mass consumption of ever better settings and commodities has been the aim and the trend. After the divergence between elite and lowbrow culture beginning in the late nineteenth century,[11] the motel helped raise lowbrow expectations to upper-middle-class sights throughout the twentieth century.

Physical and metaphoric mobility has long been a verbalized American value. The motel has increased mobility's potency by facilitating its possibility. Motels are also a large and integral contributor to the service industries, which are expected to employ more than 90 percent of the nation's labor force by the year 2000.[12] On the one hand, the motel contributes to the image of people who define their status by their level of consumption; on the other hand, the motel workers' relatively low-paying jobs leave them with limited power as consumers. Also, while the motel has provided a generally high quality of lodging because its facilities have been regularly updated, it is those who travel between motels that benefit. Market segmentation has led to clear distinctions between the various grades of "haves." Motels for the have-nots would be a patent absurdity. Keith Sculle's childhood experience of staying with relatives and minimizing motel respites perhaps typifies how many people did and still do lodge along the roadside.

For most, ease of mobility has in turn led to ephemerality, with its own debasement. Most telling in this regard is the ever-changing room geography, which is perhaps most notable to commercial travelers, who are likely to return to the same motels, where they experience upgrading as a pleasant improvement encouraging further consumption. Entire motels are razed or rebuilt in pursuit of better profits, as almost any landscape observer can affirm (see Fig. 11.6). In a materialistic culture, ephemerality for its own sake is not far from ephemerality as a business strategy. Motels have become important agents of rapid landscape change, and landscape

FIGURE 11.6 Rebranded motels, such as this Springfield, Illinois, Travelodge become a Ramada Inn, are a sign of changefulness along America's highways.

has a profound impact on human consciousness. Motels have come to be a place where guests are introduced to novelties. In the motel, many Americans saw their first color television, their first coffeemaker, their first shag rug, their first indirect lighting. It was there that the idea of swimming pools for residential purposes took hold.

The house as a symbol of security and contentment seems to have been a particular victim of the motel's rise. Motels, as surrogate homes, have simultaneously fostered the search for security and the opposing quest for adventure. J. B. Jackson reminds us that Americans have long valued not only stability and permanence but mobility and short-term occupancy, the latter actually more strongly and more visibly in recent times.[13] Might the motel be the compromise of a people moving toward a polycentric definition of residency? Or might the motel be an intermediate step for a society that will live completely on the road? Does the already great popularity of the house trailer only hint at trends to come? Will we ever willingly, without legal caveat, find equality of opportunity for all based on talent, regardless of class, gender, and race, in the turmoil of self-interested renewal? How will the motel change in a culture whose only constant seems to be change (see Figs. 11.7 and 11.8)? Amidst the swirling debates about the pluses and minuses of modernity's flux, we can do little more here than raise these questions. Motels will deserve more reflection as the future unfolds.

FIGURE 11.7 Can a town thrive without a motel? Bradlettsville, Texas, reaches out for economic opportunity through signs at the edge of town.

FIGURE 11.8 Construction of a Comfort Suites motel in Springfield, Illinois, late 1994. In places regularly visited by outsiders, such as state capitals, the building, remodeling, and changing ownership of motels are common.

Answering questions about the motel's significance, moreover, can help guide laypersons and scholars alike to a culture preferred rather than one contended. The opposites listed earlier in this concluding chapter demonstrate some critical choices. For example: Is immobility merely the necessary state of rest required physically before going forth again in pursuit of other opportunities on the road? Are parochialism's disadvantages significantly surmounted through the connectivity of local motels with a pretense of cosmopolitanism to a world beyond? Can the homey traits usually associated with mom-and-pop enterprises be adequately reproduced in the dominant corporate market? What will emerge along the road as democracy's overnight lodging for all, regardless of the emphasis on strongly defined multicultural distinctions? Is segmentation discrimination by mutual consent? Will seeking freedom on the "open road" require continual affectations of the casual in overnight lodging? How will motels—which, after all, are places of public accommodation—serve a culture set on encouraging individual expressions of lifestyle? Must America's acceptance of a desirable motel system entail repetition of the historical cycle of new building, short-lived profit, decline, and abandonment? Is lodger vulnerability at motels more sensational in the public mind than his or her vulnerability in his or her own home? Will the great mass of motels eventually be indistinguishable altogether from hotels in a culture moored to upper-middle-class travel expectations? Will the search for rest and relaxation along the American roadside always hinge on convenience primarily? Or will other values loom to configure the motel in America as a distinctive kind of place?

Notes

Chapter 1. Introduction

1. See, e.g., [T. J.] Jackson Lears, *Fables of Abundance: A Cultural History of Advertising in America* (New York: Basic Books, 1994), 3–9.

2. For discussions of postmodern scholarship in history and geography, see Joyce Appleby, Lynn Hunt, and Margaret Jacob, *Telling the Truth about History* (New York: Norton, 1994), 198–237; and [R.] Cole Harris, "Power, Modernity, and Historical Geography," *Annals of the Association of American Geographers* 81 (December 1991): 671–83.

3. A compendium of Carl Sauer's writings may be found in Carl Ortwin Sauer, *Land and Life: A Selection from the Writings of Carl Ortwin Sauer,* ed. John Leighly (Berkeley: University of California Press, 1963). For an excellent appraisal of Sauer's approach to landscape study, see J. Nicholas Entrikin, "Carl O. Sauer, Philosopher in Spite of Himself," *Geographical Review* 74 (1984): 387–408.

4. See Peirce F. Lewis, "Axioms for Reading the Landscape: Some Guides to the American Scene," in *The Interpretation of Ordinary Landscapes: Geographical Essays,* ed. D. W. Meinig (New York: Oxford University Press, 1979), 13–32; and idem, "Learning from Looking: Geographic and Other Writing about the American Cultural Landscape," *American Quarterly* 35 (1983): 242–61.

5. For a concise introduction to landscape visualization, see John A. Jakle, *The Visual Elements of Landscape* (Amherst: University of Massachusetts Press, 1987).

6. For an introduction to J. B. Jackson, see his *Discovering the Vernacular Landscape* (New Haven: Yale University Press, 1984); and D. W. Meinig, "Reading the Landscape: An Appreciation of W. G. Hoskins and J. B. Jackson," in Meinig, *Interpretation of Ordinary Landscapes,* 195–244.

7. For an excellent introduction to the study of the vernacular in landscape, see Robert E. Riley, "Vernacular Landscapes," in *Advances in Environment, Behavior, and Design, Volume One,* ed. Ervin H. Zube and Gary T. Moore (New York: Plenum, 1987), 129–58.

8. A good example is Chester H. Liebs, *Main Street to Miracle Mile: American Roadside Architecture* (Boston: Little, Brown, 1985). See also Richard Longstreth, "The

Neighborhood Shopping Center in Washington, DC, 1930–1941," *Journal of the Society of Architectural Historians* 51 (March 1922): 5–34.

9. The orientation of cultural geography is clearly evident in architect Alan Hess's *Viva Las Vegas: After-Hours Architecture* (San Francisco: Chronicle Books, 1993).

10. For an introduction to the literature on house classification, see Allen G. Noble, *Wood, Brick, and Stone: The American Settlement Landscape, Volume One — Houses* (Amherst: University of Massachusetts Press, 1984); and John A. Jakle, Robert Bastian, and Douglas Meyer, *Common Houses in America's Small Towns: The Atlantic Seaboard to the Mississippi Valley* (Athens: University of Georgia Press, 1989).

11. See, e.g., the companion volume to this book, John A. Jakle and Keith A. Sculle, *The Gas Station in America* (Baltimore: Johns Hopkins University Press, 1994).

12. John A. Jakle, "Motel by the Roadside: America's Room for the Night," *Journal of Cultural Geography* 1 (1981): 34–49. This article appears in an expanded form as chapter 2 of this book.

13. Warren J. Belasco, *Americans on the Road: From Autocamp to Motel, 1910–1945* (Cambridge: MIT Press, 1979).

14. Ibid., 33.

15. Two of the better biographies are Rufus Jarman, *A Bed for the Night: The Story of the Wheeling Bellboy, E. M. Statler and His Remarkable Hotels* (New York: Harper & Row, 1952); and Robert O'Brien, *Marriott: The J. Williard Marriott Story* (Salt Lake City: Deseret, 1977).

16. Robert H. Woods, "Hospitality's History: Who Wrote What about When," *Cornell Hotel and Restaurant Administration Quarterly* 32 (1991): 89–95.

17. [James Agee], "The Great American Roadside," *Fortune* 10 (September 1934): 53–63, 172, 174, 177.

18. Ibid., 55. See also Judith Keller, "Evans and Agee: 'The Great American Roadside' (*Fortune* 1934)," *History of Photography* 16 (summer 1992): 170–71.

19. Vladimir Nabokov, *Lolita* (New York: Olympia, 1955), 147.

20. J. Edgar Hoover with Courtney R. Cooper, "Camps of Crime," *American Magazine,* no. 160 (February 1940): 14–15, 130–32.

21. Norman Hayner, "Auto Camps in the Evergreen Playground," *Social Forces* 9 (1930): 256–66.

22. Belasco, *Americans on the Road.*

23. Elbert L. Hooker, "The Urban Tourist Camp," *Studies in Sociology* (Southern Methodist University, Department of Sociology) 1, no. 1 (1936): 12–18.

24. Geoffrey Baker and Bruno Funaro, *Motels* (New York: Reinhold, 1955).

25. Hess, *Viva Las Vegas,* 18, 31.

26. "First Motel," *Tourist Court Journal* 18 (February 1955): 11.

27. Howard E. Morgan, *The Motel Industry in the United States: Small Business in Transition* (Tucson: University of Arizona, Bureau of Business and Public Research, 1964), 185.

28. Marvin E. Irwin, "America's First Tourist Court," *Tourist Court Journal* 18 (February 1955): 80.

29. Doug Cochran, "Exclusive Interview with TraveLodge Head . . . Scott King on Co-ownership," ibid. 27 (October 1963): 14.

30. "How Big Is the Motel Industry?" *Motel/Motor Inn Journal* 37 (July, 1974): 9; U.S. Bureau of the Census, *Census of Service Industries, 1987* (Washington, D.C.: U.S. Government Printing Office, 1989), US-9.

31. "How Big Is the Motel Industry?"; Perry Garfinkel, "A Market-by-Market Battle to Tuck in the Nation," *New York Times,* September 4, 1994, F3.

32. U.S. Bureau of the Census, *Historical Statistics of the United States, Colonial Times to 1957* (Washington, D.C.: U.S. Government Printing Office, 1960); idem *Statistical Abstract of the United States* (Washington, D.C.: U.S. Government Printing Office, 1961 and 1992).

33. Bureau of the Census, *Statistical Abstract* (1961).

34. "Here's Your Guest's Profile," *Tourist Court Journal* 33 (October 1969): 69–75.

Chapter 2. The Motel as Architecture

1. This chapter is an expanded version of John A. Jakle's "Motel by the Roadside: America's Room for the Night," *Journal of Cultural Geography* 1 (1981): 34–49.

2. For a concise history of the American commercial hotel, see Karl B. Raitz and John P. Jones III, "The City Hotel As Landscape Artifact and Community Symbol," ibid. 9 (1988): 17–36.

3. Sinclair Lewis, *Free Air* (London: Jonathan Cape, 1933), 29, 30.

4. Warren Belasco, *Americans on the Road: From Autocamp to Motel, 1910–1945* (Cambridge: MIT Press, 1979), 58.

5. Ibid., 56.

6. Theodore Dreiser, *A Hoosier Holiday* (New York: John Lane, 1916), 477.

7. Belasco, *Americans on the Road,* 146.

8. Ibid., 143.

9. John A. Jakle, *The Tourist: Travel in Twentieth-Century North America* (Lincoln: University of Nebraska Press, 1985), 152.

10. John Steinbeck, *The Grapes of Wrath* (New York: Viking, 1939).

11. Belasco, *Americans on the Road,* 125.

12. See Alderson Molz, "Tourist Homes," *Hotel Monthly* 41 (January 1933): 15.

13. "Figures on Growth of Tourist Camp Business," ibid. 43 (December 1935): 24.

14. John J. McCarthy and Robert Littell, "Three Hundred Thousand Shacks: The Arrival of a New American Industry," *Harper's Magazine* 167 (July 1933): 185.

15. See, e.g., "Tourist Cabins That Get the Business," *Popular Mechanics* 64 (July 1935): 151–54.

16. "Roadside Cabins for Tourists," *Architectural Record* 72 (December 1933): 457–62.

17. Henry Schmidt, "Overnight Rest-Cabins Spreading," *Literary Digest* 117 (June 9, 1934): 40.

18. Norman Hayner, "Auto Camps in the Evergreen Playground," *Social Forces* 9 (December 1930): 257.

19. McCarthy and Littell, "Three Hundred Thousand Shacks," 183.

20. "I'll Answer Your Questions on Tourist Camps." *Hotel Management,* July 1936, 18–19.

21. "Money on the Roadside," *Fortune* 44 (August 1951): 80.

22. E. L. Barringer, "Uncle Sam Takes Census of Tourist Camps," *National Petroleum News* 29 (December 15, 1937): 44–45.

23. Ward K. Halbert, "Tourist Camps Pay Southern Jobbers as Rented Dealers Outlets," ibid. 21 (March 20, 1929): 164.

24. Ibid.

25. *Tourist Court Plan Book* (Temple, Tex.: Tourist Court Journal, 1950), 16.

26. Wallace W. True, "Significant Trends in the Motel Industry," *Appraisal Journal* 27 (April 1959): 229.

27. *Motels, Hotels, Restaurants, and Bars: An Architectural Record Book* (New York: F. W. Dodge, 1963), 25.

28. Ray Sawyer, "A Survey of Motel Chain Organizations, Part One: Referral Chains," *Motel/Motor Inn Journal* 38 (December 1974): 65.

29. C. Joseph Molinaro, "Ten Reasons Why People Buy Motels," ibid. 37 (May 1974): 49.

30. Ibid.

31. Seymour Freedgood, "The Motel Free-for-All," *Fortune* 59 (June 1959): 171.

32. David B. Carlson, "New Hotel vs. Old Code," *Architectural Forum* 113 (November 1960): 208.

33. C. Vernon Kane, *Motor Courts: From Planning to Profits* (New York: Ahrens, 1954), 62.

34. Carleton Whiting, "Gas Stations Grow to Motorists Hotels under Pierce Terminal System," *National Petroleum News* 22 (March 1930): 153.

35. See John A. Jakle and Keith A. Sculle, *The Gas Station in America* (Baltimore: Johns Hopkins University Press, 1994).

36. Carl Koch, "Design for a Franchise Chain," *Architectural Record* 123 (April 1958): 48.

37. "Motel/Hotel Architecture: The State of the Art; Part Two," *Motel/Motor Inn Journal* 38 (May 1975): 42–48; "TraveLodge Opens First Tri-Arc," *Tourist Court Journal* 33 (June 1970): 88–89.

38. Michael Messerle, "A New Decade of All-Suites Design," *Hotel and Resort Industry* 14 (September 1991): 20–26.

39. Freedgood, "Motel Free-for-All," 211.

40. Molinaro, "Ten Reasons," 49.

41. Oakley R. Bramble, "Overbuilding Seen Cause for Caution," *AMHA News* 9 (November–December 1960): 4.

42. *Financing the Lodging Industry: A Survey of Lender Attitudes* (Philadelphia: Laventhol & Horwath, 1975), 5.

43. Gerald W. Lattin, *The Lodging and Food Service Industry* (Washington, D.C.: American Hotel and Motel Association, 1989), 55. Howard Rudnitsky, "Blood in the Suites," *Forbes* 148 (October 28, 1991): 85.

44. Ibid., 86.

Chapter 3. Mom-and-Pop Enterprise

1. Two works inform the general view of culture taken in this chapter. Most important is Warren I. Susman, *Culture As History: The Transformation of American Society in the Twentieth Century* (New York: Pantheon, 1973), xix–xxx; followed by *Culture and Commitment, 1929–1945* (New York: Braziller, 1973), 1–24. Both also have specific application regarding the consumer culture's entrepreneurial choices during the motel's formative years in the 1930s. Richard Wightman Fox and T. J. Jackson Lears, in the introduction to their *Culture of Consumption: Critical Essays in American History, 1880–1980* (New York: Pantheon, 1983), vii–xvii, reinforce Susman's description of the consumer culture and amplify his explanation of it as a power structure.

2. See Berle Noggle, "The Twenties: A New Historiographical Frontier," *Journal of*

American History 53, no. 2 (1966): 307. Although he does not find the 1920s to have been a pivotal period in the consumer culture's development, Lawrence W. Levine, "Progress and Nostalgia: The Self Image of the Nineteen Twenties," in *The Unpredictable Past: Explorations in American Cultural History* (New York: Oxford University Press, 1993), 189–205, confirms the futurist-traditionalist duality of the period and its resulting tensions.

3. Susman, *Culture and Commitment,* 4–5.

4. Susman, *Culture As History,* 188–90.

5. William E. Leuchtenburg, *Perils of Prosperity, 1914–1932* (Chicago: University of Chicago Press, 1958), 225–40.

6. See, e.g., David L. Lewis, "Sex and the Automobile: From Rumble Seats to Rockin' Vans," in *The Automobile and American Culture,* ed. David L. Lewis and Laurence Goldstein (Ann Arbor: University of Michigan Press, 1980), 123–24.

7. Elbert L. Hooker, "The Urban Tourist Camp," *Studies in Sociology* (Southern Methodist University, Department of Sociology) 1, no. 1 (1936), 16.

8. For the "revolution in morals," see Leuchtenburg, *Perils of Prosperity,* 158–77. Especially regarding women, see James R. McGovern, "Woman's Pre–World War I Freedom in Manners and Morals," *Journal of American History* 55, no. 2 (1968): 315–33.

9. "'Couple Trade' in the Tourist Camps," *New Republic,* July 29, 1936, 340–41; Ray Sawyer, "How the Chandler Family Has Kept Pace with the Times," *Motel/Motor Inn Journal* 35 (February 1972): 42; George P. Gardner Jr., interview by Keith A. Sculle and Jefferson S. Rogers, Jackson, Tennessee, December 11, 1993. The George-Anna Cottages, in Jackson, begun by the senior Gardner in 1927, was operated by George Gardner Jr. from 1936 until it closed, in 1981.

10. Hoover, with Cooper, "Camps of Crime"; "America Takes to the Motor Court," *Business Week,* no. 563 (June 15, 1940): 20.

11. Hooker, "The Urban Tourist Camp," 18.

12. Susman, *Culture As History,* 109–10.

13. Paul Carter, *Another Part of the Twenties* (New York: Columbia University Press, 1977), 13–14, points out the conservative perspective that both proponents and travelers frequently brought to automobile travel.

14. T. J. Jackson Lears, "The Concept of Cultural Hegemony: Problems and Possibilities," *American Historical Review* 90 (June 1985): 586.

15. John J. McCarthy, "'Pay Dirt' in Tourist Camps," *Advertising and Selling* 42 (May 25, 1933): 26; idem, "The Market Business Forgets," *Nation's Business* 21 (August 1933): 39–40; Henry Schmidt, "Overnight Rest-Cabins Spreading," *Literary Digest* 117 (June 9, 1934): 40; John J. McCarthy and Robert Littell, "Three Hundred Thousand Shacks: The Arrival of a New American Industry," *Harper's Magazine* 167 (July 1933): 180–83; L. H. Robbins, "America Hobnobs at the Tourist Camp," *New York Times Magazine,* August 12, 1934, 9, 19.

16. McCarthy and Littell, "Three Hundred Thousand Shacks," 181.

17. McCarthy, "'Pay Dirt' in Tourist Camps," 44; "America Takes to the Motor Court," 20.

18. McCarthy and Littell, "Three Hundred Thousand Shacks," 180–81; Robbins, "America Hobnobs at the Tourist Camp."

19. "Tourist Cabins That Get the Business," *Popular Mechanics* 64 (July 1935): 151.

20. [James Agee], "The Great American Roadside," *Fortune* 10 (September 1934): 56.

21. Susman, *Culture As History,* 156–57; idem, *Culture and Commitment,* 7–8.

22. James Elliott, "T.C.O.A. To Hold Annual Confab Here," *Jackson (Tenn.) Sun,* May 3, 1937, 1. See also *Jackson (Tenn.) Sun,* May 4, 1937, 1, 12; and May 5, 1937, 1–2.

23. Frank J. Taylor, "Just What the Motorist Ordered," *Saturday Evening Post* 220 (July 5, 1947): 93; *Jackson (Tenn.) Sun,* May 4, 1937, 12.

24. For a history of the NTL-MCTA, see Warren J. Belasco, *Americans on the Road: From Autocamp to Motel, 1910–1945* (Cambridge: MIT Press, 1979), 154–56; and "Amid the Colorful Surroundings of Mexico, International Motor Court Association Launched," *Tourist Court Journal* 1 (October 1937): 5, 22–24.

25. "Tourist Court Journal Named As Official Organ International Motor Court Association," *Tourist Court Journal* 1 (October 1937): 4.

26. Dwayne Jones, "Sources and Resources: *Tourist Court Journal,*" *SCA News Journal* 12, no. 2 (1992): 22.

27. See George W. Pierson, *The Moving American* (New York: Knopf, 1973); and Wilbur Zelinsky, *The Cultural Geography of the United States* (Englewoods Cliffs, N.J.: Prentice-Hall, 1973), 53–58, 91.

28. Norman Hayner, "Auto Camps in the Evergreen Playground," *Social Forces* 9 (December 1930): 264; "Hotel Hopes Rise," *Business Week,* no. 562 (June 8, 1940): 21–22.

29. "Cabin and Cottage Building Time Is Here," *American Builder* 57 (March 1935): 40–41; "Tourist Cabins That Get the Business," 151–53; "Rustic Cabins and Filling Stations," *American Builder* 62 (July 1940): 68–69.

30. [Agee], "The Great American Roadside," 57; "I'll Answer Your Questions on Tourist Camps," *Hotel Management,* July 1936, 18.

31. [Agee], "The Great American Roadside," 56–57; "Cabin and Cottage Building Time Is Here," 40; "I'll Answer Your Questions on Tourist Camps," 19.

32. Schmidt, "Overnight Rest-Cabins Spreading," 40.

33. Keith A. Sculle, "Oral History: A Key to Writing the History of American Roadside Architecture," *Journal of American Culture* 13, no. 3 (1990): 82, 85; idem, "The Dutch Mill Village in Glasgow: A Research Note," *Register of the Kentucky Historical Society* 91, no. 1 (1993): 61; Anna Connor, telephone interview by Sculle, April 28, 1994. Clara Z. Keyton, *Tourist Camp Pioneering Experiences* (Chicago: Adams, 1960), presents a wealth of detail about the woman's role in one mom-and-pop team.

34. Sculle, "Oral History," 83, 85; idem, "Dutch Mill Village in Glasgow," 61; Sawyer, "How the Chandler Family Has Kept Pace with the Times," 38–44, 46–48.

35. Regarding female entrepreneurs, see also Velma Carson, "Bed, Bath, and Garage," *Independent Woman* 15 (July 1936), 204–6, 218–19, which gives largely generic magazine advice for prospective motel owners, except that Carson and female entrepreneurs interviewed insist on their sex's advantage in having a "woman's touch" or "talent for hospitality" and being a "homemaker to the public."

36. Rosemary Lyons Jones, "Pen Shots," newspaper clipping dated August 30, 1936, in the possession of Holst C. Beall Jr.

37. Ibid.

38. Ibid.

39. "Touristless Courts," *Business Week,* no. 659 (April 25, 1942): 28; Holst C. Beall Jr., telephone interview by Sculle, August 3, 1993.

40. For a history of the Wigwam Village chain, see Keith A. Sculle, "Frank Redford's Wigwam Village Chain: A Link in the Modernization of the American Roadside,"

in *Roadside America: The Automobile in Design and Culture,* ed. Jan Jennings (Ames: Iowa State University Press, 1990), 125–35; and idem, "Oral History," 79–88.

41. Dean Jennings, "Thrivin' Drive-Inns," *Readers Digest* 51 (September 1947): 85; Katharine Hillyer, "Bed and Butter Letter," *Tourist Court Journal* 10 (February 1947): 13; Alethia Lindsey, "What Are You Getting Into?" *Better Homes and Gardens* 26 (May 1948): 239; Richard F. Dempewolff, "Drive-In Dream Castles," *Popular Mechanics* 106 (July 1956): 99; Belasco, *Americans on the Road,* 59.

42. Regarding black ownership of automobiles, see Catherine A. Barnes, *Journey from Jim Crow: The Desegregation of Southern Transit* (New York: Columbia University Press, 1983), 17–18, 213 n. 47.

43. *The Negro Motorist Green-Book* (New York: Victor H. Green, 1942); U.S. Travel Bureau, *Directory of Negro Hotels and Guest Houses in the United States, 1939* (Washington, D.C.: National Park Service, 1939).

44. *Negro Motorist Green-Book,* 1.

45. Regarding blacks and tourist courts in Dallas, Texas, see Dwayne Jones, "From Camps to Courts: Dallas Tourist Accommodations in the Early Twentieth Century," *Legacies: A History Journal for Dallas and North Central Texas* 7 (spring 1995): 30.

46. Harry Barclay Love, *Establishing and Operating a Year-Round Motor Court,* Industrial (Small Business) Series, no. 50 (Washington, D.C.: U.S. Government Printing Office, 1945); *Tourist Court Plan Book* (Temple, Tex.: Tourist Court Journal, 1950); C. Vernon Kane, *Motor Courts: From Planning to Profits* (New York: Ahrens, 1954); Harold Whittington, *Starting and Managing a Small . . . Motel,* The Starting and Managing Series, no. 7 (Washington, D.C.: Small Business Administration, 1963).

47. For the definition and dynamics of professionalism applied here to the motel industry, see Burton J. Bledstein, *The Culture of Professionalism: The Middle Class and the Development of Higher Education in America* (New York: Norton, 1976), 80–105.

48. Love, *Establishing and Operating a Year-Round Motor Court,* 1; *Thirty-Fourth Annual Report of the Secretary of Commerce, 1946* (Washington, D.C.: U.S. Government Printing Office, 1946), 141–42; Small Business Administration, *First Semi-Annual Report of the Small Business Administration* (Washington, D.C., 1954), 1.

49. Bob Gresham, "For Courters Only," *Tourist Court Journal* 25 (September 1962): 82; Lawrence W. Ingram, telephone interview by Sculle, April 19, 1994; Harold Whittington, telephone interview by Sculle, April 20, 1994. Ingram bought the *Tourist Court Journal* in 1975–76; Whittington was the assistant editor from 1957–58 to 1963.

50. Love, *Establishing and Operating a Year-Round Motor Court,* ii; Taylor, "Just What the Motorist Ordered," 93; William L. Edmundson III to Sculle, August 17, 1993, letter in possession of Sculle.

51. Kane, *Motor Courts,* 5.

52. Love, *Establishing and Operating a Year-Round Motor Court,* 5–9.

53. *Tourist Court Plan Book,* 9.

54. Love, *Establishing and Operating a Year-Round Motor Court,* 5, 119; Whittington, *Starting and Managing a Small . . . Motel,* 59.

55. Love, *Establishing and Operating a Year-Round Motor Court,* 11.

56. Ibid., 16.

57. *Tourist Court Plan Book,* 15.

58. Kane, *Motor Courts*, 62–63; Whittington, *Starting and Managing a Small . . . Motel*, 30, 47, 49; Susan Strasser, *Satisfaction Guaranteed: The Making of the American Mass Market* (New York: Pantheon, 1989), 207, 209.

59. [R.] Cole Harris, "Power, Modernity, and Historical Geography," *Annals of the Association of American Geographers* 81 (1991): 672–75; Susman, *Culture As History*, 164–66.

60. Sharon Zukin, *Landscapes of Power: From Detroit to Disney World* (Berkeley: University of California Press, 1991).

61. Love, *Establishing and Operating a Year-Round Motor Court*, 46–47, 56–70, 86, 96; *Tourist Court Plan Book*, 5, 42; Kane, *Motor Courts*, 37–39; Whittington, *Starting and Managing a Small . . . Motel*, 14, 28–29, 32–33, 43–50.

62. Love, *Establishing and Operating a Year-Round Motor Court*, 3–4, 123; Whittington, *Starting and Managing a Small . . . Motel*, 1, 12–13, 51.

63. Howard E. Morgan, *The Motel Industry in the United States: Small Business in Transition*, Small Business Management Research Reports (Tucson: University of Arizona, Bureau of Business and Public Research, 1964), 2, 206 (table E-20); U.S. Bureau of the Census, *Census of Selected Service Industries, 1972* (Washington, D.C.: U.S. Government Printing Office, 1975), 2–7. The 1948 and 1972 censuses' "proprietorships" and "partnerships," that is, motels with, respectively, one and at least two owners, are represented above as the mom-and-pop operations, although small corporations could be added. Since the size of corporations was not distinguished in the censuses, it was impossible to represent the number of mom-and-pop motels in 1948 and 1972 more precisely.

64. William E. Leuchtenburg, *A Troubled Feast: American Society since 1945*, rev. ed. (Boston: Little, Brown, 1983), 6, 37–38; William H. Chafe, *The Unfinished Journey: America since World War II* (New York: Oxford University Press, 1986), iii; Norman L. Rosenberg and Emily S. Rosenberg, *In Our Times: America since World War II*, 3d ed. (Englewood Cliffs, N.J.: Prentice-Hall, 1987), 67.

65. Richard Polenburg, *One Nation Divisible: Class, Race, and Ethnicity in the United States since 1938* (New York: Viking, 1980), 131–32; Leuchtenburg, *A Troubled Feast*, 63; James Gilbert, *Another Chance: Post-war America, 1945–1985*, 2d ed. (Chicago: Dorsey, 1986), 120. An excellent popular history of the ways common objects were influenced by values between 1954 and 1964, a period now often looked on with nostalgia, is Tom Hine, *Populuxe* (New York: Knopf, 1986).

66. Leuchtenburg, *A Troubled Feast*, 58; Rosenberg and Rosenberg, *In Our Times*, 73.

67. Daniel Bell, *End of Ideology* (Glencoe, Ill.: Free Press, 1960); David Riesman, *The Lonely Crowd* (New Haven: Yale University Press, 1950); J. B. Jackson, "Other-Directed Houses," *Landscape* 6 (winter 1956–57): 31; Leuchtenburg, *A Troubled Feast*, 79; Rosenberg and Rosenberg, *In Our Times*, 47.

68. John E. H. Sherry, *The Laws of Innkeepers—For Hotels, Motels, Restaurants, and Clubs*, 3d ed. (Ithaca, N.Y.: Cornell University Press, 1993), 43–44, 68; John Hersey, *The Algiers Motel Incident* (New York: Knopf, 1968); Michael R. Belknap, introduction to *The Drive to Desegregate Places of Public Accommodation*, ed. Belknap, vol. 9 of *Civil Rights, the White House, and the Justice Department, 1945–1968*, ed. Belknap (New York: Garland, 1991), 48; Edward C. Koziara and Karen S. Koziara, *The Negro in the Hotel Industry* (Philadelphia: University of Pennsylvania Press, 1968), 69 (motels as well as hotels are referenced in this last work).

69. "Money on the Roadside," *Fortune* 44 (August 1951): 81; Evan M. Wylie, "Troubles of a Motel Keeper," *Saturday Evening Post* 226 (July 18, 1953): 32–33, 69–70,

73, 75; Vernon Kane, "Motel Trends," *Architectural Forum* 100 (February 1954): 112.

70. Wylie, "Troubles of a Motel Keeper," 70.

71. Ibid.; Opal Henson and Gwendolyn Gosnell, interview by Sculle, Paris, Illinois, September 7, 1994. Henson and her husband, Charles, have owned the Pinnell Motel since 1959 and managed it until 1988. Their daughter Gwendolyn lived at the motel and has leased it since 1988.

72. Wylie, "Troubles of a Motel Keeper," 73.

73. "Motel Fever," *Saturday Evening Post* 226 (August 22, 1953): 4, 6; Bernard DeVoto, "The Easy Chair: Motel Town," *Harper's Magazine* 207 (September 1953): 46; "So You Think You Want to Own a Motel," *Changing Times* 10 (December 1956): 18; Wylie, "Troubles of a Motel Keeper," 181; Carl Rieser, "Sheraton vs. Hilton: Playing Checkers with 60,000 Rooms," *Fortune* 62 (January 1961) 104; Royal Shipp and Robert Moore Fisher, *The Postwar Boom in Hotels and Motels,* Staff Economic Studies (n.p.: Board of Governors of the Federal Reserve, 1965), 5.

74. "Hotels That Look Like Motels," *Business Week,* no. 1228 (March 14, 1953), 62; "Motels Edge In to Snag the City Trade," ibid., no. 1266 (December 5, 1953), 174–78, 180, 182, 184, 186; Norman Carlisle and Madelyn Carlisle, "Luxury Hostels along the Highway," *Coronet* 46 (May 1959): 33–37; Shipp and Fisher, *Postwar Boom in Hotels and Motels,* 5.

75. William J. Carley, "Roadside Jam: Motel Failures Mount As Building Boom Adds to Excess Capacity," *Wall Street Journal,* October 27, 1961, 1.

76. U.S. Bureau of the Census, *Census of Service Industries, 1987* (Washington, D.C.: U.S. Government Printing Office, 1989), 3–3. The 1987 census's "proprietorships" and "partnerships" are represented above as the mom-and-pop motels in 1987.

77. "So You Think You Want to Own a Motel," 19.

78. Wylie, "Troubles of a Motel Keeper," 73.

79. *Independent Motels of America: Lodging Directory,* fall 1993, back cover.

Chapter 4. Remember the Alamo Plazas

1. E. O. Cypent, telephone interview by Keith A. Sculle, November 6, 1993; Hugh Jones, telephone interview by Sculle, June 30, 1993. Cypent became Torrance's bookkeeper in 1938. Jones managed the St. Francis in Montgomery, Alabama, in 1955–58.

2. Richard S. Tedlow, *New and Improved: The Story of Mass Marketing in America* (New York: Basic Books, 1990), 348–54.

3. *Waco Times-Herald,* June 6, 1971, 1.

4. Patricia W. Wallace, *Waco: Texas Crossroads* (Woodland Hills, Calif.: Windsor, 1983), 34–37, 49–50; idem, *Our Land, Our Lives: A Pictorial History of McLennan County, Texas* (Norfolk, Va.: Donning, 1986), 94, 99.

5. Wallace, *Our Land, Our Lives,* 65, 74.

6. *Waco Times-Herald,* June 6, 1971, 1; Wallace, *Waco,* 51–52.

7. Wallace, *Waco,* 44–46; idem, *Our Land, Our Lives,* 113, 149, 172; W. R. Poage, *McLennan County—Before 1980* (Waco: Texian, 1981), 210.

8. "New Court at Memphis Provides the Seventh in the Alamo Plaza Chain of Courts," *Tourist Court Journal* 3 (November 1939): 6; "A Veteran Motel Operator Speaks," *American Motel Magazine,* November 1953, 34; Dayton Kelley, ed., *The Handbook of Waco and McLennan County, Texas* (Waco: Texian, 1972), 21–22; Opal (Mrs. D. W.) Bartlett, telephone interview by Sculle, April 5, 1993.

9. The authors are indebted to W. Dwayne Jones of the Texas Historical Commission for sharing his detailed studies of Texas's early motels, especially the possibility of Alamo Plaza's architectural pedigree (W. Dwayne Jones to Sculle, May 31, 1994).

10. Warren I. Susman, *Culture As History: The Transformation of American Society in the Twentieth Century* (New York: Pantheon, 1973), 109; Richard Polenburg, *One Nation Divisible: Class, Race, and Ethnicity in the United States since 1938* (New York: Viking, 1980), 15; William B. Rhoads, "Roadside Colonial: Early American Design for the Automobile Age, 1900–1940," *Winterthur Portfolio* 21, nos. 2–3 (1986): 134–40; David Gebhard, "The American Colonial Revival in the 1930s," ibid. 22, nos. 2–3 (1987): 141.

11. Helon Torrance Hiatt to Sculle, October 22, 1990 (Hiatt is Torrance's daughter); "A Veteran Motel Operator Speaks," 34.

12. See, e.g., Alan Hess, *Viva Las Vegas: After-Hours Architecture* (San Francisco: Chronicle Books, 1993), 40–41.

13. "A Veteran Motel Operator Speaks," 34.

14. Ibid.

15. Ibid., 35; Hiatt to Sculle, February 20, 1993.

16. Susman, *Culture As History*, 108; Robert M. Craig, letter to editor, Correspondence, *Society for Commercial Archeology News* 2 (spring 1994): 9.

17. Hiatt to Sculle, March 24, 1993; Ted Farner to Sculle, November 1993 (Ted Farner is Bill Farner's oldest son).

18. Albert Woldert, *A History of Tyler and Smith County, Texas* (San Antonio: Naylor, 1948), 134–36, 153–54; Robert W. Glover, ed., *Tyler and Smith County, Texas: An Historical Survey* (n.p.: American Bicentennial Committee of Tyler-Smith County, 1976), 106, 116, 122, 141; William Norman Large, "The Hub of East Texas: A History of Tyler, Texas, 1918–1940" (Master's thesis, University of Texas at Tyler, 1992), 52, 56, 58, 107–8.

19. Frank Bronaugh, "The Blackstone Hotel," *Chronicles of Smith County, Texas* 25 (summer 1986): 35.

20. *Worley's Tyler (Smith County, Tex.) City Directory, 1932* (Dallas: John F. Worley Directory, 1932), 484.

21. *Tyler Courier-Times-Telegraph*, July 5, 1931, 7.

22. Ibid., 1, 10.

23. Warren James Belasco, *Americans on the Road: From Autocamp to Motel, 1910–1945* (Cambridge: MIT Press, 1979), 141–42.

24. Susan Strasser, *Satisfaction Guaranteed: The Making of the American Mass Market* (New York: Pantheon, 1989); Tedlow, *New and Improved.*

25. *Shreveport Times*, June 28, 1935, 6–8, September 30, 1935, 4; Viola Carruth, *Caddo: 1,000. A History of the Shreveport Area from the Time of the Caddo Indians to the 1970s*, 2d ed. (Shreveport, La.: Shreveport Magazine, 1971), 39, 99, 136, 147–48; Ann M. McLaurin, ed., *Glimpses of Shreveport* (Natchitoches, La.: Northwestern State University Press, 1985), 115–17, 147.

26. *Shreveport Times*, August 4, 1935, 3; Lilla McLure and J. Ed Howe, *History of Shreveport and Shreveport Builders* (Shreveport, La.: J. Ed Howe, 1937), 103; W. G. McGrady to Sculle, November 8, 1993; Annie Mae Johnson, telephone interview by Sculle, May 12, 1994 (Annie Mae Johnson was the wife of Mason Johnson, with whom she managed several Alamo Plazas, their longest time being at Shreveport).

27. Carruth, *Caddo*, 143, 159.

28. Farner to Sculle, November 1993.

29. Ibid.
30. Ibid., November 1993 and June 2, 1994.
31. Ibid., November 1993; Allan Turner, "Beyond Its Time," *Houston Chronicle,* June 17, 1986, 5.
32. Farner to Sculle, November 1993.
33. Ibid.; Turner, "Beyond Its Time."
34. Turner, "Beyond Its Time"; Maybelle Olsen, telephone interview by Sculle, March 1, 1993 (Olsen was at one time married to Charles H. Mooney); Farner to Sculle, November 1993.
35. "Alamo Plaza Gulfport," *Down South* 23 (September–October 1973): 16; Farner to Sculle, November 1993.
36. Judith W. Linsley and Ellen W. Rienstra, *Beaumont: A Chronicle of Promise* (Woodland Hills, Calif.: Windsor, 1982), 86, 93; John H. Walker and Gwendolyn Wingate, *Beaumont: A Pictorial History* (Norfolk, Va.: Donning, 1983), 83, 88, 115, 131.
37. *Beaumont Enterprise,* April 2, 1938, 12, April 19, 1938, 10, June 8, 1938, 16; Linsley and Rienstra, *Beaumont,* 132; Walker and Wingate, *Beaumont,* 101.
38. *Beaumont Enterprise,* May 8, 1938, 8-A; Ted Farner, telephone interview by Sculle, December 14, 1993; Farner to Sculle, November 1993.
39. Farner to Sculle, November 1993; Farner, telephone interview, December 14, 1993.
40. *Baton Rouge Morning Advocate,* May 1, 1940, 1; May 17, 1940, 8.
41. Ibid., August 17, 1940, 1.
42. See, e.g., ibid., August 27, 1940, 10.
43. Ibid, March 30, 1941, 6B-7B.
44. Advertisement, *Tourist Court Journal* 16 (April 1954): 50.
45. Agnes (Mrs. Jess) Chastain, telephone interview by Sculle, February 1, 1994; Farner, telephone interview, December 14, 1993.
46. D. B. Sharron, "To Whom It May Concern," September 8, 1949, letter in possession of Helon Hiatt.
47. Harold J. Bryant, "To Whom It May Concern," September 7, 1949, letter in possession of Helon Hiatt.
48. Advertisement, *Tourist Court Journal* 3 (September 1940): 19, 24; *1987 Oklahoma City, Oklahoma, Directory* (Dallas: R. L. Polk, 1987), 12.
49. "Hot Springs, Arkansas, Host to Dual Convention of the IMCA and UMCCD," *Tourist Court Journal* 1 (April 1938): 8; Lee Torrance, "Radio Advertising," ibid. 1 (September 1938): 23; Advertisement, ibid. 1 (November 1937): 26.
50. Hiatt to Sculle, February 20, 1993; T. S. Hickman to Jess Chastain, January 2, 1946 (Hickman was the Shreveport branch AAA manager); *This Week in Tennessee, Alabama, Georgia,* 1968, 10.
51. Hiatt to Sculle, February 20, 1993.
52. Torrance, "Radio Advertising," 23.
53. "New Court at Memphis," 6.
54. Ibid.; Hiatt to Sculle, October 22, 1990, and March 24, 1993; E. L. McLallen, telephone interview by Sculle, October 30, 1993.
55. McLallen, telephone interview, October 30, 1993.
56. See John A. Jakle and Keith A. Sculle, *The Gas Station in America* (Baltimore: Johns Hopkins University Press, 1994).
57. Wayne Jarvis, "Show Room," *Tourist Court Journal* 5 (October 1941): 8.
58. See, e.g., Eleanor N. Knowles, "Along the Roadside," *Christian Science Monitor*

Weekly Magazine, July 31, 1935, 15; and "Duncan Hines Picks Ten Best Motels in the U.S.A.," *Look* 18 (January 12, 1954): 31–34.

59. *Tourist Court Journal* 16 (February 1954): 59.

60. Advertisement, ibid. 5 (February 1941): 15; *United Motor Courts: Free Guide,* 1950, 31; McLallen, telephone interview, October 30, 1993.

61. "The Plaza Hotel Courts, New and Interesting Columbus Enterprise, Embodying a Novel Form of Construction," *Industrial Index: Columbus,* 1941, 92; *United Motor Courts: Free Guide,* 1950, 16; various business documents in the possession of Mary Wade Robinson, Columbus, Georgia.

62. Farner to Sculle, November 1993.

63. Charles L. Sullivan, *The Mississippi Gulf Coast: Portrait of a People* (Northridge, Calif.: Windsor, 1985), 41–69, 142.

64. Ibid., 151–52.

65. See, e.g., *Biloxi-Gulfport Daily Herald,* April 9, May 12, July 14, 1945, pp. 3, 3, and 8, respectively; *Gulf Coast, Miss.* telephone directory, December 1948, 83; *Biloxi-Gulfport Daily Herald,* March 2, July 8, 1948, pp. 6 and 7, respectively.

66. Farner to Sculle, November 1993.

67. Maybelle Olsen, telephone interview, March 1, 1993; Farner to Sculle, November 1993; *Polk's Savannah (Chatham County, Ga.) City Directory, 1955* (Richmond, Va.: R. L. Polk, 1955), 6.

68. *Tyler Courier-Times-Telegraph,* July 5, 1931, 7; Advertisement, *Tourist Court Journal* 15 (September 1953): 55; "A Veteran Motel Operator Speaks," 35–36; *Chattanooga Times,* June 7, 1961; *Lucite Spectrum* 1 (April 1963): 6; F. Randolph Helms, telephone interview by Sculle, November 22, 1993 (Helms was the consulting industrial engineer for the Chattanooga motel in 1961).

69. "A Veteran Motel Operator Speaks," 36; Farner to Sculle, November 1993.

70. Farner to Sculle, November 1993; Chastain, telephone interview, February 1, 1994; Johnson, telephone interview, May 12, 1994.

71. Dorothy Wade, "The Waldorf-Astoria of Tourist Courts," *Tourist Court Journal* 13 (January 1951): 9–10, 26; Ray Humbert, "What Happened at the Minneapolis American Motor Hotel Association?" ibid. 23 (December 1959): 12; *Motel News,* 9 (November–December 1960): 1; McGrady to Sculle, July 6, 1993.

72. *Alamo Plaza Hotel Courts: Free Pocket Travel Guide* [1959]; Hiatt to Sculle, February 2, 1993; Vernon W. Phillips to Keith A. Sculle, April 10, 1993; authors' survey, 1993.

73. Phillips, telephone interview by Sculle, April 4, 1993; Kemmons Wilson to Sculle, January 25, 1994.

74. *Chattanooga Times,* September 4, 1991, B1.

75. *Charlotte Observer,* March 16, 1991, 1B.

76. Olsen, telephone interview, March 1, 1993.

77. Sanford J. Ungar, *Fresh Blood: The New American Immigrants* (New York: Simon & Schuster, 1995), 29–32; Asian American Hotel Owners Association, *A Profile of the Asian American Hotel Owners Association* ([Atlanta, 1995]).

Chapter 5. The Rise of Place-Product-Packaging

1. See: John A. Jakle and Keith A. Sculle, *The Gas Station in America* (Baltimore: Johns Hopkins University Press, 1994).

2. See Thomas S. Dicke, *Franchising in America: The Development of a Business Method, 1840–1980* (Chapel Hill: University of North Carolina Press, 1992).

3. "Eppley Buys Pittsburgh Hotels," *Hotel Monthly* 36 (March 1928): 29.

4. Floyd Miller, *Statler: America's Extraordinary Hotelman* (New York: Statler Foundation, 1968), 92.

5. Henry J. Bohn, quoted in ibid., 133.

6. See, e.g., *Hotel Planning and Outfitting* (Chicago: Albert Pick–Barth, 1928).

7. "The Hotel Influence," *American Motel Magazine* 15 (October 1985): 48.

8. Donald E. Lundberg, *The Hotel and Restaurant Business* (Boston: Cahners, 1976), 276.

9. Carl Rieser, "Sheraton vs. Hilton: Playing Checkers with 60,000 Rooms," *Fortune* 62 (January 1961): 166.

10. Lundberg, *Hotel and Restaurant Business,* 277.

11. Ibid.

12. Rieser, "Sheraton vs. Hilton," 164.

13. "Motels: 'By Golly,'" *Time* 82 (July 19, 1963): 66.

14. Terry Breen, "Hilton Offers Discount to Senior," *Hotel and Motel Management* 201 (March 17, 1986): 3.

15. The Chain Report, *Lodging Hospitality* 46 (December 1990): 77.

16. Lundberg, *Hotel and Restaurant Business,* 270.

17. "Sheraton Plans Biggest Expansion," *Hotel and Motel Management* 184 (June 1969): 68.

18. Irving Zeldman, quoted in Ray Sawyer, "Sheraton's Zeldman: Expansion Is His Game," *Motel/Motor Inn Journal* 35 (July 1971): 53.

19. "Sheraton: It's Our Turn," *Hotel and Motel Management* 193 (November 1978): 21.

20. The Chain Report, 77.

21. E. L. Yordan, "Motor Camps Win New Friends," *New York Times,* July 14, 1935, sec. X, p. 1.

22. A. C. Hanson, "The Scope and Purpose of the International Motor Court Association," *Tourist Court Journal* 1 (December 1937): 9–10, 28.

23. Richard E. Gill, "Hospitality Industry Associations," in *Introduction to Hotel and Restaurant Management: A Book of Readings,* ed. Robert A. Brymer, 5th ed. (Dubuque, Iowa: Kendall/Hunt, 1988), 76–83.

24. Ibid., 79.

25. American Automobile Association, *Requirements for Recommendation of Hotels, Motels, Resorts, and Restaurants* (Washington, D.C., 1960).

26. Advertisement, *Tourist Court Journal* 27 (April 1964): 12.

27. George E. Toles, "Advertising Helps Stimulate Treadway Inns' Success," *Motel/Motor Inn Journal* 34 (September 1971): 52–54.

28. E. L. Barringer, "Tourist Camp Station Patterned After Dutch Windmills," *National Petroleum News* 22 (April 30, 1930): 105–6.

29. "Housing the Tourist," *Architectural Forum* 66 (May 1937): 438–41.

30. Frank J. Taylor, "Just What the Motorist Ordered," *Saturday Evening Post* 220 (July 5, 1947): 32–33, 90, 93.

31. "M. K. Guertin," *American Motel Magazine* 17 (August 1960): 60.

32. Doug Cochran, "Some Pointers from M. K. Guertin," *Tourist Court Journal* 26 (January 1963): 19.

33. Ibid., 21.

34. "Big Move for Best Western," *Hotel and Motel Management* 191 (June 1976): 11.

35. "Best Western Markets New Image," ibid. 191 (September 1976): 25.

36. Best Western advertising insert, *Lodging Hospitality* 36 (November 1980): 58.

37. Bill Gillette, "Best Western Sets Global Goals," *Hotel and Motel Management* 205 (June 11, 1990): 3.

38. Terry Breen, "Best Value, Superior, Magic Key Inns Combine to Form Chain: USA Inns," ibid. 200 (July 1985):

39. Bob Gresham, "Anatomy of Chain and Referral Motels," *Tourist Court Journal* 30 (August 1967): 59.

40. National Newsbeat, *Hotel and Motel Management* 192 (September 1977): 15.

Chapter 6. Motel Franchising – Part 1

1. Chekian S. Dev and Janet E. Hubbard, "A Strategic Analysis of the Lodging Industry," *Cornell Hotel and Restaurant Administration Quarterly* 30 (May 1989): 21.

2. Joseph E. Lavin and Dallas S. Lunceford, "Franchising and the Lodging Industry," in *Encyclopedia of Hospitality and Tourism,* ed. Mahmood A. Khan, Michael D. Olsen, and Turgut Var (New York: Van Nostrand Reinhold, 1993), 367.

3. U.S. House of Representatives, Committee on Small Business, *Franchising in the U.S. Economy: Prospects and Problems,* 101st Cong., 2d sess. (Washington, D.C.: U.S. Government Printing Office, 1990), 3.

4. John Gamrecki, "Franchising: Fitting the Property into Today's Marketplace," *Hotel and Motel Management* 196 (October 1981): 20.

5. Glenn Withiam, "Hotel Companies Aim for Multiple Markets," *Cornell Hotel and Restaurant Administration Quarterly* 26 (March 1985): 39.

6. Ibid., 44–45.

7. See The Chain Report, *Lodging Hospitality* 48 (August 1992): 59–66.

8. See, e.g., Margo L. Vignola and Jill S. Krutick, *The Lodging Industry in the 1990s: Confronting Crowded Markets* (New York: Salamon Brothers, 1990).

9. "10,000,000 Motorists' Dollars Help Howard Johnson Build Up Chain of 130 Company-Owned Shops," *Ice Cream Review* 23 (July 1940): 25.

10. Doug Cochran, "Exclusive Interview with TraveLodge Head . . . Scott King on Co-ownership," *Tourist Court Journal* 27 (October 1963): 11.

11. Dan Streib, "TraveLodge Has New Franchise Plan," ibid. 29 (October 1965): 84.

12. "Exclusive Interview with TraveLodge President," ibid. 31 (April 1968): 9.

13. Ibid., 13.

14. "History of Trusthouse Forte," *Lodging Hospitality* 40 (November 1984): 120.

15. Advertisement, *Tourist Court Journal* 26 (November 1962): 71.

16. G. Taninecz, "Imperial 400 Acquired by European Firm (Interpart America, Inc.)," *Hotel and Motel Management* 202 (March 30, 1984): 2.

17. R. A. Perry, "Quality Courts United Holds Convention," *Tourist Court Journal* 9 (December 1945): 15.

18. Advertisement, ibid. 23 (June 1960): 74.

19. Doug Cochran, "How Quality Courts Lives Up to Its Name," ibid. 26 (March 1963): 25.

20. Ibid., 28.

21. Ken Koepper and Christine O'Dwyer, "Chains Poise for Development at the Dawn of a New Decade," *Lodging* 15 (January 1990): 14.

22. "Mid-Priced Hotels Slugging It Out in a Shrinking Market," *Lodging Hospitality* 39 (May 1983): 46.

23. Choice Hotels International, "Fact Sheet," August 1, 1991.

24. Michael DeLuca, "Quality's Newest Entry: McSleep," *Hotel and Motel Management* 202 (September 28, 1987): 1.

25. Carlo Wolff, "Budget Chains in Catbird Seat," *Lodging Hospitality* 46 (September 1990): 63.

26. Bob Gresham, "Anatomy of Chain and Referral Motels," *Tourist Court Journal* 30 (August 1967): 59.

27. "Will Innkeeping History Repeat Itself with the Budget Motel?" *Hotel and Motel Management* 187 (November 1972): 43.

28. "Rodeway Inn: Changes Make for Success," ibid. 193 (September 1977): 28.

29. Choice Hotels International, "Fact Sheet," August 1, 1991.

30. Advertisement, *Tourist Court Journal* 24 (May 1961): 10.

31. Advertisement, ibid. 33 (July 1970): 47.

32. Ibid.

33. Frances Loeb, "How One Motel Franchise System Works," *Tourist Court Journal* 19 (February 1956): 14.

34. Gresham, "Anatomy of Chain and Referral Motels," 59.

35. Rita Koselka, "It's an Ill Wind," *Forbes* 150 (December 7, 1992), 125.

36. "Hampton Inns Announces Opening of 200th Hotel," *Hotel and Motel Management* 204 (September 1989): 129.

37. Chuck Hawkins, "Promus: Fighting for the Middle of the Road," *Business Week*, no. 3173 (August 13, 1990): 102.

38. "Hospitality Franchise System: Banking on President Frank Beletti," *Hotel and Resort International* 14 (July 1991): 22.

39. Pat Askin, "Ramada: Redefining the Mid-Priced Hotel," *Lodging Hospitality* 39 (May 1983): 38.

40. "500 Ramada Inns in a Decade," *Tourist Court Journal* 31 (November 1967): 15.

41. Ibid., 16.

42. Ray Sawyer, "Ramada Inn's New Direction in Motel Management," *Motel/Motor Inn Journal* 35 (January 1971): 47.

43. "Ramada Reaches for a Renaissance in the '80s," *Lodging Hospitality* 36 (February 1980): 6.

44. Askin, "Ramada," 38.

45. "Hospitality Franchise System," 22.

46. Ira Teinowitz, "Check-in for Budget," *Advertising Age* 62 (December 2, 1991): 12.

47. "What's Howard Johnson Up to Now?" *American Motel Magazine* 15 (April 1958): 33.

48. Robert C. Lewis, *Cases in Hospitality Marketing and Management* (New York: John Wiley & Sons, 1989), 241.

49. Howard Rudnitsky, "What Do the Sellers Know That the Buyers Don't?" *Forbes* 136 (October 7, 1985): 118.

50. Super 8 Motels, "Fact Sheet," December, 31, 1991, 1.

Chapter 7. Motel Franchising – Part 2

1. National Newsbeat, *Hotel and Motel Management* 186 (August 1971): 13.

2. Bob Gresham, "What's the Game Plan for Master Hosts and Red Carpet Inns?" *Motel/Motor Inn Journal* 35 (July 1972): 24.

3. Bob Gresham, "So Flows Master Hosts," *Tourist Court Journal* 33 (July 1970): 64.

4. "Will Innkeeping History Repeat Itself with the Budget Motel?" *Hotel and Motel Management* 187 (November 1972): 41.

5. Seymour Freedgood, "The Hotels: Time to Stop and Rest," *Fortune* 68 (July 1963): 162.

6. National Newsbeat, *Hotel and Motel Management* 187 (August 1972): 11.

7. Donald E. Lundberg, *The Hotel and Restaurant Business* (Boston: Cahners, 1976), 285.

8. "The World's Largest Motel," *American Motel Magazine* 15 (August 1958): 25–30.

9. Lundberg, *Hotel and Restaurant Business,* 288.

10. Bill Gillette, "Conservative Approach Fuels Marriott Success," *Hotel and Motel Management* 204 (June 19, 1989): 3.

11. Christopher Hart, "Product Development: How Marriott Created Courtyard," *Cornell Hotel and Restaurant Administration Quarterly* 27 (November 1986): 69–69.

12. Lodging Today, *Lodging Hospitality* 40 (July 1984): 10.

13. Christopher Muller, "The Marriott Divestment: Leaving the Past Behind," *Cornell Hotel and Restaurant Administration Quarterly* 31 (February 1990): 9.

14. Edwin McDowell, "Hotels Await the Wake-up Call," *New York Times,* September 24, 1991, D-6.

15. Megan Rowe, "Growing Pains at Marriott?" *Lodging Hospitality* 46 (February 1990): 57.

16. Edwin McDowell, "Marriott's Shareholders Back Plan to Split in 2," *New York Times,* July 24, 1993, 37.

17. Michael Porter, *Competitive Strategies* (New York: Free Press, 1980), discussed in Muller, "Marriott Divestment," 8.

18. D. Daryl Wyckoff and W. Earl Sasser, *The U.S. Lodging Industry* (Lexington, Mass.: Lexington Books, 1981), 209.

19. Ibid., 214.

20. John Gurda, *In the Light of Liberty: A History of the Marcus Company* (n.p.: Marcus, 1991), 11.

21. Ibid., 12.

22. National Newsbeat, *Hotel and Motel Management* 188 (November 1973): 11.

23. George Taninecz, "Reality Governs Budgetel Growth," ibid. 204 (May 9, 1988): 3.

24. "Following the Cardinal Rule," ibid. 194 (September 1979): 21.

25. "Jousting with Motel 6," *Lodging Hospitality* 48 (April 1992): 18.

26. "Economy Lodging: America's Top 10," *Lodging* 19 (March 1992): 22.

27. George R. Justus, "Microtel: How 'Simple' Translates into Success," *Cornell Hotel and Restaurant Administration Quarterly* 32 (December 1991): 52.

28. Tony Dela Cruz, "Choice Hotels Loses Suit Over Microtel's Design," *Hotel Business* 1 (October 21, 1992): 1.

29. Caytie Daniell, "Budget Host Aims to Top Record Year," *Hotel and Motel Management* 202 (April 27, 1987): 15.

30. Wyckoff and Sasser, *U.S. Lodging Industry,* 31.

31. "Indianapolis Dillon Inn: Prototype for New Chain," *Lodging Hospitality* 34 (July 1983): 10.

32. Gordon Kopulos, "A Chain's Proven Guide to Performance and Service," *Motel/Motor Inn Journal* 38 (March 1975): 11.

33. Kenneth R. MacDonald, "How the Hyatt Chain Has Expanded in Five Years," *Tourist Court Journal* 29 (November 1965): 48.

34. "Radisson on the Rise," *Hotel and Motel Management* 193 (September 1978): 26.

35. Loretta Ivany and Ed Watkins, "Management Companies Reach a Crossroads," *Lodging Hospitality* 38 (January 1982): 90–94, 96.

Chapter 8. The Changing Motel Room

1. "A Rougher Road for Motel Chains," *Business Week,* no. 2324 (March 30, 1974): 96.
2. Holmes A. Shepard, "Postcards for the Tourist Court," *Tourist Court Journal* 10 (November 1946): 12–13.
3. Helen P. Washburn, "Tourists Accommodated," *Christian Science Monitor Weekly Magazine,* July 19, 1941, 12.
4. See Gwendolyn Wright, *Moralism and the Model Home: Domestic Architecture and Cultural Conflict in Chicago, 1873–1912* (Chicago: University of Chicago Press, 1980), 234–35, 238, 243–46; idem, *Building the Dream: A Social History of Housing in America* (New York: Pantheon, 1981), 171; Alan Gowans, *The Comfortable House: North American Suburban Architecture, 1890–1913* (Cambridge: MIT Press, 1986), 214; and Jean Gordon and Jan McArthur, "Popular Culture, Magazines, and American Domestic Interiors, 1898–1940," *Journal of Popular Culture* 22 (1989): 49.
5. E. H. Lightfoot, "Tile Baths Can Be Constructed Economically," *Tourist Court Journal* 1 (October 1937): 9–10, 24.
6. Elizabeth Collins Cromley, "A History of American Beds and Bedrooms, 1890–1930," in *American Home Life, 1880–1930: A Social History of Spaces and Services,* ed. Jessica H. Foy and Thomas J. Schlereth (Knoxville: University of Tennessee Press, 1992), 123, 138.
7. "Portfolio of Special Building Types," *Architectural Record* 77 (February 1935): 97.
8. John J. McCarthy, "The Market Business Forgets," *Nation's Business* 21 (August 1933): 40; "Roadside Cabins for Tourists," *Architectural Record* 74:6 (December 1933): 457.
9. "Roadside Cabins for Tourists," *Architectural Record* 72 (December 1933): 462.
10. Clara Z. Keyton, *Tourist Camp Pioneering Experiences* (Chicago: Adams, 1960), 18, 19.
11. Eleanor N. Knowles, "Along the Roadside," *Christian Science Monitor Weekly Magazine,* July 31, 1935, 15.
12. Mary Anne Beecher, "The Motel in Builder's Literature and Architectural Publications: An Analysis of Design," in *Roadside America: The Automobile in Design and Culture,* ed. Jan Jennings (Ames: Iowa State University Press, 1990), 121.
13. Ewart H. Lightfoot applied for a patent on the "knockdown house" on April 11, 1931, and received patent 1,985,789 for the invention on December 25, 1934 (Knowles, "Along the Roadside," 15).
14. "Tourist Cabins That Get the Business," *Popular Mechanics* 64 (July 1935): 151–53.
15. Family scrapbook containing clipping entitled "Gov. Guy B. Park to be Invited to 'Village' Opening," from an unidentified newspaper, [1934]; "Vision in Dream to Become Real," from an unidentified newspaper, [September 12, 1934], in the possession of Mrs. Henry Ward Owen, Lebanon, Missouri.
16. Washburn, "Tourists Accommodated," 12.
17. "Portfolio of Special Building Types," 96.
18. L. H. Robbins, "America Hobnobs at the Tourist Camp," *New York Times Magazine,* August 12, 1934, 9.
19. See Alan Gowans, *Images of American Living: Four Centuries of Architecture and Furniture as Cultural Expression* (Philadelphia: J. B. Lippincott, 1964), 424.

20. Warren J. Belasco, *Americans on the Road: From Autocamp to Motel, 1910–1945* (Cambridge: MIT Press, 1979), 167–68.

21. "Deaths: T. E. Lightfoot Was an Architect for 30 Years," *Houston Press,* July 6, 1961, 24; Chester H. Liebs, *Main Street to Miracle Mile: American Roadside Architecture* (Boston: Little, Brown, 1985), 180–81. For an example of the Simmons Company's advertisements, see *Tourist Court Journal* 1 (October 1937): 26.

22. John Hocke, "Good Profits Building Tourist Camps," *American Builder and Building Age* 51 (April 1931): 88–89.

23. Henry Schmidt, "Overnight Rest-Cabins Spreading," *Literary Digest* 117 (June 9, 1934), 40.

24. E. L. Yordan, "Motor Camps Win New Friends," *New York Times,* July 14, 1935, sec. X, p. 1.

25. Wright, *Building the Dream,* 170–71.

26. "I'll Answer Your Questions on Tourist Camps," *Hotel Management,* July 1936, 19.

27. Ibid.; "Grande Vista Tourist Homes," *American Builder* 59 (June 1937): 79.

28. Liebs, *Main Street to Miracle Mile,* 180; Gordon and McArthur, "Popular Culture, Magazines, and American Domestic Interiors, 1898–1940," 47, 49, 55; Jeffrey L. Meikle, *Twentieth Century Limited: Industrial Design in America, 1925–1939* (Philadelphia: Temple University Press, 1979), 4, 209–10.

29. "Housing the Tourist," *Architectural Forum* 66 (May 1937): 464–65.

30. Ray Sawyer, "Why 'Lady Luck' Seems to Smile on the Hitching Post Inn," *Tourist Court Journal* 33 (February 1970): 12–14b, 16–20, 22; idem, "How the Chandler Family Has Kept Pace with the Times," *Motel/Motor Inn Journal* 35 (February 1972): 38–44, 46–48; advertisement, *Tourist Court Journal* 12 (April 1950): 3.

31. Knowles, "Along the Roadside," 5; *Tourist Court Plan Book* (Temple, Tex: Tourist Court Journal, 1950), 60–61.

32. Alan W. Farrant, "Why Up-Grade?" *Tourist Court Journal* 19 (June 1958): 13–16; W. L. Edmundson, "Obsolescence Is No Bane to Rex Plaza Motor Inn," ibid. 28 (April 1965): 24–28.

33. "Going DeLuxe in Phoenix," ibid. 5 (May 1942): 22; Tom E. Lightfoot, "Victory Housing," ibid. 5 (April 1942): 9.

34. W. D. Riddle, "Modern Motel," ibid. 8 (November 1944): 5.

35. Ibid.

36. Ibid., 7.

37. H. D. Lukenbill, "Profit in the North," ibid. 9 (July 1946): 6 (quotation), 19.

38. Frederic Pawley, "Motels," *Architectural Record* 107 (March 1950): 123, 124.

39. Ibid., 125, 124, 130, 126, 118 (quotations on 125 and 124).

40. "Hotel Experience Built This Motel," *American Motel Magazine* 6 (March 1953): 37.

41. Norman J. Radder, "Yording's Hides the Heat," *Tourist Court Journal* 14 (May 1951): 11–13, 34.

42. Pawley, "Motels," 128; George P. Gardner Jr., interview by Keith A. Sculle and Jefferson S. Rogers, Jackson, Tennessee, December 11, 1993.

43. Janet Smith, "Planning a Usable Room," *Tourist Court Journal* 17 (April 1954): 52.

44. Clare A. Gunn, "Planning the Motel Room," *American Motel Magazine* 10 (December 1954): 38.

45. Clare A. Gunn, *Motels and Resorts: A Guide to Better Planning* (East Lansing: Cooperative Extension Service, Michigan State University, [1960]), 6–8.

46. Gunn, "Planning the Motel Room," 40.

47. Ibid., 38, 41.

48. *The Architectural Record: Motels, Hotels, Restaurants, and Bars* (New York: F. W. Dodge, 1953), 21.

49. Geoffrey Baker and Bruno Funaro, *Motels* (New York: Reinhold, 1955), 200, 204, 210 (quotation on 210).

50. See, e.g., Clinton H. Cowgill, "Modern Travel Accommodations," *AIA Journal* 33 (March 1960): 73–92.

51. Baker and Funaro, *Motels,* 9.

52. Henry End, *Interiors Book of Hotels and Motor Hotels* (New York: Whitney Library of Design, 1963), 120, 130, 131; Carl Koch, "Design for a Franchise Chain," *Architectural Record* 123 (April 1958): 206 (quotation).

53. End, *Interiors Book of Hotels and Motels,* 120, 130.

54. "A Single Standard for Travelers," *Business Week,* no. 1784 (November 16, 1963): 120.

55. Ibid., 120.

56. Candace M. Volz, "The Modern Look of the Early Twentieth-Century House: A Mirror of Change," in Foy and Schlereth, *American Home Life, 1880–1930,* 34.

57. Regarding the impact those who were discontented with "modern living" had on domestic design, see Thomas J. Schlereth, "Conduits and Conduct: Home Utilities in Victorian America, 1876–1915," in Foy and Schlereth, *American Home Life, 1880–1930,* 238–39. Regarding the impact of gender's power over bedroom design, see Cromley, "History of American Beds and Bedrooms," 129–30.

58. Harry R. Pearson, "Modular Construction: Is It the Answer?" *Motel/Motor Inn Journal* 34 (August 1971): 15.

59. Wright, *Building the Dream,* 244–46. Anticipating prefabricated housing's postwar boom market, Alfred Bruce and Harold Sandbank, *A History of Prefabrication* (1944; reprint, New York: Arno, 1972), remains the only book on the subject of prefabrication.

60. Frederic A. Birmingham, "Kemmons Wilson: The Inn-Side Story," *Saturday Evening Post* 244 (winter 1971): 69.

61. Kemmons Wilson, *The Holiday Inn Story* (New York: Newcomen Society in North America, 1968), 14.

62. Eugene M. Hanson, "The Best Western's New Home Office," *Tourist Court Journal* 28 (September 1965): 67, 68.

63. "Best Western's New One-Stop Shopping Center," ibid. 33 (June 1970): 67.

64. "Best Western Forms Supply Arm," *Lodging Hospitality* 36 (March 1980): 6.

65. "New Motel Will Have 'Hospital Clean' Interiors," *American Motel Magazine* 13 (September 1957): 72.

66. "Here Are the Newest Factory-Built Units," *Tourist Court Journal* 25 (September 1962): 56.

67. "Following the Cardinal Rule," *Hotel and Motel Management* 194 (September 1973): 23.

68. Pearson, "Modular Construction."

69. Gordon Kopulos, "How a Budget Chain Minimizes Operating Costs For Its Motels," *Motel/Motor Inn Journal* 38 (November 1974): 11.

70. End, *Interiors Book of Hotels and Motor Hotels,* 117.

71. Henry End, *Interiors Second Book of Hotels* (New York: Whitney Library of Design, 1978), 43.

72. Faye Rice, "Hotels Fight For Business Guests," *Fortune* 121 (April 23, 1990): 268.

73. Ibid., 272.

74. Ray Sawyer, "How An Independent Motel Bucked the Tide in 'Chain Country,'" *Motel/Motor Inn Journal* 35 (August 1972): 20.

75. End, *Interiors Book of Hotels and Motor Hotels*, 12.

Chapter 9. The Nation's Innkeeper

1. Frederic A. Birmingham, "Kemmons Wilson: The Inn-Side Story," *Saturday Evening Post* 244 (winter 1971): 68.

2. Kemmons Wilson, *The Holiday Inn Story* (New York: Newcomen Society in North America, 1968), 8.

3. Ed Weathers, "Profile: Kemmons Wilson," *Memphis* 10 (September 1985): 55.

4. Ellis Moore, "Loan of $50 Starts Memphian on Modern Horatio Alger Trip," *Memphis Commercial Appeal*, September 25, 1952.

5. Weathers, "Profile," 55.

6. "Rapid Rise of the Host with the Most," *Time* 99 (June 12, 1972): 79.

7. Weathers, "Profile," 56.

8. Wilson, *Holiday Inn Story*, 9.

9. The Great Sign design was inspired by Wilson's experience in the movie theater business, where he learned the drawing power of large, colorful signs with marquees featuring movable letters (Doug Cochran, "An Interview with Kemmons Wilson," *Tourist Court Journal* 26 [August 1963]: 23).

10. Weathers, "Profile," 56, 58; Birmingham, "Kemmons Wilson," 69–70.

11. William B. Walton, "The Holiday Inn Story," *Tourist Court Journal* 26 (August 1963): 26, 28.

12. Wallace E. Johnson, *Work Is My Play* (New York: Hawthorne, 1973), 91–94; idem, "Millionaire: A Self-Portrait," *Esquire* 61 (February 1964): 164.

13. Wilson, *Holiday Inn Story*, 11.

14. Weathers, "Profile," 58; Richard Martin, "Super Salesmanship Builds Holiday Inn Motel Chain," *Memphis Sunday Times*, November 8, 1964, 15.

15. Wilson, *Holiday Inn Story*, 13–14; Walton, "Holiday Inn Story," 28.

16. Martin, "Super Salesmanship," 15, 17. See also "Holiday Inns of America," *American Motel Magazine* 14 (May 1959): 54–55.

17. William W. Bond, interview by Jefferson S. Rogers and Keith A. Sculle, Memphis, Tennessee, February 14, 1995. Bond, whose firm was independent from Holiday Inn, was the chain's principal architect until 1973.

18. Ibid.

19. Kemmons Wilson, interview by Rogers and Sculle, Memphis, Tennessee, December 10, 1993. See also David Halberstam, *The Fifties* (New York: Villard, 1993), 178–79.

20. Wilson, *Holiday Inn Story*, 18–19; "Holiday City: Home of Modern Innkeeping in an Old World Tradition," *Holiday Inn Magazine*, December 1968, 34.

21. "Innkeeping and the Computer: II," *Hotel and Motel Management* 183 (August 1968): 27–30.

22. Kemmons Wilson, interview, December 10, 1993; "Cabana Rooms," *Tourist Court Journal* 25 (September 1962): 57. The company Wilson acquired was renamed Holiday Manufacturing Company.

23. Weathers, "Profile," 58.

24. Martin, "Super Salesmanship," 18; Wilson, *Holiday Inn Story,* 18; "Holiday City," 35.

25. Kemmons Wilson, interview, December 10, 1993.

26. Ibid.; Martin, "Super Salesmanship," 17. Wilson may have been ahead of his time with the Holiday Inn Junior concept, given the relatively recent success of economy lodging chains such as Knights Inn (which uses prefabricated buildings), Sleep Inn and Microtel (which feature space-efficient rooms), and Super 8 Motels (which have built properties predominantly in America's smaller communities).

27. *Moody's Bank and Finance Manual* (New York: Moody's Investors Services, 1974), 1841; *Holiday Inns, Incorporated, 1981 Annual Report* (Memphis: Holiday Inns, 1982), 25.

28. "Rapid Rise of the Host with the Most," 82.

29. *Moody's Industrial Manual,* vol. 1 (New York: Moody's Investors Services, 1976), 681.

30. Carl Crawford, "By Cutting Its Manufacturing, HI Lifts Its Profits Dramatically," *Memphis Commercial Appeal,* April 9, 1978, B-4. The impetus for divestiture came from a perceived need not only to refocus the company's operations but also to stave off conflicts with its franchisees. By manufacturing and processing products used by its franchisees, Holiday Inn expected to maintain a loyal, captive market. After threats of antitrust litigation and the loss of business from franchisees who purchased products from lower-price vendors, the company decided to sell off those subsidiaries.

31. "Holiday Inns Takes a New Road to Profits," *Business Week,* no. 2347 (September 7, 1974): 88.

32. "Holiday Inns: Trying the Comeback Trail," ibid., no. 2439 (July 5, 1976): 65.

33. "Holiday Inns Takes a New Road to Profits," 88.

34. *Holiday Inn Worldwide Directory, May 1–Oct 31, 1974* (Memphis: Holiday Inns, 1974), 5; *Holiday Inn Worldwide Directory, Jan. 1–May 31, 1977* (Memphis: Holiday Inns, 1977), 13; *Holiday Inn Directory,* effective November 28, 1987 (Memphis: Holiday Inns, 1987).

35. Kemmons Wilson, interview, December 10, 1993.

36. Nolan Lewis, "Holiday Inns' Casino Decision Sparks Departure of Clymer," *Memphis Commercial Appeal,* September 30, 1978, 1, 5.

37. Judy Ringel, "Holiday Inns at 30," *Memphis* 7 (October 1982): 88.

38. *Moody's Industrial Manual,* vol. 1 (New York: Moody's Investors Services, 1984), 1575; *Holiday Corporation 1988 Annual Report* (Memphis: Holiday Corporation, 1989), 45.

39. See, e.g., *Holiday Inn Directory,* effective May 25, 1986 (Memphis: Holiday Inns, 1986), 3.

40. Ringel, "Holiday Inns at 30," 98. Holiday Inn has continued to force franchisees to invest considerable sums of money in renovation projects; see, e.g., Del Jones, "Hotels Push Franchisees to Remodel," *USA Today,* February 9, 1995, 1B-2B.

41. Loretta Ivany, "Crowne Plaza," *Lodging Hospitality* 39 (June 1983): 87–88, 90.

42. Joe Jancsurak, "Holiday Inn Launches Its Second Hotel Chain," *Hotel and Motel Management* 198 (June 1983): 1.

43. "Holiday Inn Orders Operators of Older Motels to Renovate," *Chicago Tribune,* September 25, 1994, sec. 7, p. 10. See also Robert A. Nozar, "Empowerment Strengthens Holiday," *Hotel and Motel Management* 208 (July 5, 1993): 18.

44. Robert A. Nozar, "Embassy Stays Ahead in All-Suite Parade," *Hotel and Motel Management* 202 (July 8, 1987): 3.

45. Sharon Donovan, "Hampton Sets Strategy to Hike Market Share," ibid. 203 (May 30, 1988): 2, 76; *Holiday Corporation 1988 Annual Report*, 2.

46. "Bye-Bye Memphis, Hello, Atlanta," *Lodging Hospitality* 47 (May 1991): 25.

47. Megan Rowe, "Holiday Inn Fat and Sassy to Lean and Mean," ibid. 48 (July 1992): 25.

48. *Holiday Inn Worldwide Directory*, effective May 26, 1991 (Atlanta: Holiday Inns, 1991), 1.

49. Alan Salomon, "Holiday Readying Two New Brands," *Hotel and Motel Management* 209 (September 19, 1994): 1, 52, 71.

50. "So, What's New? Holiday Inn Worldwide Launches on the Internet" [cited June 15, 1995]; available from http://www.holiday-inn.com; INTERNET. See also http://www.webscope.com/travel to examine the homepages of other chains, such as Best Western, Hampton Inn, and La Quinta.

Chapter 10. The Motel in Albuquerque

1. See, e.g., V. B. Price, *A City at the End of the World* (Albuquerque: University of New Mexico Press, 1992); and Marc Simmons, *Albuquerque: A Narrative History* (Albuquerque: University of New Mexico Press, 1982), 374–77.

2. The villa was named for Don Francisco Fernandez de la Cueva Enriquez, duke of Alburquerque, the thirty-fourth viceroy of New Spain. The name of the duke's home city—Alburquerque, in Badajoz, Spain—is probably derived from the Latin *albus quercus* (white oak). The letter *r* in the second syllable was dropped by English-speaking visitors and writers in the early 1800s (see T. M. Pearce, ed., *New Mexico Place Names: A Geographical Dictionary* [Albuquerque: University of New Mexico Press, 1965], 5).

3. Paul Horgan, *Great River: The Rio Grande in North American History*, vol. 1, *Indians and Spain* (New York: Rinehart, 1954), 328–30.

4. Simmons, *Albuquerque*, 225–27, 276–77.

5. Ibid., 329.

6. Ibid., 329–32.

7. Franklin T. McCann, "The Growth of the Tourist Court in the United States and Its Relationship to the Urban Development of Albuquerque, New Mexico." *Journal of the Scientific Laboratories of Denison University* 37 (May 1942): 61–62.

8. The data on the location of establishments used to create the series of maps for this chapter were compiled from *Hudspeth's Albuquerque City Directory* (El Paso: Hudspeth, 1930, 1940, 1950, 1961, 1971); and the *Albuquerque (Bernalillo County, N.M.) City Directory* (Dallas: R. L. Polk, 1980, 1990). Contemporary roads and highways are shown on all the of maps for the purpose of comparative reference.

9. Locations of establishments and residences along all city streets are recorded in *Hudspeth's Albuquerque City Directory*.

10. McCann, "Growth of the Tourist Court," 64.

11. Ibid., 62–63. See also Arthur Krim, "Mapping Route 66: A Cultural Cartography," in *Roadside America: The Automobile in Design and Culture*, ed. Jan Jennings (Ames: Iowa State University Press, 1990), 198–208, for a concise overview of U.S. Route 66's development.

12. Jerry L. Williams. "Urban Area: Albuquerque," in *New Mexico in Maps*, ed. Jerry L.

Williams and Paul E. McAllister (Albuquerque: University of New Mexico Press, 1981), 100–101.

13. Bart Ripp, "The De Anza Had It All: Turquoise Floor, No Stairs." *Albuquerque Tribune,* July 30, 1985, A-1.

14. Ibid., A-1, A-4; E. H. Lightfoot, "De Anza Motor Lodge Pueblo Designed," *Tourist Court Journal* 3 (May 1940): 5–6, 21.

15. Conrad N. Hilton, *Be My Guest* (Englewood Cliffs, N.J.: Prentice-Hall, 1957), 11, 182.

16. U.S. Bureau of the Census, *U.S. Census of Business: 1948,* vol. 7, *Service Trade— Area Statistics* (Washington, D.C.: U.S. Government Printing Office, 1951), 30.07–30.08 (tables 103C and 103D). In 1948, motels, motor hotels, and tourist courts generated more than $1.3 million in receipts in Bernalillo County, New Mexico, out of a total $3.7 million in total lodging revenues.

17. U.S. Bureau of the Census, *U.S. Census of Business: 1958,* vol. 6, *Selected Services— Area Statistics; Part 2: New Mexico* (Washington, D.C.: U.S. Government Printing Office, 1961), 31.10 (table 103). Albuquerque's motels, motor hotels, and tourist courts took in almost $4.1 million out of $6.6 million in total lodging revenues.

18. Simmons, *Albuquerque,* 373.

19. Ibid., 374.

20. Old Town, the original colonial settlement of the city, languished after 1880 and remained a separate municipality until the late 1940s. The Albuquerque City Commission designated Old Town as a historic zone in 1957 in order to prevent the destruction or modernization of its buildings. Over the past several decades, Old Town has become one of the city's most popular tourist attractions. The construction of several hotels on the western edge of the district has occurred in response to increasing tourist demand.

Chapter 11. Conclusion

1. Edith Louise Allen, *American Housing As Affected by Social and Economic Conditions* (Peoria, Ill.: Manual Arts, 1930), 144.

2. Michael Kammen, *Mystic Chords of Memory: The Transformation of Tradition in American Culture* (New York: Knopf, 1991), 704.

3. Richard P. Horwitz, *The Strip: An American Place* (Lincoln: University of Nebraska Press, 1985), 178–83.

4. Jenene G. Garey, "Women in Hospitality Management," in *Introduction to Hotel and Restaurant Management,* ed. Robert A. Brymer, 4th ed. (Dubuque, Iowa: Kendall/Hunt, 1984), 150–54.

5. John Hersey, *The Algiers Motel Incident* (New York: Knopf, 1968), 331.

6. Beth Macklin, "Tulsan Has Change of Heart about Motel," *Tulsa World,* December 8, 1982, A-1, A-4; Tom Kertscher, "Park Plaza Owner Gets Donations," ibid., March 6, 1987, D-1, D-3; Mark I. Pinsky, "'Motel People,' a New Class of Homeless on Horizon," *Los Angeles Times Magazine,* March 27, 1985, 1, 3, 24–25; Brad Kessler, "The Hidden Homeless: Down and Out in Suburbia," *The Nation,* September 25, 1989, 306, 308–9, 312–13; Jonathan Eig, "Cheap Motels Offer Poor 'Bottom-of-the-Rung' Living," *Dallas Morning News,* June 25, 1995, 1A, 9A.

7. *Charlotte Observer,* August 30, 1992, 6B.

8. Warren J. Belasco, *Americans on the Road: From Autocamp to Motel, 1910–1945* (Cambridge: MIT Press, 1979), 173.

9. Sinclair Lewis, "Adventures in Autobumming—The Great American Frying Pan," *Saturday Evening Post* 192 (January 3, 1920), 62.

10. Stefanos Polyzoides, Roger Sherwood, and James Tice, *Courtyard Housing in Los Angeles: A Topological Analysis* (Berkeley: University of California Press, 1982), 12. A rare exception to architectural history's avoidance of the motel is John S. Garner, "How Fare Thee Fair Camelot?" *Reflections: The Journal of the School of Architecture* (University of Illinois at Urbana-Champaign) 1 (fall 1983): 38–41.

11. John F. Kasson, *Amusing the Millions: Coney Island at the Turn of the Century* (New York: Hill & Wang, 1978), 4–6, 106–7; Lawrence W. Levine, *Highbrow/Lowbrow: The Emergence of Cultural Hierarchy* (Cambridge: Harvard University Press, 1988).

12. Thomas A. Bloom and Robert A. Brymer, "Careers in the Hospitality Industry," in Brymer, *Introduction to Hotel and Restaurant Management,* 29.

13. J. B. Jackson, "The Movable Dwelling and How It Came to America," in *Discovering the Vernacular Landscape,* by J. B. Jackson (New Haven: Yale University Press, 1984), 101.

Select Bibliography

Unpublished Materials

Large, William Norman. "The Hub of East Texas: A History of Tyler, Texas, 1918–1940." Master's thesis, University of Texas at Tyler, 1992.

City Directories and Statistical Sources

Albuquerque (Bernalillo County, N.M.) City Directory. Dallas: R. L. Polk, 1980, 1990.
Holiday Corporation 1988 Annual Report. Memphis: Holiday Corporation, 1989.
Holiday Inns, Incorporated, 1981 Annual Report. Memphis: Holiday Inns, 1982.
Hudspeth's Albuquerque City Directory. El Paso: Hudspeth, 1930, 1940, 1950, 1961, 1971.
Moody's Bank and Finance Manual. New York: Moody's Investors Services, 1958, 1960, 1962, 1964, 1966, 1968, 1970, 1972, 1974.
Moody's Industrial Manual. New York: Moody's Investors Services, 1976, 1980, 1982, 1984, 1986, 1989, 1994.
1987 Oklahoma City, Oklahoma, Directory. Dallas: R. L. Polk, 1987.
Polk's Savannah (Chatham County, Ga.) City Directory, 1955. Richmond, Va.: R. L. Polk, 1955.
Worley's Tyler (Smith County, Tex.) City Directory, 1932. Dallas: John F. Worley Directory, 1932.

Government Documents

Small Business Administration. *First Semi-Annual Report of the Small Business Administration.* Washington, D.C., 1954.
U.S. Bureau of the Census, *Census of Selected Service Industries, 1972.* Washington, D.C.: U.S. Government Printing Office, 1975.
———. *Census of Service Industries, 1987.* Washington, D.C.: U.S. Government Printing Office, 1989.
———. *Historical Statistics of the United States, Colonial Times to 1957.* Washington, D.C.: U.S. Government Printing Office, 1960.

————. *Statistical Abstract of the United States*. Washington, D.C.: U.S. Government Printing Office, 1961.

————. *Statistical Abstract of the United States*. Washington, D.C.: U.S. Government Printing Office, 1992.

————. *U.S. Census of Business: 1948*. Vol. 7. *Service Trade—Area Statistics*. Washington, D.C.: U.S. Government Printing Office, 1951.

————. *U.S. Census of Business: 1958*. Vol. 6. *Selected Services—Area Statistics; Part 2: New Mexico*. Washington, D.C.: U.S. Government Printing Office, 1961.

U.S. Department of Commerce. *Thirty-Fourth Annual Report of the Secretary of Commerce, 1946*. Washington, D.C.: U.S. Government Printing Office, 1946.

U.S. House of Representatives, Committee on Small Business. *Franchising in the U.S. Economy: Prospects and Problems*. 101st Cong., 2d sess. Washington, D.C.: U.S. Government Printing Office, 1990.

Books

Allen, Edith Louise. *American Housing As Affected by Social and Economic Conditions*. Peoria, Ill.: Manual Arts, 1930.

American Automobile Association. *Requirements for Recommendation of Hotels, Motels, Resorts, and Restaurants*. Washington, D.C., 1960.

The Architectural Record: Motels, Hotels, Restaurants, and Bars. New York: F. W. Dodge, 1953.

Asian American Hotel Owners Association. *A Profile of the Asian American Hotel Owners Association*. [Atlanta, 1995].

Baker, Geoffrey, and Bruno Funaro. *Motels*. New York: Reinhold, 1955.

Barnes, Catherine A. *Journey from Jim Crow: The Desegregation of Southern Transit*. New York: Columbia University Press, 1983.

Beecher, Mary Anne. "The Motel in Builder's Literature and Architectural Publications: An Analysis of Design." In *Roadside America: The Automobile in Design and Culture*, edited by Jan Jennings, 115–24. Ames: Iowa State University Press, 1990.

Belasco, Warren J. *Americans on the Road: From Autocamp to Motel, 1910–1945*. Cambridge: MIT Press, 1979.

Belknap, Michael R. Introduction to *The Drive to Desegregate Places of Public Accommodation*, edited by Michael R. Belknap. Vol. 9 of *Civil Rights, the White House, and the Justice Department, 1945–1968*, edited by Michael R. Belknap. New York: Garland, 1991.

Bell, Daniel. *End of Ideology*. Glencoe, Ill.: Free Press, 1960.

Bledstein, Burton J. *The Culture of Professionalism: The Middle Class and the Development of Higher Education in America*. New York: Norton, 1976.

Bloom, Thomas A., and Robert A. Brymer. "Careers in the Hospitality Industry." In *Introduction to Hotel and Restaurant Management*, edited by Robert A. Brymer, 29–36. 4th ed. Dubuque, Iowa: Kendall/Hunt, 1984.

Brimmer, Frank E. "Fundamentals of Motor Camping." In *Official AAA Camp Directory*, 5–24. Washington D.C.: American Automobile Association, 1928.

Bruce, Alfred, and Harold Sandbank. *A History of Prefabrication*. 1944. Reprint. New York: Arno, 1972.

Carruth, Viola. *Caddo: 1,000. A History of the Shreveport Area from the Time of the Caddo Indians to the 1970s*. 2d ed. Shreveport, La.: Shreveport Magazine, 1971.

Carter, Paul. *Another Part of the Twenties*. New York: Columbia University Press, 1977.

Chafe, William H. *The Unfinished Journey: America since World War II.* New York: Oxford University Press, 1986.

Cromley, Elizabeth Collins. "A History of American Beds and Bedrooms, 1890–1930." In *American Home Life, 1880–1930: A Social History of Spaces and Services,* edited by Jessica H. Foy and Thomas J. Schlereth, 120–41. Knoxville: University of Tennessee Press, 1992.

Dicke, Thomas S. *Franchising in America: The Development of a Business Method, 1840–1980.* Chapel Hill: University of North Carolina Press, 1992.

Dreiser, Theodore. *A Hoosier Holiday.* New York: John Lane, 1916.

End, Henry. *Interiors Book of Hotels and Motor Hotels.* New York: Whitney Library of Design, 1963.

———. *Interiors Second Book of Hotels.* New York: Whitney Library of Design, 1978.

Financing the Lodging Industry: A Survey of Lender Attitudes. Philadelphia: Laventhol & Horwath, 1975.

Fox, Richard Wightman, and T. J. Jackson Lears. Introduction to *The Culture of Consumption: Critical Essays in American History, 1880–1980,* edited by Richard W. Fox and T. J. Jackson Lears, vii–xvii. New York: Pantheon, 1983.

Garey, Jenene G. "Women in Hospitality Management." In *Introduction to Hotel and Restaurant Management,* edited by Robert A. Brymer, 150–54. 4th ed. Dubuque, Iowa: Kendall/Hunt, 1984.

Gilbert, James. *Another Chance: Post-war America, 1945–1985.* 2d ed. Chicago: Dorsey, 1986.

Gill, Richard E. "Hospitality Industry Associations." In *Introduction to Hotel and Restaurant Management: A Book of Readings,* edited by Robert A. Brymer, 76–83. 5th ed. Dubuque, Iowa: Kendall/Hunt, 1988.

Glover, Robert W., ed. *Tyler and Smith County, Texas: An Historical Survey.* N.p.: American Bicentennial Committee of Tyler-Smith County, 1976.

Gowans, Alan. *The Comfortable House: North American Suburban Architecture, 1890–1913.* Cambridge: MIT Press, 1986.

———. *Images of American Living: Four Centuries of Architecture and Furniture as Cultural Expression.* Philadelphia: J. B. Lippincott, 1964.

Gunn, Clare A. *Motels and Resorts: A Guide to Better Planning.* East Lansing: Cooperative Extension Service, Michigan State University, [1960].

Gurda, John. *In the Light of Liberty: A History of the Marcus Company.* N.p: Marcus, 1991.

Halberstam, David. *The Fifties.* New York: Villard, 1993.

Hersey, John. *The Algiers Motel Incident.* New York: Knopf, 1968.

Hess, Alan. *Viva Las Vegas: After-Hours Architecture.* San Francisco: Chronicle Books, 1993.

Hine, Tom. *Populuxe.* New York: Knopf, 1986.

Hilton, Conrad N. *Be My Guest.* Englewood Cliffs, N.J.: Prentice-Hall, 1957.

Horgan, Paul. *Great River: The Rio Grande in North American History.* Vol. 1. *Indians and Spain.* New York: Rinehart, 1954.

Horwitz, Richard P. *The Strip: An American Place.* Lincoln: University of Nebraska Press, 1985.

Hotel Planning and Outfitting. Chicago: Albert Pick–Barth, 1928.

Jackson, J. B. *Discovering the Vernacular Landscape.* New Haven: Yale University Press, 1984.

———. "The Moveable Dwelling and How It Came to America." In *Discovering the Vernacular Landscape*, by J. B. Jackson, 91–101. New Haven: Yale University Press, 1984.

Jakle, John A. *The Tourist: Travel in Twentieth-Century North America.* Lincoln: University of Nebraska Press, 1985.

———. *The Visual Elements of Landscape.* Amherst: University of Massachusetts Press, 1987.

Jakle, John A., Robert Bastian, and Douglas Meyer. *Common Houses in America's Small Towns: The Atlantic Seaboard to the Mississippi Valley.* Athens: University of Georgia Press, 1989.

Jakle, John A., and Keith A. Sculle. *The Gas Station in America.* Baltimore: Johns Hopkins University Press, 1994.

Jarman, Rufus. *A Bed for the Night: The Story of the Wheeling Bellboy, E. M. Statler and His Remarkable Hotels.* New York: Harper & Row, 1952.

Johnson, Wallace E. *Work Is My Play.* New York: Hawthorne, 1973.

Kammen, Michael. *Mystic Chords of Memory: The Transformation of Tradition in American Culture.* New York: Knopf, 1991.

Kane, C. Vernon. *Motor Courts: From Planning to Profits.* New York: Ahrens, 1954.

Kasson, John F. *Amusing the Millions: Coney Island at the Turn of the Century.* New York: Hill & Wang, 1978.

Kelley, Dayton, ed. *The Handbook of Waco and McLennan County, Texas.* Waco: Texian, 1972.

Keyton, Clara Z. *Tourist Camp Pioneering Experiences.* Chicago: Adams, 1960.

Koziara, Edward C., and Karen S. Koziara. *The Negro in the Hotel Industry.* Philadelphia: University of Pennsylvania Press, 1968.

Krim, Arthur. "Mapping Route 66: A Cultural Cartography." In *Roadside America: The Automobile in Design and Culture,* edited by Jan Jennings, 198–208. Ames: Iowa State University Press, 1990.

Lattin, Gerald W. *The Lodging and Food Service Industry.* Washington, D.C.: American Hotel and Motel Association, 1989.

Lavin, Joseph E., and Dallas S. Lunceford. "Franchising and the Lodging Industry." In *Encyclopedia of Hospitality and Tourism,* edited by Mahmood A. Khan, Michael D. Olsen, and Turgut Var, 366–71. New York: Van Nostrand Reinhold, 1993.

Leuchtenburg, William E. *Perils of Prosperity, 1914–1932.* Chicago: University of Chicago Press, 1958.

———. *A Troubled Feast: American Society since 1945.* Rev. ed. Boston: Little, Brown, 1983.

Levine, Lawrence W. *Highbrow/Lowbrow: The Emergence of Cultural Hierarchy.* Cambridge: Harvard University Press, 1988.

———. *The Unpredictable Past: Explorations in American Cultural History.* New York: Oxford University Press, 1993.

Lewis, David L. "Sex and the Automobile: From Rumble Seats to Rockin' Vans." In *The Automobile and American Culture,* edited by David L. Lewis and Laurence Goldstein, 123–33. Ann Arbor: University of Michigan Press, 1980.

Lewis, Peirce F. "Axioms for Reading the Landscape: Some Guides to the American Scene." In *The Interpretation of Ordinary Landscapes: Geographical Essays,* edited by D. W. Meinig, 13–32. New York: Oxford University Press, 1979.

Lewis, Robert C. *Cases in Hospitality Marketing and Management.* New York: John Wiley & Sons, 1989.

Lewis, Sinclair. *Free Air*. London: Jonathan Cape, 1933.

Liebs, Chester H. *Main Street to Miracle Mile: American Roadside Architecture*. Boston: Little, Brown, 1985.

Linsley, Judith W., and Ellen W. Rienstra. *Beaumont: A Chronicle of Promise*. Woodland Hills, Calif.: Windsor, 1982.

Love, Henry Barclay. *Establishing and Operating a Year-Round Motor Court*. Industrial (Small Business) Series, no. 50. Washington, D.C.: U.S. Government Printing Office, 1945.

Lundberg, Donald E. *The Hotel and Restaurant Business*. Boston: Cahners, 1976.

McLaurin, Ann M., ed. *Glimpses of Shreveport*. Natchitoches, La.: Northwestern State University Press, 1985.

McLure, Lilla, and J. Ed Howe. *History of Shreveport and Shreveport Builders*. Shreveport, La.: J. Ed Howe, 1937.

Meikle, Jeffrey L. *Twentieth Century Limited: Industrial Design in America, 1925–1939*. Philadelphia: Temple University Press, 1979.

Meinig, D. W. "Reading the Landscape: An Appreciation of W. G. Hoskins and J. B. Jackson." In *The Interpretation of Ordinary Landscapes: Geographical Essays,* edited by D. W. Meinig, 195–244. New York: Oxford University Press, 1979.

Miller, Floyd. *Statler: America's Extraordinary Hotelman*. New York: Statler Foundation, 1968.

Morgan, Howard E. *The Motel Industry in the United States: Small Business in Transition*. Tucson: University of Arizona, Bureau of Business and Public Research, 1964.

Motels, Hotels, Restaurants, and Bars: An Architectural Record Book. New York: F. W. Dodge, 1963.

Nabokov, Vladimir. *Lolita*. New York: Olympia, 1955.

Noble, Allen G. *Wood, Brick, and Stone: The American Settlement Landscape, Volume One—Houses*. Amherst: University of Massachusetts Press, 1984.

O'Brien, Robert. *Marriott: The J. Willard Marriott Story*. Salt Lake City: Deseret, 1977.

Pearce, T. M., ed. *New Mexico Place Names: A Geographical Dictionary*. Albuquerque: University of New Mexico Press, 1965.

Pierson, George W. *The Moving American*. New York: Knopf, 1973.

Poage, W. R. *McLennan County—Before 1980*. Waco: Texian, 1981.

Polenburg, Richard. *One Nation Divisible: Class, Race, and Ethnicity in the United States since 1938*. New York: Viking, 1980.

Polyzoides, Stefanos, Roger Sherwood, and James Tice. *Courtyard Housing in Los Angeles: A Topological Analysis*. Berkeley: University of California Press, 1982.

Porter, Michael. *Competitive Strategies*. New York: Free Press, 1980.

Price, V. B. *A City at the End of the World*. Albuquerque: University of New Mexico Press, 1992.

Riesman, David. *The Lonely Crowd*. New Haven: Yale University Press, 1960.

Riley, Robert E. "Vernacular Landscapes." In *Advances in Environment, Behavior, and Design, Volume One,* edited by Ervin H. Zube and Gary T. Moore, 129–58. New York: Plenum, 1987.

Rosenberg, Norman L., and Emily S. Rosenberg. *In Our Times: America since World War II*. 3d ed. Englewood Cliffs, N.J.: Prentice-Hall, 1987.

Sauer, Carl Ortwin. *Land and Life: A Selection from the Writings of Carl Ortwin Sauer*. Edited by John Leighly. Berkeley: University of California Press, 1963.

Schlereth, Thomas J. "Conduits and Conduct: Home Utilities in Victorian America, 1876–1915." In *American Home Life, 1880–1930: A Social History of Spaces and*

Services, edited by Jessica H. Foy and Thomas J. Schlereth, 225–41. Knoxville: University of Tennessee Press, 1992.

Sculle, Keith A. "Frank Redford's Wigwam Village Chain: A Link in the Modernization of the American Roadside." In *Roadside America: The Automobile in Design and Culture,* edited by Jan Jennings, 125–35. Ames: Iowa State University Press, 1990.

Sherry, John E. H. *The Laws of Innkeepers—For Hotels, Motels, Restaurants, and Clubs.* 3d ed. Ithaca, N.Y.: Cornell University Press, 1993.

Shipp, Royal, and Robert Moore Fisher. *The Postwar Boom in Hotels and Motels."* Staff Economic Studies. N.p.: Board of Governors of the Federal Reserve, 1965.

Simmons, Marc. *Albuquerque: A Narrative History.* Albuquerque: University of New Mexico Press, 1982.

Steinbeck, John. *The Grapes of Wrath.* New York: Viking, 1939.

Strasser, Susan. *Satisfaction Guaranteed: The Making of the American Mass Market.* New York: Pantheon, 1989.

Sullivan, Charles L. *The Mississippi Gulf Coast: Portrait of a People.* Northridge, Calif.: Windsor, 1985.

Susman, Warren I. *Culture and Commitment, 1929–1945.* New York: Braziller, 1973.

———. *Culture As History: The Transformation of American Society in the Twentieth Century.* New York: Pantheon, 1973.

Tedlow, Richard S. *New and Improved: The Story of Mass Marketing in America.* New York: Basic Books, 1990.

Tourist Court Plan Book. Temple, Tex.: Tourist Court Journal, 1950.

Ungar, Sanford J. *Fresh Blood: The New American Immigrants.* New York: Simon & Schuster, 1995.

Vignola, Margo L., and Jill S. Krutick. *The Lodging Industry in the 1990s: Confronting Crowded Markets.* New York: Salomon Brothers, 1990.

Volz, Candace M. "The Modern Look of the Early Twentieth-Century House." In *American Home Life, 1880–1930: A Social History of Spaces and Services,* edited by Jessica H. Foy and Thomas J. Schlereth, 25–48. Knoxville: University of Tennessee Press, 1992.

Walker, John H., and Gwendolyn Wingate. *Beaumont: A Pictorial History.* Norfolk, Va.: Donning, 1983.

Wallace, Patricia W. *Our Land, Our Lives: A Pictorial History of McLennan County, Texas.* Norfolk, Va.: Donning, 1986.

———. *Waco: Texas Crossroads.* Woodland Hills, Calif.: Windsor, 1983.

Whittington, Harold. *Starting and Managing a Small . . . Motel.* The Starting and Managing Series, no. 7. Washington, D.C.: Small Business Administration, 1963.

Williams, Jerry L. In *New Mexico in Maps,* edited by Jerry L. Williams and Paul E. McAllister. Albuquerque: University of New Mexico Press, 1981.

Wilson, Kemmons. *The Holiday Inn Story.* New York: Newcomen Society in North America, 1968.

Woldert, Albert. *A History of Tyler and Smith County, Texas.* San Antonio: Naylor, 1948.

Wright, Gwendolyn. *Building the Dream: A Social History of Housing in America.* New York: Pantheon, 1981.

———. *Moralism and the Model Home: Domestic Architecture and Cultural Conflict in Chicago, 1873–1912.* Chicago: University of Chicago Press, 1980.

Wyckoff, D. Daryl, and W. Earl Sasser. *The U.S. Lodging Industry.* Lexington, Mass.: Lexington Books, 1981.

Zelinsky, Wilbur. *The Cultural Geography of the United States*. Englewood Cliffs, N.J.: Prentice-Hall, 1973.

Zukin, Sharon. *Landscapes of Power: From Detroit to Disney World*. Berkeley: University of California Press, 1991.

Periodicals

[Agee, James]. "The Great American Roadside." *Fortune* 10 (September 1934).

"Alamo Plaza Gulfport." *Down South* 23 (September–October 1973).

"America Takes to the Motor Court." *Business Week*, no. 563 (June 15, 1940).

"Amid the Colorful Surroundings of Mexico, International Motor Court Association Launched." *Tourist Court Journal* 1 (October 1937).

Askin, Pat. "Ramada: Redefining the Mid-Priced Hotel." *Lodging Hospitality* 39 (May 1983).

Barringer, E. L. "Tourist Camp Station Patterned After Dutch Windmills." *National Petroleum News* 22 (April 30, 1930).

———. "Uncle Sam Takes Census of Tourist Camps." *National Petroleum News* 29 (December 15, 1937).

"Best Western Forms Supply Arm." *Lodging Hospitality* 36 (March 1980).

"Best Western Markets New Image." *Hotel and Motel Management* 191 (September 1976).

"Best Western's New One-Stop Shopping Center." *Tourist Court Journal* 33 (June 1970).

"Big Move for Best Western." *Hotel and Motel Management* 191 (June 1976).

Birmingham, Frederic A. "Kemmons Wilson: The Inn-Side Story." *Saturday Evening Post* 244 (winter 1971).

Bramble, Oakley R. "Overbuilding Seen Cause for Caution." *AMHA News* 9 (November–December 1960).

Breen, Terry. "Best Value, Superior, Magic Key Inns Combine to Form Chain: USA Inns." *Hotel and Motel Management* 200 (July 1985).

———. "Hilton Offers Discount to Seniors." *Hotel and Motel Management* 201 (March 17, 1986).

Bronaugh, Frank. "The Blackstone Hotel." *Chronicles of Smith County, Texas* 25 (summer 1986).

"Bureau of Census Report of Courts." *Tourist Court Journal* 13 (September 1950).

"Bye-Bye Memphis, Hello, Atlanta." *Lodging Hospitality* 47 (May 1991).

"Cabana Rooms." *Tourist Court Journal* 25 (September 1962).

"Cabin and Cottage Building Time Is Here." *American Builder* 57 (March 1935).

Carley, William J. "Roadside Jam: Motel Failures Mount As Building Boom Adds to Excess Capacity." *Wall Street Journal*, October 27, 1961.

Carlisle, Norman, and Madelyn Carlisle. "Luxury Hostels along the Highway." *Coronet* 46 (May 1959).

Carlson, David B. "New Hotel vs. Old Code." *Architectural Forum* 113 (November 1960).

Carson, Velma. "Bed, Bath, and Garage." *Independent Woman* 15 (July 1936).

The Chain Report. *Lodging Hospitality* 46 (December 1990) and 48 (August 1992).

Clark, Jack J. "Holiday Inn: New Rooms in the Inn." *Cornell Hotel and Restaurant Administration Quarterly* 34 (October 1993).

Cochran, Doug. "Exclusive Interview with TraveLodge Head . . . Scott King on Co-ownership." *Tourist Court Journal* 27 (October 1963).

———. "How Quality Courts Lives Up to Its Name." *Tourist Court Journal* 26 (March 1963).

———. "An Interview with Kemmons Wilson." *Tourist Court Journal* 26 (August 1963).

———. "Some Pointers from M. K. Guertin." *Tourist Court Journal* 26 (January 1963).

"Complete Court Census Released." *Tourist Court Journal* 5 (February 1942).

"'Couple Trade' in the Tourist Camps." *New Republic,* July 29, 1936.

Cowgill, Clinton H. "Modern Travel Accommodations." *AIA Journal* 33 (March 1960).

Craig, Robert M. Letter to editor. Correspondence. *Society for Commercial Archeology News* 2 (spring 1994).

Crawford, Carl. "By Cuttings Its Manufacturing, HI Lifts Its Profits Dramatically." *Memphis Commercial Appeal,* April 9, 1978.

Daniell, Caytie. "Budget Host Aims to Top Record Year." *Hotel and Motel Management* 202 (April 27, 1987).

Dela Cruz, Tony. "Choice Hotels Loses Suit Over Microtel's Design." *Hotel Business* 1 (October 21, 1992).

DeLuca, Michael. "Quality's Newest Entry: McSleep." *Hotel and Motel Management* 202 (September 28, 1987).

Dempewolff, Richard F. "Drive-In Dream Castles." *Popular Mechanics* 106 (July 1956).

Dev, Chekian S., and Janet E. Hubbard. "A Strategic Analysis of the Lodging Industry." *Cornell Hotel and Restaurant Administration Quarterly* 30 (May 1989).

DeVoto, Bernard. "The Easy Chair: Motel Town." *Harper's Magazine* 207 (September 1953).

Donovan, Sharon. "Hampton Sets Strategy to Hike Market Share." *Hotel and Motel Management* 203 (May 30, 1988).

"Duncan Hines Pickets Ten Best Motels in the U.S.A." *Look* 18 (January 12, 1954).

"Economy Lodging: America's Top 10." *Lodging* 19 (March 1992).

Edmundson, W. L. "Obsolescence Is No Bane to Rex Plaza Motor Inn." *Tourist Court Journal* 28 (April 1965).

Elliott, James. "T.C.O.A. To Hold Annual Confab Here." *Jackson (Tenn.) Sun,* May 3, 1937.

Entrikin, J. Nicholas. "Carl O. Sauer, Philosopher in Spite of Himself." *Geographical Review* 74 (1984).

"Eppley Buys Pittsburgh Hotels." *Hotel Monthly* 36 (March 1928).

"Exclusive Interview with TraveLodge President." *Tourist Court Journal* 31 (April 1968).

Farrant, Alan W. "Why Up-Grade?" *Tourist Court Journal* 19 (June 1958).

"Figures on Growth of Tourist Camp Business." *Hotel Monthly* 43 (December 1935).

"First Motel." *Tourist Court Journal* 18 (February 1955).

"500 Ramada Inns in a Decade." *Tourist Court Journal* 31 (November 1967).

"Following the Cardinal Rule." *Hotel and Motel Management* 194 (September 1979).

Freedgood, Seymour. "The Motel Free-for-All." *Fortune* 59 (June 1959).

———. "The Hotels: Time to Stop and Rest." *Fortune* 68 (July 1963).

Gamrecki, John. "Franchising: Fitting the Property into Today's Marketplace." *Hotel and Motel Management* 196 (October 1981).

Garfinkel, Perry. "A Market-by-Market Battle to Tuck in the Nation." *New York Times,* September 4, 1994.

Garner, John S. "How Fare Thee Fair Camelot?" *Reflections: The Journal of the School of Architecture* (University of Illinois at Urbana-Champaign) 1 (fall 1983).

Gebhard, David. "The American Colonial Revival in the 1930s." *Winterthur Portfolio* 22, nos. 2–3 (1987).

Gillette, Bill. "Best Western Sets Global Goals." *Hotel and Motel Management* 205 (June 11, 1990).

———. "Conservative Approach Fuels Marriott Success." *Hotel and Motel Management* 204 (June 19, 1989).

"Going DeLuxe in Phoenix." *Tourist Court Journal* 5 (May 1942).

Gordon, Jean, and Jan McArthur. "Popular Culture, Magazines, and American Domestic Interiors, 1898–1940." *Journal of Popular Culture* 22 (1989).

"Grande Vista Tourist Homes." *American Builder* 59 (June 1937).

Gresham, Bob. "Anatomy of Chain and Referral Motels." *Tourist Court Journal* 30 (August 1967).

———. "For Courters Only." *Tourist Court Journal* 25 (September 1962).

———. "So Flows Master Hosts." *Tourist Court Journal* 33 (July 1970).

———. "What's the Game Plan for Master Hosts and Red Carpet Inns?" *Motel/Motor Inn Journal* 35 (July 1972).

Gunn, Clare A. "Planning the Motel Room." *American Motel Magazine* 10 (December 1954).

Halbert, Ward K. "Tourist Camps Pay Southern Jobbers as Rented Dealer Outlets." *National Petroleum News* 21 (March 20, 1929).

"Hampton Inns Announces Opening of 200th Hotel." *Hotel and Motel Management* 204 (September 1989).

Hanson, A. C. "The Scope and Purpose of the International Motor Court Association." *Tourist Court Journal* 1 (December 1937).

Hanson, Eugene M. "The Best Western's New Home Office." *Tourist Court Journal* 28 (September 1965).

Harris, [R.] Cole. "Power, Modernity, and Historical Geography." *Annals of the Association of American Geographers* 81 (December 1991).

Hart, Christopher. "Product Development: How Marriott Created Courtyard." *Cornell Hotel and Restaurant Administration Quarterly* 27 (November 1986).

Hawkins, Chuck. "Promus: Fighting for the Middle of the Road." *Business Week,* no. 3173 (August 13, 1990).

Hayner, Norman. "Auto Camps in the Evergreen Playground." *Social Forces* 9 (December 1930).

"Here Are the Newest Factory-Built Units." *Tourist Court Journal* 25 (September 1962).

"Here's Your Guest's Profile." *Tourist Court Journal* 33 (October 1969).

Hillyer, Katherine. "Bed and Butter Letter." *Tourist Court Journal* 10 (February 1947).

"History of Trusthouse Forte." *Lodging Hospitality* 40 (November 1984).

Hocke, John. "Good Profits Building Tourist Camps." *American Builder and Building Age* 51 (April 1931).

"Holiday City: Home of Modern Innkeeping in an Old World Tradition." *Holiday Inn Magazine,* December 1968.

"Holiday Inn Orders Operators of Older Motels to Renovate." *Chicago Tribune*, September 25, 1994.

"Holiday Inns of America." *American Motel Magazine* 14 (May 1959).

"Holiday Inns' Second Generation." *Hotel and Motel Management* 192 (June 1977).

"Holiday Inns Takes a New Road to Profits." *Business Week*, no. 2347 (September 7, 1974).

"Holiday Inns: Trying the Comeback Trail." *Business Week*, no. 2439 (July 5, 1976).

Hooker, Elbert L. "The Urban Tourist Camp." *Studies in Sociology* (Southern Methodist University, Department of Sociology) 1, no. 1 (1936).

Hoover, J. Edgar, with Courtney R. Cooper. "Camps of Crime." *American Magazine*, no. 160 (February 1940).

"Hospitality Franchise System: Banking on President Frank Beletti." *Hotel and Resort International* 14 (July 1991).

"Hotel Experience Built This Motel." *American Motel Magazine* 6 (March 1953).

"Hotel Hopes Rise." *Business Week*, no. 562 (June 8, 1940).

"The Hotel Influence." *American Motel Magazine* 15 (October 1985).

"Hotels: 'By Golly.'" *Time* 82 (July 19, 1963).

"Hotels That Look Like Motels." *Business Week*, no. 1228 (March 14, 1953).

"Hot Springs, Arkansas, Host to Dual Convention of the IMCA and UMCCD." *Tourist Court Journal* 1 (April 1938).

"Housing the Tourist." *Architectural Forum* 66 (May 1937).

"How Big Is the Motel Industry?" *Motel/Motor Inn Journal* 37 (July 1974).

"How Big Is Your Motel Industry?" *Tourist Court Journal* 25 (July 1962).

Humbert, Ray. "What Happened at the Minneapolis American Motor Hotel Association?" *Tourist Court Journal* 23 (December 1959).

"I'll Answer Your Questions on Tourist Camps." *Hotel Management*, July 1936.

"Indianapolis Dillon Inn: Prototype for New Chain." *Lodging Hospitality* 34 (July 1983).

"Innkeeping and the Computer: II." *Hotel and Motel Management* 183 (August 1968).

Irwin, Marvin E. "America's First Tourist Court." *Tourist Court Journal* 18 (February 1955).

Ivany, Loretta. "Crowne Plaza." *Lodging Hospitality* 39 (June 1983).

Ivany, Loretta, and Ed Watkins. "Management Companies Reach a Crossroads." *Lodging Hospitality* 38 (January 1982).

Jackson, John B. "Other-Directed Houses." *Landscape* 6 (winter 1956–57).

Jakle, John A. "Motel by the Roadside: America's Room for the Night." *Journal of Cultural Geography* 1 (1981).

Jancsurak, Joe. "Holiday Inn Launches Its Second Hotel Chain." *Hotel and Motel Management* 198 (June 1983).

Jarvis, Wayne. "Show Room." *Tourist Court Journal* 5 (October 1941).

Jennings, Dean. "Thrivin' Drive-Inns." *Reader's Digest* 51 (September 1947).

Johnson, Wallace E. "Millionaire: A Self-Portrait." *Esquire* 61 (February 1964).

Jones, Del. "Hotels Push Franchisees to Remodel." *USA Today*, February 9, 1995.

Jones, Dwayne. "From Camps to Courts: Dallas Tourist Accommodations in the Early Twentieth Century." *Legacies: A History Journal for Dallas and North Central Texas* 7 (spring 1995).

———. "Sources and Resources: *Tourist Court Journal*." *S[ociety for] C[ommercial] A[rcheology] News Journal* 12, no. 2 (1992).

"Jousting with Motel 6." *Lodging Hospitality* 48 (April 1992).

Justus, George R. "Microtel: How 'Simple' Translates into Success." *Cornell Hotel and Restaurant Administration Quarterly* 32 (December 1991).

Kane, C. Vernon. "Motel Trends." *Architectural Forum* 100 (February 1954).

Knowles, Eleanor N. "Along the Roadside." *Christian Science Monitor Weekly Magazine*, July 31, 1935.

Koch, Carl. "Design for a Franchise Chain." *Architectural Record* 123 (April 1958).

Koepper, Ken, and Christine O'Dwyer. "Chains Poise for Development at the Dawn of a New Decade." *Lodging* 15 (January 1990).

Kopulos, Gordon. "A Chain's Proven Guide to Performance and Service." *Motel/Motor Inn Journal* 38 (March 1975).

———. "How a Budget Chain Minimizes Operating Costs For Its Motels." *Motel/Motor Inn Journal* 38 (November 1974).

Koselka, Rita. "It's an Ill Wind." *Forbes* 150 (December 7, 1992).

"Latest Motel Census." *American Motel Magazine* 14 (January 1957).

Lears, T. J. Jackson. "The Concept of Cultural Hegemony: Problems and Possibilities." *American Historical Review* 90 (June 1985).

Lewis, Nolan. "Holiday Inns' Casino Decision Sparks Departure of Clymer." *Memphis Commercial Appeal*, September 30, 1978.

Lewis, Peirce F. "Learning from Looking: Geographic and Other Writing about the American Cultural Landscape." *American Quarterly* 35 (1983).

Lewis, Sinclair. "Adventures in Autobumming—The Great American Frying Pan." *Saturday Evening Post* 192 (January 3, 1920).

Lightfoot, E. H. "De Anza Motor Lodge Pueblo Designed." *Tourist Court Journal* 3 (May 1940).

———. "Tile Baths Can Be Constructed Economically." *Tourist Court Journal* 1 (October 1937).

Lightfoot, Tom E. "Victory Housing." *Tourist Court Journal* 5 (April 1942).

Lindsey, Alethia. "What Are You Getting Into?" *Better Homes and Gardens* 26 (May 1948).

"Lodging Industry Census." *Lodging Hospitality* 46 (December 1990).

"Lodging Today." *Lodging Hospitality* 40 (July 1984).

Loeb, Frances. "How One Motel Franchise System Works." *Tourist Court Journal* 19 (February 1956).

Lukenbill, H. D. "Profit in the North." *Tourist Court Journal* 9 (July 1946).

MacDonald, Kenneth R. "How the Hyatt Chain Has Expanded in Five Years." *Tourist Court Journal* 29 (November 1965).

Martin, Richard. "Super Salesmanship Builds Holiday Inn Motel Chain." *Memphis Sunday Times*, November 8, 1964.

McCann, Franklin T. "The Growth of the Tourist Court in the United States and Its Relationship to the Urban Development of Albuquerque, New Mexico." *Journal of the Scientific Laboratories of Denison University* 37 (May 1942).

McCarthy, John J. "The Market Business Forgets." *Nation's Business* 21 (August 1933).

———. "'Pay Dirt' in Tourist Camps." *Advertising and Selling* 42 (May 25, 1933).

McCarthy, John J., and Robert Littell. "Three Hundred Thousand Shacks: The Arrival of a New American Industry." *Harper's Magazine* 167 (July 1933).

McDowell, Edwin. "Hotels Await the Wake-up Call." *New York Times*, September 24, 1991.

———. "Marriott's Shareholders Back Plan to Split in 2." *New York Times*, July 24, 1993.

McGovern, James R. "Woman's Pre–World War I Freedom in Manners and Morals." *Journal of American History* 55, no. 2 (1968).

Messerle, Michael. "A New Decade of All-Suites Design." *Hotel and Resort Industry* 14 (September 1991).

"Mid-Priced Hotels Slugging It Out in a Shrinking Market." *Lodging Hospitality* 39 (May 1983).

"M. K. Guertin." *American Motel Magazine* 17 (August 1960).

Molinaro, C. Joseph. "Ten Reasons Why People Buy Motels." *Motel/Motor Inn Journal* 37 (May 1974).

Molz, Alderson. "Tourist Homes." *Hotel Monthly* 41 (January 1933).

"Money on the Roadside." *Fortune* 44 (August 1951).

Moore, Ellis. "Loan of $50 Starts Memphian on Modern Horatio Alger Trip." *Memphis Commercial Appeal,* September 25, 1952.

"Motel/Hotel Architecture: The State of the Art; Part Two." *Motel/Motor Inn Journal* 38 (May 1975).

"Motel Census Completed." *Tourist Court Journal* 19 (September 1956).

"Motel Fever." *Saturday Evening Post* 226 (August 22, 1953).

"Motels Edge In to Snag the City Trade." *Business Week,* no. 1266 (December 5, 1953).

Muller, Christopher. "The Marriott Divestment: Leaving the Past Behind." *Cornell Hotel and Restaurant Administration Quarterly* 31 (February 1990).

National Newsbeat. *Hotel and Motel Management* 186 (August 1971); 187 (August 1972); 188 (November 1973); 192 (September 1977).

"New Court at Memphis Provides the Seventh in the Alamo Plaza Chain of Courts." *Tourist Court Journal* 3 (November 1939).

"New Motel Will Have 'Hospital Clean' Interiors." *American Motel Magazine* 13 (September 1957).

Noggle, Berle. "The Twenties: A New Historiographical Frontier." *Journal of American History* 53, no. 2 (1966).

Nozar, Robert A. "Embassy Stays Ahead in All-Suite Parade." *Hotel and Motel Management* 202 (July 8, 1987).

———. "Empowerment Strengthens Holiday." *Hotel and Motel Management* 208 (July 5, 1993).

Pawley, Frederic. "Motels." *Architectural Record* 107 (March 1950).

Pearson, Harry R. "Modular Construction: Is It the Answer?" *Motel/Motor Inn Journal* 34 (August 1971).

Perry, R. A. "Quality Courts United Holds Convention." *Tourist Court Journal* 9 (December 1945).

"The Plaza Hotel Courts, New and Interesting Columbus Enterprise, Embodying a Novel Form of Construction." *Industrial Index: Columbus,* 1941.

"Portfolio of Special Building Types." *Architectural Record* 77 (February 1935).

Radder, Norman J. "Yording's Hides the Heat." *Tourist Court Journal* 14 (May 1951).

"Radisson on the Rise." *Hotel and Motel Management* 193 (September 1978).

Raitz, Karl B., and John P. Jones III. "The City Hotel As Landscape Artifact and Community Symbol." *Journal of Cultural Geography* 9 (1988).

"Ramada Reaches for a Renaissance in the '80s." *Lodging Hospitality* 36 (February 1980).

"Rapid Rise of the Host with the Most." *Time* 99 (June 12, 1972).

Rhoads, William B. "Roadside Colonial: Early American Design for the Automobile Age, 1900–1940." *Winterthur Portfolio* 21, nos. 2–3 (1986).

Rice, Faye. "Hotels Fight for Business Guests." *Fortune* 121 (April 23, 1990).

Riddle, W. D. "Modern Motel." *Tourist Court Journal* 8 (November 1944).

Rieser, Carl. "Sheraton vs. Hilton: Playing Checkers with 60,000 Rooms." *Fortune* 62 (January 1961).

Ringel, Judy. "Holiday Inns at 30." *Memphis* 7 (October 1982).

Ripp, Bart. "The De Anza Had It All: Turquoise Floor, No Stairs." *Albuquerque Tribune*, July 30, 1985.

"Roadside Cabins for Tourists." *Architectural Record* 72 (December 1933).

Robbins, L. H. "America Hobnobs at the Tourist Camp." *New York Times Magazine*, August 12, 1934.

"Rodeway Inn: Chances Make for Success." *Hotel and Motel Management* 193 (September 1977).

"A Rougher Road for Motel Chains." *Business Week*, no. 2324 (March 30, 1974).

Rowe, Megan. "Growing Pains at Marriott?" *Lodging Hospitality* 46 (February 1990).

———. "Holiday Inn Fat and Sassy to Lean and Mean." *Lodging Hospitality* 48 (July 1992).

Rudnitsky, Howard. "Blood in the Suites." *Forbes* 148 (October 28, 1991).

———. "What Do the Sellers Know That the Buyers Don't?" *Forbes* 136 (October 7, 1985).

"Rustic Cabins and Filling Stations." *American Builder* 62 (July 1940).

Salomon, Alan. "Holiday Readying Two New Brands." *Hotel and Motel Management* 209 (September 19, 1994).

Sawyer, Ray. "How An Independent Motel Bucked the Tide in 'Chain Country.'" *Motel/Motor Inn Journal* 33 (August 1972).

———. "How the Chandler Family Has Kept Pace with the Times." *Motel/Motor Inn Journal* 35 (February 1972).

———. "Ramada Inns's New Direction in Motel Management." *Motel/Motor Inn Journal* 35 (January 1971).

———. "Sheraton's Zeldman: Expansion Is His Game." *Motel/Motor Inn Journal* 35 (July 1971).

———. "A Survey of Motel Chain Organizations, Part One: Referral Chains." *Motel/Motor Inn Journal* 38 (December 1974).

———. "Why 'Lady Luck' Seems to Smile on the Hitching Post Inn." *Tourist Court Journal* 33 (February 1970).

Schmidt, Henry. "Overnight Rest-Cabins Spreading." *Literary Digest* 117 (June 9, 1934).

Sculle, Keith A. "The Dutch Mill Village in Glasgow: A Research Note." *Register of the Kentucky Historical Society* 91, no. 1 (1993).

———. "Oral History: A Key to Writing the History of American Roadside Architecture." *Journal of American Culture* 13, no. 3 (1990).

Shepard, Holmes A. "Postcards for the Tourist Court." *Tourist Court Journal* 10 (November 1946).

"Sheraton: It's Our Turn." *Hotel and Motel Management* 193 (November 1978).

"Sheraton Plans Biggest Expansion." *Hotel and Motel Management* 184 (June 1969).

"A Single Standard for Travelers." *Business Week*, no. 1784 (November 16, 1963).

Smith, Janet. "Planning a Usable Room." *Tourist Court Journal* 17 (April 1954).

"So You Think You Want to Own a Motel." *Changing Times* 10 (December 1956).

Streib, Dan. "TraveLodge Has New Franchise Plan." *Tourist Court Journal* 29 (October 1965).

Taninecz, George. "Imperial 400 Acquired by European Firm (Interpart America, Inc.)." *Hotel Motel Management* 202 (March 30, 1984).

———. "Reality Governs Budgetel Growth." *Hotel and Motel Management* 204 (May 9, 1988).

Taylor, Frank J. "Just What the Motorist Ordered." *Saturday Evening Post* 220 (July 5, 1947).

Teinowitz, Ira. "Check-in for Budget." *Advertising Age* 62 (December 2, 1991).

"10,000,000 Motorists' Dollars Help Howard Johnson Build Up Chain of 130 Company-Owned Shops." *Ice Cream Review* 23 (July 1940).

Toles, George E. "Advertising Helps Stimulate Treadway Inns' Success." *Motel/Motor Inn Journal* 34 (September 1971).

"Top Management Companies." *Lodging* 18 (August 1992).

Torrance, Lee. "Radio Advertising." *Tourist Court Journal* 1 (September 1938).

"Tourist Cabins That Get the Business." *Popular Mechanics* 64 (July 1935).

"Tourist Court Journal Named as Official Organ International Motor Court Association." *Tourist Court Journal* 1 (October 1937).

"Touristless Courts." *Business Week,* no. 659 (April 25, 1942).

"TraveLodge Opens First Tri-Arc." *Tourist Court Journal* 33 (June 1970).

True, Wallace W. "Significant Trends in the Motel Industry," *Appraisal Journal* 27 (April 1959).

Turner, Allan. "Beyond Its Time." *Houston Chronicle,* June 17, 1986.

"A Veteran Motel Operator Speaks." *American Motel Magazine,* November 1953.

Wade, Dorothy. "The Waldorf-Astoria of Tourist Courts." *Tourist Court Journal* 13 (January 1951).

Walton, William B. "The Holiday Inn Story." *Tourist Court Journal* 26 (August 1963).

Washburn, Helen P. "Tourists Accommodated." *Christian Science Monitor Weekly Magazine,* July 19, 1941.

Watkins, Edward. "Do Conversions Make Sense?" *Lodging Hospitality* 47 (November 1991).

Weathers, Ed. "Profile: Kemmons Wilson." *Memphis* 10 (September 1985).

"What's Howard Johnson Up to Now?" *American Motel Magazine* 15 (April 1958).

Whiting, Carleton. "Gas Stations Grow to Motorists Hotels under Pierce Terminal System." *National Petroleum News* 22 (March 1930).

"Will Innkeeping History Repeat Itself with the Budget Motel?" *Hotel and Motel Management* 187 (November 1972).

Willett, Norris. "Wayside Inns: The Big Hotel Chains Are Plunging into the Motel Business." *Barron's,* November 26, 1956.

Witham, Glenn. "Hotel Companies Aim for Multiple Markets." *Cornell Hotel and Restaurant Administration Quarterly* 26 (November 1985).

Wolff, Carlo. "Budget Chains in Catbird Seat." *Lodging Hospitality* 46 (September 1990).

Woods, Robert H. "Hospitality's History: Who Wrote What about When." *Cornell Hotel and Restaurant Administration Quarterly* 32 (August 1991).

"The World's Largest Motel." *American Motel Magazine* 15 (August 1958).

Wylie, Evan M. "Troubles of a Motel Keeper." *Saturday Evening Post* 226 (July 18, 1953).

Yordan, E. L. "Motor Camps Win New Friends." *New York Times,* July 14, 1935.

Index

National Recovery Admin-
   istration (NRA), 66, 131
*National Register of Historic
   Places*, 9, 10
National Tourist
   Lodge–Motor Court
   Trade Association (NTL-
   MCTA), 66, 131–32
Nelson, Arthur T., 61
Nelson's Dream Village,
   235
New Image Realty, Inc.,
   170–71
New Orleans, La., 44
Newport, Ark., 47
New York, N.Y., 4
Niagara Falls, 6, 7
Nims, Rufus, 250, 252
North Shore Hilton,
   126–27

Oaks Tourist Court, 42
Ohio and Northwestern
   Hotel Association, 123
Oil industry, economic im-
   pact of, 101
Oklahoma City, Okla., 106,
   107
Old Forge, N.Y., 6
Oleander Court, 75
Olshan, Alfred, 168
Omaha, Neb., 158
Omni Hotels, 223
Onawa, Iowa, 38
Orange, Tex., 48

Paducah, Ky., 283
Palmer House, 126, 127
Palmyra, Ind., 41
Paris, Ill., 9
Park Consolidated Motels,
   163
Park Hotel (Chattanooga,
   Tenn.), 25
Park Hotel (Lake Orion,
   Mich.), 23
Park Inns, 193
Park Mo-tel, 239–40
Park Plaza Hotel Court, 44
Park Sheraton Hotel, 4, 129

Park Suites, 179
Passport Inns, 199
Pensacola, Fla., 268
Perkins Pancake House,
   198
Petersen, C. A., 242
Pfister, 207
Philadelphia Sheraton, 129
Philadelphia, Pa., 4
Phillips, Vernon W., 116
Pick Americana Company,
   125
Pickett Suite Hotel Com-
   pany, 188, 221
Pierce Petroleum Corpora-
   tion, 49
Pines Motel, 48
Pinnell Motel, 9
Place-product-packaging:
   in franchising, 152; in
   hotel chains, 123; in
   motel industry, 22, 120,
   136–38, 149, 174, 179,
   184–85, 193, 195, 213,
   225–26, 229–30; and
   room geography,
   250–60
Plaza Hotel, 127, 222
Porter, Michael, 204
Poussin, Nicholas, 14
Prime Hospitality Corpo-
   ration, 223
Prime Motor Inns, 172,
   184, 187, 203, 218
Promus Companies,
   179–82, 282
Psycho, 17

Quality Courts United,
   140, 162–65, 166, 200
Quality Inns, 13, 165, 166,
   172
Quality Inns International,
   165
Quality International, 154
Quality Royale, 165
Quebec City, Canada, 5

Radisson-Cadillac Hotel, 27
Radisson Hotels, 222–23

Raleigh Hotel, 92
Ramada Inns, 172,
   182–84, 185
Ramada Renaissance
   Hotels, 184
Ravy, Fred, 87
Recommendation services.
   See Motel recommenda-
   tion services
Red Apple Motel, 84
Red Carpet Inns, 196, 197,
   198
Redford, Frank, 69, 72, 237
Redford, Vetra, 69
Red Hat Tourist Camp, 40
Red Lion Inns, 219–20
Red Roof Inns, 213, 214
Referral chains, 138–49,
   174; converted to fran-
   chising, 162–73
Regal 8, 256
Reliance Capital Group,
   190
Residence Inns, 178,
   200–203, 220
Resort hotels, 29–30
Revere Furniture Com-
   pany, 165
Richfield Hotel Manage-
   ment, Inc., 223
Richmond, Va., 36
Riesman, David, 82
Ringel, Judy, 278
Ritz-Carlton Hotels, 223
River Boat Casino, Inc.,
   277
Roadside Holiday Inns,
   267–70, 284
Robinson, Mary W., 109
Robinson, William P., 109
Rocky Mountain Lake
   Park, 32
Rodeway Inns, 154, 165,
   171–72, 184, 206
Rogers, Jefferson, motel ex-
   periences of, 10–13, 21
Room geography, 231–32;
   in the 1920s and 1930s,
   232–40; from the 1940s
   to the 1960s, 240–50;

LIBRARY OF CONGRESS CATALOGING-IN-PUBLICATION DATA

Jakle, John A.
   The motel in America / John A. Jakle, Keith A. Sculle & Jefferson S. Rogers.
     p.   cm.
   Includes bibliographical references and index.
   ISBN 0-8018-5383-4 (hc : alk. paper)
   1. Motels—United States—History.   2. Architecture, Modern—20th century—
United States.   3. Roadside architecture—United States.   I. Sculle, Keith A.
II. Rogers, Jefferson S.   III. Title.
TX909.J35   1996
647.9473′02—dc20
                                          96-14762